Understanding Forgiveness and Addiction

This book integrates and synthesizes numerous empirically supported positive psychological constructs and psychotherapeutic theories to help understand addiction and facilitate recovery through the lens of forgiveness.

Proposing forgiveness as an alternative and critical tool to understanding the process of addiction and recovery, whether in the context of substance use, compulsive behavior, and/or suicidal behavior, the book discusses multiple theoretical points of view regarding the process of forgiveness. Additionally, foundational theories underlying the process of recovery, the psychological and spiritual nature of forgiveness, and the nature of the association of forgiveness with health all receive detailed coverage. Considerable attention is also paid to the extant empirical support for the association of forgiveness with addiction and recovery.

The text's comprehensive integration of theory, research, and clinical application, including guidelines regarding forgiveness as a treatment for recovery from addiction, provide a roadmap forward for addiction counselors and other recovery specialists.

Jon R. Webb, Ph.D., is a licensed clinical psychologist, a tenured associate professor, and the Addictive Disorders and Recovery Studies Program Director in the Department of Community, Family, and Addiction Sciences at Texas Tech University.

"In Understanding Forgiveness and Addiction: Theory, Research, and Clinical Application, Jon Webb is masterful at taking a massive hodge-podge of research and molding it into both a researcher's and clinician's dream. There's enough detail to fuel theory and new research ideas for years. Yet the writing is clear enough that clinicians can find evidence-based interventions that they might not have been familiar with. And apply them with clients. The title aptly captures the book's contents. Authoritative and usable. This book will be read and cited for years."

Everett L. Worthington, Jr., PhD, Commonwealth professor emeritus, Virginia Commonwealth University, Richmond, Virginia

"Forgiveness is an area that holds great potential in addiction recovery. This volume does an excellent job of bringing together the theory, research, and clinical relevance/application into one place. Whether a student, academic, researcher, clinician, or person struggling with addictive and/or suicidal behavior, this book serves as the comprehensive repository of authoritative information on all things related to the role of forgiveness in healing from problems with addiction including in the context of substance use, compulsive behaviors, and suicidal behavior."

Harold G. Koenig, MD, professor of Psychiatry & Behavioral Sciences, associate professor of Medicine, Duke University Medical Center, Durham, North Carolina

"Forgiveness, a principle shared by positive psychology and spirituality, is a powerful and essential tool to address the relational and inner issues commonly experienced in the struggle for addiction recovery. In this book, Dr. Webb compellingly provides researchers, clinicians, and people struggling with addictions and related compulsive behaviors and suicidality with theory integration, scientific evidence, and clinical application to prioritize the inclusion of forgiveness in treatment."

Lisa J. Miller, PhD, professor and founder, Spirituality Mind Body Institute, Columbia University, New York, New York.

Understanding Forgiveness and Addiction

Theory, Research, and Clinical Application

Jon R. Webb

Routledge
Taylor & Francis Group
NEW YORK AND LONDON

First published 2021
by Routledge
52 Vanderbilt Avenue, New York, NY 10017

and by Routledge
2 Park Square, Milton Park, Abingdon, Oxon OX14 4RN

Routledge is an imprint of the Taylor & Francis Group, an informa business

Library of Congress Cataloging-in-Publication Data
Names: Webb, Jon R., author.
Title: Understanding forgiveness and addiction: : theory, research, and clinical application / Jon R. Webb.
Description: New York : Routledge, 2021. | Includes bibliographical references and index. |
Identifiers: LCCN 2020048611 (print) | LCCN 2020048612 (ebook) |
ISBN 9780367190835 (hardback) | ISBN 9780367190842 (paperback) |
ISBN 9780429200274 (ebook)
Subjects: LCSH: Forgiveness–Psychological aspects. | Substance abuse.
Classification: LCC BF637.F67 W37 2021 (print) | LCC BF637.F67 (ebook) |
DDC 155.9/2–dc23
LC record available at https://lccn.loc.gov/2020048611
LC ebook record available at https://lccn.loc.gov/2020048612

ISBN: 978-0-367-19083-5 (hbk)
ISBN: 978-0-367-19084-2 (pbk)
ISBN: 978-0-429-20027-4 (ebk)

Typeset in Times New Roman
by Taylor & Francis Books

To the person who helped me understand and know that I was worthwhile and lovable – my mother. I love you and I miss you terribly.

Contents

Illustrations

Figures

Tables

Acknowledgements

I want to express my sincere thankfulness and appreciation to Routledge for the opportunity to publish this book and to the people who have assisted me and shepherded the process to its completion – and for your patience with me – including, Amanda Devine, Clare Ashworth, Grace McDonnell, Victoria Day, Reanna Young, and any others working behind the scenes to prepare this manuscript for publication. For most of my adult life, I have dreamed of writing books. Little did I know what kind of an undertaking it is. Even after having written and published many scientific journal articles and edited-book chapters, the experience of writing a book has been quite a bit different for me. Again, thank you to those responsible for agreeing that this book idea was worthwhile and for putting all the pieces together and making this dream come true for me.

I also want to take this opportunity to express my gratitude to particular people in my life who have helped make something like this possible for me. Going all the way back to High School, during my somewhat wayward teen years, one of my teachers, George Baljevich, took me under his wing and provided me shelter from the storm, so to speak. Also, during this time, I found myself sitting across from a psychologist, Robert B. Field, Ph.D. I can recall thinking about what was going on between us and wondering how effective it was and yet, also admiring him for what he was trying to do. I believe he was my first inspiration for wanting to be a psychologist.

As an undergraduate and graduate student, I had instructors and professors, particularly I. Reed Payne, Ph.D., and Edward P. Shafranske, Ph.D., who sparked in me the desire to pursue academia and persist in otherwise unpopular topics in psychology (i.e., issues related to spirituality) by showing me that it could be done. Although much remains to be done, things have improved quite a bit over the years, thanks to their work in helping push it forward. My doctoral mentor, Seymour L. Zelen, Ph.D., was exactly the right person at the right time for me. He was pivotal in inspiring me to pursue my developing dream of having an academic, research-based career. What a mind, I could sit and listen to and learn from him forever!

Particular pre- and post-doctoral clinical supervisors, John Irby, LMFT, Stevan Lars Nielsen, Ph.D., and Spencer Schein, Ph.D., taught me that I had something unique to offer. Post-doctoral research mentors and trainers, Denise G. Tate, Ph.D., Elizabeth, A. R. Robinson, Ph.D., Kirk J. Brower, MD, and Robert A. Zucker, Ph.D., took a chance on me as an inexperienced, rough-around-the-edges idealist with a fairly vague idea about forgiveness being associated with health and addiction recovery. And, shared with me their expertise, and encouraged me both directly and through their passion for excellence to likewise pursue *my* academic, research, and professional interests. Consistently throughout my career, Loren L. Toussaint, Ph.D., and Everett L. Worthington, Jr., Ph.D., have each had a profound and inspiring effect on me in my pursuit of the psychology of forgiveness – and also more broadly in my pursuit of the science of psychology. Each and every one of these individuals has helped instill in me the desire to persevere in the pursuit of my dreams.

Importantly, without the sacrifices, dedication, support, and love of my family – my spouse, children, parents, and siblings – I would not have had the privilege to engage in these pursuits. And, without my faith, nothing good and decent I may do would be possible. Indeed, in the context of writing this book (and related professional pursuits), and consistent with the eleventh step of the Twelve Step Model (see Chapter 9), I have noticed many seemingly out-of-nowhere thoughts, ideas, and impressions guiding my work. Because my God forgives me and I feel its healing and transformative power, I am inspired to seek to understand the thing called forgiveness.

> We love him, because he first loved us. … And this commandment have we from him, That he who loveth God love his brother also.
>
> – *1 John* 4:19,21

About the Author

Jon R. Webb, Ph.D., a licensed psychologist, is a tenured associate professor in the Department of Community, Family, and Addiction Sciences at Texas Tech University, where he serves as the Addictive Disorders and Recovery Studies Program Director. He is a past president of the Tennessee Psychological Association. He received his American Psychological Association accredited doctorate in Clinical Psychology from the California School of Professional Psychology, Los Angeles, and completed two Research Postdoctoral Fellowships at the University of Michigan Medical School – one in the Department of Psychiatry (Substance Abuse Section, Addiction Research Center) and one in the Department of Physical Medicine and Rehabilitation (Division of Rehabilitation Psychology and Neuropsychology). Dr. Webb also completed a Clinical Postdoctoral Fellowship at the Kaiser Permanente Medical Center in San Rafael, California in the Department of Psychiatry, Chemical Dependency Services. Dr. Webb's primary professional interests are in the area of spirituality and health; including, ritualistic, theistic, and existential spirituality, forgiveness, temptation, psychache, existangst, addiction recovery, suicidal behavior, and medical rehabilitation. He has published more than 50 peer-reviewed articles and edited-book chapters on these topics.

About the Author

1 Introduction

Identifying the Problem of Addiction and the Relevance of Spirituality as a Solution

As an academic clinical psychologist, an activity that I typically use when teaching university courses on addiction-related topics involves spending 10–15 minutes each week near the beginning or ending of a class session discussing "Addiction in the News." I usually alternate between different online national news websites, in an effort to tap into various political perspectives, and otherwise balance any perceived, news-based biases. As I never have difficulty finding relevant articles prior to class, for dramatic effect, I am often tempted to do a quick "cold" search of the national news during class, in real-time. The few times I have given into this temptation, as luck would have it, it seems to take longer than expected and the dramatic effect is progressively lost with each successive click required to find an article. Such is life!

As I started writing this introductory chapter, I decided to Google "addiction stories in the news" – on August 1, 2019. The search returned about 256,000,000 hits, with the first dedicated link to a specific story on a national news website (published by foxnews.com on June 15, 2019) being found near the bottom of the first page of results. The story was entitled "Addicted to meds: One nurse's story of addiction and recovery" and it originated at Healthline.com. At the end of the article (Campbell, 2019), the subject of the story, Samantha, pointed to the role of self-forgiveness in her recovery from addiction and stated:

> I'm still working on forgiving myself for the mistakes I've made, and I think that will continue for a long time. But I wake up every day and I try to be a better person than I was the day before. I try to remind myself of the successes so that I can quiet my fears and slowly rebuild my self-esteem. It's a process, but I'm not giving up.

The reason I engage in this activity at the beginning of my classes, and here at the beginning of this book, is to illustrate how ever-present addiction is in our society. Indeed, current events, as reported in the news, are saturated with the story of addiction such that the struggle (public and private) with addiction and addictive behavior in everyday life is seemingly inescapable. Of note, this exercise only provides anecdotal evidence for the ubiquitous nature of the problem of addiction. Moreover, the American Psychological Association (2015, p. 55) defines the *anecdotal method* as: "an investigational technique in which informal verbal reports of incidents casually observed are accepted as useful information. The anecdotal method is scientifically inadequate but can offer clues as to areas of investigation that warrant more systematic, controlled research."

In the remainder of this introductory chapter, I will provide an overview of this book, including scientifically justifying the need for a book focused on addiction and the role of forgiveness (i.e., an aspect of spirituality) in recovery from addiction. Information will be presented (as available) in the context of the world in general, and the United States in particular, regarding: (1) the societal problems of addiction (i.e., alcohol, drugs, and compulsive behaviors) and suicidal behavior (sometimes thought of as consistent with addiction), including material related to problem frequency and economic burden, and (2) the universal relevance of spirituality.

Societal-Level Problems Related to Alcohol and Drugs

Using the most recent, publicly available data from 2016 (see Table 1.1 & Table 1.2) provided by the World Health Organization (WHO), an agency of the United Nations, regarding disease burden and mortality (WHO, 2016a, 2016b; see also, GBD, 2018a, 2018b), it is estimated that, worldwide (see Table 1.1), about 1.95 deaths per 100,000 population can be attributed to alcohol use *disorders*, and about 2.15 deaths per 100,000 population can be attributed to drug use *disorders* (i.e., opioid, cocaine, amphetamine, cannabis, and other drug use disorders, combined). Likewise, that per 1,000 population, about 2.47 DALYs are lost in the context of alcohol use disorders (i.e., disability-adjusted life years lost – time lost because of poor health and early death), and about 2.93 DALYs are lost in the context of drug use disorders. With a worldwide population in 2016 of about 7,461,884,000 (7.46 billion[1]) (WHO, 2016a), these estimates suggest that, *each year*: (1) over 145,500 individuals die from alcohol use disorders and over 160,000 individuals die from drug use disorders, and (2) over 18,250,000 DALYs are lost due to alcohol use disorders and over 21,750,000 DALYs are lost due to drug use disorders.[2]

Based on biological sex, for alcohol use disorders, the WHO also estimates about 1.63 deaths per 100,000 population for males and about .32 deaths per 100,000 population for females, and about 1.82 DALYs per 1,000 population for males and about .65 DALYs per 1,000 population for females. And, for drug use disorders, the estimates are about 1.46 deaths per 100,000 population for males and about .68 deaths per 100,000 population for females, and about 1.91 DALYs per 1,000 population for males and about 1.02 DALYs per 1,000 population for females. According to these estimates, based on biological sex, worldwide, each year: (1) over 121,500 males and over 24,000 females die from alcohol use disorders, and over 109,250 males and over 50,750 females die from drug use disorders, and (2) over 13,500,000 DALYs for males and over 4,750,000 DALYs for females are lost due to alcohol use disorders, and over 14,250,000 DALYs for males and over 7,500,000 DALYs for females are lost due to drug use disorders. In sum, it appears that there is a worldwide, sex-based health disparity in the context of death and disability related to alcohol and drug use disorders. That is, males seem to experience more negative health related outcomes due to alcohol and drug use disorders than do females.

In the United States more particularly[3] (see Table 1.2; WHO, 2016a, 2016b), per 100,000 population, it is estimated that, about 3.29 deaths can be attributed to alcohol use disorders, and about 11.17 deaths can be attributed to drug use disorders. Likewise, that per 1,000 population, about 3.75 DALYs are lost in the context of alcohol use disorders and about 12.76 DALYs are lost in the context of drug use disorders. With the population of the United States in 2016 at about 322,180,000 (i.e., 322 million) (WHO, 2016a), these estimates suggest that, *each year*: (1) over 10,500 individuals die from alcohol use disorders and over 35,750 individuals die from drug use disorders, and (2) over 1,200,000 DALYs are lost due to alcohol use disorders and over 4,000,000 DALYs are lost due to drug use disorders.

Table 1.1 Global[a] Estimates of Death and Disability for the Year: 2016

Cause	*Deaths*			*DALYs[b]*		
	Total	*Male*	*Female*	*Total*	*Male*	*Female*
Alcohol Use Disorders	145,565	121,557	24,008	18,454,879	13,613,720	4,841,159
Drug Use Disorders	160,235	109,274	50,960	21,891,978	14,285,422	7,606,555
- Opioid	118,622	83,207	35,416	16,636,604	10,867,688	5,768,916
- Cocaine	9,434	6,662	2,772	1,238,919	858,424	380,494
- Amphetamine	7,102	5,513	1,589	999,708	698,407	301,301
- Cannabis	0	0	0	646,380	441,163	205,216
- Others, combined	25,076	13,893	11,184	2,370,368	1,419,740	950,628
Intentional Injuries	1,453,897	1,020,885	433,012	82,235,860	57,563,869	24,671,990
- Self-Harm	793,307	507,730	285,577	37,563,741	23,801,135	13,762,606
- Interpersonal Violence	476,898	381,829	95,069	31,236,573	24,322,495	6,914,079
- Collective Violence & Legal Intervention	183,691	131,326	52,365	13,435,545	9,440,239	3,995,306
Unintentional Injuries	3,429,298	2,243,812	1,185,486	215,158,431	141,310,595	73,847,836
- Road Injury	1,402,302	1,037,142	365,160	82,538,052	60,615,714	21,922,337
- Poisonings	106,683	60,881	45,802	6,268,554	3,606,139	2,662,415
- Falls	660,320	363,454	296,866	38,162,438	22,209,548	15,952,890
- Fire, Heat, & Hot Substances	152,601	68,856	83,744	10,609,679	4,895,841	5,713,839
- Drowning	322,149	215,184	106,965	20,134,352	13,536,598	6,597,754
- Exposure to Mechanical Forces	149,974	105,772	44,202	13,224,605	9,117,437	4,107,168
- Natural Disasters	1,822	1,088	734	360,717	222,916	137,801
- Other	633,448	391,434	242,013	43,860,035	27,106,403	16,753,632
Eating Disorders	1,845	411	1,434	2,260,725	540,139	1,720,587

[a] Global population = about 7,461,884,000 (i.e., 7.46 billion).
[b] Disability-Adjusted Life Years Lost (i.e., time lost because of poor health and early death).
Source: Adapted from World Health Organization (2016a, 2016b).

Based on biological sex, for alcohol use disorders, the WHO also estimates that, per 100,000 population, about 2.51 deaths for males and about .76 deaths for females, and that, per 1,000 population, about 2.49 DALYs for males and about 1.26 DALYs for females. For drug use disorders, the estimates are about 7.26 deaths for males and about 3.88 deaths for females, and about 8.02 DALYs for males and about 4.74 DALYs for females. According to these estimates, based on biological sex, in the United States[4]

Table 1.2 United States[a] Estimates of Death and Disability for the Year: 2016

Cause	*Deaths*			*DALYs*[b]		
	Total	*Male*	*Female*	*Total*	*Male*	*Female*
Alcohol Use Disorders	10,600	8,080	2,519	1,207,799	801,430	406,369
Drug Use Disorders	35,986	23,442	12,544	4,110,199	2,582,252	1,527,947
- Opioid	24,111	16,160	7,951	2,851,674	1,813,664	1,038,010
- Cocaine	4,592	2,971	1,621	462,264	298,189	164,075
- Amphetamine	1,804	1,237	566	190,533	113,439	77,093
- Cannabis	0	0	0	77,514	52,274	25,240
- Others, combined	5,478	3,072	2,405	528,212	304,685	223,527
Intentional Injuries	71,019	55,031	15,988	3,772,688	2,913,935	858,753
- Self-Harm	49,393	37,647	11,745	2,277,522	1,726,089	551,432
- Interpersonal Violence	21,058	16,839	4,219	1,436,076	1,132,267	303,808
- Collective Violence & Legal Intervention	567	544	23	59,089	55,578	3,511
Unintentional Injuries	112,561	69,662	42,898	6,760,493	4,107,441	2,653,051
- Road Injury	38,203	26,834	11,368	2,394,349	1,633,386	760,962
- Poisonings	2,912	1,561	1,351	160,453	90,272	70,181
- Falls	36,157	18,466	17,691	1,998,602	944,106	1,054,495
- Fire, Heat, & Hot Substances	3,154	1,863	1,291	246,946	144,148	102,797
- Drowning	4,568	3,606	962	253,492	198,668	54,823
- Exposure to Mechanical Forces	3,754	3,089	665	529,211	380,025	149,185
- Natural Disasters	121	76	44	10,432	6,254	4,178
- Other	23,688	14,165	9,522	1,167,005	710,578	456,426
Eating Disorders	292	40	251	215,312	43,775	171,537

[a] United States population = about 322,180,000 (i.e., 322.18 million).
[b] Disability-Adjusted Life Years Lost (i.e., time lost because of poor health and early death).
Source: Adapted from World Health Organization (2016a, 2016b).

alone, each year: (1) over 8,000 males and over 2,500 females die from alcohol use disorders, and over 23,000 males and over 12,500 females die from drug use disorders, and (2) over 800,000 DALYs for males and over 400,000 DALYs for females are lost due to alcohol use disorders, and over 2,500,000 DALYs for males and over 1,500,000 DALYs for females are lost due to drug use disorders. In sum, consistent with worldwide levels of death and disability due to alcohol and drug use disorders, in the United States, males seem to experience disparately worse health related outcomes than do females.

Related to this, in regard to alcohol *consumption* (i.e., not necessarily rising to the level of an alcohol use disorder), additional data from 2016 suggests that, worldwide, of all such related deaths (i.e., about 3 million[5]), 28.7 percent were linked to injuries (20.9

percent unintentional; 7.8 intentional), 21.3 percent to digestive diseases, 19.0 percent to cardiovascular diseases and diabetes, 12.9 percent to infectious diseases, 12.6 percent to cancers, 4.9 percent to alcohol use disorders, and .6 percent to epilepsy (WHO, 2018b). Likewise, of all such related DALYs (i.e., about 133 million[6]), 39.5 percent were linked to injuries (30.0 percent unintentional; 9.5 intentional), 17.6 percent to digestive diseases, 13.9 percent to alcohol use disorders, 11.2 percent to infectious diseases, 9.0 percent to cardiovascular diseases and diabetes, 7.7 percent to cancers, and 1.1 percent to epilepsy (WHO, 2018b).

Regarding economic impact, Rehm et al. (2009) summarized several studies conducted between 1997 and 2006 across the following six countries (with population estimates during the study year in parentheses): France (58.6 million), United States (280.6 million), Scotland (5.1 million), Canada (31.9 million), South Korea (47.5 million), and Thailand, (64.6 million). The annual burden (i.e., direct and indirect costs) related to alcohol use (e.g., health care, law enforcement, productivity) is estimated to be over $305,250,000,000 (i.e., $305.25 billion). In the context of illicit drug use, according to the International Narcotics Control Board (INCB), an affiliate of the United Nations, and regarding the costs of drug treatment alone, an estimated 1 in 6 problematic drug users receives treatment, costing about $35 billion on an annual basis, extrapolated to about $200 billion to $250 billion if all those in need actually received treatment (INCB, 2014). In the United States alone, the direct and indirect economic impact of: (1) alcohol use is estimated to be over $234.75 billion (Rehm et al., 2009), and (2) illicit drug use is estimated to be over $193 billion (NDIC, 2011). Of note, of the six countries reviewed by Rehm et al. (2009), the United States (i.e., its national population), while acounting for 57.46 percent of the sample(s) studied, accounted for 76.94 percent of the economic impact observed.

In sum, regarding the societal-level association of alcohol use and illicit drug use with death, disability, and economic burden, it is clear that the anecdotal evidence readily available in the news (e.g., Campbell, 2019) is overwhelmingly supported by the empirical[7] evidence freely available to the public via the World Health Organization (see INCB, 2014; WHO, 2016a, 2016b, 2018b) and other scientific resources (e.g., NDIC, 2011; Rehm et al., 2009). Indeed, worldwide (WHO, 2016a, 2016b), alcohol use disorders and drug use disorders together account for: (1) over 300,000 deaths, every single year, and (2) over 40 million years lost because of poor health and early death (i.e., DALYs), every single year. In terms of the worldwide negative health related consequences of the mere consumption of alcohol,[8] about 3 million related deaths occur every single year, and about 133 million years are lost every single year because of poor health and early death (WHO, 2018b). Lastly, the worldwide economic burden of alcohol and illicit drug use together rises to at least[9] $500,000,000,000 (i.e., $500 billion, or $.5 trillion), every single year (INCB, 2014; Rehm et al., 2009).

Societal-Level Problems Related to Compulsive Behaviors

Unlike for alcohol and illicit drug use, and for suicidal behavior (see below), the World Health Organization largely does not report data regarding death and disability related to compulsive behavioral sets otherwise known as process, or behavioral addictions. Indeed, the recognition of behavioral addictions as formal and official diagnostic possibilities is a controversial topic (see Chapter 2). Nevertheless, to better understand the potential societal impact of behavioral addictions, it is useful to gain perspective on the frequency of such problematic compulsive behavioral sets. Sussman et al. (2011; see also, Sussman, 2017) conducted a comprehensive review of the scientific literature regarding 11 addictive behaviors in an effort to provide estimates of 12-month prevalence rates in the United States population (i.e., the rate of occurrence within a given 12-month period). The 11 addictive behaviors examined were in the context of: cigarettes,[10] alcohol use, illicit drug use, binge eating,[11] gambling, the internet, love, sex, exercise, working, and shopping (see Table 1.3 and Table 1.4). The 12-month prevalence rate estimates for these

Table 1.3 Behavioral Addictions Related Estimates[a] for the Year: 2016 – Part 1

	Estimated Prevalence[b]			*Estimated Population*[c]		
	Alone	*With Alcohol*	*With Drugs*	*Alone*	*With Alcohol*	*With Drugs*
Alcohol Abuse/ Dependence	10%	–	50%			
- Global[d]				746,188,400	–	373,094,200
- United States				32,218,000	–	16,109,000
Drug Abuse/ Dependence	5%	50%	–			
- Global[d]				373,094,200	186,547,100	–
- United States				16,109,000	8,054,500	–
Binge Eating Disorder[e]	2%	25%	25%			
- Global[d]				149,237,680	37,309,420	37,309,420
- United States				6,443,600	1,610,900	1,610,900
Gambling Addiction[e]	2%	30%	20%			
- Global[d]				149,237,680	44,771,304	29,847,536
- United States				6,443,600	1,933,080	1,288,720
Internet Addiction[e]	2%	10%	10%			
- Global[d]				149,237,680	14,923,768	14,923,768
- United States				6,443,600	644,360	644,360
Love Addiction[e]	3%	40%	40%			
- Global[d]				223,856,520	89,542,608	89,542,608
- United States				9,665,400	3,866,160	3,866,160
Sex Addiction[e]	3%	40%	40%			
- Global[d]				223,856,520	89,542,608	89,542,608
- United States				9,665,400	3,866,160	3,866,160

[a] 12-month prevalence.
[b] Estimated prevalence of abuse/dependence in the United States (Sussman et al., 2011).
[c] Based on World Health Organization (2016a, 2016b) Global (i.e., ± 7.46 billion) and United States (i.e., ± 322.18 million) population estimates.
[d] Estimated population values extrapolated from Sussman et al. (2011) United States prevalence estimates.
[e] When Sussman et al. (2011) United States prevalence estimates were published, the *DSM-5* (American Psychiatric Association, 2013) was not yet published and the addictions listed under this note were broadly defined (i.e., not formal diagnoses, as were alcohol abuse/dependence, and drug abuse/dependence). Currently, Gambling Disorder is the only non-substance behavioral addiction included in the *DSM-5*. Eating disorders (often considered a behavioral addiction) also are included in the *DSM-5*; however, as a distinct category.

Table 1.4 Behavioral Addictions Related Estimates[a] for the Year: 2016 – Part 2

	Estimated Prevalence[b]			*Estimated Population[c]*		
	Alone	*With Alcohol*	*With Drugs*	*Alone*	*With Alcohol*	*With Drugs*
Exercise Addiction[e]	3%	15%	15%			
- Global[d]				223,856,520	33,578,478	33,578,478
- United States				9,665,400	1,449,810	1,449,810
Workaholism[e]	10%	20%	20%			
- Global[d]				746,188,400	149,237,680	149,237,680
- United States				32,218,000	6,443,600	6,443,600
Shopping/Buying Addiction[e]	6%	20%	20%			
- Global[d]				447,713,040	89,542,608	89,542,608
- United States				19,330,800	3,866,160	3,866,160
Total		46% (33.5%)[f]				
- Global[d]				3,432,466,640	734,995,574	906,618,906
- United States				148,202,800	31,734,730	39,144,870
Total (not Alcohol/Drugs)		31% (23.5%)[g]				
- Global[d]				2,313,184,040	548,448,474	533,524,706
- United States				99,875,800	23,680,230	23,035,870

[a] 12-month prevalence.
[b] Estimated prevalence of abuse/dependence in the United States (Sussman et al., 2011).
[c] Based on World Health Organization (2016a, 2016b) Global (i.e., ± 7.46 billion) and United States (i.e., ± 322.18 million) population estimates.
[d] Estimated population values extrapolated from Sussman et al. (2011) United States prevalence estimates.
[e] When Sussman et al. (2011) United States prevalence estimates were published, the *DSM-5* (American Psychiatric Association, 2013) was not yet published and the addictions listed under this note were broadly defined (i.e., not formal diagnoses, as were alcohol abuse/dependence, and drug abuse/dependence). Currently, Gambling Disorder is the only non-substance behavioral addiction included in the *DSM-5*. Eating disorders (often considered a behavioral addiction) also are included in the *DSM-5*; however, as a distinct category.
[f] Sussman et al. (2011) recommend, rather than basing an estimate of overall addiction prevalence (% of the population) on the sum of the individual estimates, to remove the average of the co-occurring based estimates (i.e., $n = 18$ estimates; $\bar{X} = 27.22\%$) from the sum of the individual estimates. As such, regarding this unadjusted estimate of 46%, the adjusted estimate of the overall addiction prevalence rate would be about 33.48% (i.e., 46% − 12.52% (i.e., 46% × 27.22%) = 33.48). Or, about 33.5% of the population is estimated to have an addiction, of some sort, during any given 12-month period. That is, when considering behavioral addictions in conjunction with alcohol and/or drug addictions (but not behavioral addictions in conjunction with each other), the overall prevalence estimate is 33.5%.
[g] Similar to note f, regarding this unadjusted estimate of 31%, the adjusted estimate of the overall addiction prevalence rate would be about 23.44% (i.e., 31% − 7.56% (i.e., 31% × 24.38%) = 23.44). Or, about 23.5% of the population is estimated to have a behavioral addiction, of some sort, during any given 12-month period. That is, when considering behavioral addictions on their own (i.e., not in conjunction with alcohol and/or drug addictions, nor in conjunction with each other), the overall prevalence estimate is 23.5%.

non-substance related addictive behaviors ranged from 2 percent to 10 percent, each. With the population of the United States in 2016 at about 322 million people, these estimates suggest that, *each year* nearly 100,000,000 (i.e., 100 million) individuals are struggling with a non-substance related behavioral addiction, of some sort (see Table 1.4, Total (not Alcohol/Drugs), Estimated Population, Alone).

Although Sussman et al. (2011; see also, Sussman, 2017) explicitly provided their 12-month prevalence estimates for behavioral addictions in the context of the United States population, it may be useful to apply them to the global population in order to gain a preliminary understanding of the worldwide societal impact of behavioral addictions (see Table 1.3 and Table 1.4). In this regard, with a worldwide population in 2016 of about 7.46 billion people, these estimates suggest that, *each year* over 2,250,000,000 (2.25 billion) individuals are struggling with a non-substance related behavioral addiction (see Table 1.4, Total (not Alcohol/Drugs), Estimated Population, Alone).

Regarding economic impact, few studies exist regarding the financial burden associated with behavioral addictions. This is likely due to the controversy related to their formal and official recognition as diagnostic possibilities (see Chapter 2). However, reports are available estimating the economic impact of gambling disorders and eating disorders, as these are two diagnoses contained in the *DSM-5* [12] (American Psychiatric Association, 2013), both of which are also considered behavioral addictions (see Petry, 2016; Rosenberg & Feder, 2014; Sussman, 2017).

In the context of gambling disorders, Rodriguez-Monguio et al. (2018) provided United States based annual estimates of average health care costs per patient with a diagnosis of pathological gambling between 2009–2012. For 2009, the per patient cost was \$7,993 (95 percent confidence interval[13] (95 CI): ± \$11,847); for 2010, \$10,054 (95 CI: ± \$14,555); for 2011, \$9,093 (95 CI: ± \$13,422); and for 2012, \$9,523 (95 CI: ± \$14,505). Thompson and Beruhard (2010) discussed the social costs of gambling, or the "costs that are imposed upon people other than the gambler and his or her family, that is people who do not participate in the gambling process" (p. 178). In this regard, consistent with Thompson and Beruhard's (2010) estimate of the individual level *social cost* (as opposed to per patient healthcare cost) of pathological gambling (i.e., \$10,053 per pathological gambler) and formula for extrapolating such to the larger population, but using the Sussman et al. (2011) estimate of United States prevalence (i.e., 2 percent), the annual social cost of problematic gambling may be as high as over \$64,750,000,000 (i.e., 64.75 billion; about 322.18 million population ×.02 = 6,443,600, and 6,443,600 × \$10,053 = over \$64.75 billion). Likewise extrapolating to the global population (i.e., over 7.46 billion), the annual social cost of problematic gambling may be as high as nearly \$1,500,000,000,000 (i.e., \$1.5 trillion; about 7.46 billion population ×.02 = 149.2 million, and 149.2 million × \$10,053 = nearly \$1.5 trillion). Of note, worldwide annual losses due to gambling itself recently have been estimated to be as high as \$400,000,000,000 (i.e., \$400 billion) (see Abbott, 2017).

Regarding eating disorders, Stuhldreher et al. (2012) examined the available scientific literature and summarized relevant studies conducted in the United States, Canada, and Germany. Including Anorexia Nervosa (AN), Bulimia Nervosa (BN), Binge Eating Disorder (BED), and Eating Disorder – not otherwise specified (EDNOS), the estimated overall cost per patient, per year, ranged from \$127 (BN; Germany) to \$8,042 (AN; United States; women). The average annual estimate provided was \$4,276, with a standard deviation[14] (SD) of \$2,387. More recently in Canada (de Oliveira et al., 2017), average total direct costs per patient in Canadian dollars were \$10,022.8 (95 CI: \$9,390.9 to \$10,654.6). And, more recently in the United States (Samnaliev et al., 2015), average annual health care costs were \$5,779 (data related to SD was not reported).

Of note, the World Health Organization (2016a, 2016b) provides data regarding death and disability in the context of eating disorders (see Table 1.1 & Table 1.2). Globally, an estimated 1,845 deaths occur each year (411 males; 1,434 females) due to eating disorders as a broad category (i.e., not broken into sub-types), and about 2.26 million years are lost each year (over 500,000 for males; over 1.5 million for females) due to death and disability (i.e., DALYs). In the United States alone, an estimated 292 deaths occur each year (40 males; 251 females) due to eating disorders, and over 200,000 years are lost each year (over 40,000 for males; over 150,000 for females) due to death and disability. These WHO-based worldwide and United States estimates of death and disability in the context of eating disorders suggest a biological sex-based health disparity such that females appear to experience more negative outcomes related to eating disorders than do males.

Societal-Level Problems Related to Suicide and Suicidal Behavior

The World Health Organization collects data regarding death and disability related to injuries, and distinguishes between those of unintentional versus intentional origin (see Table 1.1 & Table 1.2; WHO, 2016a, 2016b). From this most recent, publicly available data, it is estimated that, worldwide, about 10.63 deaths per 100,000 population can be attributed to intentional self-harm; that is, death by suicide.[15] Also, that per 1,000 population, about 5.03 DALYs are lost. With a worldwide population in 2016 of about 7.46 billion people, these estimates suggest that, *each year*: (1) over 775,000[16] individuals die by suicide and (2) over 37,500,000 DALYs are lost due to suicidal behavior.

Based on biological sex, the WHO also estimates that about 6.80 deaths per 100,000 population for males and about 3.83 deaths per 100,000 population for females can be attributed to suicide. And, about 3.19 DALYs per 1,000 population for males and about 1.84 DALYs per 1,000 population for females. According to these estimates, based on biological sex, worldwide, each year: (1) over 500,000 males and over 275,000 females die by suicide, and (2) over 23,750,000 DALYs for males and over 13,750,000 DALYs for females are lost due to suicidal behavior.

In the United States more particularly (WHO, 2016a, 2016b), per 100,000 population, it is estimated that, about 15.33 deaths can be attributed to suicide, and per 1,000 population, about 7.07 DALYs are lost due to suicidal behavior. With the population of the United States in 2016 at about 322 million people, these estimates suggest that, *each year*: (1) over 49,250 individuals die by suicide, and (2) over 2,250,000 DALYs are lost due to suicidal behavior.

Based on biological sex, the WHO also estimates that, per 100,000 population, about 11.69 deaths for males and about 3.65 deaths for females can be attributed to suicide. And, per 1,000 population, about 5.36 DALYs for males and about 1.71 DALYs for females. According to these estimates, based on biological sex, in the United States[17] alone, each year, (1) over 37,500 males and over 11,500 females die by suicide, and (2) over 1,500,000 DALYs for males and over 500,000 DALYs for females are lost due to suicidal behavior.

As with alcohol use disorders and drug use disorders, whether based on worldwide or United States levels of death and disability, there again appears to be a sex-based health disparity in the context of suicide and suicidal behavior. That is, males likewise appear to experience disparately worse health-related outcomes than do females.

Related to this, when comparing annual unintentional injuries versus annual intentional injuries (Table 1.1 & Table 1.2), the worldwide total number of deaths, for both the world and the United States, due to all unintentional injuries combined (over

3,250,000 and over 100,000, respectively) easily outnumbers the worldwide total number of deaths due to all intentional injuries combined (over 1,250,000 and over 70,000, respectively). However, *death by suicide* outnumbers all other single-cause deaths due to injury, regardless of intentionality, except for worldwide deaths due to road injury (Table 1.1 & Table 1.2). That is, among all types of injury, worldwide, death by suicide is second to death by road injury. And, in the United States alone, death by suicide occurs more often than death due to any other single type of injury. Also, every year, worldwide and in the United States, suicide accounts for more intentional deaths due to injury (793,307 and 49,393, respectively) than all other intentional deaths due to injury (660,589 and 21,625, respectively). That is, each year, more individuals die by suicide than by interpersonal violence, collective violence, and legal intervention, *combined.* [18] Regarding suicide attempts, compared to deaths by suicide, up to 20 times as many attempts may occur (WHO, 2018c). This suggests that, each year: (1) worldwide, there are up to over 15.5 million suicide attempts, and (2) in the United States alone, there are up to over 985,000 suicide attempts.

Regarding economic impact, McDaid (2016) summarized several studies published between 1999 and 2015 across the following six countries (see Table 1.5 for relevant suicide related estimates): Australia, Canada, Ireland, New Zealand, Scotland, and United States. The annual burden (i.e., direct and indirect costs) related to death by suicide (e.g., health care and productivity) is estimated to be over $66,750,000,000 (i.e., $66.75 billion). In the United States alone, the direct and indirect economic impact of suicide *and* nonfatal suicide attempts, combined, has been estimated to be between about $58.5 billion and about $93.5 billion[19] (Shepard et al., 2016). Of note, of the six countries reviewed by McDaid (2016; see also Table 1.5), the United States (i.e., its national population), while accounting

Table 1.5 Suicide Related Estimates for Six Countries for the Year: 2016

Country	*Deaths by Suicide*[a]	*Cost per Suicide*[b]	*Total Cost of Suicide*[c]	*Population*[d]	*Rate*[e]
Australia	3,186	$1,471,600	$4,688,517,600	24,126,000	7,572
Canada	4,525	$1,000,400	$4,526,810,000	36,290,000	8,019
Ireland	542	$2,540,400	$1,376,896,800	4,726,000	8,719
New Zealand	565	$2,099,000	$1,185,935,000	4,661,000	8,249
Scotland[f]	728	$2,342,000	$1,704,976,000	5,404,700	7,424
United States	49,393	$1,079,700	$53,329,622,100	322,180,000	6,522
Total	58,939	$10,533,100	$66,812,757,500	397,387,700	6,742[g]
Average	9,823	$1,755,516	$11,135,459,583	66,231,283	7,751
(SD)[h]	(19,454)[i]	($661,138)[j]	($20,730,370,321)[k]	(126,057,727)[l]	(762)[m]

[a] Except for Scotland, World Health Organization (2016a, 2016b).
[b] Cost per *individual* death by suicide (see McDaid, 2016).
[c] Total cost of all individual deaths by suicide (i.e., [Deaths] × [Cost per Suicide]).
[d] Except for Scotland, World Health Organization (2016a, 2016b).
[e] Suicide rate in the population (e.g., Australia = about 1 per 7,572 population).
[f] Scottish Public Health Observatory (2019) and National Records of Scotland (2017).
[g] Overall suicide rate for the six countries (i.e., 397,387,700 / 58,939 = 6,742; or, about 1 per 6,742 population).
[h] Standard Deviation; see note 14.
[i] ± 1SD = −9,631 to 29,277
[j] ± 1SD = $1,094,378 to $2,416,654
[k] ± 1SD = −$9,594,910,738 to $31,865,829,904
[l] ± 1SD = −59,826,444 to 192,289,010
[m] ± 1SD = 6,989 to 8,513

for 81.07 percent of the sample(s) studied, accounted for 79.82 percent of the economic impact observed. Related to this, when comparing among the six countries: (1) the cost per individual death by suicide, and (2) the suicide rate within the country, meaningful discrepancies arise. The average cost per suicide is equal to about \$1.75 million, with the standard deviation[14], [20] equal to about \$660,000. As such, the cost per suicide for Canada and the United States (i.e., about \$1 million each) was atypically lower than the average, and for Ireland (i.e., about \$2.5 million) was atypically higher than the average. The average suicide rate, or frequency of suicide within each country's population, is equal to about 1 individual death by suicide per 7,751 population, with the standard deviation equal to about 762. As such, the frequency of suicide for Ireland (i.e., about 1 per 8,719) was atypically lower (i.e., less frequent) than the average, and for the United States (i.e., about 1 per 6,522) was atypically higher (i.e., more frequent) than the average.

In sum, regarding the societal-level association of suicidal behavior with death, disability, and economic burden, it is clear, based on the empirical evidence available, that there is a distinct and present public health problem related to suicide. Indeed, worldwide (WHO, 2016a, 2016b; see also, Naghavi, 2019), suicidal behavior accounts for: (1) nearly 800,000 deaths, every single year, and (2) over 37.5 million years lost because of poor health and early death (i.e., DALYs), every single year. In terms of death due to all types of injury, whether unintentional or intentional, suicide is a leading cause of death due to injury worldwide, and *the* leading cause of death due to injury in the United States. Lastly, the worldwide economic burden of suicidal behavior rises to at least[21] \$66.75 billion, every single year (McDaid, 2016).

Co-Occurrence of Substance Addictions, Behavioral Addictions, and Suicidal Behavior

Experts also have estimated rates of co-occurrence between various addictive and compulsive behavior sets; that is, substance addictions, behavioral addictions, and suicidal behaviors. Based on Sussman et al.'s (2011) United States prevalence rate estimates (see Table 1.3 & Table 1.4), nearly half of those struggling with a particular behavioral addiction are likely also struggling with an alcohol or drug addiction. That is, over 1 billion individuals worldwide, including over 46.5 million individuals in the United States (see Table 1.4, Total (not Alcohol/Drugs), Estimated Population, with Alcohol + with Drugs). Similarly, up to 40 percent of those struggling with substance related addiction and seeking treatment have also attempted suicide (see Yuodelis-Flores & Ries, 2015), and in a study among 99 individuals struggling with pathological gambling and seeking help through Gamblers Anonymous, over 65 percent engaged in planning a suicide attempt and over 27 percent attempted suicide (see Thompson & Beruhard, 2010).

Societal Relevance of Religiousness and Spirituality

The International Social Survey Programme (ISSP) collects worldwide data on a variety of topics including a module on religion (GESIS, 2018; ISSP Research Group, 2018). From its most recent, publicly available data[22] (i.e., collected between 2007 and 2010), Table 1.6 and Table 1.7 include Global (i.e., among 40 participating countries) and United States specific participant responses to several religiously and spiritually oriented questions contained within the aforementioned module. For each of the 12 ISSP questions presented in Table 1.6 and Table 1.7, response options and their corresponding tallies are provided (see GESIS, 2018; ISSP Research Group, 2018). Additionally, for our purposes here, the response tallies have been collapsed to calculate estimates regarding overall levels of

Table 1.6 Spirituality Related Estimates[a,b] – Part 1

Survey Item	*Response Options*								*Respondents*		*Spirituality*[c]	
13b. Respect all Religions[d]	(SA)	(A)	(NAND)	(D)	(SD)	–	(CC[e])	(NA[e])	N[e]	Nv[e]	% +	% –
- Global	20,176	26,245	6,210	3,445	2,099	–	1,377	430	59,982	58,175	79.80	20.20
- United States	433	666	116	106	31	–	8	5	1,365	1,352	81.29	18.71
16. Belief about God[f]	(1)	(2)	(3)	(4)	(5)	(6)	(DN[e])	(NA)				
- Global	6,267	5,204	7,744	5,545	9,814	24,631	370	407	59,982	59,205	80.62	19.38
- United States	38	68	140	48	229	830	5	7	1,365	1,353	92.17	7.83
17. Belief about God[g]	(1)	(2)	(3)	(4)	–	–	(CC)	(NA)				
- Global	8,082	5,100	4,022	34,070	–	–	6,891	797	59,982	51,274	74.29	25.71
- United States	56	72	96	1,099	–	–	30	12	1,365	1,323	90.33	9.67
18a. Life after Death[h]	(1)	(2)	(3)	(4)	–	–	(CC)	(NA)				
- Global	16,604	15,165	10,434	11,961	–	–	5,212	606	59,982	54,164	58.65	41.35
- United States	745	279	152	127	–	–	54	8	1,365	1,303	78.59	21.41
18b. Heaven[h]	(1)	(2)	(3)	(4)	–	–	(CC)	(NA)				
- Global	17,095	14,496	9,971	12,562	–	–	5,088	770	59,982	54,124	58.37	41.63
- United States	853	276	117	80	–	–	33	6	1,365	1,326	85.14	14.86
18c. Hell[h]	(1)	(2)	(3)	(4)	–	–	(CC)	(NA)				
- Global	13,258	11,792	12,024	16,629	–	–	5,365	914	59,982	53,703	46.65	53.35
- United States	698	270	196	163	–	–	30	8	1,365	1,327	72.95	27.05
18d. Religious Miracles[h]	(1)	(2)	(3)	(4)	–	–	(CC)	(NA)				
- Global	14,823	15,605	11,490	12,754	–	–	4,363	947	59,982	54,672	55.66	44.34
- United States	738	311	183	101	–	–	29	3	1,365	1,333	78.69	21.31

[a] (GESIS, 2018; see also, ISSP Research Group, 2018)
[b] Data collected between 2007 and 2010, from 40 participating countries.
[c] Spirituality: % + = Spiritual (i.e., religious and/or spiritual responses / Nv); % – = Non-Spiritual (i.e., non-religious and/or non-spiritual responses / Nv).
[d] SA = strongly agree; A = agree; NAND = neither agree nor disagree; D = disagree; SD = strongly disagree
[e] CC = can't choose; NA = no answer; DN = don't know; N = overall sample size; Nv = valid sample size (i.e., not including CC, NA, and/or DN)
[f] 1 = no belief; 2 = no belief and no way to find out; 3 = not a personal god, but a higher power of some kind; 4 = belief in God, at times; 5 = have doubts, but believe; 6 = believe and no doubts
[g] 1 = no belief now and never have; 2 = no belief now, but used to; 3 = believe now, but didn't used to; 4 = believe now and always have
[h] 1 = yes, definitely; 2 = yes, probably; 3 = no, probably not; 4 = no, definitely not

Table 1.7 Spirituality Related Estimates[a,b] – Part 2

Survey Item	Response Options													Respondents		Spirituality[c]	
19a. God concerned with every human being personally[d]	(SA)		(A)		(NAND)		(D)		(SD)		–	(CC[e])	(NA[e])	N[e]	Nv[e]	% +	% –
- Global	13,509		15,113		9,372		8,828		8,769		–	3,650	741	59,982	55,591	51.49	48.51
- United States	578		368		185		136		76		–	16	6	1,365	1,343	70.44	29.56
19f. Connect with God without church / religious services[d]	(SA)		(A)		(NAND)		(D)		(SD)		–	(CC)	(NA)				
- Global	10,960		17,841		9,978		8,393		8,033		–	3,829	948	59,982	55,205	52.17	47.83
- United States	339		543		155		194		118		–	9	7	1,365	1,349	65.38	34.62
27. How Often Pray[i]	(1)	(2)	(3)	(4)	(5)	(6)	(7)	(8)	(9)	(10)	(11)	(DN[e])	(NA)				
- Global	15,317	2,588	3,181	5,682	2,202	2,811	2,766	3,049	6,006	8,985	5,327	424	629	59,982	57,914	53.78	46.22
- United States	138	28	25	68	38	63	27	66	149	356	391	6	10	1,365	1,349	80.80	19.20
31. Religiousness[j]	(1)		(2)	(3)		(4)	(5)		(6)	(7)		(CC)	(NA)				
- Global	2,006		7,756	21,607		11,350	6,171		5,049	4,507		1,173	363	59,982	58,446	53.67	46.33
- United States	91		271	678		96	97		52	70		4	6	1,365	1,355	76.75	23.25
32. Religious and/or Spiritual[k]	(1)		(2)		(3)		(4)		–		–	(CC)	(NA)				
- Global	14,345		18,743		9,275		11,690		–		–	5,347	582	59,982	54,053	78.37	21.63
- United States	528		304		312		154		–		–	48	19	1,365	1,298	88.14	11.86

[a] (GESIS, 2018; see also, ISSP Research Group, 2018).
[b] Data collected between 2007 and 2010, from 40 participating countries.
[c] Spirituality: % + = Spiritual (i.e., religious and/or spiritual responses / Nv); % – = Non-Spiritual (i.e., non-religious and/or non-spiritual responses / Nv).
[d] SA = strongly agree; A = agree; NAND = neither agree nor disagree; D = disagree; SD = strongly disagree
[e] CC = can't choose; NA = no answer; DN = don't know; N = overall sample size; Nv = valid sample size (i.e., not including CC, NA, and/or DN)
[f] 1 = no belief; 2 = no belief and now way to find out; 3 = not a personal god, but a higher power of some kind; 4 = belief in God, at times; 5 = have doubts, but believe; 6 = believe and no doubts
[g] 1 = no belief now and never have; 2 = no belief now, but used to; 3 = believe now, but didn't used to; 4 = believe now and always have
[h] 1 = yes, definitely; 2 = yes, probably; 3 = no, probably not; 4 = no, definitely not
[i] 1 = never; 2 = less than once a year; 3 = about once or twice a year; 4 = several times a year; 5 = about once a month; 6 = 2–3 times a month; 7 = nearly every week; 8 = every week; 9 = several times a week; 10 = once a day; 11 = several times a day
[j] 1 = extremely religious; 2 = very religious; 3 = somewhat religious; 4 = neither religious nor non-religious; 5 = somewhat non-religious; 6 = very non-religious; 7 = extremely non-religious
[k] 1 = follow a religion and spiritual; 2 = follow a religion, but not spiritual; 3 = don't follow a religion, but spiritual; 4 = don't follow a religion and not spiritual

spirituality versus non-spirituality among the respondents.[23] That is, for each survey item[24] there is a percentage estimate of religious and/or spiritual oriented responses (i.e., % +) versus a percentage estimate of non-religious and/or non-spiritual oriented responses (i.e., % −). For example, regarding the importance of respecting all religions[25] (see Table 1.6, survey item 13b), at the Global level of analysis, the tallies for the response options of "strongly agree" and "agree" were added together and divided by the valid sample size (i.e., 20,176 + 26,245 = 46,421, and 46,421 / 58,175 = .7980) in order to calculate a "Spirituality % +" estimate of 79.80. Likewise, the tallies for the response options of "neither agree nor disagree," "disagree," and "strongly disagree" were added together and divided by the valid sample size (i.e., 6,210 + 3,445 + 2,099 = 11,754, and 11,754 / 58,175 = .2020) in order to calculate a "Spirituality % −" estimate of 20.20. As such, at the Global level of analysis, nearly 80 percent of the respondents from 40 countries considered respect for all religions to be important, whereas about 20 percent did not. That is, on this particular question regarding the level of spirituality among the respondents, 80 percent versus 20 percent were spiritual versus non-spiritual, respectively. Through the same calculation process, for the United States, the Spirituality estimates for this item (i.e., respect for all religions) were about 81 percent versus about 19 percent, respectively – suggesting consistency between the United States and the rest of the world.

Considering the 12 ISSP items included in Table 1.6 and Table 1.7 as a group, at the Global level of analysis (i.e., all 40 participating countries), the average Spirituality % + score was 61.96, with a standard deviation of 12.53. The highest score of 80.62 percent was for belief in God or a higher power of some kind (i.e., item 16) and the lowest score of 46.65 percent was for belief in Hell (i.e., item 18c.). Also, except for belief in Hell being below 50 percent, seven of the 11 other scores were between 51.49 percent and 58.65 percent, with the four remaining scores at or above 74.29 percent. At the United States level of analysis, the average Spirituality + score was 80.06, with a standard deviation of 8.08.[26] The highest score of 92.17 percent was for belief in God or a higher power and the lowest score of 65.38 percent was for connecting with God without church or religious services (i.e., item 19f). Also, except for connecting with God without church or religious services at 65.38 percent, five of the 11 other scores were between 70.44 percent and 78.69 percent, four more scores were between 80.80 percent and 88.14 percent, with the two remaining scores above 90 percent.

Regarding belief in God or a higher power (i.e., item 16; see Table 1.6), the top Spirituality % + score at both the Global and United States levels of analysis (i.e., 80.62 percent and 92.17 percent, respectively), a more conservative estimate may be more appropriate. That is, the initial estimate for this item included response option 4 (see note 24, and Table 1.6 and its footnote f); that is, a belief in God, at times, or "I find myself believing in God some of the time, but not at others" (see GESIS, 2018, p. 67). If this response option is removed from the calculation, the Spirituality % + scores for this item become 71.26[27] and 88.62, respectively. Also, using this more conservative estimate (i.e., the sum of response options 3, 5, and 6), of the 40 participating countries (see GESIS, 2018, p. 68), two countries reported a belief rate below 50 percent (i.e., Czech Republic = 40.33 percent and Japan = 39.71 percent), and five countries reported a belief rate above 90 percent (i.e., Chile = 94.51 percent, Dominican Republic = 94.38 percent, Philippines = 94.58 percent, Turkey = 96.27 percent, and Venezuela = 96.00 percent).

Regarding frequency of prayer (i.e., item 27; see Table 1.7), the Spirituality % + analysis revealed scores of 53.78 and 80.80 at the Global and United States levels of analysis, respectively. Of note, the estimate for this item included response options 5–11 (see note 24, and Table 1.7 and its footnote i); that is, a frequency of prayer of about once per month or more. Of note, when considering only response options 9, 10, and

11 (i.e., several times a week, once a day, and several times a day, respectively), at both the Global and United States levels of analysis, the Spirituality % + scores would be 35.08 percent and 66.42 percent, respectively. The *modal* response (i.e., the most frequent response) regarding frequency of prayer at both the Global and United States levels of analysis was 1 or never, and 11 or several times a day, respectively; that is, the polar opposite response options. Indeed, worldwide, while 26.45 percent of the respondents reported that they never pray, 9.20 percent pray several times per day; whereas, in the United States, while 10.23 percent of the respondents never pray, 28.98 percent pray several times per day.

More recent United States polling, from 2017 (see Gallup Poll, 2019), suggests that while 87 percent report a *belief* in God, 80 percent report thinking that there is at least a *high probability* that God exists (i.e., convinced that God exists = 64 percent; think God probably exists, but have a little doubt = 16 percent). And, that 74 percent consider religion to be at least fairly important in their lives (i.e., very important = 51 percent; fairly important = 23 percent).

In sum, when considering the 12 ISSP items presented in Table 1.6 and Table 1.7, individually (i.e., 11 of 12 items above 50 percent and 12 of 12 items above 65 percent, respectively) and as a group (i.e., about 62 percent and about 80 percent, respectively), both globally and within the United States, human beings appear to be spiritual in nature. Indeed, there is evidence to suggest that spirituality is an aspect of human nature (Pargament, 2013; Piedmont & Wilkins, 2013; see also, Chapter 4). However, the United States appears to be more spiritual than the world as a whole – given the discrepancy in the overall Spirituality % + scores, in general, and the discrepancies in the belief in God and frequency of prayer scores, in particular (see above).

In light of the societal relevance and prevalence of spirituality, the centrality of forgiveness to mainstream spiritual belief systems / world religions (see Webb et al., 2012; see also, Chapter 4), and the healthful association of forgiveness with addiction and suicidal behavior (see Webb & Toussaint, 2020; see also Chapter 6 and Chapter 7), it becomes important to understand as much as possible about the Forgiveness–Addiction–Recovery Association. Indeed, to put an electron microscope,[28] so to speak, on the theory, research, and clinical application of forgiveness as a means of addressing the clear and present public health problems – in truth, crises – posed by addictive behaviors; that is, substance addiction, behavioral addiction, and suicidal behavior. In this regard, the remainder of this chapter will provide a brief overview of the content of this book.

Understanding Forgiveness and Addiction: Theory

Chapter 2 provides comprehensive overviews of diagnostic related issues, the subject matter of addiction, and theories of recovery. Regarding diagnosis, *DSM* and *ICD* categorical systems are discussed and contrasted with the dimensional perspective on addiction. That is, the debate (see Helzer et al., 2006) between a categorical system (yes/no) of diagnosis versus a dimensional understanding (more/less, or intensity) of addiction is addressed. Regarding the subject matter of addiction, the following categories are addressed in terms of the content and whether or not they "should" be considered addictions: substances (i.e., alcohol and various illegal and legal drugs), compulsive behaviors (e.g., gambling, overeating, sexual activity), and other activities (e.g., suicide). Regarding theories of recovery, a variety of theories are presented, including: abstinence-based (e.g., Wallace, 2012), harm reduction (e.g., MacCoun, 1998), and natural recovery (e.g., Bischof et al., 2012). Chapter 2 also includes a discussion regarding addiction versus dependence versus abuse; that is, there is debate about which term(s) are best to use (e.g., meaningful, relevant, appropriate; Albanese & Shaffer, 2012).

Chapter 3 provides comprehensive discussions of: (1) the multidimensional nature of forgiveness and (2) definitions for the multiple dimensions of forgiveness. For example, forgiveness can involve a variety of targets (e.g., of self, of others, of deity, of uncontrollable situations) and methods (e.g., offering, seeking, and feeling) and each dimension can be considered in the context of a particular offense or as a general tendency (Toussaint & Webb, 2005; Webb et al., 2017).

Chapter 4 discusses larger issues about the nature of forgiveness. For example, is it a spiritual construct (or only a spiritual construct), a positive psychological construct, or both (including discussion of other parallels between spirituality and positive psychology)? Is it (in its multiple dimensions) morally justifiable (e.g., Enright & The Human Development Study Group, 1996)? Regarding the spiritual nature of forgiveness, aspects of spirituality are discussed, including: the search for the sacred and whether spirituality requires belief in deity (e.g., Pargament, 2013), the multidimensional nature of spirituality; for example, ritualistic, theistic, and existential spirituality (Webb et al., 2014) and relational spirituality (Worthington & Sandage, 2016), spirituality as a distinct, inherent trait common to the human condition, akin to the so-called Big 5 personality traits (e.g., Piedmont & Wilkins, 2013), the nature of spiritual struggle (e.g., Exline, 2013), and incorporating spirituality into treatment (e.g., Toussaint et al., 2012).

Chapter 5 discusses a variety of theoretical models progressively applicable to the association between forgiveness, health, and addiction. For example, Worthington's stress-and-coping theory of forgiveness (Worthington, 2006), Worthington et al.'s general model of the forgiveness–health association, including the notion of forgiveness as a component of the larger relationship between spirituality and health (Lavelock et al., 2015; Worthington et al., 2001), other models of the relationship between spirituality and health (e.g., Baetz & Toews, 2009; Koenig & Larson, 2001), and ultimately the expansion of Worthington's general model of the forgiveness–health association to explicitly address addiction/recovery as a particular manifestation of health and well-being (Webb et al., 2015). Updated forgiveness–health association modeling also is provided regarding additional issues particularly relevant to addiction/recovery; for example, anger (Webb et al., 2012), psychache (Webb et al., 2015), and temptation (Webb, 2014). Also, research regarding demographic differences in forgiveness is discussed in general terms.

Understanding Forgiveness and Addiction: Research

Chapter 6 reviews the empirical evidence regarding the association of forgiveness with substance (ab)use (Webb et al., 2011; Webb & Jeter, 2015; Webb & Toussaint, 2018, 2020; Webb et al., 2017) and the empirical evidence regarding the association of forgiveness with compulsive behaviors; for example, gambling and sexual activity (Webb & Toussaint, 2018, 2020). Chapter 7 reviews the empirical evidence regarding the association of forgiveness with suicidal behavior (e.g., Webb et al., 2015; Webb & Toussaint, 2020). Most theories of suicide do not conceptualize suicidal behavior as addictive behavior. However, the Twelve-Step Model of addiction and recovery (Alcoholics Anonymous, 1981, 1998, 2001) has been adapted to suicide (Suicide Anonymous, 2010) and has drawn many parallels between other forms of addictive behavior and suicidal behavior. Other models of suicidal behavior and their relevance to forgiveness are also discussed (e.g., Joiner et al., 2009; Shneidman, 1993).

Understanding Forgiveness and Addiction: Clinical Application

Chapter 8 provides comprehensive overviews of stand-alone forgiveness intervention modalities, which are then applied to subsequent chapters. For example, Enright's four-phase model of forgiveness therapy (Coyle & Enright, 1998; Enright & Fitzgibbons, 2015) involves *uncovering*, an awareness of the problem and emotional pain following an offense; *decision*, realizing the need for an alternate resolution; *work*, engaging in processes such as, reframing, empathy, and acceptance of pain; and *deepening*, finding meaning and universality. Also, Worthington's REACH Model of forgiveness psychoeducation (Worthington, 2006, 2020; Worthington & Sandage, 2016) involves: (r)ecalling an offense, developing (e)mpathy, choosing forgiveness as an (a)ltruistic gift, making a public, formal (c)ommitment to forgive, and (h)olding on to progress. Of note, both of these models are empirically-supported.

Chapter 9 builds upon previous reviews of the conceptual similarities between the process of forgiveness and the process/features of the Twelve-Step Model, including Twelve-Step Facilitation therapy (TSF) (Webb et al., 2015; Webb & Jeter, 2015; Webb & Toussaint, 2018; Webb et al., 2017; Webb & Trautman, 2010; see also, Lyons et al., 2010). For example, the interplay between resentments and forgiveness in addiction and recovery (Alcoholics Anonymous, 2001). Also, deliberate discussion of the application of principles and techniques is provided. For example, explicitly incorporating models of the forgiveness process (see Chapter 8) into Step 8 and Step 9 of the Twelve-Step Model, labeled the forgiveness steps (Hart, 1999), which involve becoming willing to make amends and actually making amends when possible and appropriate.

Chapter 10 builds upon previous reviews of the conceptual similarities between the process of forgiveness and the process/features of Motivational Enhancement Therapy / Motivational Interviewing, and the Stages-of-Change Model (see Webb & Jeter, 2015). For example, enhancing internal motivation, in terms of making progress in readiness for change, through developing awareness of problematic circumstances and facilitating cognitive resolve to address such. Also, deliberate discussion of the application of principles and techniques is provided. For example, explicitly incorporating models of the forgiveness process (see Chapter 8) in the context of developing discrepancy and recognizing the need to choose alternative options more likely to lead to growth.

Chapter 11 builds upon previous reviews of the conceptual similarities between the process of forgiveness and the process/features of Cognitive-Behavioral Coping Skills Therapy (see Webb & Jeter, 2015) and other traditional cognitive-behavioral approaches to treatment (e.g., REBT; see Ellis & Dryden, 1997). For example, developing stress management and problem solving skills. Also, deliberate discussion of the application of principles and techniques is provided. For example, integrating Socratic-style questioning and other disputation styles with models of the forgiveness process (see Chapter 8).

Chapter 12 addresses other counseling and psychotherapy modalities and related processes and their similarities to the process of forgiveness. Including, acceptance/mindfulness-based modalities (i.e., Acceptance and Commitment Therapy, Dialectical Behavior Therapy, and Mindfulness-based Cognitive Therapy), systemic-based modalities (i.e., Structural Family Therapy, Internal Family Systems Therapy, and Alcohol-focused Behavioral Couples Therapy), and psychodynamic-based modalities. Also, models of aggression are discussed, as related to forgiveness and addiction.

Chapter 13 provides a review and synthesis of the main points of each chapter and outlines future directions for the theory, research, and clinical application of forgiveness to addiction recovery. Indeed, such comprehensive integration of theory, research, and clinical application results in a roadmap forward; that is, guidelines regarding forgiveness as a treatment for recovery from addiction.

Notes

1 It is generally considered to be "bad form" to switch between numerical formats (e.g., 7,461,884,000 versus 7.46 billion). However, when describing the frequency-related information in this chapter, I intentionally use both formats for effect. The former to illustrate and remind the reader of the overwhelming nature of the number [of digits], and the latter for readability.

2 Remember, each DALY refers to a year's worth of lost time. That is, each year, over 18.25 million *and* over 21.75 million years' worth of time are lost due to alcohol use disorders and drug use disorders, respectively.

3 In addition to the United States, for 2016, the World Health Organization (2016a, 2016b) collected data regarding many forms of death and disability related thereto from 185 other countries, areas, or territories.

4 Even closer to home for me, I live in Lubbock, Texas – a city of about 240,000 people. Based on these estimates, about 34 people will die this and every year (23 males and 11 females) due to alcohol and drug use disorders. Likewise, nearly 4,000 DALYs will be lost this and every year (2,522 for males and 1,440 for females) due to alcohol and drug use disorders.

5 Recall that the World Health Organization estimates that over 145,500 people die each year due to alcohol use *disorders* (WHO, 2016a). Here, the estimated number of deaths per year, of about 3,000,000, is due to the mere *consumption* of alcohol (WHO, 2018b), whether it leads to an alcohol use disorder or not. If we subtract the number of people with alcohol use disorders from the overall number of people who consume alcohol, we are left with about 2,854,500 individuals whose death is related to their drinking but *do not* have an alcohol use disorder, versus about 145,500 individuals whose death is related to their drinking and *do* have an alcohol use disorder. This discrepancy is by a factor of 19.62 (i.e., 2,854,500 / 145,500 = 19.62). That is, there are 19.62 times as many deaths attributable to merely consuming alcohol, as opposed to deaths attributable to being clinically diagnosed with an alcohol use disorder.

6 As with note 5, recall that the World Health Organization estimates that over 18,250,000 DALYs are lost each year due to alcohol use *disorders* (WHO, 2016b). Here, the estimated number of DALYs lost per year, of about 133,000,000, is due to the mere *consumption* of alcohol (WHO, 2018b), whether it leads to an alcohol use disorder or not. If we subtract the number of DALYs based on people with alcohol use disorders from the overall number of DALYs based on people who consume alcohol, we are left with about 114,750,000 DALYs related to drinking among people who *do not* have an alcohol use disorder, versus about 18,250,000 DALYs related to drinking among people who *do* have an alcohol use disorder. This discrepancy is by a factor of 6.29 (i.e., 114,750,000 / 18,250,000 = 6.29). That is, there are 6.92 times as many DALYs attributable to merely consuming alcohol, as opposed to DALYs attributable to being clinically diagnosed with an alcohol use disorder.

7 The American Psychological Association (2015, p. 366; capitalization as in original) defines the *empirical method* as: "any procedure for conducting an investigation that relies upon experimentation and systematic observation rather than theoretical speculation. The term is sometimes used as a vague synonym for SCIENTIFIC METHOD."

8 It is important to acknowledge the meaningful distinction between alcohol consumption/alcohol use, versus alcohol problems/alcohol use disorders. Indeed, it is difficult and unfair to conclude that any/all alcohol use is a problem. That is, individuals and society at large can drink without otherwise having a problem (e.g., cultural, social, and economic related desirable effects; see Babor et al., 2010; Dunbar et al., 2017) and there can be healthful effects (albeit very limited; i.e., related to diabetes, ischaemic stroke, and coronary heart disease; Babor et al., 2010; WHO, 2018b), such that it is not reasonable to expect our society to stop drinking, or to assume that drinking *itself* is otherwise a problem among individuals or necessarily in society. However, it also is clear that alcohol use causes problems aside from those directly and indirectly associated with *addiction* (i.e., problems related to mere *consumption*). As such, it is likewise difficult, based on the comprehensive data available regarding the societal impact of alcohol (at a minimum as a health related outcome; both direct and indirect consequences), to conclude that the *net effect* of alcohol can be considered good, or even neutral. Based on the scientific evidence (as briefly outlined in this chapter), it is fair to conclude that alcohol, as an entity (so to speak), is highly problematic for humans – whether in terms of addiction as an issue of individual or public health, or in terms of being counterproductive to healthful living [particularly in the context of the World Health Organization's comprehensive definition of health; that is, "health is a state of complete physical,

mental and social well-being and not merely the absence of disease or infirmity" (WHO, 2018a, p. 1)]. Indeed, some have argued that the only safe level of alcohol consumption is *none* (Burton & Sheron, 2018; see also, GBD, 2018b). A fair, scientifically informed bottom line for alcohol is: although there can be otherwise innocuous and even desirable effects, use alcohol at your own risk. A reasonable corollary is: although there can be otherwise desirable effects, if you do not already drink alcohol, do not start, as such effects can be obtained in other, more healthy and less risky ways (see Harvard, 2019; USDHHS and USDA, 2015; see also, Perreault et al., 2017).

9 Keep in mind, this worldwide annual estimate of [at least] $500 billion, in the context of the portion related to: (1) alcohol, only includes six out of the nearly 200 countries in the world, and (2) drugs, only includes drug treatment costs. As such, this estimate is likely to be very low.

10 Although cigarette addiction is a diagnosable disorder (i.e., Tobacco Use Disorder; see American Psychiatric Association, 2013, p. 571), is a serious and consequential addiction in its own right (see Nutt et al., 2007), and certainly contributes to death and disability (see Britton, 2017; GBD, 2017; WHO, 2015), as an addiction, it is not addressed in this volume and thus not included in Table 1.3 and Table 1.4. When addiction treatment services are provided (i.e., for alcohol use disorder, opioid use disorder, etc.), for better or worse, it is not uncommon to deprioritize tobacco use disorders when otherwise incorporating harm reduction related principles in addiction recovery (see Chapter 2). Indeed, there is a popular saying in regard to tobacco addiction; that is, something along the lines of, "after smoking cigarettes, people do not get in their cars and kill people." A crass statement, to be sure, but illustrative of meaningful differences compared to the otherwise more proximal, or immediate negative implications and consequences associated with many addictive behaviors.

11 The World Health Organization (2016a, 2016b) does provide information regarding death and disability for eating disorders as a broad category (i.e., not broken into sub-types; see Table 1.1 and Table 1.2).

12 See Chapter 2 for an overview of the *Diagnostic and Statistical Manual of Mental Disorders* (DSM) – the primary resource/system utilized by mental healthcare professions (e.g., psychiatry; psychology; couple, marriage, and family therapy; social work; counseling) when assessing for and diagnosing mental illness.

13 The American Psychological Association (2015) defines *confidence interval* (and the related term confidence level) as:

> a range of values … that is estimated from a sample with a preset, fixed probability … that the range will contain the true value …. The width of the confidence interval provides information about the precision of the estimate, such that a wider interval indicates relatively low precision and a narrower interval indicates relatively high precision.
>
> (p. 231)

The fixed probability referred to above is the *confidence level*:

> a value expressing the frequency with which a given CONFIDENCE INTERVAL contains the true value … being estimated. For example, a 95 percent confidence level associated with a confidence interval for estimating [a value] indicates that in 95 percent of all estimates … the confidence interval will contain the true value.
>
> (p. 231)

14 When considering an average score or value, it is important also to consider its standard deviation; that is, its standard deviation score or value enhances the information conveyed by an average score. The statistical formula used to calculate a standard deviation is: $\sqrt{[\Sigma(X_i - \bar{X})^2/(n - 1)]}$; where X_i is a particular individual score in a set of scores, $\bar{X}$ is the average of the set of scores, and n is the number of individual scores in the set of scores (see American Psychological Association (APA), 2015, p. 1024). For example, consider the age (in years) of each person in a group of five friends: 26, 28, 31, 31, and 34. The average age of this group of friends is: 30.00. The respective distance from the average age of each individual friend (i.e., each $X_i - \bar{X}$) is: −4, −2, 1, 1, and 4. Each respective distance squared, i.e. $(X_i - \bar{X})^2$ is: 16, 4, 1, 1, 16. This sum of squares, i.e. ($\Sigma(X_i - \bar{X})^2$, 16 + 4 + 1 + 1 + 16 = 38) divided by n − 1 (i.e., 5 [friends] − 1) is: 38 / 4 = 9.5. Lastly, the square root of 9.5 is: 3.08 (i.e., $\sqrt{9.5} = 3.08$). As such, the average age of this group of friends is 30 years, with a standard deviation of ± 3.08 years. That is, on average, each friend is about 3 years older or younger than the average age of the group.

Though not precise, a simplified, otherwise sufficient, conceptual description of a standard deviation is: the average distance of each individual score in a set of scores, from the mean score (i.e., average score) for said set of individual scores. The APA (2015, p. 1024) defines *standard deviation* (SD), based on the statistical formula outlined above, as:

a measure of the variability of a set of scores or values within a group, indicating how narrowly or broadly they deviate from the MEAN [i.e., average score]. A small [SD] indicates data points that cluster around the mean, whereas a large [SD] indicates data points that are dispersed across many different values.

In this regard, the bottom line for the notion of a standard deviation is that a small SD suggests consistency between the average score and its component scores, and a large SD suggests a lack of consistency between the average score and its component scores.

Another aspect of understanding the relationship between an average score and its standard deviation is in the context of the *central limit theorem* (see APA, 2015, p. 169) and a *normal distribution* (see APA, 2015, pp. 715–716), or the *normal curve.* That is, basic statistical theory suggests that large enough samples of any given variable (e.g., age; that is, the age of all living human beings at any given point in time), when charted on a graph, will resemble a symmetrical, *bell-shaped curve,* with the top of the curve representing the average score (as well as the median and modal scores). Moreover, calculating the standard deviation for the average score in the context of this symmetrical, bell-shaped curve, and mapping it onto the curve (i.e., plus or minus (±) 1 standard deviation around the average score), accounts for 34.13 percent of the scores included in the graph above the average score and 34.13 percent of the scores included in the graph below the average score. That is, the range of ± 1 SD includes over 68 percent of all of the scores included in the graph. Given that the range of scores covered by ± 1 SD includes over 68 percent of all of the scores, if an individual score falls within ± 1 SD, it is sometimes referred to as a typical score. Also, if an individual score falls outside of ± 1 SD, it can be considered an atypical score.

As such, by knowing the average score, along with its standard deviation score, we are more able to understand at least two things. First, how consistent an average score is, or how well an average score represents its component scores (i.e., small versus large SD). Second, whether a particular component score is typical or atypical when compared to the average score (i.e., whether or not a particular component score falls within ± 1 SD), or, in effect, when compared to the other component scores.

When considering the average score or value and the corresponding standard deviation score or value in the context of the example given in the text referenced by this note, we are able to gain useful perspective about the annual cost of eating disorders per patient. In this case, the standard deviation was just over half the size of the average score ($2,387 / $4,276 = 55.82), suggesting a moderately large sized standard deviation and thus, a fair amount of inconsistency between the annual cost estimates. Related to this, the range of scores within ± 1 SD was $1,889 to $6,663, suggesting that the lowest estimate of $127 for the component scores is clearly atypical compared to the other component scores, as is the highest estimate of $8,042 for the component scores (two other higher side scores were also above the range).

15 As also stated in Chapter 13, definitions and language used when researching and discussing suicide and suicidal behavior are important (see Ackerman et al., 2018; O'Carroll et al., 1996; Silverman et al., 2007a, 2007b). In particular, the American Association of Suicidology (AAS) has developed guidelines for appropriate language to use, in order to describe suicide and suicidal behavior in an ethical, respectful, and constructive manner (Ackerman et al., 2018). For example, rather than using the phrase *commit* suicide (and its variations), it is better to use *die by* suicide, or *death by* suicide, etc. That is, this and other *traditional* types of phrasing reinforce stigma associated with suicide, including implications regarding criminalization and moral failure (see Ackerman et al., 2018).

16 The worldwide number of individuals who die by suicide each year has also been estimated to be over 1,000,000 (Värnik, 2012).

17 As with note 4, based on these estimates, in Lubbock, Texas, about 36 people will die by suicide this and every year (28 males and 8 females). Likewise, nearly 1,700 DALYs will be lost this and every year (1,286 for males and 410 for females) due to suicidal behavior.

18 Of note, the worldwide-based discrepancy here represents about a 20 percent difference or increase (i.e., 793,307 / 660,589 = 1.20090858 [if this number were 1.0, it would indicate an equal rate; therefore, the .20 portion of this number indicates an increase], or the suicide rate is about .20 higher than the rate of death due to all other deaths by intentional injury). Whereas, the United States-based discrepancy represents about a 128 percent difference or increase (i.e., 49,393 / 21,625 = 2.28406936 [minus 1.0 to account for the indication of an equal rate], or the suicide rate is about 1.28 higher than the rate of death due to all other

deaths by intentional injury). In this regard, the ratio of death by suicide to other forms of death due to intentional injury is over six times as high (i.e., 1.28 /.20 = 6.4) in the United States as it is in the rest of the world.

19 Generally speaking, the lower end of this range is what was used in the global estimate cited above (see also, Table 1.5).

20 When considering the average scores or values and their corresponding standard deviation scores or values in the context of the examples given in the text referenced by this note, we are able to gain meaningful perspective about cost per suicide and suicide rates (as described in the text). Of note, when considering such in the context of the other variables in Table 1.5, the respective standard deviation scores allow us to realize that the average scores are not particularly helpful. For example, in the context of total individual deaths by suicide across the six countries, the average was 9,823 and the standard deviation was 19,454; that is, the standard deviation was nearly twice as large as the average (19,454 / 9,823 = 1.98). This standard deviation is very large and thus, the average score is not consistent with, or a good representation of, its component scores; indeed none of the component scores is conceptually/meaningfully close to the average score. Related to this, although the United States' total number of deaths by suicide easily falls outside of the ± 1 SD target range and thus, is atypical, it is difficult to determine whether the totals for the other countries are conceptually/meaningfully typical or atypical. That is, this standard deviation is too large such that the other countries' totals easily fit within the ± 1 SD target range, even though, aside from the United States' total, there appears to be relatively higher and lower totals (Similarly, without considering the total population for each country, comparing the total deaths by suicide between countries is not useful). As such, for these reasons, the categories of Death by Suicide, Total Cost of Suicide, and Population in Table 1.5 were not similarly elaborated upon in the section of text referenced by this note.

21 Keep in mind, this worldwide annual estimate of [at least] $66.75 billion, is in the context of: (1) including the low end of the estimate for the United States, and (2) only includes six out of the nearly 200 countries in the world. As such, and consistent with the global estimate for the economic burden of alcohol and illicit drug use, this estimate is likely to be very low.

22 This most recent ISSP module on religion is labeled as *ISSP 2008 – Religion III* (see GESIS, 2018; ISSP Research Group, 2018). That is, this is the third time the module has been collected and it is considered as from the year 2008 (although the data was collected between 2007 and 2010). The first two times the religion module was collected were 1991 and 1998. The module has been collected for a fourth time (i.e., 2018), but the data have not been publicly released yet (see http://w.issp.org/data-download/by-topic/).

23 To be clear, this process of collapsing the response categories to calculate estimates of overall spirituality versus non-spirituality is unique to this chapter. That is, I have done this for the purpose of further analysis.

24 For the first item regarding respecting all religions (i.e., ISSP item 13b), the response options that were collapsed (i.e., added together, and then divided by Nv, or the valid sample size) to calculate the "Spirituality % +" estimate are described in the next sentences of the main text. For the remaining 11 items in Table 1.6 and Table 1.7, I will provide said information here (by inference, the "Spirituality % −" estimates are comprised of the remaining response options for a given item). For item 16, Spirituality % + is comprised of response options 3, 4, 5, and 6. For item 17, Spirituality % + is comprised of response options 3 and 4. For item 18a, Spirituality % + is comprised of response options 1 and 2. For item 18b, Spirituality % + is comprised of response options 1 and 2. For item 18c, Spirituality % + is comprised of response options 1 and 2. For item 18d, Spirituality % + is comprised of response options 1 and 2. For item 19a, Spirituality % + is comprised of response options strongly agree and agree. For item 19f, Spirituality % + is comprised of response options strongly agree and agree. For item 27, Spirituality % + is comprised of response options 5, 6, 7, 8, 9, 10, and 11. For item 31, Spirituality % + is comprised of response options 1, 2, and 3. For item 32, Spirituality % + is comprised of response options 1, 2, and 3.

25 Of the 12 survey items included in Table 1.6 and Table 1.7, this question regarding *respect* for all religions is arguably the least religiously and/or spiritually oriented. Nevertheless, I included it in the tables as an assessment of the respondents' openness to religiousness and spirituality and thus an indirect perspective on their level of spirituality versus non-spirituality.

26 An informal comparison of the Global versus United States average Spirituality % + scores suggests that the United States scores are relatively higher by 29 percent (80.06 / 61.96 = 1.2921), and relatively more consistent. That is, the standard deviation for the United States

average score is 8.08, whereas the standard deviation for the Global average score is 12.53. That is, since the average scores are both percentage scores (and thus, on the same scale of measurement), the relative difference between standard deviation scores meaningfully suggests more consistency among the United States component scores (see note 14, above).

27 This Spirituality % + score is the raw sum of response options 3, 5, and 6 for ISSP item 16 (i.e., 7,744 + 9,814 + 24,631 = 42,189, and 42,189 / 59,205 = 71.26). When *averaging* the individual rates of belief in God (based on item 16) for each of the 40 participating countries, the average rate of belief in God is 71.43 percent, with a standard deviation of 15.60.

28 Used in psychotherapy/counseling (see Kopp, 1995), religion (e.g., the parables of Jesus in the New Testament; KJV, 1983), and everyday life/communication, metaphors can be uniquely effective facilitators of understanding. Merriam-Webster defines *metaphor* as: "a figure of speech in which a word or phrase literally denoting one kind of object or idea is used in place of another to suggest a likeness or analogy between them (as in *drowning in money*)" (https://www.merriam-webster.com/dictionary/metaphor).

In this regard, Merriam-Webster defines *electron microscope* as: "an electron-optical instrument in which a beam of electrons is used to produce an enlarged image of a minute object" (https://www.merriam-webster.com/dictionary/electron%20microscope). I use this metaphor, here (and often with my patients, and students), to convey the image of looking deeply into a subject; that is, more deeply than might otherwise be the case with a standard microscope.

References

Abbott, M. (2017). The epidemiology and impact of gambling disorder and other gambling-related harm: Discussion paper for the 2017 WHO Forum on alcohol, drugs and addictive behaviours. Geneva: World Health Organization. Retrieved August 31, 2019, from https://www.who.int/substance_abuse/activities/fadab/abbot_gambling_forum.pdf?ua=1.

Ackerman, J., Cannon, E. A., Stage, D. R. L., Singer, J. B., & Young, N. (2018). Suicide reporting recommendations: Media as partners in suicide prevention. Washington, DC: American Association of Suicidology. Retrieved August 16, 2019, from https://suicidology.org/wp-content/uploads/2018/12/Suicide-Media-Reporting-Extended-4-merged-1.pdf.

Albanese, M. J., & Shaffer, H. J. (2012). Addiction: The genesis and evolution of an idea and its consequences. In H. J. Shaffer, D. A. LaPlante, & S. E. Nelson (Eds.), *APA addiction syndrome handbook, Vol. 1: Foundations, influences, and expressions of addiction.* (pp. 3–25). Washington, DC: American Psychological Association.

Alcoholics Anonymous (1981). *Twelve steps and twelve traditions.* New York, NY: Author. See https://www.aa.org/pages/en_US/twelve-steps-and-twelve-traditions.

Alcoholics Anonymous (1998). *Living sober.* New York, NY: Author.

Alcoholics Anonymous (2001). *Alcoholics Anonymous* (4th ed.). New York, NY: Author. See https://www.aa.org/pages/en_US/alcoholics-anonymous.

American Psychiatric Association (2013). *Diagnostic and statistical manual of mental disorders* (5th ed.). Washington, DC: Author.

American Psychological Association (2015). *APA dictionary of psychology* (2nd ed.). Washington, DC: Author.

Babor, T., Caetano, R., Casswell, S., Edwards, G., Giesbrecht, N., Graham, K., … Rossow, I. (2010). *Alcohol: No ordinary commodity: Research and public policy* (2nd ed.). New York, NY: Oxford University Press.

Baetz, M., & Toews, J. (2009). Clinical implications of research on religion, spirituality, and mental health. *The Canadian Journal of Psychiatry / La Revue canadienne de psychiatrie*, 54 (5), 292–301.

Bischof, G., Rumpf, H.-J., & John, U. (2012). Natural recovery from addiction. In H. J. Shaffer, D. A. LaPlante, & S. E. Nelson (Eds.), *APA addiction syndrome handbook, Vol. 2: Recovery, prevention, and other issues.* (pp. 133–155). Washington, DC: American Psychological Association.

Britton, J. (2017). Death, disease, and tobacco. *The Lancet*, 389(10082), 1861–1862. doi:10.1016/S0140-6736(17)30867-X.

Burton, R., & Sheron, N. (2018). No level of alcohol consumption improves health. *The Lancet*, 392(10152), 987–988. doi:10.1016/S0140-6736(18)31571-X.

Campbell, L. (2019). Addicted to meds: One nurse's story of addiction and recovery. *Healthline.com*. Retrieved from: https://www.foxnews.com/health/addicted-to-meds-one-nurses-story-of-addiction-and-recovery.

Coyle, C., & Enright, R. D. (1998). Forgiveness education with adult learners. In M. Smith (Ed.). In *Adult learning and development: Perspectives from educational psychology* (pp. 219–238). Mahwah, NJ: Lawrence Erlbaum Associates.

de Oliveira, C., Colton, P., Cheng, J., Olmsted, M., & Kurdyak, P. (2017). The direct health care costs of eating disorders among hospitalized patients: A population-based study. *International Journal of Eating Disorders*, 50(12), 1385–1393. doi:10.1002/eat.22797.

Dunbar, R. I. M., Launay, J., Wlodarski, R., Robertson, C., Pearce, E., Carney, J., & MacCarron, P. (2017). Functional benefits of (modest) alcohol consumption. *Adaptive Human Behavior and Physiology*, 3, 118–133. doi:10.1007/s40750-016-0058-4.

Ellis, A., & Dryden, W. (1997). *The practice of rational emotive behavior therapy* (2nd ed.). New York, NY: Springer.

Enright, R. D., & Fitzgibbons, R. P. (2015). *Forgiveness therapy: An empirical guide for resolving anger and restoring hope* (2nd ed.). Washington, DC: American Psychological Association.

Enright, R. D., & The Human Development Study Group (1996). Counseling within the forgiveness triad: On forgiving, receiving forgiveness, and self-forgiveness. *Counseling and Values*, 40(2), 107–126. doi:10.1002/j.2161-007X.1996.tb00844.x.

Exline, J. J. (2013). Religious and spiritual struggles. In K. I. Pargament, J. J. Exline, & J. W. Jones (Eds.), *APA handbook of psychology, religion, and spirituality* (Vol. 1, pp. 459–475). Washington, DC: American Psychological Association.

Gallup Poll (2019). Religion. Retrieved September 3, 2019, from https://news.gallup.com/poll/1690/Religion.aspx#1.

GBD (2017). [GBD 2015 Tobacco Collaborators] Smoking prevalence and attributable disease burden in 195 countries and territories, 1990–2015: A systematic analysis from the Global Burden of Disease Study 2015. *The Lancet*, 389, 1885–1906. doi:10.1016/S0140-6736(17)30819-X.

GBD (2018a). [GBD 2016 Alcohol and Drug Use Collaborators] The global burden of disease attributable to alcohol and drug use in 195 countries and territories, 1990–2016: A systematic analysis for the global burden of disease study 2016. *The Lancet Psychiatry*, 5(12), 987–1012. doi:10.1016/S2215-0366(18)30337-7.

GBD (2018b). [GBD 2016 Alcohol Collaborators] Alcohol use and burden for 195 countries and territories, 1990–2016: A systematic analysis for the Global Burden of Disease Study 2016. *The Lancet*, 392(10152), 1015–1035. doi:10.1016/S0140-6736(18)31310-2.

GESIS (Ed.) (2018). ISSP 2008 – Religion III. Variable Report: Documentation release 2018/10/26, related to the international dataset Archive-Study-No. ZA4950 Version 2.3.0 Variable Reports 2018|17. Cologne: Author.

Hart, K. E. (1999). A spiritual interpretation of the 12-steps of Alcoholics Anonymous: From resentment to forgiveness to love. *Journal of Ministry in Addiction & Recovery*, 6(2), 25–39. doi:10.1300/J048v06n02_03.

Harvard T. H. Chan School of Public Health (2019). Alcohol: Balancing risks and benefits. Boston, MA: Author. Retrieved August 14, 2019, from https://www.hsph.harvard.edu/nutritionsource/healthy-drinks/drinks-to-consume-in-moderation/alcohol-full-story/.

Helzer, J. E., van den Brink, W., & Guth, S. E. (2006). Should there be both categorical and dimensional criteria for the substance use disorders in DSM-V? *Addiction*, 101(Suppl 1), 17–22. doi:10.1111/j.1360-0443.2006.01587.x.

International Narcotics Control Board (INCB) (2014). Report of the International Narcotics Control Board for 2013. Vienna, Austria: United Nations. Retrieved August 9, 2019, from https://www.incb.org/documents/Publications/AnnualReports/AR2013/English/AR_2013_E.pdf.

ISSP Research Group (2018). *International Social Survey Programme: Religion III - ISSP 2008*. GESIS Data Archive, Cologne. ZA4950 Data file Version 2.3.0, doi:10.4232/1.13161.

Joiner, T. E., Jr., Van Orden, K. A., Witte, T. K., & Rudd, M. D. (2009). *The interpersonal theory of suicide: Guidance for working with suicidal clients.* Washington, DC: American Psychological Association.

King James Version (KJV) (1983). *Holy Bible.* Salt Lake City, UT: Church of Jesus Christ of Latter-day Saints. (Original work published 1769).

Koenig, H. G., & Larson, D. B. (2001). Religion and mental health: Evidence for an association. *International Review of Psychiatry*, 13(2), 67–78. doi:10.1080/09540260124661.

Kopp, R. R. (1995). *Metaphor therapy: Using client-generated metaphors in psychotherapy.* New York, NY: Brunner-Routledge.

Lavelock, C. R., Snipes, D. J., Griffin, B. J., Worthington, E. L., Jr., Davis, D. E., Hook, J. N., … Ritter, J. (2015). A conceptual model of forgiveness and health. In L. L. Toussaint, E. L. Worthington, Jr., & D. R. Williams (Eds.), *Forgiveness and health: Scientific evidence and theories relating forgiveness to better health* (pp. 29–42). New York, NY: Springer.

Lyons, G. C. B., Deane, F. P., & Kelly, P. J. (2010). Forgiveness and purpose in life as spiritual mechanisms of recovery from substance use disorders. *Addiction Research & Theory*, 18(5), 528–543. doi:10.3109/16066351003660619.

MacCoun, R. J. (1998). Toward a psychology of harm reduction. *American Psychologist*, 53(11), 1199–1208. doi:10.1037/0003-066X.53.11.1199.

McDaid, D. (2016). Making an economic case for investing in suicide prevention: Quo vadis? In R. C. O'Connor & J. Pirkis (Eds.), *The international handbook of suicide prevention* (2nd ed., pp. 775–790). Malden, MA: John Wiley & Sons.

Naghavi, M. (2019). Global, regional, and national burden of suicide mortality 1990 to 2016: Systematic analysis for the Global Burden of Disease Study 2016. *British Medical Journal*, 364, 394.

National Drug Intelligence Center (NDIC) (2011). The economic impact of illicit drug use on American society. Washington, DC: United States Department of Justice. Retrieved August 7, 2019, from http://www.justice.gov/archive/ndic/pubs44/44731/44731p.pdf.

National Records of Scotland (2017). Mid-year population estimates Scotland, Mid-2016: Population estimates by sex, age and area. Edinburgh: Author. Retrieved August 18, 2019, from https://www.nrscotland.gov.uk/files//statistics/population-estimates/mid-year-2016/16mype-cahb.pdf.

Nutt, D., King, L. A., Saulsbury, W., & Blakemore, C. (2007). Development of a rational scale to assess the harm of drugs of potential misuse. *The Lancet*, 369(9566), 1047–1053. doi:10.1016/S0140-6736(07)60464-4.

O'Carroll, P. W., Berman, A., Maris, R. W., Moscicki, E. K., Tanney, B. L., & Silverman, M. M. (1996). Beyond the tower of Babel: A nomenclature for suicidology. *Suicide and Life-Threatening Behavior*, 26(3), 237–252.

Pargament, K. I. (2013). Searching for the sacred: Toward a nonreductionistic theory of spirituality. In K. I. Pargament, J. J. Exline, & J. W. Jones (Eds.), *APA handbook of psychology, religion, and spirituality (Vol 1): Context, theory, and research* (pp. 257–273). Washington, DC: American Psychological Association.

Perreault, K., Bauman, A., Johnson, N., Britton, A., Rangul, V., & Stamatakis, E. (2017). Does physical activity moderate the association between alcohol drinking and all-cause, cancer and cardiovascular diseases mortality? A pooled analysis of eight British population cohorts. *British Journal of Sports Medicine*, 51, 651–657. doi:10.1136/bjsports-2016-096194.

Petry, N. M. (Ed.) (2016). *Behavioral addictions: DSM-5® and beyond.* New York, NY: Oxford University Press.

Piedmont, R. L., & Wilkins, T. A. (2013). Spirituality, religiousness, and personality: Theoretical foundations and empirical applications. In K. I. Pargament, J. J. Exline, & J. W. Jones (Eds.), *APA handbook of psychology, religion, and spirituality (Vol 1): Context, theory, and research.* (pp. 173–186). Washington, DC: American Psychological Association.

Rehm, J., Mathers, C., Popova, S., Thavorncharoensap, M., Teerawattananon, Y., & Patra, J. (2009). Global burden of disease and injury and economic cost attributable to alcohol use and alcohol-use disorders. *The Lancet*, 373(9682), 2223–2233. doi:10.1016/S0140-6736(09)60746-7.

Rodriguez-Monguio, R., Brand, E., & Volberg, R. (2018). The economic burden of pathological gambling and co-occurring mental health and substance use disorders. *Journal of Addiction Medicine*, 12(1), 53–60. doi:10.1097/ADM.0000000000000363.

Rosenberg, K. P., & Feder, L. C. (Eds.). (2014). *Behavioral addictions: Criteria, evidence, and treatment*. San Diego, CA: Elsevier Academic Press.

Samnaliev, M., Noh, H. L., Sonneville, K. R., & Austin, S. B. (2015). The economic burden of eating disorders and related mental health comorbidities: An exploratory analysis using the U.S. Medical Expenditures Panel Survey. *Preventative Medicine Reports*, 2, 32–34. doi:10.1016/j.pmedr.2014.12.002.

Scottish Public Health Observatory (2019). Suicide: Scotland overview 2019. Glasgow/Edinburgh: Author. Retrieved August 18, 2019, from https://www.scotpho.org.uk/health-wellbeing-and-disease/suicide/data/scottish-trends/.

Shepard, D. S., Gurewich, D., Lwin, A. K., Reed, G. A., Jr., & Silverman, M. M. (2016). Suicide and suicidal attempts in the United States: Costs and policy implications. *Suicide and Life-Threatening Behavior*, 46(3), 352–362. doi:10.1111/sltb.12225.

Shneidman, E. S. (1993). *Suicide as psychache: A clinical approach to self-destructive behavior*. Northvale, NJ: Jason Aronson.

Silverman, M. M., Berman, A. L., Sanddal, N. D., O'Carroll, P. W., & Joiner, T. E., Jr. (2007a). Rebuilding the Tower of Babel: A revised nomenclature for the study of suicide and suicidal behaviors: Part 1: Background, rationale, and methodology. *Suicide and Life-Threatening Behavior*, 37(3), 248–263. doi:10.1521/suli.2007.37.3.248.

Silverman, M. M., Berman, A. L., Sanddal, N. D., O'Carroll, P. W., & Joiner, T. E., Jr. (2007b). Rebuilding the Tower of Babel: A revised nomenclature for the study of suicide and suicidal behaviors: Part 2: Suicide-related ideations, communications and behaviors. *Suicide and Life-Threatening Behavior*, 37(3), 264–277. doi:10.1521/suli.2007.37.3.264.

Stuhldreher, N., Konnopka, A., Wild, B., Herzog, W., Zipfel, S., Löwe, B., & König, H. H. (2012). Cost-of-illness studies and cost-effectiveness analyses in eating disorders: A systematic review. *International Journal of Eating Disorders*, 45(4), 476–491. doi:10.1002/eat.20977.

Suicide Anonymous (2010). *Suicide Anonymous, the little book*. Memphis, TN: Author. Retrieved August 7, 2018, from http://www.suicideanonymous.net/uploads/SA_BOOKLET_ok_copy.pdf.

Sussman, S. (2017). *Substance and behavioral addictions: Concepts, causes, and cures*. New York, NY: Cambridge University Press.

Sussman, S., Lisha, N., & Griffiths, M. (2011). Prevalence of the addictions: A problem of the majority or the minority? *Evaluation & the Health Professions*, 34(1), 3–56. doi:10.1177/0163278710380124.

Thompson, W. N., & Beruhard, B. (2010). Problem gambling. In W. N. Thompson (Ed.), *The international encyclopedia of gambling* (Vol. 1, pp. 171–186). Santa Barbara, CA: ABC-CLIO.

Toussaint, L. L., & Webb, J. R. (2005). Theoretical and empirical connections between forgiveness, mental health, and well-being. In E. L.Worthington, Jr. (Ed.), *Handbook of forgiveness* (pp. 349–362). New York, NY: Routledge.

Toussaint, L. L., Webb, J. R., & Keltner, W. (2012). Religion, spirituality, and mental health. In J. D. Aten, K. A. O'Grady, & E. L.Worthington, Jr. (Eds.), *The psychology of religion and spirituality for clinicians: Using research in your practice* (pp. 331–356). New York, NY: Routledge.

U. S. Department of Health and Human Services and U. S. Department of Agriculture (2015). *2015–2020 dietary guidelines for Americans*. (8th ed.). Washington, DC: Author. Retrieved August 14, 2019, from https://health.gov/dietaryguidelines/2015/resources/2015-2020_Dietary_Guidelines.pdf.

Värnik, P. (2012). Suicide in the world. *International Journal of Environmental Research and Public Health*, 9(3), 760–771. doi:10.3390/ijerph9030760.

Wallace, J. (2012). Theory of 12-step-oriented treatment. In S. T. Walters, & F. Rotgers (Eds.), *Treating substance abuse: Theory and technique*. (3rd ed., pp. 167–190). New York, NY: Guilford Press.

Webb, J. R. (2014). Incorporating spirituality into the psychology of temptation: Conceptualization, measurement, and clinical implications. *Spirituality in Clinical Practice*, 1(3), 231–241. doi:10.1037/scp0000028.

Webb, J. R., & Jeter, B. R. (2015). Forgiveness and problematic substance use. In L. L. Toussaint, E. L.Worthington, Jr., & D. R. Williams (Eds.), *Forgiveness and health: Scientific evidence and theories relating forgiveness to better health* (pp. 139–154). New York, NY: Springer.

Webb, J. R., & Toussaint, L. L. (2018). Self-forgiveness as a critical factor in addiction and recovery: A 12-step model perspective. *Alcoholism Treatment Quarterly*, 36(1), 15–31. doi:10.1080/07347324.2017.1391057.

Webb, J. R., & Toussaint, L. L. (2020). Forgiveness, well-being, and mental health. In E. L. Worthington, Jr. & N. G. Wade (Eds.), *Handbook for forgiveness* (2nd ed., pp. 188–197). New York, NY: Routledge.

Webb, J. R., & Trautman, R. P. (2010). Forgiveness and alcohol use: Applying a specific spiritual principle to substance abuse problems. *Addictive Disorders & Their Treatment*, 9(1), 8–17. doi:10.1097/ADT.0b013e318195000d.

Webb, J. R., Dula, C. S., & Brewer, K. (2012). Forgiveness and aggression among college students. *Journal of Spirituality in Mental Health*, 14(1), 38–58. doi:10.1080/19349637.2012.642669.

Webb, J. R., Hirsch, J. K., & Toussaint, L. L. (2011). Forgiveness and alcohol problems: A review of the literature and a call for intervention-based research. *Alcoholism Treatment Quarterly*, 29(3), 245–273. doi:10.1080/07347324.2011.585922.

Webb, J. R., Hirsch, J. K., & Toussaint, L. L. (2015). Forgiveness as a positive psychotherapy for addiction and suicide: Theory, research, and practice. *Spirituality in Clinical Practice*, 2(1), 48–60. doi:10.1037/scp0000054.

Webb, J. R., Toussaint, L. L., & Conway-Williams, E. (2012). Forgiveness and health: Psycho-spiritual integration and the promotion of better healthcare. *Journal of Health Care Chaplaincy*, 18(1–2),57–73. doi:10.1080/08854726.2012.667317.

Webb, J. R., Toussaint, L. L., & Dula, C. S. (2014). Ritualistic, theistic, and existential spirituality: Initial psychometric qualities of the RiTE measure of spirituality. *Journal of Religion & Health*, 53(4), 972–985. doi:10.1007/s10943-013-9697-y.

Webb, J. R., Toussaint, L. L., & Hirsch, J. K. (2017). Self-forgiveness, addiction, and recovery. In L. Woodyatt, E. L.Worthington, Jr., M. Wenzel, & B. J. Griffin (Eds.), *Handbook of the psychology of self-forgiveness* (pp. 265–277). New York, NY: Springer.

Webb, J. R., Bumgarner, D. J., Conway-Williams, E., Dangel, T., & Hall, B. B. (2017). A consensus definition of self-forgiveness: Implications for assessment and treatment. *Spirituality in Clinical Practice*, 4(3), 216–227. doi:10.1037/scp0000138.

World Health Organization (WHO) (2015). WHO global report on trends in prevalence of tobacco smoking 2015. Geneva: Author. Retrieved September 1, 2019, from https://www.who.int/tobacco/publications/surveillance/reportontrendstobaccosmoking/en/index4.html.

World Health Organization (WHO) (2016a). Health statistics and information systems: Disease burden and mortality estimates: Cause-specific mortality, 2000–2016. Geneva: Author. Retrieved August 8, 2019, from https://www.who.int/healthinfo/global_burden_disease/estimates/en/.

World Health Organization (WHO) (2016b). Health statistics and information systems: Disease burden and mortality estimates: Disease burden, 2000–2016. Geneva: Author. Retrieved August 8, 2019, from https://www.who.int/healthinfo/global_burden_disease/estimates/en/index1.html.

World Health Organization (WHO) (2018a). Constitution of the World Health Organization. Geneva: Author. Retrieved July 28, 2018, from http://apps.who.int/gb/bd/PDF/bd47/EN/constitution-en.pdf?ua=1.

World Health Organization (WHO) (2018b). Global status report on alcohol and health (2018). Executive Summary. Geneva: Author. Retrieved August 7, 2019, from https://apps.who.int/iris/bitstream/handle/10665/274603/9789241565639-eng.pdf?ua=1.

World Health Organization (WHO) (2018c). LIVE LIFE: Preventing suicide. Geneva: Author. Retrieved August 8, 2019, from https://www.who.int/publications-detail/live-life-preventing-suicide.

Worthington, E. L., Jr. (2006). *Forgiveness and reconciliation: Theory and application*. New York, NY: Routledge.

Worthington, E. L., Jr. (2020). Forgiveness intervention manuals. Accessed June 19, 2020 from: http://www.people.vcu.edu/~eworth/ & https://evworthington.squarespace.com/diy-workbooks.

Worthington, E. L., Jr., & Sandage, S. J. (2016). *Forgiveness and spirituality in psychotherapy: A relational approach*. Washington, DC: American Psychological Association.

Worthington, E. L., Jr., Berry, J. W., & Parrott, L., III. (2001). Unforgiveness, forgiveness, religion, and health. In T. G. Plante, & A. C. Sherman (Eds.), *Faith and health: Psychological perspectives.* (pp. 107–138). New York, NY: Guilford Press.

Yuodelis-Flores, C., & Ries, R. K. (2015). Addiction and suicide: A review. *The American Journal on Addictions*, 24(2), 98–104. doi:10.1111/ajad.12185.

2 Theory: Addiction and Recovery

What is the phenomenological[1] experience of a person struggling with addiction? Obviously, there is not one simple answer. To the extent that interpersonal[2] and intrapersonal[3] issues and/or conflicts are a concern for addiction and recovery, a sentiment expressed by Layne Staley, the former lead singer for the band Alice In Chains (see Rothman, 2002), may be relevant – particularly so to forgiveness. That is, "At the end of the day or at the end of the party, when everyone goes home, you're stuck with yourself" (Wiederhorn, 1996, p. 13). Before we can examine the role of forgiveness in addiction recovery, it is important to understand what is meant by *addiction* and *recovery*. How is addiction diagnosed, including the most meaningful and useful descriptors (e.g., addiction, dependence, abuse, or use) and perspectives (e.g., categorical or dimensional)? What can be identified as an addiction, or what can a person be considered to be addicted to – substances, behaviors, suicide? Why does addiction develop and persist? What constitutes sobriety or recovery from addiction – abstinence, sufficiently reduced use or harm, treatment-based improvements (as opposed to improvement without professional treatment)?

Diagnosing Addiction

Whether arriving at one's own personal conclusion that a friend, family member, or stranger has an addiction or the clinical diagnosis of addiction by a trained professional, the underlying assumptions regarding commonly used – sometimes otherwise synonymously – descriptive terms are important to consider. Although related to each other, the terms of *addiction, dependence, abuse,* and *use,* can lead to public confusion and negative outcomes (e.g., unnecessary treatment, increased costs, and mistrust of healthcare providers) among those struggling with addiction (Albanese & Shaffer, 2012; Shaffer, 2012a). Beyond inconsequential *use* for otherwise innocuous social or recreational purposes, or use consistent with medical advice, *abuse* entails use, likely excessive (though not necessarily), with negative consequences, albeit less intense than dependence or addiction (Albanese & Shaffer, 2012). *Dependence* includes physiological neuroadaptation; that is, (1) tolerance, or increased dosing becomes required to attain a desired effect, and (2) withdrawal, or the pain, agitation, sickness, etc. associated with decreased use (Shaffer, 2012a). An important distinction between dependence and *addiction* is that physiological dependence may or may not be problematic (e.g., a post-operative patient may develop physiological dependence to opioids during the course of pain management, but will not necessarily continue opioid use when pain is no longer an issue), whereas addiction is essentially intensely problematic and may involve, but importantly *does not require*, physiological dependence (Albanese & Shaffer, 2012; Shaffer, 2012a; see also, American Psychiatric Association, 2013). Albanese and Shaffer (2012) identify the essence of addiction not as a quality inherent to or arising from a substance [or behavioral set], but an experiential relationship. That is, "experience is the currency of addiction. When a particular pattern of behavior reliably and robustly changes emotional experience, the potential for addiction emerges. … *Addiction* is the description of a relationship between organisms and objects within their environment" (emphasis in original; Albanese & Shaffer, 2012, p. 6).

The *Diagnostic and Statistical Manual of Mental Disorders* (DSM) is published by the American Psychiatric Association (https://www.psychiatry.org/) and is the primary resource/system utilized by mental healthcare professions (e.g., psychiatry; psychology; couple, marriage, and family therapy; social work; counseling) when assessing for and diagnosing mental illness, including addiction-related disorders. The first edition (i.e., DSM-I) was published nearly 70 years ago in 1952, and the most recent edition (i.e., DSM-5) was published in 2013 (American Psychiatric Association, 1952, 2013). Although the DSM is utilized across the globe, the *International Classification of Diseases* (ICD) system, published by the World Health Organization (https://www.who.int/), in addition to physical disorders, also includes mental, behavioral, and addictive disorders. The first edition of what became the ICD was published over 125 years ago in 1893 and was adopted by the World Health Organization in 1948. The current, 10th edition (i.e., ICD-10) was adopted in 1990 and the 11th edition (i.e., ICD-11) is set to be fully adopted in 2022 (WHO, 2019). Importantly, the ICD system largely overlaps with the DSM system (see WHO, 1992), and thus these resources are essentially interchangeable when diagnosing mental, behavioral, and addictive disorders.

Early Versions of the DSM

While addictive disorders are included in the DSM system (and thus the ICD system), when making a professionally trained clinical *diagnosis*, the term *addiction*, although used historically, is not included in the *current* terminology. In the DSM-I (American Psychiatric Association, 1952), classified under Personality Disorders, Addiction was further classified as either Alcoholism or Drug addiction. Alcoholism "included … cases in which there is well established addiction to alcohol" and Drug addiction was explicitly stated to be "usually symptomatic of a personality disorder" (p. 39). In the DSM-II (American Psychiatric Association, 1968), Alcoholism and Drug dependence were classified under Personality Disorders and Certain Other Non-Psychotic Mental Disorders. Alcoholism included sub-types such as different manifestations of excessive drinking and Alcohol addiction, which was evidenced by "the inability of the patient to go one day without drinking" (p. 45). Drug dependence included sub-types referring to the particular substance (i.e., opium, synthetic analgesics, barbiturates, other hypnotics and sedatives, cocaine, cannabis sativa, other psycho-stimulants, and hallucinogens) (see p. 46). Both the DSM-I and the DSM-II provided few diagnostic details and limited guidance regarding the diagnostic decision-making process.

The DSM-III (American Psychiatric Association, 1980) divided the classification of Substance Use Disorders (SUDs) into Substance Abuse (i.e., a pattern of pathological use) and Substance Dependence (i.e., physiological dependence – either tolerance or withdrawal) and provided subjective guidance regarding the course of the disorder (i.e., continuous, episodic, in remission, or unspecified) (see pp. 166–167). A diagnosis of abuse and/or dependence applied to five substances; that is, "alcohol, barbiturates or similarly acting sedatives or hypnotics, opioids, amphetamines or similarly acting [stimulants], and cannabis," whereas Substance Abuse only applied to "cocaine, phencyclidine (PCP) or similarly acting [substances] and hallucinogens" … "because physiological dependence has not been demonstrated" (pp. 165–166). Consistent with the DSM-III, the DSM-III-Revised (DSM-III-R; American Psychiatric Association, 1987), divided the classification of Psychoactive Substance Use Disorders into Psychoactive Substance Abuse and Psychoactive Substance Dependence. More importantly, the substantive revisions to the DSM-III in the context of addictive disorders were the addition of several diagnostic criteria and minimums for abuse versus dependence, and subjective guidance for determining dependence-related severity and course. The DSM-IV and DSM-IV-Text Revision (DSM-IV-TR; American Psychiatric Association, 1994, 2000) divided the classification of Substance-Related Disorders into Substance Abuse (i.e., maladaptive use and negative consequences) and Substance Dependence (i.e., continued abuse, often with tolerance, withdrawal, and/or compulsive behavior). A specifier was added to Substance Dependence regarding with or without physiological dependence in recognition of the fact that dependence sufficiently can be "characterized by a pattern of compulsive use" (American Psychiatric Association, 1994, p. 179). Also, while severity was no longer formally designated, course specifiers were expanded and objective criteria for such were provided.

Current Version of the DSM

With the publication of the current edition of the DSM (i.e., DSM-5) (American Psychiatric Association, 2013), *abuse* and *dependence* are no longer utilized in the diagnostic terminology for Substance-Related and Addictive Disorders. Beginning in 1980 with the DSM-III (see above), abuse and dependence were used as the two categorical diagnostic options available for any particular addiction-related disorder. That is, if an addiction-related problem met diagnostic criteria to be considered a disorder, it was designated as abuse or dependence. Although the formal distinction between abuse and dependence was warranted, perhaps due to practical difficulties in making the distinction (e.g., diagnosable abuse likely almost always turned into dependence), the categorical diagnostic distinction of abuse versus dependence was discontinued in the DSM-5 and replaced with a categorical diagnosis of [Substance] Use Disorder with a severity qualifier of mild, moderate, or severe, and course specifiers. Also, legal problems were removed as an option from the DSM-IV (and DSM-IV-TR) criteria (for substance abuse), and cravings were added as an option to the DSM-5 criteria for a substance use disorder. In sum, the number of criteria met, whether related to abuse or dependence, are now tabulated to determine the severity of a substance *use* disorder – representing a return to DSM-III-R (severity) and DSM-III (SUD) terminology, respectively.

The DSM-5 (American Psychiatric Association, 2013) is the first edition to deliberately include an explicit addictive disorder not otherwise related to substances – Gambling Disorder. Importantly, Gambling Disorder is evaluated by the same diagnostic criteria as the other addictive disorders (i.e., substance related) in the DSM-5. Although other behavioral addictions are thought to exist (see below), they have not been included in the DSM system "because *at this time* there is insufficient peer-reviewed evidence to establish the diagnostic criteria and course descriptions needed to identify these behaviors as mental disorders" (emphasis added; American Psychiatric Association, 2013, p. 481). Nevertheless, aside from tolerance and withdrawal, "neuroadaptation [also] reflects changes in the brain neurotransmitter receptors. … [Indeed], the biological substrate is similar for both substance and behavioral addictions" (Albanese & Shaffer, 2012, p. 5; see also, Shaffer, 2012b). "As far as the brain is concerned, a reward's a reward, regardless of whether it comes from a chemical or an experience. And where there's a reward, there's the risk of the vulnerable brain getting trapped in a compulsion" (Holden, 2001, p. 890; also cited in Albanese & Shaffer, 2012, p. 4). It is likely simply a matter of time before additional behavioral addictions are included in the DSM system (i.e., a function of continued research, including improved conceptualization, and measurement tools and techniques).

Physiological Issues

Related to the notion that tolerance and withdrawal are a function of physiological dependence and not necessarily needed in order to constitute an addiction, when diagnosing a DSM-based addictive disorder (whether a [Substance] Use Disorder, or Gambling Disorder), there are 11 diagnostic criteria to consider. Only two of the 11 symptoms are required for a diagnosis of [Substance] Use / Gambling Disorder, Mild (severity), four of 11 for Moderate, and six of 11 for Severe. Moreover, only two of the 11 symptoms are necessarily physiological (#10 – Tolerance, and #11 – Withdrawal), such that an individual could receive a diagnosis of [Substance] Use / Gambling Disorder, Severe, *without experiencing any physiological symptoms.*

To be clear, one way to minimize public confusion (including stigma) and negative outcomes among those struggling with addiction (see above; Albanese & Shaffer, 2012; Shaffer, 2012a) is to *educate* the public and *remind* healthcare professionals that addictive disorders do not need to include explicit physiological markers or symptoms. Addiction can be constituted entirely by psychological processes or emotional experiences. Moreover, any physiological components of addiction can be managed with medication, particularly in the context of physiological withdrawal from substances, such that once any substances are removed from the body (or the immediate problematic activities of a behavioral addiction are otherwise under control), the remaining psychological or emotional components of the addiction (i.e., the *long-term* risk factors of addiction) are what need to be addressed in order to sufficiently facilitate healthy recovery therefrom (see Leshner, 1997).

Recognizing the psychological and emotional underpinnings of long-term addiction does not imply that addiction is a weakness (as is often the default assumption in society). Rather, the psychological and emotional underpinnings of addiction (and all difficult behavior change) are a function of human nature. An individual spends their age in years learning how to live their life – skills related to problem solving, stress management, coping, etc. – and it takes time to relearn how to live life, or to develop more adaptive skills to replace the dysfunctional patterns resulting from years of addiction. Fortunately, the amount of time required to make changes is not the same as the time spent learning and developing such dysfunctional patterns in the first place.

Categorical versus Dimensional Diagnosis

The DSM system for diagnosing mental illness, including Substance-Related and Addictive Disorders, is categorical in nature. Although disorders and their diagnostic criteria (i.e., symptoms) have been identified and defined, minimum symptom counts have been determined, and disorder-level severity specifiers have been designated, the disorder-level diagnostic question is fundamentally categorical such that an individual either does or does not meet the criteria for any particular disorder (i.e., yes or no). While minimum symptom counts and disorder-level severity specifiers do suggest a dimensional diagnostic continuum (i.e., more or less of a disorder), each possible symptom is judged as present or not and then tallied to determine two yes/no, either/or categorical questions: (1) are the minimum number of symptoms present in order to warrant an overall diagnosis? and (2) what is the particular level of severity based on the number of symptoms present?

Categorical information is useful and important for diagnostic, and thus treatment related purposes. However, with categorical information there is no indication as to the severity, intensity, or *dimensionality* of each potential symptom; that is, (1) any given symptom may or may not be present, (2) if a symptom is present, it may or may not warrant diagnosis (as a symptom for a given disorder), and (3) all symptoms (for a given disorder) rising to the level of warranting diagnosis (and thus contributing to the symptom count for said disorder) are not equal in their severity and/or intensity (Helzer, 2011). Both disorders and symptoms can be considered sub-clinical, or present but not sufficient for formal diagnosis. And, because something is sub-clinical does not necessarily mean that there are not any negative implications or consequences, nor does meeting a clinical threshold (whether diagnosis of a disorder, or a disorder-level severity designation of mild, moderate, or severe) mean that each individual meeting said threshold will have or manifest the same experience. Related to this, though the DSM system provides increasingly objective guidance, and thus increasingly consistent resolution for the diagnostic decision-making process, the use of categorical criteria and decision-making allows for *subjective* evaluation of whether or not the threshold for a given symptom has been met. That is, diagnosing clinicians are faced with the challenge of deciding whether or not a particular state of affairs meets the yes/no threshold for a particular diagnostic criterion and thus, diagnosis.

Consider the case of Frank,[4] a 64-year-old multi-ethnic male presenting for counseling following the untimely death of his life-partner about 3 months ago – with concerns that his grief is spiraling out of control. After a few counseling sessions, he discloses that for about 30 years he has been in abstinence-based natural recovery (i.e., never received formal treatment for addiction; see below) from self-reported problematic use of marijuana. And, although he has periodically experienced cravings over the course of his recovery time, he is becoming concerned because the cravings have been gradually, yet consistently increasing lately – both in terms of frequency and intensity. Upon further exploration, the clinician has been unable to identify any additional symptoms in the context of a Substance Use Disorder. Although Frank arguably meets criteria for Cannabis Use Disorder, in sustained remission (which allows for cravings), he is in very long-term recovery and a formal diagnosis may be irrelevant at this point. Nevertheless, Frank is very stressed that he is headed for relapse if he does not resolve his grief. He feels like he is caught in a vicious cycle of ever-increasing grief↔craving↔stress, etc. Otherwise, Frank does not report any significant impairment or distress in the context of his day-to-day functioning, etc. As such, in practical terms, Frank appears to be sub-clinical. However, the frequency and intensity of his cravings indicates that continued treatment is warranted and likely critical; indeed, his need for treatment may inform his diagnosis. In sum, while Frank does not meet categorically-based criteria for an active substance use disorder (i.e., he only meets one criteria – cravings), the severity and intensity of his one symptom suggests that dimensional issues may be relevant to treatment, and thus diagnosis.

Dimensional considerations may be critical in our effort to gain a thorough understanding of the *entire* effect of addiction on health and well-being, and thus more accurate diagnosis and treatment planning, *and better outcomes* (see Webb et al., 2017). Dimensional aspects of addiction are complex, inevitable, and unavoidable, and require our full attention. Easy-to-recognize dimensional aspects include the immediate implications for addiction related to quantity, frequency, and/or intensity of addictive behavior. Less obvious dimensional aspects of addiction include those otherwise removed (i.e., distal) complications related to health, financial strain, and legal problems, difficulties associated with prevention, recovery, and relapse, and the impact of addiction on family, friends, and accidental or incidental others. Of note, Helzer, Bucholz, and colleagues provide comprehensive discussions of the relevance of dimensional considerations for formal diagnosis (see Helzer, 2011; Helzer, Bucholz, et al., 2006; Helzer, Bucholz, et al., 2008; Helzer, van den Brink, et al., 2006; Jackson et al., 2014; see also, Helzer, Kraemer, et al., 2008).

Descriptive Labels

Making a professional diagnosis and the terminology related thereto is important to consider; indeed, it is critical to accurately defining the problem, understanding its course, and planning for and implementing effective treatment and aftercare. Also important is the terminology we, as a society, use to describe a person struggling with addiction. The terms we use can influence the stigma associated with addiction – they can lead to, maintain, and strengthen stigma, thereby exacerbating or intensifying the already difficult struggle for recovery, or they can dismantle stigma, thereby removing an unnecessary barrier to recovery (see Broyles et al., 2014; Kelly et al., 2016; Richter & Foster, 2014; Saitz, 2016). In this regard, research has shown that terms such as "substance abuser" are problematic (Ashford et al., 2019; Kelly & Westerhoff, 2010), and that even the term "recovery" can be problematic and stigmatizing (Kelly et al., 2018). Robinson (2017) argues that clinicians also must be careful about the negative impact of terminology on patients, including in the context of charting (i.e., the official notes written in a patient's healthcare chart, in order to track the course of treatment), and recommends against using words such as "clean" and "dirty" in reference to people struggling with addiction. Terms such as "addict" (and "alcoholic") and "addiction" have also been described as problematic given their potential for judgmental and nonclinical implications (Petry, 2016a; Robinson, 2017). The common recommendation for how to describe *a person struggling with an addiction*, is just that – person-centered language (e.g., Broyles et al., 2014; Robinson, 2017; Saitz, 2016), allowing for a person *to have* a problem rather than *to be* a problem (Kelly et al., 2016). In sum, the "consistent use of agreed-upon terminology will aid precise and unambiguous clinical and scientific communication and help reduce stigmatizing and discriminatory public health and social policies" (Kelly et al., 2016, p. 116).

Identifying an Addiction

What can be considered an addiction? Does addiction occur only in the context of substance use, or can it include other behaviors? As mentioned previously, Albanese and Shaffer (2012) identify the essence of addiction as being an experiential relationship. That is, "experience is the currency of addiction. When a particular pattern of behavior reliably and robustly changes emotional experience, the potential for addiction emerges. … *Addiction* is the description of a relationship between organisms and objects within their environment" (emphasis in original; Albanese & Shaffer, 2012, p. 6). As such, the objects of addiction may be ever increasing (see Sussman, 2017, Chapter 5 in particular). Although popular culture may overestimate, some may argue that the DSM system underestimates what can be considered an addiction. Indeed, the DSM system currently only recognizes substance use and gambling as having the potential to be addictive disorders (American Psychiatric Association, 2013). It is important to note, however, that the DSM system has left the door open for other behaviors to be considered addictions as it recognizes that compulsive/excessive behavior is sufficient for a diagnosis (see above; i.e., physiological/pharmacological criteria are not necessary for diagnosis), and that additional compulsive/excessive behavioral sets may warrant diagnosis pending additional research, or empirical support (American Psychiatric Association, 2013, see pp. 481, 483–484).

Many scholars explicitly identify various compulsive/excessive behavioral sets, in addition to substance use and gambling, as addictive behaviors (see Petry, 2016b; Rosenberg & Feder, 2014b; Sussman, 2017). If such addictive behaviors are not recognized by the DSM system (yet), what kind of criteria are or should be used to identify said behaviors as addictive in nature? Griffiths (2005; see also, Griffiths et al., 2014; Király et al., 2014) describes six features of addictive behaviors: (1) salience; that is, an activity governs and dictates one's thinking, feelings, and behavior, (2) mood modification; that is, an activity produces subjective feelings of arousal (e.g., "buzz" or "high" or "rush") and/or tranquility (e.g., "escape" or "numbing"), (3) tolerance, (4) withdrawal symptoms; whether psychological or physiological, (5) conflict related to the activity; whether interpersonal or intrapsychic, and (6) relapse (see Griffiths, 2005, pp. 193–195). Similarly, Sussman and Sussman (2011; see also, Sussman, 2017) describe five features of addictive behaviors: (1) feeling different; that is, "[pursuit of] some course of action for appetitive effects or motives (e.g., pain reduction, affect enhancement, arousal manipulation, or fantasy)," (2) preoccupation with the behavior, (3) temporary satiation, (4) loss of control, and (5) negative consequences (see Sussman & Sussman, 2011, pp. 4026–4030). In sum, "the *individual's inability to curtail the activity despite the negative consequences* is what stands as the hallmark of the addiction process" (emphasis in original; Rosenberg & Feder, 2014a, p. 4).

Behavioral addictions have been conceptualized as *Impulsive-Compulsive Disorders* (Cuzen & Stein, 2014) given "the impulsive features (arousal) that initiate the behavior, and the compulsive drive that causes the behaviors to persist over time" (Dell'Osso et al., 2006, p. 464). Also, given the co-morbidity of addictions (i.e., co-occurrence, or more than one addiction occurring at the same time) and synergistic interaction, individuals struggling with addiction have been conceptualized as having an *Addiction Interaction Disorder* (Carnes et al., 2005; Rosenberg & Feder, 2014a; Rosenberg et al., 2014; Sussman et al., 2011). Of note, Impulsive-Compulsive Disorders and Addiction Interaction Disorders are not terms or diagnoses formally recognized in the DSM system.

Behavioral Addictions

Sussman (2017), in his book *Substance and Behavioral Addictions: Concepts, Causes, and Cures*, identifies 16 categories of addictive behavior (only one of which includes substance use) with some 63 subcategories, yet comprehensively addresses only 11 *focal* addictions given their informal status as having the most research, discussion, and highest prevalence. That is, (1) cigarette smoking, (2) alcohol use, (3) illicit drug use (including marijuana), (4) eating/food, (5) gambling, (6) Internet, (7) love, (8) sex, (9) exercise, (10) work, and (11) shopping (see pp. 91 & 101). Petry (2016b), in her edited book *Behavioral Addictions: DSM-5® and Beyond*, includes chapters on seven non-substance or traditional gambling related behavioral addictions: (1) Internet gaming, (2) Internet, (3) sexual behavior, (4) shopping, (5) exercise, (6) food, and (7) tanning. Rosenberg and Feder (2014b), in their edited book *Behavioral Addictions: Criteria, Evidence, and Treatment*, include chapters on eight non-substance or traditional gambling related behavioral addictions: (1) online gaming, (2) Internet, (3) social networking, (4) food, (5) sex, (6) love, (7) buying [shopping], and (8) exercise.

Suicide

Although suicidal ideation and attempts (i.e., suicidal behavior) are recognized as *consequences* of addiction (see Black et al., 2012; Rehbein et al., 2016; Rumpf et al., 2016;

Sussman, 2017, Chapters 4 & 5) and as *comorbid* with addiction (Yuodelis-Flores & Ries, 2015) and non-suicidal self-injury (NSSI) has been recognized/conceptualized as an addiction (see Sussman, 2017, Chapter 5), suicide and suicidal behavior have *not* been identified as addictions in and of themselves in otherwise seminal resources on addiction (e.g., Petry, 2016b; Rosenberg & Feder, 2014b; Shaffer, 2012b; Sussman, 2017). Nevertheless, addiction has been described as a microsuicidal behavior (Firestone, 2006; Firestone, 1986; Firestone & Seiden, 1987). And, the cognitive processes involved in the "self-attacks" (i.e., self-talk, or an internal voice) inherent to suicidal behavior have been described as analogous to the cognitive processes involved in the cycle of addiction (Firestone, 2006, see pp. 123–124). Moreover, theory has been developed and empirical evidence observed in support of suicidal behavior as addictive behavior (Blasco-Fontecilla, 2016; Blasco-Fontecilla et al., 2014; Blasco-Fontecilla et al., 2016; Hatteschweiler et al., 2015; Tullis, 1998; see also, da Silva et al., 2018; Ellis, 2006; Shneidman, 1993). Indeed, Suicide Anonymous (2010), a grass-roots, community-based, mutual-help group patterned after the Twelve-Step Model of addiction and recovery has been established to support individuals struggling with suicidal behavior (see https://suicideanonymous.net/).

Models of Addiction and Recovery

Models of the Origins of Addiction

Albanese and Shaffer (2012, see pp. 11–12) provide a comprehensive overview of the vast literature (going back over 200 years to 1812) regarding the development and persistence of addiction, organized into five model-based categories: (1) Moral, (2) Biological, (3) Psychological, (4) Social, and (5) Etiological Multidimensional. The Moral model views addiction as a moral failing or an issue of depravity. Biological models view addiction as a disease, illness, or disorder and consider biogenetic vulnerability, reward system deficiency, and neurophysiological adaptation. Psychological models view addiction as a function of behavioral excess, poor judgment, distorted cognition, intrapsychic conflict, and/or personality and emotional vulnerability. Social models view addiction as the product of a variety of psychosocial and/or public health related issues. And, the Etiological Multidimensional model views addiction as a syndrome or the confluence of various multifaceted pressures on a vulnerable individual. Consistent with the Etiological Multidimensional model, the American Psychological Association's two-volume *Addiction Syndrome Handbook* (Shaffer et al., 2012a, 2012b) explicitly addresses a variety of specific contributors to addiction and barriers to recovery. For example, neurobiology, psychiatric comorbidity, self-control, personality, and externalizing spectrum related issues, as well as, social, sociological, developmental, infectious disease, homelessness, and technology related issues.

Alternative models regarding the origins of addiction also exist – models less likely to be espoused in academic circles, but not necessarily less likely to be supported by science. Of note, and of particular relevance to forgiveness, the Twelve-Step model of addiction and its overarching emphasis on resentments and self-centeredness (e.g., Alcoholics Anonymous, 2001) and Carnes' view of addiction as a cyclical process driven by self-condemnation (Carnes, 2001; see also, Hook et al., 2015; Hook et al., 2008). Also, family and relational dynamics are important when considering the development and persistence of addiction (see Miller et al., 2019; Reiter, 2019; Thombs & Osborn, 2019).

Models of Recovery from Addiction

Each of the aforementioned models of the development and persistence of addiction provide a platform from which to derive models of recovery from addiction, or a return to otherwise healthy, addiction-free living (i.e., sobriety). The evidence-based assumptions foundational to each of these models regarding the origins and maintenance of addiction likely can be transformed into effective catalysts of recovery from addiction. When applied to recovery, said models of the etiology of addiction arguably work from the inside to facilitate the outcome of recovery. Or, by working to resolve or reverse such predictors or underlying processes of addiction, the result of recovery can be facilitated. Additional models of recovery can be described as directly focused on the result of recovery itself. That is, models concentrated on first addressing the negative consequences associated with addiction, whether through abstinence, relapse prevention, harm reduction, or motivation.

Abstinence

The lifetime cessation of use of substances and/or engagement in other addictive behaviors, is commonly associated with the Twelve-Step Model of addiction and recovery (e.g., Alcoholics Anonymous (https://www.aa.org/), Narcotics Anonymous (https://www.na.org/), Gamblers Anonymous (http://www.gamblersanonymous.org/ga/), etc.). However, abstinence is also a core component of Self-Management and Recovery Training (SMART Recovery; https://www.smartrecovery.org/) and other grass-roots, community-based, mutual-help support groups such as LifeRing Secular Recovery (https://www.lifering.org/), Secular Organizations for Sobriety (SOS; http://www.sossobriety.org/), and Women for Sobriety (WFS; https://womenforsobriety.org/) (see Miller et al., 2019). In particular, the Twelve-Step Model is otherwise focused on acceptance, surrender, making amends, spiritual awakening, and comprehensive lifestyle change (AA, 1981, 1998, 2001). SMART Recovery (2019) is otherwise focused on motivation to change, coping with urges, managing thoughts, feelings, and behaviors, and balanced living. Of note, SMART Recovery, LifeRing, SOS, and WFS largely arose as secular alternatives to the Twelve-Step Model in general, and its spiritual focus in particular. However, aside from the secular versus spirituality component, it is fair to say that each of these mutual-help based models of recovery not only share the priority of abstinence, but also many other principles and values of recovery. Indeed, research has shown similar effectiveness for recovery between SMART Recovery, LifeRing, WFS, and the Twelve-Step Model among people with Alcohol Use Disorders (Zemore et al., 2018).

Relapse Prevention

A focus on preventing a return to problematic use and/or other addictive behaviors once abstinence has been reasonably established is known as Relapse Prevention (RP). RP is based in the biopsychosocial model of the determinants of addiction (i.e., a combination of biological, psychological, and social factors) and incorporates a variety of cognitive-behavioral skills and interventions (see Hsu & Marlatt, 2012). A major component of RP is understanding, recognizing, and addressing the Abstinence Violation Effect (AVE), including conceptualizing and clarifying whether a return to problematic behaviors is a lapse or a relapse (Hsu & Marlatt, 2012; Marlatt, 1996; Marlatt & Donovan, 2007; see also, Miller, 1996). The AVE is thought to arise from the pressure for abstinence in conjunction with all-or-nothing thinking when seeking recovery.

Once a person struggling with addiction returns to an addictive behavior (i.e., *any* quantity, frequency, and/or intensity thereof) it is common to return to "full-blown" activity, or a return to one's dysfunctional pattern of addictive behaviors and their attendant negative consequences. In this context, distinguishing between a *lapse* (i.e., a return that is brief in frequency, small in quantity, and mild in intensity) and a *relapse* (i.e., an otherwise "full-blown" return) becomes important. That is, depending on the nature of the return (and a lapse usually occurs first),

> it can be dealt with in a pragmatic manner as an error, a lapse, a slip or temporary setback, and [likely] not an inevitable collapse on the road to recovery. Teaching people about high-risk situations and how to cope with them more effectively is the essence of relapse prevention.
>
> (Marlatt, 1996, p. S47)

Indeed, given the common occurrence of (re)lapse (see Hsu & Marlatt, 2012), it is *critical* to distinguish between lapse and relapse in order to foster RP, and thus *prolapse*; that is, "getting back on track in the direction of positive change" (Hsu & Marlatt, 2012, p. 106).

Consider the case of Maggie, a 61-year-old Caucasian female with 19 years of abstinence-based sobriety seeking treatment for generalized anxiety. During a session with her mental health therapist, she reported having been to a large work party the night before – during the winter holiday season. She had taken a sip of a drink given to her by a server walking through the party with a tray of drinks. As she was engrossed in conversation, without thinking she took a drink off of the tray and as soon as the beverage touched her lips she recognized that it contained alcohol. Maggie was very stressed and worried because she consumed alcohol and felt very guilty because she did so without paying attention to her surroundings; that is, she typically was very mindful of these types of situations and was always careful to ask a server what types of drinks were being offered. Maggie was afraid that she had "thrown away" her 19 years of sobriety and felt that she was "teetering on the edge of a cliff toward the old days." After discussing, with her therapist, principles and activities consistent with relapse prevention, including the Abstinence Violation Effect and differences between lapsing versus relapsing, Maggie was able to leave the session feeling a measure of confidence that a full-blown relapse was no longer "right around the corner." In the coming weeks and counseling sessions she reported consistently increasing confidence for recovery as she continued to contemplate the circumstances of her lapse, particularly her recognition that in addition to it being a one-time, otherwise random occurrence, it was also purely accidental with absolutely no intention on her part. In sum, through practicing relapse prevention concepts and skills, Maggie was able to maintain her long-term recovery.

Harm Reduction

Focusing on managing and reducing addictive behaviors, high-risk behaviors, and/or the negative consequences of such behaviors in a pragmatic fashion is known as Harm Reduction (HR; see Marlatt et al., 2011). Indeed, the HR approach to recovery is designed to:

> reduce the harmful consequences of alcohol and drug use or other high-risk activities by incorporating several strategies that cut across the spectrum from safer use

> to managed use to abstinence. The primary goal of most harm reduction approaches is to meet individuals "where they are at" and not to ignore or condemn the harmful behaviors but rather to work with the individual or community to minimize the harmful effects of a given behavior.
>
> (Marlatt & Witkiewitz, 2010, p. 591)

An example of an HR program is that of needle exchange programs (see Weinmeyer, 2016). Not without controversy (see Knight, 2019), needle exchange programs are designed to reduce the spread of infectious disease associated with intravenous (IV) drug use and the sharing of needles. Rather than share potentially contaminated needles, people struggling with IV drug use can access sterile and new needles available through community services and resources. Likewise, methadone clinics are an additional example of an HR program (see Roberts, 2009). Also not without controversy (see https://www.johnsoncitypress.com/tags/gray-methadone-clinic), in order to reduce crime associated with opioid use, risk for overdose, as well as dangers associated with contaminated needles, methadone clinics are designed to replace shorter acting opioids (e.g., heroin) with a longer acting opioid, as well as to administer and monitor methadone use – a pharmaceutical grade medicine – in a highly controlled environment.

Moderation Management

A grass-roots, community-based, mutual-help program, Moderation Management (MM) is consistent with the harm reduction model of recovery (https://www.moderation.org/). It was developed in response to the Twelve-Step Model (see Humphreys, 2004) and designed to assist:

> problem drinkers who are not alcohol-dependent. MM members pursue a goal of moderate drinking as defined by specific guidelines for frequency and quantity of alcohol consumption. MM's program for change is based primarily on cognitive restructuring and behavioral self-control enhancement and has no inherent spiritual component. MM's definition of the "nondependent" problem drinker is based on the individual's ability to adhere to MM guidelines, which include an initial 30-day abstinence period followed by limits on daily consumption.
>
> (Lembke & Humphreys, 2012, p. 130)

The United States National Institute on Alcohol Abuse and Alcoholism (NIAAA) guidelines regarding alcohol consumption are: less than or equal to three or four standard drinks[5] per day and seven or 14 per week for females or males, respectively (NIAAA, 2005). Roughly consistent with NIAAA's guidelines, MM's drinking-related limits are three or four standard drinks per occasion and nine or 14 per week for females or males, respectively, and both sexes are to abstain from drinking 3–4 days per week (MM, 2019a). If any given individual subsequently decides or discovers that moderated drinking is not a self-determined practical outcome, abstinence is encouraged and supported by the MM program and community (MM, 2019b).

Motivation

Deliberate and systematic efforts to facilitate and leverage individual motivation to effect behavior change have been developed – most notably Motivational Interviewing (MI; see Miller & Rollnick, 2013). Importantly, MI is not a technique to use, but a way of interacting with clients that can be incorporated into any formalized treatment modality. Miller and Rollnick (2013) define MI from a clinical perspective as "a person-centered counseling *style* for addressing the common problem of ambivalence about change" (emphasis added; p. 21). From a more general, technical perspective, Miller and Rollnick (2013) define MI as:

> a collaborative, goal-oriented style of communication with particular attention to the language of change. It is designed to strengthen personal motivation for and commitment to a specific goal by eliciting and exploring the person's own reasons for change within an atmosphere of acceptance and compassion.
>
> (p. 29)

Though separate from the Transtheoretical Model of Change (TTM; e.g., Prochaska & DiClemente, 1984), often referred to as the Stages of Change Model (SofC; e.g., Connors et al., 2013), MI is sometimes confused as to be part of the SofC Model. Indeed, MI is viewed as a good fit with SofC (Miller & Rollnick, 2013), including as a method to help individuals progress through the stages of change (i.e., precontemplation, contemplation, preparation, action, maintenance) (Connors et al., 2013), such that the relationship between MI and SofC has been described as "'kissing cousins who never married'" (Miller & Rollnick, 2013, pp. 35–36). Both MI and SofC have been game-changers and thus, widely incorporated into the treatment of addiction (see Connors et al., 2013; DiClemente et al., 2017). See Chapter 10 for more discussion regarding MI and SofC.

Self-Medication and Natural Recovery

Two additional approaches to understanding addiction and recovery are important to consider as potentially useful and fungible alternative perspectives. That is, the role of self-medication in addiction and attempts at recovery, and whether or not formal treatment from professionally trained providers is required in order for remission from addiction to occur.

Self-Medication

Given the common occurrence of relapse (see above discussion regarding Relapse Prevention) and the typical co-occurrence of various addictive behaviors (see Chapter 1), all the while facing the inevitable return and presence of myriad negative consequences, the societal question often arises of why a person struggling with addiction would willfully engage in addictive behavior. The Self-Medication Hypothesis (SMH) suggests that:

> addiction is a special adaptation and means to cope with a range of human psychological problems. … Individuals discover that in the short term they can reduce or control their suffering by self-medicating a range of distressful states, and there is a considerable degree of psychopharmacologic specificity in a person's preferred drug. … [Such that addiction can be viewed as a] self-regulation disorder.
>
> (Khantzian, 2003, p. 17)

The aforementioned psychological problems can derive from diagnosable DSM-5 disorders, related sub-clinical conditions, and everyday emotional struggles that "make a substance or behavior especially desirable as a vehicle to shift and attenuate [i.e., reduce] these painful subjective states" (Albanese & Shaffer, 2012, p. 10). The SMH is controversial as its research-base is conflicted (see Khantzian, 2018; Miller et al., 2019; Suh et al., 2008), including whether or not pharmacologic mechanisms of action are consistent with desired effects. However, as Miller et al. (2019) astutely point out, "it is not necessary that the drug [or addictive behavior] *actually* yields the desired effect, but only that the person believes [or perceives that] it does so" (emphasis in original; p. 313).

Related to the notion and process of self-medicating, is the notion of replacing one addiction with another. Indeed, Hsu and Marlatt (2012) provide an overview of the common occurrence of addiction substitution – particularly in the context of tobacco as the substitute. As another example, it is not unusual for Twelve-Step Model adherents to engage is *13th Stepping*, or substituting a sexual compulsion in place of one's original addictive behavior (see Sussman, 2017). Also, a common critique of the Twelve-Step Model is that it replaces one's addiction to substance use and/or other addictive behaviors with an addiction to God. As such, it is fair to say that not only is self-medication a potentially useful alternative conceptualization of addiction and attempts at recovery, but *self-treatment* through addiction substitution may be as well.

Natural Recovery

The reality is that most people struggling with addictive behavior do not seek treatment (Bischof et al., 2012; see also Cohen et al., 2007); moreover, "most [expressions of] addictive behavior, … resolve in the general population without [the] use of formal treatment" (Bischof et al., 2012, p. 150). As such, the predictors of Natural Recovery must be understood, prioritized, and disseminated to the population at large through targeted public health campaigns. For example, public service announcements, grade school and high school prevention programs, and college-campus outreach programs.

Although the empirical evidence regarding the occurrence of Natural Recovery is quite clear, why it happens and how it happens is less clear. Research does support various predictors of the remission of addiction without treatment. For example, and of particular relevance to forgiveness, committed relationships, less avoidance coping, better self-esteem, cognitive appraisal analyses, and development of social skills, social networking, and a healthy self-image (see Bischof et al., 2012; LaPlante, 2012). However, mixed results and research design limitations currently preclude drawing *definitive* conclusions regarding what leads to Natural Recovery (Bischof et al., 2012). For example, inconsistent use of definitions, lack of prospective, longitudinal data, use of non-representative samples, and sampling concerns related to snowball sampling and media solicitation (i.e., selection bias).

Formal Treatment

This reality, that most people struggling with addiction do not seek treatment and yet many still find some level of healthy resolution, may lead some that are struggling with addiction to conclude that treatment for addictive behavior is therefore unnecessary. Given the effectiveness of treatment for addiction (see Blonigen et al., 2015; Grant et al., 2015; McKay et al., 2015; Miller et al., 2019; Renner, 2012; Witkiewitz et al., 2012), it becomes short-sighted at best and self-destructive at worst to decline treatment when the opportunity is available. Importantly, those predictors of Natural Recovery (see above), otherwise empirically identified in *hindsight* (i.e., after the fact) among those attaining said resolution without first having had formal treatment, are consistent with the principles and practice of recovery attained through evidence-based treatments (see immediately above regarding treatment effectiveness; see also Miller & Brown, 1997). In sum, when struggling with addiction, whether or not one recognizes or admits to be struggling therewith, declining to seek or accept formal treatment because science tells us that Natural Recovery can and does occur (and what the predictors of successful Natural Recovery are) is counter-productive and self-defeating. Rather, seeking and obtaining formalized treatment from professionally trained and licensed/certified therapists can serve to proactively facilitate and quicken the recovery process, particularly when those seeking treatment are or become motivated to progress through the stages of change and implement the treatment received.

Lastly, when seeking formal treatment, a logical consideration is whether or not the treatment provider needs a personal background in addiction in order to be an effective addiction therapist. Although the scientific research is clear that this is *not necessary* (see Miller & Brown, 1997; Miller et al., 2019), it is important to remember that the nature of research regarding behavior change is such that the findings are identifying generalities and not necessarily specificities. That is, the research conclusions drawn from statistical reasoning identify what works for *most* people, *most* of the time. However, as clinicians are working at the individual level (whether working with individual persons, in a group setting, or with couples, families, etc.), it may be that the particular individual in treatment may be "an exception to the rule." As such, clinicians/therapists need to be open to the fact that a particular client/patient, though not very likely, may in actuality need a provider with a personal background in addiction. This does not mean that as soon as a client claims the need and makes the request (as will inevitably occur), that clinicians are automatically and immediately to make the change. However, if over time a therapeutic alliance in this context does not develop, then clinicians must be open to making the change for the sake of the client. Keep in mind, however, that a sufficient therapeutic alliance in this regard usually can/will develop and a change will not be necessary. In the event that a change does become warranted, it is not necessarily an issue of a lack of therapist expertise or even competence, but rather an issue of unique client need.

Related to this is the metaphor of the *Procrustean Bed* (see Hoffman & Rosman, 2003). Rather than artificially forcing a client into a therapist-preferred approach to treatment, clinicians must be prepared to allow their clients reasonably to pull from them what is needed, and sometimes what is needed is a referral to another therapist for fit-related purposes – whether related to having personal experience with addiction and recovery, or more broadly to other therapeutic alliance issues and/or treatment modality characteristics.

Notes

1 The American Psychological Association (APA, 2015, p. 789) defines *phenomenological theory* as: "an approach to personality theory that places questions of individuals' current experiences of themselves and their world at the center of analyses of personality functioning and change."

2 The APA defines *interpersonal* as: "pertaining to actions, events, and feelings between two or more individuals" (2015, p. 554) and *interpersonal conflict* as: "disagreement or discord between people with respect to goals, values, or attitudes". In more simple language, the terms *interpersonal* and *interpersonal conflict* are in reference to the relationships an individual has with other people.

3 The APA (2015) defines *intrapersonal* as: "describing factors operating or constructs occurring within the person, such as attitudes, decisions, self-concept, self-esteem, or self-regulation" (p. 559) and *intrapersonal conflict* as: "see INTRAPSYCHIC CONFLICT" or "in psychoanalytic theory, the clash of opposing forces within the psyche, such as conflicting drives, wishes, or agencies". In

more simple language, the terms *intrapersonal* and *intrapersonal conflict* are in reference to the relationship an individual has with the self. For example, based on my performance on a major assignment at work, I may be happy with myself, I may be disappointed in myself, etc.

4 Here and elsewhere throughout the book, whenever particular persons are discussed in clinical terms, demographic and case-oriented details have been modified to protect the identities of said individuals. Related to this, some clinical scenarios may be composite in nature. That is, one or more individuals with similar circumstances may comprise, or contribute to, the description of a particular "individual."

5 The NIAAA (2005) defines one (1) standard drink as 14 grams of pure alcohol (i.e., about .6 fluid ounces or 1.2 tablespoons), or 12 ounces of beer (5% alcohol), 8–9 ounces of malt liquor (7% alcohol), 5 ounces of wine (12% alcohol), or 1.5 ounces of 80-proof spirits (so-called hard liquor/alcohol; 40% alcohol).

References

Albanese, M. J., & Shaffer, H. J. (2012). Addiction: The genesis and evolution of an idea and its consequences. In H. J. Shaffer, D. A. LaPlante, & S. E. Nelson (Eds.), *APA addiction syndrome handbook, Vol. 1: Foundations, influences, and expressions of addiction* (pp. 3–25). Washington, DC: American Psychological Association.

Alcoholics Anonymous (AA) (1981). *Twelve steps and twelve traditions.* New York, NY: Author. See https://www.aa.org/pages/en_US/twelve-steps-and-twelve-traditions.

Alcoholics Anonymous (AA) (1998). *Living sober.* New York, NY: Author.

Alcoholics Anonymous (AA) (2001). *Alcoholics Anonymous* (4th ed.). New York, NY: Author. See https://www.aa.org/pages/en_US/alcoholics-anonymous.

American Psychiatric Association (1952). *Diagnostic and statistical manual of mental disorders.* Washington, DC: Author.

American Psychiatric Association (1968). *Diagnostic and statistical manual of mental disorders* (2nd ed.). Washington, DC: Author.

American Psychiatric Association (1980). *Diagnostic and statistical manual of mental disorders* (3rd ed.). Washington, DC: Author.

American Psychiatric Association (1987). *Diagnostic and statistical manual of mental disorders* (3rd ed., revised). Washington, DC: Author.

American Psychiatric Association (1994). *Diagnostic and statistical manual of mental disorders* (4th ed.). Washington, DC: Author.

American Psychiatric Association (2000). *Diagnostic and statistical manual of mental disorders* (4th ed., text revision). Washington, DC: Author.

American Psychiatric Association (2013). *Diagnostic and statistical manual of mental disorders* (5th ed.). Washington, DC: Author.

American Psychological Association (APA) (2015). *APA dictionary of psychology* (2nd ed.). Washington, DC: Author.

Ashford, R. D., Brown, A. M., & Curtis, B. (2019). 'Abusing addiction': Our language still isn't good enough. *Alcoholism Treatment Quarterly*, 37(2), 257–272. doi:10.1080/07347324.2018.1513777.

Bischof, G., Rumpf, H.-J., & John, U. (2012). Natural recovery from addiction. In H. J. Shaffer, D. A. LaPlante, & S. E. Nelson (Eds.), *APA addiction syndrome handbook, Vol. 2: Recovery, prevention, and other issues* (pp. 133–155). Washington, DC: American Psychological Association.

Black, D. W., Kuzma, J., & Shaw, M. (2012). Unique consequences of behavioral expressions of addiction. In H. J. Shaffer, D. A. LaPlante, & S. E. Nelson (Eds.), *APA addiction syndrome handbook, Vol. 1: Foundations, influences, and expressions of addiction* (pp. 329–351). Washington, DC: American Psychological Association.

Blasco-Fontecilla, H. (2016). The addiction to suicidal behavior. In P. Courtet (Ed.), *Understanding suicide: From diagnosis to personalized treatment* (pp. 53–61). New York, NY: Springer.

Blasco-Fontecilla, H., Artieda-Urrutia, P., Berenguer-Elias, N., Garcia-Vega, J., Fernandez-Rodriguez, M., Rodriguez-Lomas, C., … de Leon, J. (2014). Are major repeater patients addicted to suicidal behavior? *Adicciones*, 26(4), 321–333. doi:10.20882/adicciones.38.

Blasco-Fontecilla, H., Fernández-Fernández, R., Colino, L., Fajardo, L., Perteguer-Barrio, R., & de Leon, J. (2016). The addictive model of self-harming (non-suicidal and suicidal) behavior. *Frontiers in Psychiatry*, 7. doi:10.3389/fpsyt.2016.00008.

Blonigen, D. M., Finney, J. W., Wilbourne, P. L., & Moos, R. H. (2015). Psychosocial treatments for substance use disorders. In P. E. Nathan & J. M. Gorman (Eds.), *A guide to treatments that work* (4th ed., pp. 731–761). New York, NY: Oxford University Press.

Broyles, L. M., Binswanger, I. A., Jenkins, J. A., Finnell, D. S., Faseru, B., Cavaiola, A., … Gordon, A. J. (2014). Confronting inadvertent stigma and pejorative language in addiction scholarship: A recognition and response. *Substance Abuse*, 35(3), 217–221. doi:10.1080/08897077.2014.930372.

Carnes, P. J. (2001). *Out of the shadows: Understanding sexual addiction*. (3rd ed.). Center City, MN: Hazelden Foundation.

Carnes, P. J., Murray, R. E., & Charpentier, L. (2005). Bargains with chaos: Sex addicts and Addiction Interaction Disorder. *Sexual Addiction & Compulsivity*, 12(2–3), 79–120. doi:10.1080/10720160500201371.

Cohen, E., Feinn, R., Arias, A., & Kranzler, H. R. (2007). Alcohol treatment utilization: Findings from the National Epidemiologic Survey on Alcohol and Related Conditions. *Drug and Alcohol Dependence*, 86(2–3), 214–221. doi:10.1016/j.drugalcdep.2006.06.008.

Connors, G. J., DiClemente, C. C., Velasquez, M. M., & Donovan, D. M. (2013). *Substance abuse treatment and the stages of change: Selecting and planning interventions* (2nd ed.). New York, NY: Guilford Press.

Cuzen, N. L., & Stein, D. J. (2014). Behavioral addiction: The nexus of impulsivity and compulsivity. In K. P. Rosenberg & L. C. Feder (Eds.), *Behavioral addictions: Criteria, evidence, and treatment* (pp. 19–34). San Diego, CA: Elsevier Academic Press.

da Silva, A. G., Malloy-Diniz, L. F., Garcia, M. S., Figueiredo, C. G. S., Figueiredo, R. N., Diaz, A. P., & Palha, A. P. (2018). Cognition as a therapeutic target in the suicidal patient approach. *Frontiers in Psychiatry*, 9(Article 31). doi:10.3389/fpsyt.2018.00031.

Dell'Osso, B., Altamura, A. C., Allen, A., Marazziti, D., & Hollander, E. (2006). Epidemiologic and clinical updates on impulse control disorders: A critical review. *European Archives of Psychiatry and Clinical Neuroscience*, 256(8), 464–475. doi:10.1007/s00406-006-0668-0.

DiClemente, C. C., Corno, C. M., Graydon, M. M., Wiprovnick, A. E., & Knoblach, D. J. (2017). Motivational interviewing, enhancement, and brief interventions over the last decade: A review of reviews of efficacy and effectiveness. *Psychology of Addictive Behaviors*, 31(8), 862–887. doi:10.1037/adb0000318.

Ellis, T. E. (2006). *Cognition and suicide: Theory, research, and therapy*. Washington, DC: American Psychological Association.

Firestone, L. (2006). Suicide and the Inner Voice. In T. E. Ellis (Ed.), *Cognition and suicide: Theory, research, and therapy* (pp. 119–147). Washington, DC: American Psychological Association.

Firestone, R. W. (1986). The 'inner voice' and suicide. *Psychotherapy: Theory, Research, Practice, Training*, 23(3), 439–447. doi:10.1037/h0085636.

Firestone, R. W., & Seiden, R. H. (1987). Microsuicide and suicidal threats of everyday life. *Psychotherapy: Theory, Research, Practice, Training*, 24(1), 31–39. doi:10.1037/h0085688.

Grant, J. E., Odlaug, B. L., & Potenza, M. N. (2015). Treatments for gambling disorder and impulse control disorders. In P. E. Nathan & J. M. Gorman (Eds.), *A guide to treatments that work* (4th ed.) (pp. 801–826). New York, NY: Oxford University Press.

Griffiths, M. D. (2005). A 'components' model of addiction within a biopsychosocial framework. *Journal of Substance Use*, 10(4), 191–197. doi:10.1080/14659890500114359.

Griffiths, M. D., Kuss, D. J., & Demetrovics, Z. (2014). Social networking addiction: An overview of preliminary findings. In K. P. Rosenberg & L. C. Feder (Eds.), *Behavioral addictions: Criteria, evidence, and treatment* (pp. 119–141). San Diego, CA: Elsevier Academic Press.

Hatteschweiler, C., Graziani, P., Bon, M., & Charbonnier, E. (2015). Addiction et passage à l'acte suicidaire: Des processus cognitifs similaires? = Addiction and passage to the suicidal act: Similar cognitive processes? *Revue Francophone de Clinique Comportementale et Cognitive*, 20(3), 35–44.

Helzer, J. E. (2011). A proposal for incorporating clinically relevant dimensions into DSM-5. In D. A. Regier, W. E. Narrow, E. A. Kuhl, & D. J. Kupfer (Eds.), *The conceptual evolution of DSM-5* (pp. 81–96). Arlington, VA: American Psychiatric Publishing.

Helzer, J. E., Bucholz, K. K., & Gossop, M. (2008). A dimensional option for the diagnosis of substance dependence in DSM-V. In J. E. Helzer, H. C. Kraemer, R. F. Krueger, H.-U. Wittchen, P. J. Sirovatka, & D. A. Regier (Eds.), *Dimensional approaches in diagnostic classification: Refining the research agenda for DSM-V* (pp. 19–34). Washington, DC: American Psychiatric Association.

Helzer, J. E., van den Brink, W., & Guth, S. E. (2006). Should there be both categorical and dimensional criteria for the substance use disorders in DSM-V? *Addiction*, 101(Suppl 1), 17–22. doi:10.1111/j.1360-0443.2006.01587.x.

Helzer, J. E., Bucholz, K. K., Bierut, L. J., Regier, D. A., Schuckit, M. A., & Guth, S. E. (2006). Should DSM-V include dimensional diagnostic criteria for alcohol use disorders? *Alcoholism: Clinical and Experimental Research*, 30(2), 303–310. doi:10.1111/j.1530-0277.2006.00028.x.

Helzer, J. E., Kraemer, H. C., Krueger, R. F., Wittchen, H.-U., Sirovatka, P. J., & Regier, D. A. (Eds.). (2008). *Dimensional approaches in diagnostic classification: Refining the research agenda for DSM-V.* Arlington, VA: American Psychiatric Association.

Hoffman, S., & Rosman, L. (2003). 'Procrustean psychotherapy' or differential therapeutics: Teaching treatment selection to trainees. *Journal of Contemporary Psychotherapy*, 33(4), 341–347. doi:10.1023/B:JOCP.0000004503.15006.d0.

Holden, C. (2001). 'Behavioral' addictions: Do they exist? *Science*, 294(5544), 980–982. doi:10.1126/science.294.5544.980.

Hook, J. N., Farrell, J. E., Davis, D. E., Van Tongeren, D. R., Griffin, B. J., Grubbs, J., … Bedics, J. D. (2015). Self-forgiveness and hypersexual behavior. *Sexual Addiction & Compulsivity*, 22 (1), 59–70. doi:10.1080/10720162.2014.1001542.

Hook, J. N., Hook, J. P., & Hines, S. (2008). Reach out or act out: Long-term group therapy for sexual addiction. *Sexual Addiction & Compulsivity*, 15(3), 217–232. doi:10.1080/10720160802288829.

Hsu, S. H., & Marlatt, G. A. (2012). Addiction syndrome: Relapse and relapse prevention. In H. Shaffer, D. A. LaPlante, & S. E. Nelson (Eds.), *APA addiction syndrome handbook, Vol. 2: Recovery, prevention, and other issues* (pp. 105–132). Washington, DC: American Psychological Association.

Humphreys, K. (2004). *Circles of recovery: Self-help organizations for addictions.* New York, NY: Cambridge University Press.

Jackson, K. M., Bucholz, K. K., Wood, P. K., Steinley, D., Grant, J. D., & Sher, K. J. (2014). Towards the characterization and validation of alcohol use disorder subtypes: Integrating consumption and symptom data. *Psychological Medicine*, 44(1), 143–159. doi:10.1017/S0033291713000573.

Kelly, J. F., & Westerhoff, C. M. (2010). Does it matter how we refer to individuals with substance-related conditions? A randomized study of two commonly used terms. *International Journal of Drug Policy*, 21(3), 202–207. doi:10.1016/j.drugpo.2009.10.010.

Kelly, J. F., Saitz, R., & Wakeman, S. (2016). Language, substance use disorders, and policy: The need to reach consensus on an 'addiction-ary'. *Alcoholism Treatment Quarterly*, 34(1), 116–123. doi:10.1080/07347324.2016.1113103.

Kelly, J. F., Abry, A. W., Milligan, C. M., Bergman, B. G., & Hoeppner, B. B. (2018). On being 'in recovery': A national study of prevalence and correlates of adopting or not adopting a recovery identity among individuals resolving drug and alcohol problems. *Psychology of Addictive Behaviors*, 32(6), 595–604. doi:10.1037/adb0000386.

Khantzian, E. J. (2003). Understanding addictive vulnerability: An evolving psychodynamic perspective. *Neuropsychoanalysis*, 5(1), 5–21. doi:10.1080/15294145.2003.10773403.

Khantzian, E. J. (2018). *Treating addiction: Beyond the pain.* Lanham, MD: Rowman & Littlefield.

Király, O., Nagygyörgy, K., Griffiths, M. D., & Demetrovics, Z. (2014). Problematic online gaming. In K. P. Rosenberg & L. C. Feder (Eds.), *Behavioral addictions: Criteria, evidence, and treatment* (pp. 61–97). San Diego, CA: Elsevier Academic Press.

Knight, V. (2019). Needle exchanges find new champions among republicans. *Kaiser Health News*. Retrieved December 14, 2019from https://khn.org/news/needle-exchanges-find-new-champions-among-republicans/.

LaPlante, D. A. (2012). Technology and its relationship to the addiction syndrome. In H. J. Shaffer, D. A. LaPlante, & S. E. Nelson (Eds.), *APA addiction syndrome handbook, Vol. 2: Recovery, prevention, and other issues* (pp. 273–296). Washington, DC: American Psychological Association.

Lembke, A., & Humphreys, K. (2012). Moderation management: A mutual-help organization for problem drinkers who are not alcohol-dependent. *Journal of Groups in Addiction & Recovery*, 7(2–4), 130–141. doi:10.1080/1556035X.2012.705657.

Leshner, A. I. (1997). Addiction is a brain disease, and it matters. *Science*, 278(5335), 45–47. doi:10.1126/science.278.5335.45.

Marlatt, G. A. (1996). Taxonomy of high-risk situations for alcohol relapse: Evolution and development of a cognitive-behavioral model. *Addiction*, 91(12), S37–S49. doi:10.1080/09652149638791.

Marlatt, G. A., & Donovan, D. M. (Eds.). (2007). *Relapse prevention: Maintenance strategies in the treatment of addictive behaviors.* (2nd ed.). New York, NY: Guilford Press.

Marlatt, G. A., & Witkiewitz, K. (2010). Update on harm-reduction policy and intervention research. *Annual Review of Clinical Psychology*, 6, 591–606. doi:10.1146/annurev.clinpsy.121208.131438.

Marlatt, G. A., Larimer, M. E., & Witkiewitz, K. (Eds.). (2011). *Harm reduction: Pragmatic strategies for managing high-risk behaviors* (2nd ed.). New York, NY: Guilford Press.

McKay, J. R., Kranzler, H. R., Kampman, K. M., Ashare, R. L., & Schnoll, R. A. (2015). Psychopharmacological treatments for substance use disorders. In P. E. Nathan & J. M. Gorman (Eds.), *A guide to treatments that work* (4th ed.) (pp. 763–800). New York, NY: Oxford University Press.

Miller, W. R. (1996). What is a relapse? Fifty ways to leave the wagon. *Addiction*, 91(12), S15–S27. doi:10.1080/09652149638773.

Miller, W. R., & Brown, S. A. (1997). Why psychologists should treat alcohol and drug problems. *American Psychologist*, 52(12), 1269–1279. doi:10.1037/0003-066x.52.12.1269.

Miller, W. R., & Rollnick, S. (2013). *Motivational interviewing: Helping people change* (3rd ed.). New York, NY: Guilford Press.

Miller, W. R., Forcehimes, A. A., & Zweben, A. (2019). *Treating addiction: A guide for professionals* (2nd ed.). New York, NY: Guilford Press.

Moderation Management (MM) (2019a). Guide to moderation management steps of change. Retrieved December 15, 2019, from https://www.moderation.org/about_mm/steps_of_change.html.

Moderation Management (MM) (2019b). What is moderation management? Retrieved December 15, 2019, from https://www.moderation.org/about_mm/whatismm.html#.

National Institute on Alcohol Abuse and Alcoholism (NIAAA) (2005). *A pocket guide for alcohol screening and brief intervention*. Rockville, MD: Author.

Petry, N. M. (2016a). Introduction to behavioral addictions. In N. M. Petry (Ed.), *Behavioral addictions: DSM-5® and beyond.* New York, NY: Oxford University Press.

Petry, N. M. (Ed.) (2016b). *Behavioral addictions: DSM-5® and beyond.* New York, NY: Oxford University Press.

Prochaska, J. O., & DiClemente, C. C. (1984). *The transtheoretical approach: Crossing the traditional boundaries of therapy.* Malabar, FL: Krieger.

Rehbein, F., Kühn, S., Rumpf, H.-J., & Petry, N. M. (2016). Internet gaming disorder: A new behavioral addiction. In N. M. Petry (Ed.), *Behavioral addictions: DSM-5® and beyond* (pp. 43–69). New York, NY: Oxford University Press.

Reiter, M. D. (2019). *Substance abuse and the family: Assessment and treatment* (2nd ed.). New York, NY: Routledge.

Renner, J. A. (2012). Drug substitution treatments and addiction pharmacotherapies: Integrating pharmacotherapy into the addiction syndrome treatment paradigm. In H. Shaffer, D. A. LaPlante, & S. E. Nelson (Eds.), *APA addiction syndrome handbook, Vol. 2: Recovery, prevention, and other issues* (pp. 55–86). Washington, DC: American Psychological Association.

Richter, L., & Foster, S. E. (2014). Effectively addressing addiction requires changing the language of addiction. *Journal of Public Health Policy*, 35(1), 60–64. doi:10.1057/jphp.2013.44.

Roberts, J. R. (2009). How methadone clinics work. *Emergency Medicine News*, 31(4), 8–10. doi:10.1097/01.EEM.0000349230.55009.49.

Robinson, S. M. (2017). 'Alcoholic' or 'Person with alcohol use disorder'? Applying person-first diagnostic terminology in the clinical domain. *Substance Abuse*, 38(1), 9–14. doi:10.1080/08897077.2016.1268239.

Rosenberg, K. P., & Feder, L. C. (2014a). An introduction to behavioral addictions. In K. P. Rosenberg & L. C. Feder (Eds.), *Behavioral addictions: Criteria, evidence, and treatment* (pp. 1–17). San Diego, CA: Elsevier Academic Press.

Rosenberg, K. P., & Feder, L. C. (Eds.). (2014b). *Behavioral addictions: Criteria, evidence, and treatment*. San Diego, CA: Elsevier Academic Press.

Rosenberg, K. P., O'Connor, S., & Carnes, P. (2014). Sex addiction: An overview. In K. P. Rosenberg & L. C. Feder (Eds.), *Behavioral addictions: Criteria, evidence, and treatment* (pp. 215–236). San Diego, CA: Elsevier Academic Press.

Rothman, R. A. (2002). Layne Staley found dead. *Rolling Stone*. Retrieved from: https://www.rollingstone.com/music/music-news/layne-staley-found-dead-178694/.

Rumpf, H.-J., Tao, R., Rehbein, F., & Petry, N. M. (2016). Internet addiction: A future addictive disorder? In N. M. Petry (Ed.), *Behavioral addictions: DSM-5® and beyond* (pp. 71–99). New York, NY: Oxford University Press.

Saitz, R. (2016). International statement recommending against the use of terminology that can stigmatize people. *Journal of Addiction Medicine*, 10(1), 1–2. doi:10.1097/ADM.0000000000000178.

Shaffer, H. J. (2012a). Introduction. In H. J. Shaffer, D. A. LaPlante, & S. E. Nelson (Eds.), *APA addiction syndrome handbook* (pp. xxvii–lx). Washington, DC: American Psychological Association.

Shaffer, H. J. (Ed.) (2012b). *APA addiction syndrome handbook* (Vol. 1 & 2). Washington, DC: American Psychological Association.

Shaffer, H. J., LaPlante, D. A., & Nelson, S. E. (Eds.). (2012a). *APA addiction syndrome handbook, Vol. 1: Foundations, influences, and expressions of addiction*. Washington, DC: American Psychological Association.

Shaffer, H. J., LaPlante, D. A., & Nelson, S. E. (Eds.). (2012b). *APA addiction syndrome handbook, Vol. 2: Recovery, prevention, and other issues.* Washington, DC: American Psychological Association.

Shneidman, E. (1993). *Suicide as psychache: A clinical approach to self-destructive behavior.* Northvale, NJ: Jason Aronson.

SMART Recovery (2019). SMART Recovery: About, history, and FAQs. Retrieved December 14, 2019, from https://www.smartrecovery.org/.

Suh, J. J., Ruffins, S., Robins, C. E., Albanese, M. J., & Khantzian, E. J. (2008). Self-medication hypothesis: Connecting affective experience and drug choice. *Psychoanalytic Psychology*, 25(3), 518–532. doi:10.1037/0736-9735.25.3.518.

Suicide Anonymous (2010). *Suicide Anonymous, the little book*. Memphis, TN: Author. Retrieved August 7, 2018, from http://www.suicideanonymous.net/uploads/SA_BOOKLET_ok_copy.pdf.

Sussman, S. (2017). *Substance and behavioral addictions: Concepts, causes, and cures.* New York, NY: Cambridge University Press.

Sussman, S., & Sussman, A. N. (2011). Considering the definition of addiction. *International Journal of Environmental Research and Public Health*, 8, 4025–4038. doi:10.3390/ijerph8104025.

Sussman, S., Lisha, N., & Griffiths, M. (2011). Prevalence of the addictions: A problem of the majority or the minority? *Evaluation & the Health Professions*, 34(1), 3–56. doi:10.1177/0163278710380124.

Thombs, D. L., & Osborn, C. J. (2019). *Introduction to addictive behaviors* (5th ed.). New York, NY: Guilford Press.

Tullis, K. (1998). A theory of suicide addiction. *Sexual Addiction & Compulsivity*, 5(4), 311–324. doi:10.1080/10720169808402339.

Webb, J. R., Toussaint, L. L., & Hirsch, J. K. (2017). Self-forgiveness, addiction, and recovery. In L. Woodyatt, E. L.Worthington, Jr., M. Wenzel, & B. J. Griffin (Eds.), *Handbook of the psychology of self-forgiveness* (pp. 265–277). New York, NY: Springer.

Weinmeyer, R. (2016). Needle exchange programs' status in US politics. *American Medical Association Journal of Ethics*, 18(3), 252–257. doi:10.1001/journalofethics.2016.18.3.hlaw1-1603.

Wiederhorn, J. (1996). Alice in Chains: To hell and back. *Rolling Stone*. Retrieved from: http://www.rollingstone.com/music/news/alice-in-chains-to-hell-and-back-19960208.

Witkiewitz, K., Steckler, G., Gavrishova, A., Jensen, B., & Wilder, M. (2012). Psychotherapies for addiction: Empirically supported interventions for the addiction syndrome. In H. Shaffer, D. A. LaPlante, & S. E. Nelson (Eds.), *APA addiction syndrome handbook, Vol. 2: Recovery, prevention, and other issues* (pp. 87–103). Washington, DC: American Psychological Association.

World Health Organization (WHO) (1992). ICD-10 classification of mental and behavioural disorders: Diagnostic criteria for research. Geneva: Author. Retrieved September 1, 2019, from https://www.who.int/classifications/icd/en/ and https://www.who.int/classifications/icd/en/GRNBOOK.pdf?ua=1.

World Health Organization (WHO) (2019). Classifications: ICD-10 online versions: International Classification of Diseases, 11th Revision (ICD-11). Geneva: Author. Retrieved September 1, 2019, from https://www.who.int/classifications/icd/icdonlineversions/en/ and https://www.who.int/classifications/icd/en/.

Yuodelis-Flores, C., & Ries, R. K. (2015). Addiction and suicide: A review. *The American Journal on Addictions*, 24(2), 98–104. doi:10.1111/ajad.12185.

Zemore, S. E., Lui, C., Mericle, A., Hemberg, J., & Kaskutas, L. A. (2018). A longitudinal study of the comparative efficacy of Women for Sobriety, LifeRing, SMART Recovery, and 12-step groups for those with AUD. *Journal of Substance Abuse Treatment*, 88, 18–26. doi:10.1016/j.jsat.2018.02.004.

3 Theory: Definitions and Dimensions of Forgiveness

The principle and practice of forgiveness are commonly acknowledged as worthwhile and honorable, so much so that many may argue that everyone knows what forgiveness means. During his Nobel Peace Prize acceptance speech, Martin Luther King, Jr. (1964, p. 1) lamented:

> There is a sort of poverty of the spirit which stands in glaring contrast to our scientific and technological abundance. … We have learned to fly the air like birds and swim the sea like fish, but we have not learned the simple art of living together as brothers.

One implication here is that although humanity otherwise values the notion of forgiveness (see Chapter 4), we may not be very good at it, in part because too many may not really know what it actually means.

What *does* it mean to forgive? When encouraging someone to consider forgiveness, what are we asking them to do? Is the nature of the task of forgiveness different based on who is considering it? That is, is what is meant by the notion of forgiveness different if considered between loved ones (e.g., parent/child, siblings, spouses, etc.), friends, or strangers, or encouraged by clinicians or spiritual leaders? Can we forgive ourselves? Can we forgive deity?

For any given individual, the question of whether to forgive or not may or may not be a difficult one. Sometimes those considering the question may rely on faulty information about what forgiveness is, what it means to forgive, or what is expected of those who forgive. An inaccurate understanding of forgiveness may prevent a person from pursuing it. Also, forgiveness may not occur even if a person otherwise agrees to do it. Similarly, a person may believe that they have forgiven when, in actuality, they have not.

Brief Historical Context

While historically utilizing the concept or effect of forgiveness (but not necessarily the *term*), the field of psychology, until fairly recently, has largely stayed away from researching forgiveness as a formal construct, such that essentially it was overlooked during the first century of scientific psychology (McCullough, 2000). Nevertheless, its therapeutic value was widely recognized (DiBlasio, 1992), including as a key factor when working with anger and depression (Fitzgibbons, 1986), adult survivors of childhood abuse or neglect (Hope, 1987), and fractured marital relationships (Worthington & DiBlasio, 1990). Until the recent boon occurred (beginning in the 1980s and then in earnest in the 1990s and continuing currently), a good portion of the literature noted the lack of (McCullough & Worthington, 1994) and need for an understanding of the dynamics of forgiveness (Richards & Bergin, 1997), including the development of theory (Worthington, 1998). The reason for the historical dearth of research has been suggested to be its close association to religion and consequent subjective nature; therefore, understanding the process was to be avoided and not explored (Levin & Vanderpool, 1991; Shontz & Rosenak, 1988). Please see Chapter 4 for a more detailed discussion of historical issues surrounding the scientific study of forgiveness.

The Multidimensional Nature of Forgiveness

Forgiveness is a broad construct consisting of multiple dimensions. It can be considered in trait-based terms (i.e., dispositional) and/or state-based terms (i.e., situational) (Toussaint & Webb, 2005). That is, a person may (or may not) forgive most of the time and in most circumstances (trait or dispositional forgiveness – sometimes referred to as *forgivingness* (see Roberts, 1995; Worthington et al., 2001)), or a person may (or may not) forgive in a manner entirely dependent on the context of the circumstances under consideration (state or situational forgiveness). Also, a given individual may (or may not) have high levels of dispositional forgiveness, but in a particular situation may not (or may) engage in forgiveness. For example, I may easily forgive my next door neighbor for leaving their garbage cans on the street all week, putting their extra garbage into my garbage cans at least once per month, not maintaining the landscaping in their front yard, and allowing their swimming pool to drain onto my property, but I may struggle to forgive this same neighbor for coming and borrowing my ladder out of my open garage on a Saturday morning without asking. Indeed, a person may have a general tendency toward engaging in forgiveness, but may have difficulty in the context of particular offenses.

Likewise, forgiveness can involve a variety of targets (e.g., self, others, deity) and methods (e.g., offering, seeking, feeling) (Toussaint & Webb, 2005). In this regard, one can offer, seek, and/or feel forgiveness in the context of the self, others, and/or conceptions of deity – whether in trait-based and/or state-based terms. Other targets and methods of forgiveness can include: forgiveness of uncontrollable situations (e.g., natural disasters; Thompson et al., 2005), healthy family functioning as contingent upon forgiveness (DiBlasio & Proctor, 1993), group-level forgiveness (i.e., inter-group, as opposed to inter-individual; Enright et al., 2016), community-based forgiveness (i.e., cultural particularities regarding forgiveness; Sandage et al., 2003), pseudoforgiveness (Baumeister et al., 1998), unforgiveness (Worthington, 1998), and forgiveness forecasting (i.e., predicted versus actual forgiveness; Barnes & Brown, 2010). Additional dimensions of forgiveness might involve issues of: (1) a priori forgiveness-dispositional, or forgiveness, in effect, may be unnecessary as one, in a healthy manner, does not develop grudges, (2) a priori forgiveness-situational,[1] or pre-meditated forgiveness of specific events that may happen (e.g., children not maintaining a parent's gravesite), (3) feeling others have accepted one's forgiveness, (4) feeling one's conception of deity has accepted one's forgiveness, (5) feeling forgiveness is being sought by others, (6) allowing forgiveness to occur,[2] and (7) valuing the notion of forgiveness.

Defining Forgiveness

Forgiveness has been receiving increasing scientific attention over the past 30+ years and is currently burgeoning, both in general (see Woodyatt et al., 2017; Worthington & Wade, 2020) and in the particular context of health and well-being (see Toussaint et al., 2015). However, acceptance of and agreement upon common definitions has remained elusive. Although nuanced definitional differences among the various dimensions ostensibly are acknowledged, the definition of forgiveness of others (i.e., other-forgiveness) largely has served as the default definition for all dimensions of forgiveness (Webb et al., 2013). Indeed, much of the historical discussion of definitional issues to follow is based on other-forgiveness.

This otherwise de facto use of other-forgiveness as the definition for the broad multidimensional construct of forgiveness may be generally innocuous. For example, multiple dimensions of forgiveness (i.e., of self, of others, and by God) have been included together and measured as total forgiveness (see Fetzer Institute, 1999). Although convenient, this may be overly simplistic and thus erroneous. At the very least, different dimensions of forgiveness are differently related to health-related outcomes (Webb et al., 2012; see also, Toussaint et al., 2015; Toussaint et al., 2020; Webb & Toussaint, 2020) and for the sake of accuracy in general and efficient treatment in particular, clarity of association is critical. Moreover, in the particular case of forgiveness of self (i.e., self-forgiveness), the default, de facto definition is problematic given critical differences based on the self being both the offender and the offended, such as the inability to avoid the self and the need for self-reconciliation (Enright & The Human Development Study Group, 1996; Tangney et al., 2005). Of note, a recent meta-analysis indicated only a modest to moderate statistical association between other-forgiveness and self-forgiveness (Davis et al., 2015).

Early discussions of definitional issues defined forgiveness as: an emotive change away from anger (Brandsma, 1982), giving up the right to hurt the offender (Pingleton, 1989), not retaliating and wishing the offender well (Rosenak & Harnden, 1992), willingly pardoning without demanding restitution (Wahking, 1992), releasing resentment (Hargrave, 1994), and reducing negative (Gassin & Enright, 1995) and *perhaps* increasing positive responses to offense (Worthington et al., 2001). Conversely, forgiveness has been equated with a state of denial or sense that what happened must now be okay or a good event and the conclusion that the offender is no longer at fault or responsible, thereby condoning the action (Brümmer, 1993; Gordon et al., 2000) and necessitating reconciliation and a return to vulnerability. Forgiveness does not include these erroneous assumptions (Enright et al., 1998) as it is a conscious, reasoned choice (Enright, 2001), an intrapsychic process undertaken by the offended (Worthington et al., 2000) irrespective of the offender, and except for self-forgiveness, does not require reconciliation (Enright & The Human Development Study Group, 1996). As accountability differs from retaliation and restitution, one can forgive while still requiring responsibility for the incident – whether criminally, personally, or otherwise. As such, forgiveness involves various cognitive, affective, and behavioral components (i.e., thoughts, feelings, and behaviors; Enright & The Human Development Study Group, 1991) and is a motivationally and volitionally unique coping mechanism (Toussaint & Webb, 2005).

Given the aforementioned use of other-forgiveness as a default, de facto definition for the broad multidimensional construct of forgiveness and the particular difficulties associated with applying it to self-forgiveness, Webb, Bumgarner, et al. (2017) reviewed the extant scientific psychological literature in an effort to reliably distinguish self-forgiveness from other-forgiveness in explicit and succinct definitional terms. Of the 177 unique, peer-reviewed articles focused on self-forgiveness identified, 121 provided explicit definition-related material. Of these 121, 36 articles provided definitional information based on forgiveness as a broad construct and 85 articles provided definitional information for self-forgiveness in the context of it being a distinct dimension of forgiveness. A review of the 121 articles providing any definitional material identified recurrent conceptual themes, many of which reflected elements of forgiveness as a broad construct. When distinctive components of self-forgiveness were addressed, five unique qualities became apparent. That is, of the 19 consistently identified definitional components of forgiveness drawn from the extant literature, 14 were in the context of forgiveness in general, and five were in the context of self-forgiveness in particular. That is, (1) self-reconciliation, (2) self-acceptance, (3) personal accountability, (4) re-connection with humanity, and (5) genuine efforts to change (Webb, Bumgarner, et al., 2017).

Webb, Bumgarner, et al. (2017) concluded that, in definitional terms, all dimensions of forgiveness derive from the 14 general aspects and that particular dimensions incorporate unique components, as necessary. As such, as a broad construct – that is, applicable to all dimensions of forgiveness, including other-forgiveness – Webb, Bumgarner, et al. (2017) defined *forgiveness* such that it:

> occurs over time and is a deliberate, volitional process involving a fundamental shift in affect, cognition, and/or behavior in response to negative feelings regarding an acknowledged offensive experience, without condoning, excusing, or denying the transgression(s) – at a minimum, an absence of ill will toward an offender.
>
> (p. 220)

In the context of the five otherwise unique qualities identified, and building upon their general definition, Webb, Bumgarner, et al. (2017) defined *self-forgiveness* as:

> initiated in response to one's own negative feelings in the context of a personally acknowledged self-instigated wrong, that results in ready accountability for said wrong and a fundamental, constructive shift in one's relationship to, reconciliation with, and acceptance of the self through human-connectedness and commitment to change.
>
> (p. 221)

In this regard, Webb, Bumgarner, et al. (2017) have laid a foundation for the basic definition of the broad multidimensional construct of forgiveness, and provided specific definitions for other-forgiveness and self-forgiveness. Using said basic definition, at its core applicable to other-forgiveness, and building upon it further, initial definitions of select additional dimensions of forgiveness are herein proposed.

Contextually-Sacred Forgiveness

As with self-forgiveness, spiritual and/or theological issues may come into play when considering definitions of forgiveness in relation to the divine or sacred; for example, forgiveness of God (i.e., conceptions of deity; see Fincham & May, 2019a, 2019b), feeling God has accepted one's forgiveness, seeking forgiveness from God, and feeling forgiven by God. In the context of self-forgiveness, research suggests that religious people may not feel that it is their place to forgive themselves, but God's prerogative (Walker & Gorsuch, 2002). Related to this, there is some evidence to suggest that feeling forgiven by God may lead to self-forgiveness, and that seeking forgiveness from God, under certain circumstances, may play a role in this relationship (Webb, Hirsch, et al., 2017). Also, the notion of forgiving God implies that conceptions of deity and/or the sacred can (1) do things that will offend humans and (2) make mistakes and/or do wrong. Some may struggle with the idea that God (or, deity or deities) could and/or would do something offensive or could and/or would allow something offensive to occur. That is, some may prefer the interpretation of such to be that God will only do things to help humans, and we may have difficulty recognizing and accepting these types of experiences as being helpful or positive. However, it seems much more likely that many otherwise theistic people will question the idea that God has the ability to make mistakes and/or do wrong, given the archetypal assumption that deity is perfect.

The aforementioned broad definition of forgiveness seems applicable here, but cultural, spiritual, and theological differences in understanding the nature of deity/the sacred may preclude *or* enable the practice of the different dimensions of contextually-sacred forgiveness. Any related unique definitional components to incorporate into the broad definition will likely be highly nuanced; based on particular spiritual belief systems and individualized interpretations and applications thereof (see Richards & Bergin, 2005, 2014; Toussaint et al., 2012). As such, those considering contextually-sacred forgiveness are encouraged first to clarify for themselves – whether through self-reflection or reasonably assisted by friends, loved ones, clergy, or clinicians – their own, personal, autonomously-derived conception and understanding of deity and/or the sacred.

Seeking Forgiveness

When seeking forgiveness, it is important (1) that the seeker understands what they are asking for and (2) that the person(s) being asked to forgive understand(s) what is being asked of them. For example, if I seek forgiveness from my co-worker for losing my temper in a meeting, and I expect my co-worker immediately to say that it is okay and that it was not a problem anyway then I am not asking for forgiveness, but asking my co-worker to overlook what happened and likely expecting our relationship to return to what it was before as if nothing happened. Likewise and regardless of my intention when asking, if my co-worker believes that forgiveness means that it must now be the case that the incident is a good thing and that reconciliation is expected then my co-worker may not be willing to consider my request for forgiveness. In this regard, a unique definitional component to incorporate into the aforementioned broad definition of forgiveness when considering dimensions related to seeking forgiveness is that *seeking forgiveness* occurs (i.e., is requested) only after a meaningful discussion between the requestor and the potential forgiver regarding the definition and nature of forgiveness such that both parties are clear about what is and is not being asked, including expectations regarding reconciliation.

Feeling Forgiveness

After having sought forgiveness, when considering whether or not forgiveness has occurred, it is important to reflect on the nature of the interactions between the offender and the offended. Although reconciliation is neither required nor expected (except in the context of self-forgiveness), one can evaluate the extent to which the potential forgiver has changed or modified their thoughts, feelings, and behaviors toward the seeker of forgiveness. Indeed, forgiveness involves a change in thoughts, feelings, and behaviors from negative to neutral, and perhaps further to include positive, love-based emotions (see Gassin & Enright, 1995; Worthington et al., 2001). In this regard, a unique definitional component to incorporate into the aforementioned broad definition of forgiveness when considering dimensions related to feeling forgiveness is that *feeling forgiveness* occurs when the seeker of forgiveness, without expectations for reconciliation, perceives meaningful changes in their interactions with the potential forgiver, if and when they occur, especially in the context of the forgiver's thoughts, feelings, and behaviors, such that at a minimum there is an absence of ill will.

Determinants of Forgiveness

McCullough (2000) provided an early overview of important determinants of the ability to forgive; that is, empathy and perspective taking, rumination and suppression of rumination, relational closeness, commitment, and satisfaction, as well as apology have been shown to influence the likelihood for forgiveness (of others) to occur (see also, Koutsos et al., 2008; Welton et al., 2008). Additional factors predicting higher or lower levels of forgiveness include: emotions (Stackhouse, 2016), justice (Lucas et al., 2010), personality (Hodge et al., 2020), religiousness/spirituality (Choe et al., 2020), and time (Krentzman et al., 2018; McCullough et al., 2010).

The Process of Forgiveness

Much work has been completed in describing the steps or "how-to"s of forgiveness (e.g., Enright et al., 1998; Worthington, 2006). Enright et al. (1998) provide a summarization of 20 steps or units of forgiveness described in the literature and divide them into four broad phases. *Uncovering* refers to the awareness of the problem and emotional pain following an offense, including anger and insight; *Decision* includes realizing the need for an alternate resolution; *Work* includes processes such as, reframing, empathy, and acceptance of pain; and *Deepening* includes finding meaning and universality. Worthington's (2006) REACH model involves *recalling* an offense, developing *empathy* for the offender, choosing to give the *altruistic* gift of forgiveness to the offender, making a public, formal *commitment* to forgive, and *holding on* to progress made toward forgiveness, which is likely facilitated through said commitment. The steps or "how-to"s of forgiveness are thorough, and likely to be challenging, profound, and, at times, difficult.

In addition to broad, over-arching conceptual consistency, these models of forgiveness also share important assumptions about the nature of forgiveness. That is, nothing about the offense itself, the experience of the offense, or the offender is to be overlooked or minimized. Also, the outcome of forgiveness is not likely to be arrived at in a linear fashion, as an event, or as an all-or-nothing experience. See Chapter 8 for more detailed discussion regarding the overall process of forgiveness, or models of how forgiveness is facilitated.

The Task of Forgiveness

Without an accurate understanding of forgiveness *as a task*, it may not occur. The task of forgiveness not only involves understanding and implementing the steps of forgiveness, but perhaps most critically understanding and applying the definition of forgiveness. Indeed, the definition of forgiveness underlies all else when considering, attempting, and succeeding at the practice of any/all dimension(s) of forgiveness. A person may perceive that they have high levels of forgiveness and yet they may not actually be very forgiving. For example, a Christian may ostensibly engage in forgiveness and otherwise believe that their practice of it is genuine because God has commanded them to forgive any given individual on "seventy times seven" occasions (see Matthew 18:22; KJV, 1983). And, as such, when asked if they forgive, the response may very well be "of course I forgive" with little evaluative thought, self-reflection, or self-awareness. Similarly, whether spiritual or not, a person may agree that the positive psychological, prosocial principle and practice of forgiveness is important, socially desirable, and the sign of a good person. Nevertheless, if the core principles of the broad definition of forgiveness, and any necessary additional definitional components needed for dimensions other than forgiveness of others, are unknown, misunderstood, or otherwise missing, then genuine forgiveness may not be and likely is not occurring. As such, applying the definition of forgiveness and implementing the steps of forgiveness can be difficult.

Another critical issue that permeates all aspects of the task of forgiveness is that of the timing of forgiveness. As mentioned above, forgiveness typically is not an event or an all-or-nothing process; indeed, not only does the task of forgiveness take time, it fluctuates over time. Moreover, as with the particulars of what it means to forgive (i.e., definition(s) and steps), many may otherwise erroneously expect the outcome or result of forgiveness to occur instantaneously, or at the very least sooner rather than later. In sum, if one is engaging in the process of offering, seeking, or feeling forgiveness – whether in the context of self, others, deity/the sacred, etc. – it is likely not going to be an easy task or a quick task.

The Who of Forgiveness

Does the definition of forgiveness and/or the process of forgiveness change based on who is offering, seeking, or feeling forgiveness? Importantly, the answer to this question is a friendly, but definite, "No!" That is, there are no special circumstances, viable short-cuts, or easy-fixes when considering and pursuing the outcome of forgiveness. Particular determinants of forgiveness may vary in substance and magnitude (i.e., which determinants apply and the strength of association, respectively) for any given individual (see Chapter 2 discussion regarding statistical reasoning and generalities versus specificities (in the context of Formal Treatment)), but this does not change the definition or process of forgiveness. For example, relational closeness and commitment may make a difference in forgiveness (see McCullough, 2000; McCullough et al., 2010); however, this facilitated difference in forgiveness is related to the likelihood of forgiveness to occur (or, in this context of a valuable relationship, one's motivation to engage in forgiveness and be successful therein) rather than a change in the definition or process of forgiveness. In sum, regardless of the nature of the relationship between the offender and the offended (i.e., family, friends, strangers, professional, etc.), both the definition and the process of forgiveness, in its multiple dimensions, remain the same.

Notes

1 I acknowledge and thank Jameson K. Hirsch, Ph.D. (http://faculty.etsu.edu/hirsch/) for contributing this additional dimension of forgiveness during a conversation many years ago.
2 I acknowledge and thank Dana Skaggs, M.A. (https://danaskaggs.com/) for contributing this additional dimension of forgiveness during a conversation many years ago.

References

Barnes, C. D., & Brown, R. P. (2010). A value-congruent bias in the forgiveness forecasts of religious people. *Psychology of Religion and Spirituality*, 2(1), 17–29. doi:10.1037/a0017585.

Baumeister, R. F., Exline, J. J., & Sommer, K. L. (1998). The victim role, grudge theory, and two dimensions of forgiveness. In E. L.Worthington, Jr. (Ed.), *Dimensions of forgiveness: Psychological research and theological perspectives* (pp. 79–104). Philadelphia: Templeton Foundation Press.

Brandsma, J. M. (1982). Forgiveness: A dynamic, theological and therapeutic analysis. *Pastoral Psychology*, 31(1), 40–50. doi:10.1007/BF01744463.

Brümmer, V. (1993). *The model of love: A study in philosophical theology.* New York, NY: Cambridge University Press.

Choe, E., McLaughlin, A., McElroy-Heltzel, S. E., & Davis, D. E. (2020). Forgiveness and religion/spirituality. In E. L.Worthington, Jr. & N. G. Wade (Eds.), *Handbook of forgiveness* (2nd ed., pp. 107–116). New York, NY: Routledge.

Davis, D. E., Ho, M. Y., Griffin, B. J., Bell, C., Hook, J. N., Van Tongeren, D. R., … Westbrook, C. J. (2015). Forgiving the self and physical and mental health correlates: A meta-analytic review. *Journal of Counseling Psychology*, 62(2), 329–335. doi:10.1037/cou0000063.

DiBlasio, F. A. (1992). Forgiveness in psychotherapy: Comparison of older and younger therapists. *Journal of Psychology and Christianity*, 11(2), 181–187.

DiBlasio, F. A., & Proctor, J. H. (1993). Therapists and the clinical use of forgiveness. *The American Journal of Family Therapy*, 21(2), 175–184. doi:10.1080/01926189308250915.

Enright, R. D. (2001). *Forgiveness is a choice: A step-by-step process for resolving anger and restoring hope.* Washington, DC: American Psychological Association.

Enright, R. D., & The Human Development Study Group. (1991). The moral development of forgiveness. In W. Kurtines & J. Gewirtz (Eds.), *Handbook of moral behavior and development* (Vol. 1, pp. 123–152). Hillsdale, NJ: Lawrence Erlbaum.

Enright, R. D., & The Human Development Study Group. (1996). Counseling within the forgiveness triad: On forgiving, receiving forgiveness, and self-forgiveness. *Counseling and Values*, 40(2), 107–126. doi:10.1002/j.2161-007X.1996.tb00844.x.

Enright, R. D., Freedman, S., & Rique, J. (1998). The psychology of interpersonal forgiveness. In R. D. Enright & J. North (Eds.), *Exploring forgiveness* (pp. 46–62). Madison, WI: University of Wisconsin Press.

Enright, R. D., Lee, Y.-R., Hirshberg, M. J., Litts, B. K., Schirmer, E. B., Irwin, A. J., … Song, J. Y. (2016). Examining group forgiveness: Conceptual and empirical issues. *Peace and Conflict: Journal of Peace Psychology*, 22(2), 153–162. doi:10.1037/pac0000153.

Fetzer Institute (1999). Multidimensional measurement of religiousness/spirituality for use in health research: A report of the Fetzer Institute/National Institute on Aging working group, with additional psychometric data. October. Kalamazoo, MI: Corporate.

Fincham, F. D., & May, R. W. (2019a). Divine, interpersonal and self-forgiveness: Independently related to depressive symptoms? *The Journal of Positive Psychology*, 15(4), 448–454. doi:10.1080/17439760.2019.1639798.

Fincham, F. D., & May, R. W. (2019b). Self-forgiveness and well-being: Does divine forgiveness matter? *The Journal of Positive Psychology*, 14(6), 854–859. doi:10.1080/17439760.2019.1579361.

Fitzgibbons, R. (1986). The cognitive and emotive uses of forgiveness in the treatment of anger. *Psychotherapy: Theory, Research, Practice, Training*, 23(4), 629–633. doi:10.1037/h0085667.

Gassin, E. A., & Enright, R. D. (1995). The will to meaning in the process of forgiveness. *Journal of Psychology and Christianity*, 14(1), 38–49.

Gordon, K. C., Baucom, D. H., & Snyder, D. K. (2000). The use of forgiveness in marital therapy. In M. E. McCullough, K. I. Pargament, & C. E. Thoresen (Eds.), *Forgiveness: Theory, research, and practice.* New York, NY: Guilford Press.

Hargrave, T. D. (1994). *Families and forgiveness: Healing wounds in the intergenerational family.* New York, NY: Brunner/Mazel Publishers.

Hodge, A. S., Captari, L. E., Mosher, D. K., Kodali, N., Hook, J. N., Davis, D. E., & Van Tongeren, D. R. (2020). Personality and forgiveness: A meta-analytic review. In E. L.Worthington, Jr. & N. G. Wade (Eds.), *Handbook of forgiveness* (2nd ed., pp. 97–106). New York, NY: Routledge.

Hope, D. (1987). The healing paradox of forgiveness. *Psychotherapy: Theory, Research, Practice, Training*, 24(2), 240–244. doi:10.1037/h0085710.

King James Version (1983). *Holy Bible.* Salt Lake City, UT: Church of Jesus Christ of Latter-day Saints.

King, M. L., Jr. (1964). Martin Luther King Jr. – Nobel Lecture. Retrieved January 4, 2018, from https://www.nobelprize.org/nobel_prizes/peace/laureates/1964/king-lecture.html.

Koutsos, P., Wertheim, E. H., & Kornblum, J. (2008). Paths to interpersonal forgiveness: The roles of personality, disposition to forgive and contextual factors in predicting forgiveness. *Personality and Individual Differences*, 44(2), 337–348. doi:10.1016/j.paid.2007.08.011.

Krentzman, A. R., Webb, J. R., Jester, J. M., & Harris, J. I. (2018). Longitudinal relationship between forgiveness of self and forgiveness of others among individuals with alcohol use disorders. *Psychology of Religion and Spirituality*, 10(2), 128–137. doi:10.1037/rel0000152.

Levin, J. S., & Vanderpool, H. Y. (1991). Religious factors in physical health and the prevention of illness. *Prevention in Human Services*, 9(2), 41–64. doi:10.1300/J293v09n02_03.

Lucas, T., Young, J. D., Zhdanova, L., & Alexander, S. (2010). Self and other justice beliefs, impulsivity, rumination, and forgiveness: Justice beliefs can both prevent and promote forgiveness. *Personality and Individual Differences*, 49(8), 851–856. doi:10.1016/j.paid.2010.07.014.

McCullough, M. E. (2000). Forgiveness as human strength: Theory, measurement, and links to well-being. *Journal of Social & Clinical Psychology*, 19(1), 43–55. doi:10.1521/jscp.2000.19.1.43.

McCullough, M. E., & Worthington, E. L., Jr. (1994). Encouraging clients to forgive people who have hurt them: Review, critique, and research prospectus. *Journal of Psychology and Theology*, 22(1), 3–20. doi:10.1177/009164719402200101.

McCullough, M. E., Luna, L. R., Berry, J. W., Tabak, B. A., & Bono, G. (2010). On the form and function of forgiving: Modeling the time-forgiveness relationship and testing the valuable relationships hypothesis. *Emotion*, 10(3), 358–376. doi:10.1037/a0019349.

Pingleton, J. P. (1989). The role and function of forgiveness in the psychotherapeutic process. *Journal of Psychology and Theology*, 17(1), 27–35. doi:10.1177/009164718901700106.

Richards, P. S., & Bergin, A. E. (1997). *A spiritual strategy for counseling and psychotherapy.* Washington, DC: American Psychological Association.

Richards, P. S., & Bergin, A. E. (2005). *A spiritual strategy for counseling and psychotherapy* (2nd ed.). Washington, DC: American Psychological Association.

Richards, P. S., & Bergin, A. E. (Eds.). (2014). *Handbook of psychotherapy and religious diversity* (2nd ed.). Washington, DC: American Psychological Association.

Roberts, R. C. (1995). Forgivingness. *American Philosophical Quarterly*, 32(4), 289–306.

Rosenak, C. M., & Harnden, G. M. (1992). Forgiveness in the psychotherapeutic process: Clinical applications. *Journal of Psychology and Christianity*, 11(2), 188–197.

Sandage, S. J., Hill, P. C., & Vang, H. C. (2003). Toward a multicultural positive psychology: Indigenous forgiveness and Hmong culture. *The Counseling Psychologist*, 31(5), 564–592. doi:10.1177/0011000003256350.

Shontz, F. C., & Rosenak, C. (1988). Psychological theories and the need for forgiveness: Assessment and critique. *Journal of Psychology and Christianity*, 7(1), 23–31.

Stackhouse, M. R. D. (2016). Paths to not forgiving: The roles of social isolation, retributive orientation, and moral emotions. *Personality and Individual Differences*, 97, 50–54. doi:10.1016/j.paid.2016.03.023.

Tangney, J. P., Boone, A. L., & Dearing, R. (2005). Forgiving the self: Conceptual issues and empirical findings. In E. L.Worthington, Jr. (Ed.), *Handbook of forgiveness* (pp. 143–158). New York, NY: Routledge.

Thompson, L. Y., Snyder, C. R., Hoffman, L., Michael, S. T., Rasmussen, H. N., Billings, L. S., … Roberts, D. J. (2005). Dispositional forgiveness of self, others, and situations. *Journal of Personality*, 73(2), 313–359. doi:10.1111/j.1467-6494.2005.00311.x.

Toussaint, L. L., & Webb, J. R. (2005). Theoretical and empirical connections between forgiveness, mental health, and well-being. In E. L.Worthington, Jr. (Ed.), *Handbook of forgiveness* (pp. 349–362). New York, NY: Routledge.

Toussaint, L. L., Webb, J. R., & Keltner, W. (2012). Religion, spirituality, and mental health. In J. D. Aten, K. A. O'Grady, & E. L.Worthington, Jr. (Eds.), *The psychology of religion and spirituality for clinicians: Using research in your practice* (pp. 331–356). New York, NY: Routledge.

Toussaint, L. L., Worthington, E. L., Jr., & Williams, D. R. (Eds.). (2015). *Forgiveness and health: Scientific evidence and theories relating forgiveness to better health.* New York, NY: Springer.

Toussaint, L. L., Worthington, E. L., Jr., Williams, D. R., & Webb, J. R. (2020). Forgiveness and physical health. In E. L.Worthington, Jr. & N. G. Wade (Eds.), *Handbook of forgiveness* (2nd ed., pp. 178–187). New York, NY: Routledge.

Wahking, H. (1992). Spiritual growth through grace and forgiveness. *Journal of Psychology and Christianity*, 11(2), 198–206.

Walker, D., & Gorsuch, R. (2002). Forgiveness within the Big Five personality model. *Personality and Individual Differences*, 32(7), 1127–1138. doi:10.1016/S0191-8869(00)00185-9.

Webb, J. R., & Toussaint, L. L. (2020). Forgiveness, well-being, and mental health. In E. L. Worthington, Jr. & N. G. Wade (Eds.), *Handbook of forgiveness* (2nd ed., pp. 188–197). New York, NY: Routledge.

Webb, J. R., Hirsch, J. K., & Toussaint, L. L. (2017). Self-forgiveness and pursuit of the sacred: The role of pastoral-related care. In L. Woodyatt, E. L.Worthington, Jr., M. Wenzel, & B. J. Griffin (Eds.), *Handbook of the psychology of self-forgiveness* (pp. 309–325). New York, NY: Springer.

Webb, J. R., Toussaint, L. L., & Conway-Williams, E. (2012). Forgiveness and health: Psycho-spiritual integration and the promotion of better healthcare. *Journal of Health Care Chaplaincy*, 18(1–2), 57–73. doi:10.1080/08854726.2012.667317.

Webb, J. R., Hirsch, J. K., Visser, P. L., & Brewer, K. G. (2013). Forgiveness and health: Assessing the mediating effect of health behavior, social support, and interpersonal functioning. *The Journal of Psychology: Interdisciplinary and Applied*, 147(5), 391–414. doi:10.1080/00223980.2012.700964.

Webb, J. R., Bumgarner, D. J., Conway-Williams, E., Dangel, T., & Hall, B. B. (2017). A consensus definition of self-forgiveness: Implications for assessment and treatment. *Spirituality in Clinical Practice*, 4(3), 216–227. doi:10.1037/scp0000138.

Welton, G. L., Hill, P. C., & Seybold, K. S. (2008). Forgiveness in the trenches: Empathy, perspective taking, and anger. *Journal of Psychology and Christianity*, 27(2), 168–177.

Woodyatt, L., Worthington, E. L., Jr., Wenzel, M., & Griffin, B. J. (Eds.). (2017). *Handbook of the psychology of self-forgiveness.* New York, NY: Springer.

Worthington, E. L., Jr. (1998). Empirical research in forgiveness: Looking backward, looking forward. In E. L.Worthington, Jr. (Ed.), *Dimensions of forgiveness: Psychological research and theological perspectives* (pp. 321–339). Philadelphia, PA: Templeton Foundation Press.

Worthington, E. L., Jr. (2006). *Forgiveness and reconciliation: Theory and application*. New York, NY: Routledge.

Worthington, E. L., Jr., & DiBlasio, F. A. (1990). Promoting mutual forgiveness within the fractured relationship. *Psychotherapy: Theory, Research, Practice, Training*, 27(2), 219–223. doi:10.1037/0033-3204.27.2.219.

Worthington, E. L., Jr., & Wade, N. G. (Eds.). (2020). *Handbook of forgiveness* (2nd ed.). New York, NY: Routledge.

Worthington, E. L., Jr., Berry, J. W., & Parrott, L., III. (2001). Unforgiveness, forgiveness, religion, and health. In T. G. Plante & A. C. Sherman (Eds.), *Faith and health: Psychological perspectives* (pp. 107–138). New York, NY: Guilford Press.

Worthington, E. L., Jr., Sandage, S. J., & Berry, J. W. (2000). Group interventions to promote forgiveness: What researchers and clinicians ought to know. In M. E. McCullough, K. I. Pargament, & C. E. Thoresen (Eds.), *Forgiveness: Theory, research, and practice* (pp. 228–253). New York, NY: Guilford Press.

4 Theory: What is Forgiveness?

Is forgiveness a religious/spiritual principle *or* is it a positive psychological scientific construct? Can it be both? Regarding whether forgiveness is a religious/spiritual principle, is it more accurate to consider forgiveness as a religious principle *or* as a spiritual principle, or can it be both? Arthur C. Clarke (2019), a prolific author of science fiction, surmised that "Two possibilities exist: Either we are alone in the Universe or we are not. Both are equally terrifying." Although Clarke's dichotomous proposition – with implications for both science *and* religion/spirituality – seems profoundly accurate, often times in popular culture a related dichotomy is presented wherein science and religion are pitted against each other; such that, one must declare which set of principles governs one's life – science *or* religion. Likewise, it has become common to pit religion and spirituality against each other; such that, religion is bad and spirituality is good. While Clarke's dichotomy seems reasonable, is it reasonable to dichotomize science versus religion, or religion versus spirituality? Or, are these *artificial* dichotomies? That is, can religion and science, and religion and spirituality coexist? Can forgiveness be studied in the context of science, religion, and spirituality? The short answer is: Of course it can!

As a graduate student in the mid-1990s, I began to explore the idea of studying the relationship between forgiveness and happiness. I speculated, based on my personal experiences and my understanding of various spiritual belief systems, that people who were more forgiving of others would be happier in life. The response of my doctoral mentor, Seymour L. Zelen,[1] was tepid as he lamented the unlikely prospect for the successful empirical examination of such, given the difficulties associated with operationally defining and accurately measuring the notion of happiness.[2] As I delved into the then-current scientific literature, it became clear that forgiveness largely was considered a by-product of religion. Although the explicit scientific psychological study of forgiveness was still in its beginning stages in the mid-1990s (having started in the 1980s and then in earnest in the 1990s; see McCullough et al., 2000b; Webb & Toussaint, 2020), the scientific psychological study of religion was established and ostensibly mature, yet perpetually struggling to maintain traction and relevance in the broader field of secular psychology.[3] Related to this, the struggle for recognition, through peer-reviewed scientific publication, of the fledgling field of the psychology of forgiveness seemed to be a function of common assumptions regarding the close, and thus problematic association[4] of forgiveness with religion and religious practices (e.g., Enright & Zell, 1989; Hope, 1987; Levin & Vanderpool, 1991; Pingleton, 1989; Shontz & Rosenak, 1988). In those early days, DiBlasio (1992) stated that "although few would argue with the benefits of forgiveness, it is one of the least studied phenomena in the therapeutic literature" (p. 182). The lack of research regarding forgiveness was thought to be due to it being too closely associated with theology, such that it was to be avoided and not explored (Levin & Vanderpool, 1991; Shontz & Rosenak,

1988) – that work which *was* published was mostly found in religiously oriented journals (Hargrave & Sells, 1997). Indeed, whether for neutral (see Fincham, 2000; McCullough et al., 1997) or biased (see above) reasons, in order to publish empirical research regarding the psychology of forgiveness, it appeared that scholars had to acknowledge the inherent connection between forgiveness and religion, while also explicating (indeed, justifying) the otherwise secular applicability of forgiveness (e.g., Fincham, 2000; Hope, 1987; McCullough & Worthington, 1994; McCullough et al., 1997; Webb, 2003; Worthington & DiBlasio, 1990).

Over the past 30+ years the psychological study of forgiveness has been receiving consistent and increasing attention in the scientific literature (see Enright, 2001; Enright & North, 1998; McCullough et al., 2000a; Worthington, 1998, 2005), such that currently it is flourishing (see Enright & Fitzgibbons, 2015; Toussaint et al., 2015; Woodyatt et al., 2017; Worthington & Sandage, 2016; Worthington & Wade, 2020). Moreover, the construct[5] of forgiveness is now readily accepted as a human strength and virtue; a core construct in the field of positive psychology (see Snyder et al., 2016; Tsang & Martin, 2018; Webb et al., 2015). Indeed, the non-religious/spiritual nature and applicability of forgiveness has become a given. In this regard, during the last few years, I have received fairly consistent publishing-based reviewer feedback critical of my implicit presentation of forgiveness as a construct common to religion/spirituality and requesting or requiring explicit justification of forgiveness as *relevant* to religion/spirituality. As such, when seeking to publish forgiveness-based work contextually grounded in religion/spirituality in scientific psychological journals, including such journals focused on religion/spirituality, it seems to be increasingly the case that scholars need now stipulate the broad, secular nature and applicability of forgiveness, while also justifying forgiveness as a construct germane to religion/spirituality. That is, in an ironic turn of events, scholars now must deliberately explicate the religious/spiritual nature of forgiveness.[4]

The scientific study of forgiveness has found a home in the field of positive psychology. However, it appears that although it unquestionably was considered a religious/spiritual construct until quite recently, currently there is debate as to where, as a construct, forgiveness best belongs. Now that it is considered a positive psychological human strength, is forgiveness still a religious/spiritual construct, or can it be both? A better understanding of (1) the historical relationship between psychology and religion/spirituality, (2) the nature of spirituality, including its parallels with positive psychology, and (3) the central role of forgiveness in spiritual belief systems likely will help answer these and other related questions (see below).

The Relationship Between Psychology and Religion/Spirituality

The relationship between psychology and religion/spirituality can be traced back to the emergence of psychology as its own field of inquiry. In an effort to distinguish itself from philosophy and establish its grounding in empiricism, in the late 1800s psychology claimed its role in the study and explanation of human behavior as independent of religion and religious teachings (see Levin & Vanderpool, 1991). Indeed, in 1927 Freud argued that "[n]o, our science is no illusion. But an illusion it would be to suppose that what science cannot give us we can get elsewhere" (1989, p. 722). Nevertheless, there have been consistent efforts to understand the effect of religion, religiousness, and spirituality on human behavior – the psychology of religion and spirituality.[3] With the relatively recent emergence of spirituality as its own field of inquiry, separate from religion/religiousness (see Oman, 2013; Zinnbauer & Pargament, 2005), distinctions between the two fields have developed. Humans can be described as (1) religious and spiritual, (2) religious, but not spiritual, (3) spiritual, but not religious, and (4) not religious and not spiritual (see Connors et al., 1996; GESIS, 2018). Related to this, an all-too-often polarizing, albeit artificial dichotomy has arisen – religiousness *versus* spirituality – religiousness tends to be viewed as bad, whereas spirituality tends to be viewed as good (see Hood, 2003; Pargament et al., 2013; Webb et al., 2014).

Although religion is regarded as an important aspect of human culture (Cohen, 2009) and American Psychological Association policy (APA, 2008) and ethical standards (APA, 2002) recognize and respect religion and religiousness, the capacity for the application of scientific rigor to the study of religion/spirituality remains questionable (McMinn et al., 2009). Perhaps this tension underlies the question of and ironic shift in determining where the construct of forgiveness best fits within the field of psychology. Is forgiveness a religious/spiritual construct or is it a secular construct? Is it reasonable for the field of psychology to continually call into question the legitimacy of religious/spiritual issues? Are religious/spiritual issues endogenous (i.e., inherent) or exogenous (i.e., extraneous) to the human condition?

Transcendent Thread

Beginning with Freud (1989), maintained by Ellis (1980), [3] and continuing today,[4] meaningful segments of psychology, and society as a whole (e.g., Dawkins, 2006; Hitchens, 2007), have not only dismissed religion, but often virulently so. However, the fields of psychology and religion/spirituality, while assuredly different, are strikingly similar. Both psychology and religion/spirituality have attempted to address the human condition in an analogous fashion. Like psychology, sometimes referred to as the *secular priesthood* (see Reisner & Lawson, 1992), religion/spirituality:

> concerns itself with human action and experience, whether it be in philosophical ways, such as treatises on the nature of the soul and on the proper ends of human action and life, or in more practical ways, such as disciplines of character formation and in the education of children.
>
> (Kugelmann & Belzen, 2009, pp. 125–126)

Indeed, psychology and religion share a common origin and over the course of history have otherwise largely worked in concert with one another (Koenig, 2009; see also, Koenig et al., 2001; Thielman, 1998).

Moreover, scholars have identified spirituality, conceptually and empirically, as a fundamental component of human nature – part of what it means to be human – and, importantly, that a belief in deity is not a prerequisite for healthy spirituality (Pargament, 2013a; Piedmont & Wilkins, 2013; Webb et al., 2014). The Five-Factor Model of Personality (i.e., the so-called Big 5 personality traits of: openness to experience, conscientiousness, extraversion, agreeableness, and neuroticism (or emotional (in)stability)) uniquely ties together humanity throughout history, as it is common to all human beings regardless of ethnicity, geographic locale, or Eastern versus Western culture (see Widiger & Costa, 2013). Likewise, the ubiquity of spirituality as a cultural value throughout the world (see GESIS, 2018; ISSP Research Group, 2018), together with the identification of spirituality as a personality characteristic, consistently separate and independent of the Big 5 (Piedmont, 1999; Piedmont & Wilkins, 2013), warrants the description of spirituality as a *Transcendent Thread*. That is, the Transcendent Thread consists of those apparent – though sometimes vague – external, guiding, empowering, and unifying aspects of the human condition which are beyond ordinary experience and explanation, yet are commonly and seemingly universally accessible.[6] Related to this, at its most basic (not necessarily theistic) level, spirituality has been defined as a search for the sacred (Pargament, 2013a; Pargament & Mahoney, 2017).Indeed, religiousness/spirituality holds a place of near-matchless power and influence in human history and society (see Pincus, 1998). For example, as a source and force (for better or worse) of: motivation, affiliation, identity, meaning, purpose, resilience, health, and well-being, etc. (see Koenig et al., 2012; Miller, 2012; Paloutzian & Park, 2013; Pargament, 2013b).

Target-Based Spirituality

Over the years, religion and spirituality have been variously defined and parsed (see Oman, 2013; Zinnbauer & Pargament, 2005). In an effort to bring clarity and parsimony[7] to the definitional conundrum of religion/spirituality, Webb et al. (2014; see also, Webb, 2007, 2003) collapsed the otherwise common dichotomy of *religion* versus *spirituality* (see above) into an overarching singular term *Spirituality*[8] – consisting of three inter-related sub-constructs – defined as "the salient, searching pursuit of the transcendently sacred ritualistic, theistic, and/or existential aspects of the human condition." (p. 974). That is, (1) *Ritualistic Spirituality*, a structured connection with deity; (2) *Theistic Spirituality*, a non-structured connection with deity; and (3) *Existential Spirituality*, a transcendent, yet non-theistic search for meaning and purpose.

These three dimensions (Ritualistic, Theistic, and Existential) – that is, targets – of the overarching construct of Spirituality (i.e., the RiTE Model of Spirituality; see Figure 4.1) share critical characteristics, and yet there are also important distinctions among the three (Webb et al., 2014). All three include belief and practice related components. Each dimension includes a fundamental belief in the transcendent and/or sacred quality of an entity or entities external to the self. For Ritualistic Spirituality and Theistic Spirituality this belief typically involves deity, whereas for Existential Spirituality, knowledge, nature (or aspects thereof), or the Universe often are imbued with transcendently sacred qualities. Importantly, each dimension also includes an emphasis on behavioral practices or activities tied to said beliefs.

In addition to these common, underlying characteristics regardless of dimension, each pair of dimensions shares a particular emphasis which points to an essential difference from the third (Webb et al., 2014). Ritualistic Spirituality and Theistic Spirituality revere the divine, whereas Existential Spirituality typically does not. Ritualistic Spirituality and Existential Spirituality prioritize observance of principle, whereas Theistic Spirituality largely does not. And, Theistic Spirituality and Existential Spirituality focus on the pursuit of meaning and purpose, whereas Ritualistic Spirituality may not. Additionally, the intersection of: (1) Ritualistic Spirituality with Theistic Spirituality as opposed to Existential Spirituality indicates a theistic versus non-theistic quality to spirituality, (2) Ritualistic Spirituality with Existential Spirituality as opposed to Theistic Spirituality indicates a structured versus non-structured quality to spirituality, and (3) Theistic Spirituality with Existential Spirituality as opposed to Ritualistic Spirituality indicates a contemplative versus non-contemplative quality to spirituality. Accordingly, the RiTE Model of Spirituality is broadly conceptualized to be multidirectional and proportional such that higher levels of a particular dimension typically contrast with lower levels of another dimension. Of note, this model of spirituality largely addresses generalities rather than specificities. For example, an individual otherwise characterized as having Theistic Spirituality, may also engage in observance of principle in a structured fashion.

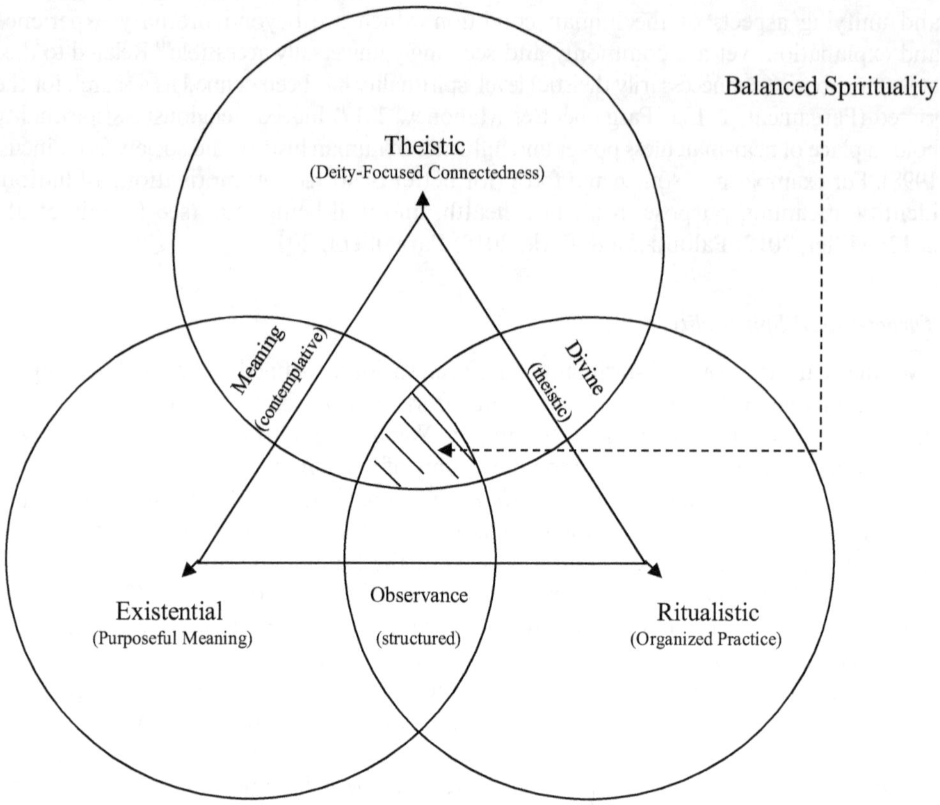

Figure 4.1 The RiTE Model of Spirituality.
Source: Adapted from Webb et al. (2014)

In this regard, constructive or healthy spirituality (i.e., good relationships with the self and others) is conceptualized to be a relatively balanced point in the center portion of this triangular model (Webb et al., 2014; see Figure 4.1). Although an individual may be characterized as or self-identify with a particular dimension of spirituality, respect and veneration for the other dimensions and individuals characterized thereby is vital. As such, optimal spirituality likely includes reasonable levels of each dimension, rather than the domination of one dimension at the expense of the others. For example, a clergy person may be a devout and effective leader of their congregation, and thus have high levels of Ritualistic Spirituality (and/or Theistic Spirituality). However, the extent to which this person disregards or disrespects other dimensions of spirituality (e.g., the atheist or agnostic who may not otherwise believe in God, but can still exhibit high levels of Existential Spirituality) may lead to dysfunctional or separated spirituality through intolerance, prejudice, and hostility.

Relation-Based Spirituality

Consistent with target-based spirituality, an approach to the role and influence of the sacred in everyday life has been developed by Worthington, Sandage, and colleagues and termed *Relational Spirituality* (see Davis et al., 2008; Davis et al., 2009; Sandage & Shults, 2007; Shults & Sandage, 2006; Worthington & Sandage, 2016). In this model, *spirituality* is defined as "a person's experience of relationship with the Sacred" (Davis et al., 2009, p. 249) or "sacred objects" (Worthington & Sandage, 2016, p. 62). That which constitutes *the sacred* for any given individual can vary and is broadly conceptualized to include "God or humanity or nature or simply the aspects of life that are beyond comprehension and seen as 'higher' or 'transcendent'" (Worthington & Sandage, 2016, p. 68). Importantly, the sacred can include myriad personally relevant notions, whether derived from theistic origins or not, such as "the marriage or family, the country, the right to privacy or self-determination, the right to life, or the right to freedom from coercion. ... [and other] transcendent goals, ... [or] political, social, or economic objects" (Worthington & Sandage, 2016, p. 68), as well as "a close friend, a partner, or a parent" (Davis et al., 2009, p. 249). Relational Spirituality draws upon systemic, contextual, attachment, and coping related psychological theories in order to understand one's relationship(s) with the self, others, and/or the sacred (see Worthington & Sandage, 2016).

In the particular context of forgiveness (see Davis et al., 2009; Worthington & Sandage, 2016), when an offense occurs in relationship, whether in the context of self, other, or the sacred, a variety of victim-based appraisals occur. The content, implications, and outcomes of these appraisals are driven by the victim's underlying Relational Spirituality. That is, based on their sense, and experience, of the sacred, the victim of the offense evaluates not only their relationship with the offender, but their relationship with the transgression itself, their perception of the relationship between the offender and the transgression, *and* the self in context. That is, the victim engages in a self-evaluative process regarding "their own beliefs and values about [spirituality], about forgiveness, about other people, and about interactions" (Worthington & Sandage, 2016, p. 64). Importantly, the victim *also* evaluates their relationship with the sacred, the relationship between the transgression and the sacred, and their perception of the relationship between the offender and the sacred. Each of these appraisals plays a role and likewise all work together (i.e., Relational Spirituality) in driving whether or not forgiveness is an option and whether or not forgiveness, if attempted, will occur. Indeed, "it is the nature of those relationships that *governs* whether people can forgive" (emphasis added; Worthington & Sandage, 2016, p. 8). As such, for clinical purposes, each appraisal dynamic can serve as a point of intervention.

Parallels Between Spirituality and Positive Psychology

As mentioned previously, although the science of forgiveness has found a home in the field of positive psychology (Snyder et al., 2016; Tsang & Martin, 2018), there is some debate, albeit ironic (see above), as to whether or not forgiveness is or remains a spiritual construct. Prior to finding its home in positive psychology and when needing to justify the secular relevance of forgiveness in scientific endeavors, forgiveness was argued to be common to psychology and philosophy (McCullough & Worthington, 1994), although expressed in different terms, such as: working through, acceptance (Hope, 1987; Pingleton, 1989), letting go (Davenport, 1991; Wahking, 1992), reframing (Cunningham, 1985), and coming to terms with (Webb, 2007/2003). Over the years, scholars have explicitly outlined the commonality of forgiveness within mainstream spiritual belief systems (e.g., Rye et al., 2000; Webb et al., 2012). That is, the principle of forgiveness is central to all mainstream spiritual belief systems in the world (i.e., Judeo-Christian, Islamic, Buddhist, Hindu), whether Eastern or Western, monotheistic or polytheistic, attested to by religious scholars, or found within sacred text/scripture (Webb et al., 2012). Forgiveness, although having found a scientific home in the field of positive psychology, clearly originates in spirituality (see also, McCullough & Worthington, 1999; "deep religious roots," p. 1143), and thus is both a religious/spiritual principle and a scientific construct.

Forgiveness is not the only spiritual principle found within positive psychology. Others include (see Tables 4.1, 4.2, 4.3, & 4.4): spirituality itself (Pargament & Mahoney, 2017),

Table 4.1 Outline of Similarities between Judeo-Christian[a] and Positive Psychological and Psychotherapeutic Principles – Part 1*

Principle	*Scriptural Reference[b]*	*Scientific Reference[c]*
action-oriented (goal-directed) / commitment / dedication	Isaiah 1:19; Zechariah 6:15; John 7:17; James 1:22; Deuteronomy 10:12; Joshua 22:5; Luke 9:62; Job 2:3, 27:5; 2 Timothy 4:7	Locke (2002)
altruism / empathy	Luke 10:25–37; John 9:1–3	Batson et al. (2009)
awareness of feelings / thoughts (being mindful)	Genesis 3:5; John 8:9; Acts 2:37; Ephesians 4:19; 1 Timothy 4:2; 1 Peter 1:13, 5:8	Langer and Ngnoumen (2019)
communal reliance / social support	Leviticus 19:18, 34; Luke 22:32; 2 Corinthians 8:4; Ephesians 4:11–16	Hooker et al. (2018)
compassion	Zechariah 7:9; Luke 10:33; 1 Peter 3:8	Cassell (2017)
courage	Deuteronomy 31:6; Joshua 1:7; 2 Timothy 1:7	Pury et al. (2016)
forgiveness	Leviticus 19:18; Matthew 18:21–22; Luke 6:37	Tsang and Martin (2018)
gratitude	Psalms 100:4; Colossians 3:15	Watkins and McCurrach (2017)

[a] For similar information regarding other religious and spiritual traditions of the world, please see Richards and Bergin (2014), Koenig (2018), and Koenig et al. (2012).
[b] References are taken from the King James Version (KJV, 1983) of *The Bible.*
[c] see also, Snyder et al. (2016), Lopez and Snyder (2009), and Snyder and Lopez (2002).
* In sum, one is always to treat others as one would want to be treated (Leviticus 19:18, 19:34; Deuteronomy 10:19, 15:12–15; Matthew 7:12, 19:19, 22:39). Additionally, The Bible uses/is full of parables and metaphors to intensify learning of principles. Psalms and Proverbs are full of psychological wisdom; that is, ways of being, living, understanding, inter-relating.

Table 4.2 Outline of Similarities between Judeo-Christian[a] and Positive Psychological and Psychotherapeutic Principles – Part 2*

Principle	*Scriptural Reference[b]*	*Scientific Reference[c]*
happiness	Proverbs 16:20; John 16:33	Oishi et al. (2018)
hope	Jeremiah 17:7; Hebrews 3:6, 6:19	Rand and Touza (2018)
humility	Proverbs 15:33, 18:22, 27:2; Matthew 23:12; Colossians 3:12	Tangney (2009)
integrity; non-hypocrisy / honesty	Job 13:16; Luke 11:39; Exodus 20:16; Matthew 19:18	Harter (2002)
knowledge	Proverbs 14:18, 15:14, 24:5; Romans 15:14; 2 Peter 1:5	Schulman (2002b)
meaning / purpose	Proverbs 3:13,18; Proverbs 21:21; Matthew 10:39; John 6:35; Romans 8:6; Philippians 2:16; Ecclesiastes 3:1; Daniel 1:8; Acts 11:23; 2 Corinthians 9:7	Steger (2018)
meditation	Psalms 19:14; 1 Timothy 4:15	Shapiro et al. (2016)
moderate behavior / personal control	Psalms 119:101; Proverbs 15:1, 25:28; 1 Corinthians 9:25, 13:5; Philippians 4:5; Mark 8:34	Thompson (2017)

* See notes a, b, c, and * in Table 4.1.

Table 4.3 Outline of Similarities between Judeo-Christian[a] and Positive Psychological and Psychotherapeutic Principles – Part 3*

Principle	*Scriptural Reference*[b]	*Scientific Reference*[c]
morality / ethics	Leviticus 19:18; Matthew 22:39	Schulman (2002a) Handelsman et al. (2009)
other-oriented love	Leviticus 19:18; Matthew 22:39; John 13:34–35	Gable and Maisel (2019)
optimism	Proverbs 15:13, 17:22	Mens et al. (2016)
self-aware love / self-regard / self-esteem	Leviticus 19:18; Deuteronomy 15:12–15; Matthew 7:12, 22:39	North and Swann (2016)
self-reliance / self-efficacy / self-determination	Proverbs 24:27; Luke 14:28–30	Maddux and Kleiman (2016) Wehmeyer et al. (2017)
spirituality (including God / love of God); faith	Romans 8:6 (Deuteronomy 6:5; Matthew 22:37); Deuteronomy 32:20; Matthew 9:29	Pargament and Mahoney (2017)
wisdom	Psalms 37:30; Proverbs 4:7; Ephesians 1:17; Colossians 4:5	Scheibe and Kunzmann (2018)

* See notes a, b, c, and * in Table 4.1.

Table 4.4 Outline of Similarities between Judeo-Christian[a] and Positive Psychological and Psychotherapeutic Principles – Part 4*

Principle	*Scriptural Reference*[b]	*Scientific Reference*[c]
addressing personal issues before others'	Matthew 7:1–5	
non-judgmental / righteous judgment	Leviticus 19:15; Psalms 58:1; Isaiah 11:3–5; Matthew 7:1–5; Luke 6:37; John 7:24	
organization / order	Psalms 37:23, 119:133; Isaiah 9:7; 1 Corinthians 14:40; Ephesians 4:11–16; Titus 1:5	
rational perfectionism (i.e., not trying to do more than one is capable of)	Isaiah 5:27, 40:31; 1 Corinthians 9:24	
responsibility	Joshua 7:19; Luke 16:2; Romans 2:6	

* See notes a, b, c, and * in Table 4.1.

optimism (Mens et al., 2016), hope (Rand & Touza, 2018), gratitude (Watkins & McCurrach, 2017), and compassion (Cassell, 2017). Related to this, in the context of addiction, not only is forgiveness relevant as a spiritual principle and positive psychological construct (e.g., Webb et al., 2015; Webb & Toussaint, 2020), but others include: hope (e.g., Kimball et al., 2017; Shumway et al., 2017; see also, Shumway & Kimball, 2012), gratitude (e.g., Chen, 2017; Krentzman, 2019), spirituality, altruism, and meaning and purpose in life (see Krentzman, 2013).

Forgiveness and Particular Issues Related to Spirituality

In the context of spirituality as a transcendent thread running through humanity, society, and culture, and thereby the search for connection with the sacred (see also, Pargament, 2013a; Pargament & Mahoney, 2017), whether ritualistically, theistically, and/or existentially targeted (i.e., the RiTE Model of Spirituality; Webb et al., 2014), underlying all of our relationships (i.e., Relational Spirituality; Worthington & Sandage, 2016), forgiveness becomes critically relevant to consider (as do many other positive psychological constructs) in regard to various other issues related to spirituality. For example, morality, spiritual struggle, and incorporating spirituality into clinical treatment.

Morality

Is forgiveness always a moral activity or morally justifiable – whether engaging in the process or succeeding in the outcome? Enright and colleagues have discussed the moral underpinnings and justifiability of forgiveness (Enright & Fitzgibbons, 2015; Enright & The Human Development Study Group, 1996; Kim & Enright, 2016), as have North (1998), Satne (2016), and Yandell (1998). One of the underlying issues regarding whether or not it is always appropriate to forgive is the question of control. Are we giving up control if we forgive others? Coleman (1998) argues that although many assume control – over the offender and the consequences and implications of an offensive experience – is maintained through *unforgiveness* (i.e., by engaging in forgiveness one *forfeits* control over the offender and the offense), in actuality, through forgiveness one is able to regain control through ending the counterproductive cycle of rumination and anger associated with unforgiveness, and thus develop the ability again to more fully experience love, trust, and joy.

Another underlying issue is the question of whether or not forgiveness, particularly self-forgiveness, is a narcissistic or self-serving process? Tangney et al. (2005) cautioned of findings regarding associations between self-forgiveness and self-centeredness, insensitivity, and narcissism such that self-forgivers may be unaware of and unscathed by their negative impact on others. In seeking to bring parsimony and clarity to the definition of self-forgiveness, Webb, Bumgarner, et al. (2017; see also, Chapter 3) emphasized the importance of "acknowledged self-instigated wrong-doing, personal responsibility, and ready accountability, thereby precluding narcissistic escape" (p. 224). Finally, from a religious point of view, Walker and Gorsuch (2002) have argued that it may be inappropriate to consider self-forgiveness; that is, religious people may not feel that it is their place, but God's, to do so. Related to this, Webb, Hirsch, et al. (2017) have found evidence to support the notion that feeling forgiven by God may then facilitate self-forgiveness.

Not only is it important to understand what forgiveness is (see Chapter 3), but understanding what forgiveness *is not* sheds light on its moral justification as well. Evidence-based models of genuine forgiveness (e.g., Enright & Fitzgibbons, 2015; Worthington, 2006) underscore the critical reality and necessity that any and all negative experiences, consequences, or implications related to the offense or being offended are never to be overlooked or minimized by the victim. Related to this, the outcome of forgiveness does not inherently require the offense or the offender now to be viewed as good or inconsequential. Indeed, the offender can still be held accountable and the offense can still be recognized as unjustifiable and unnecessary. Although forgiveness may be viewed by some as the ideal (e.g., the overtly spiritual), in practical terms, it is useful and adaptive to view forgiveness as a choice (see Enright, 2001), rather than as an obligation – whether the forgiver is overtly spiritual or not.

Spiritual Struggle

In the context of spiritual and religious issues, Exline (2013) defines struggle as "something in a person's current belief, practice, or experience [that] is causing or perpetuating distress" (p. 459), which can manifest as a particular negative emotion, or as a difficult to reconcile internal conflict. Although there is likely to be considerable overlap (Exline, 2013), *spiritual* struggles are driven by "relationships with God or with a transcendent or sacred realm", whereas *religious* struggles "center on teachings, practices, or group dynamics of an organized religious group" (p. 460). Exline et al. (2014) describe six empirically identified types of spiritual/religious struggle to include *divine, demonic, interpersonal, moral, doubt*, and *ultimate meaning*.

Forgiveness, in its many dimensions, is likely a relevant option when seeking to address spiritual/religious struggle, regardless of the given nature of said struggle. As examples, being angry at God or the universe, doubting the existence of God or the relevance of the transcendent, or being taken advantage of by a member of one's spiritual or religious in-group may necessitate one to consider forgiveness of God or the universe, self-forgiveness, or other-forgiveness, respectively. The process and experience of forgiveness in addressing and/or resolving spiritual/religious struggle could be one reason why such struggles may very well be a gift or an opportunity for growth, and may ultimately improve one's life (Exline & Rose, 2005, 2013).

Incorporating Spirituality into Treatment

During the course of a professional discussion with clinical psychologist colleagues regarding training graduate students to be clinicians (i.e., mental health therapists), I recall being taken aback by a comment made by one of my colleagues (something to the effect of): "I guess religion isn't all bad." Although there is evidence to suggest that religion/spirituality can be counterproductive to otherwise healthy and constructive functioning (e. g., positive versus negative religious coping (see Pargament, 1997)), it appears the association of religiousness/spirituality with health and well-being is salubrious and robust (see Koenig, 2018; Koenig et al., 2012). An examination of the quantitative empirical literature through 2009 found 70 percent of studies showing at least one beneficial association between religiousness/spirituality and mental health (i.e., 413 / 591 = .699) versus 7 percent showing at least one deleterious association (i.e., 44 / 591 = .074), with the rest of the studies showing either mixed associations, complex associations, or no association (Toussaint et al., 2012). The most consistent and frequent support was in the context of substance use (87 percent; i.e., 153 / 176 = .869) and suicide (83 percent; i.e., 77 / 93 = .828), as opposed to depression (63 percent; i.e., 115 / 182 = .632), anxiety (50 percent; i.e., 57 / 113 = .504), and psychotic disorders (41 percent; i.e., 11 / 27 = .407).

While the public is very likely to value religion/spirituality (and thus individuals seeking mental healthcare; see Chapter 1), it appears mental healthcare providers are comparatively less likely to do so. For example, psychologists consistently have been found to show lower levels of belief and religiousness than the general public (Bergin & Jensen, 1990; Delaney et al., 2007). Psychologists are likely to question the importance of religious/spiritual issues and to be reluctant to address them with their clients, as well as during professional consultation (Frazier & Hansen, 2009). Also, psychologists are likely to view as pathological those religious beliefs considered to be less mainstream in their nature (O'Connor & Vandenberg, 2005).

As such, although religion/spirituality is important to a considerable majority of the population and religiousness/spirituality largely is conducive to mental health, mental

Table 4.5 Example Resources for Incorporating Spirituality into Treatment

1. *Spirituality and the Psychotherapeutic Process: A Comprehensive Resource from Intake to Termination*
   - Aten and Leach (2008)
2. *The Psychology of Religion and Spirituality for Clinicians: Using Research in your Practice*
   - Aten, O'Grady, and Worthington (2012)
3. *Spiritually Oriented Interventions for Counseling and Psychotherapy*
   - Aten, McMinn, and Worthington (2011)
4. *Spiritually Oriented Psychotherapy*
   - Sperry and Shafranske (2005)
5. *Spiritually Integrated Psychotherapy: Understanding and Addressing the Sacred*
   - Pargament (2007)
6. *Trauma, Meaning, and Spirituality: Translating Research into Clinical Practice*
   - Park, Currier, Harris, and Slattery (2017)
7. *Spiritual Interventions in Child and Adolescent Psychotherapy*
   - Walker and Hathaway (2013)
8. *Counseling and Psychotherapy with Religious Persons: A Rational Emotive Behavior Therapy Approach*
   - Nielsen et al. (2001)
9. *Handbook of Psychotherapy and Religious Diversity*
   - Richards and Bergin (2014)
10. *APA Handbook of Psychology, Religion, and Spirituality*
   - Pargament (2013b)
11. American Psychological Association (APA) *Psychotherapy Video Series: Spirituality*
   - APA (2005)

healthcare providers may not be motivated or prepared to address such issues during treatment. Whether a "believer" or not, a mental health therapist can facilitate growth and healing for their "believing" clients through focused, explicit, and purposeful utilization of the client's religious/spiritual belief system (Toussaint et al., 2012) – always being careful not to impose their own belief system on the client, whether the therapist is a believer or not. Related to this, such therapists can assist their clients to identify, recognize, and apply the specific aspects of the client's belief system(s) that promote healthy motivation, socialization, interpretation, coping, and problem solving. The most important thing for mental healthcare providers to remember when "working with religious and spiritual issues and clients is to approach the client with genuine sensitivity, respect, and flexibility and to recognize that numerous resources exist to educate and assist psychotherapists in this important component of their work" (Toussaint et al., 2012, p. 343). See Table 4.5 for a listing of example resources.

Notes

1 Obituary published in the *Los Angeles Times* (2001):

Zelen, Seymour, Noted Psychologist, author and Professor, known for his work in Attribution Theory, has died August 11, of complications from a stroke, in Northridge [California], while completing his latest book. He was 78. Zelen, who had taught at UCLA and most recently at the California School of Professional Psychology in South Pasadena, was the consummate mentor, advising and directing over 100 Psychology dissertations during his tenure. His many students are among the newest generation of Psychologists in the Southland. In addition to his teaching credits, Zelen had been the Chief Psychologist at Patton State Hospital, a staff psychologist at the Veteran's Administration in the San Fernando Valley, and conducted a private psycho-therapy practice. Born in New York City, he attended Boy's High, and after his academic career was interrupted by enlistment in the Army, he returned to college after World War II, and obtained his Bachelor's Degree from New York University, his Master's Degree from Ohio State University, and his Ph.D. from UCLA. His works include, "A Sound Beginning", a book and tape promoting communication between parents and their unborn child in the womb, and numerous works in the area of Attribution Theory and Psychology. He is survived by his wife Marilyn, sons Gary, David, Brian, Steven, daughter Julie, and grandchildren Ross and Sarah-Rose. Funeral services were held on Sunday, August 12, at Hillside Memorial Jewish Cemetery.

2 Fast forward to 2000 and the founding of the scientific *Journal of Happiness Studies* (Veenhoven et al., 2000), 2006 and the founding of the scientific *Journal of Positive Psychology* (Emmons, 2006), and thus, the full-fledged [re]establishment of the scientific field of positive psychology (see Seligman, 1998; Snyder et al, 2016).

3 APA's Division 36 (Society for the Psychology of Religion and Spirituality) originated in 1946 (http://www.apadivisions.org/division-36/about/history.pdf) and scientific journals such as the *Journal of Religion & Health* (Anderson, 1961) and the *Journal for the Scientific Study of Religion* (1961) have long been established. Nevertheless, it was not until the 1980s that a debate between Allen Bergin (1980a, 1980b) and Albert Ellis (1980) regarding the existence and relevance of values in psychotherapy (Bergin argued that religiosity [i.e., religiousness] and values were important and unavoidable factors in mental health and Ellis argued that religiosity was at the root of psychological dysfunction. Ellis later tempered his stance (see Nielsen et al., 2001)) led to the permanency of the scientific psychological study of religion and spirituality through the founding of such journals as the *International Journal for the Psychology of Religion* (Brown & Malony, 1991) and *Mental Health, Religion & Culture* (Dein & Loewenthal, 1998). More recently, the growing vibrancy of the field is evidenced by the founding of Division 36's journal, *Psychology of Religion and Spirituality* (Piedmont, 2009) and the independent APA journal, *Spirituality in Clinical Practice* (Sperry & Miller, 2014).

4 Although religious/spiritual issues are considered germane to cultural diversity (APA, 2002, 2008; Cohen, 2009), capacity for scientific rigor remains in question (McMinn et al., 2009). Moreover, a meaningful subset of scholars continue to question the importance of such issues (Frazier & Hansen, 2009), consider less mainstream religious beliefs to be pathological (O'Connor & Vandenberg, 2005), and promulgate negative assumptions regarding the origin, function, and implication of religion/spirituality (e.g., Carone & Barone, 2001; Lynn et al., 2009; see also, Cummings et al., 2009).

5 The APA (2015) defines *construct* as "a complex idea or concept formed from a synthesis of simpler ideas" (p. 239).

6 For a different, but related discussion on the transcendent mind, see Barušs & Mossbridge (2017).

7 The APA (2015) defines *parsimony* as "the principle that the simplest explanation of an event or observation is the preferred explanation" (p. 591).

8 Given this work, the term spirituality (and variants) largely will be used henceforth, rather than religion (and variants), or religion/spirituality (and variants), etc.

References

American Psychological Association (APA) (2002). Ethical principles of psychologists and code of conduct. *American Psychologist*, 57(12), 1060–1073. doi:10.1037/0003-066X.57.12.1060.

American Psychological Association (APA) (2008). Resolution on religious, religion-based, and/or religion-derived prejudice. *American Psychologist*, 63(5), 431–434. doi:10.1037/0003-066X.63.5.360.

American Psychological Association (APA) (2015). *APA dictionary of psychology* (2nd ed.). Washington, DC: Author.

American Psychological Association (APA) (Producer). (2005). *Psychotherapy video series: Spirituality* [DVD]. Available from: http://www.apa.org/pubs/videos/index.aspx.

Anderson, G. C. (1961). Editorial. *Journal of Religion & Health*, 1(1), 9–11. doi:10.1007/BF01532008.

Aten, J. D., & Leach, M. M. (Eds.). (2008). *Spirituality and the therapeutic process: A comprehensive resource from intake to termination*. Washington, DC: American Psychological Association.

Aten, J. D., McMinn, M. R., & Worthington, E. L., Jr. (Eds.) (2011). *Spiritually oriented interventions for counseling and psychotherapy*. Washington, DC: American Psychological Association.

Aten, J. D., O'Grady, K. A., & Worthington, E. L., Jr. (Eds.). (2012). *The psychology of religion and spirituality for clinicians: Using research in your practice.* New York, NY: Routledge.

Baruŝs, I., & Mossbridge, J. (2017). *Transcendent mind: Rethinking the science of consciousness.* Washington, DC: American Psychological Association.

Batson, C. D., Ahmad, N., & Lishner, D. A. (2009). Empathy and altruism. In S. J. Lopez & C. R. Snyder (Eds.), *Oxford handbook of positive psychology* (2nd ed.). New York, NY: Oxford University Press.

Bergin, A. E. (1980a). Psychotherapy and religious values. *Journal of Consulting and Clinical Psychology*, 48(1), 95–105. doi:10.1037/0022-006X.48.1.95.

Bergin, A. E. (1980b). Religious and humanistic values: A reply to Ellis and Walls. *Journal of Consulting and Clinical Psychology*, 48(5), 642–645. doi:10.1037/0022-006X.48.5.642.

Bergin, A. E., & Jensen, J. P. (1990). Religiosity of psychotherapists: A national survey. *Psychotherapy: Theory, Research, Practice, Training*, 27(1), 3–7. doi:10.1037/0033-3204.27.1.3.

Brown, L. B., & Malony, H. N. (1991). Editor's note. *International Journal for the Psychology of Religion*, 1(1), 1–4. doi:10.1207/s15327582ijpr0101_1.

Carone, D. A., Jr., & Barone, D. F. (2001). A social cognitive perspective on religious beliefs: Their functions and impact on coping and psychotherapy. *Clinical Psychology Review*, 21(7), 989–1003. doi:10.1016/S0272-7358(00)00078-7.

Cassell, E. J. (2017). Compassion. In C. R. Snyder, S. J. Lopez, L. M. Edwards, & S. C. Marques (Eds.), *Oxford handbook of positive psychology* (3rd ed.). New York, NY: Oxford University Press.

Chen, G. (2017). Does gratitude promote recovery from substance misuse? *Addiction Research & Theory*, 25(2), 121–128. doi:10.1080/16066359.2016.1212337.

Clarke, A. C. (2019). Aurthur C. Clarke: Biography: Quotes. Retrieved September 9, 2019, from https://www.clarkefoundation.org/arthur-c-clarke-biography/.

Cohen, A. B. (2009). Many forms of culture. *American Psychologist*, 64(3), 194–204. doi:10.1037/a0015308.

Coleman, P. W. (1998). The process of forgiveness in marriage and the family. In R. D. Enright & J. North (Eds.) *Exploring forgiveness* (pp. 75–94). Madison, WI: University of Wisconsin Press.

Connors, G. J., Tonigan, J. S., & Miller, W. R. (1996). A measure of religious background and behavior for use in behavior change research. *Psychology of Addictive Behaviors*, 10(2), 90–96. doi:10.1037/0893-164x.10.2.90.

Cummings, N., O'Donohue, W., & Cummings, J. (Eds.) (2009). *Psychology's war on religion.* Phoenix, AZ: Zeig, Tucker, & Theisen.

Cunningham, B. B. (1985). The will to forgive: A pastoral theological view of forgiving. *Journal of Pastoral Care*, 39(2), 141–149. doi:10.1177/002234098503900206.

Davenport, D. S. (1991). The functions of anger and forgiveness: Guidelines for psychotherapy with victims. *Psychotherapy: Theory, Research, Practice, Training*, 28(1), 140–144. doi:10.1037/0033-3204.28.1.140.

Davis, D. E., Hook, J. N., & Worthington, E., Jr. (2008). Relational spirituality and forgiveness: The roles of attachment to God, religious coping, and viewing the transgression as a desecration. *Journal of Psychology and Christianity*, 27(4), 293–301.

Davis, D. E., Worthington, E. L., Jr., Hook, J. N., Van Tongeren, D. R., Green, J. D., & Jennings, D. J., II. (2009). Relational spirituality and the development of the Similarity of the Offender's Spirituality Scale. *Psychology of Religion and Spirituality*, 1(4), 249–262. doi:10.1037/a0017581.

Dawkins, R. (2006). *The God delusion.* New York, NY: Houghton Mifflin.

Dein, S., & Loewenthal, K. M. (1998). Editorial. *Mental Health, Religion & Culture*, 1(1), 5–9. doi:10.1080/13674679808406492.

Delaney, H. D., Miller, W. R., & Bisonó, A. M. (2007). Religiosity and spirituality among psychologists: A survey of clinician members of the American Psychological Association. *Professional Psychology: Research and Practice*, 38(5), 538–546. doi:10.1037/0735-7028.38.5.538.

DiBlasio, F. A. (1992). Forgiveness in psychotherapy: Comparison of older and younger therapists. *Journal of Psychology and Christianity*, 11(2), 181–187.

Ellis, A. (1980). Psychotherapy and atheistic values: A response to A. E. Bergin's 'Psychotherapy and religious values'. *Journal of Consulting and Clinical Psychology*, 48(5), 635–639. doi:10.1037/0022-006X.48.5.635.

Emmons, R. A. (2006). Editorial. *The Journal of Positive Psychology*, 1(1), 1–2. doi:10.1080/17439760500372622.

Enright, R. D. (2001). *Forgiveness is a choice: A step-by-step process for resolving anger and restoring hope*. Washington, DC: American Psychological Association.

Enright, R. D., & Fitzgibbons, R. P. (2015). *Forgiveness therapy: An empirical guide for resolving anger and restoring hope* (2nd ed.). Washington, DC: American Psychological Association.

Enright, R. D., & The Human Development Study Group (1996). Counseling within the forgiveness triad: On forgiving, receiving forgiveness, and self-forgiveness. *Counseling and Values*, 40(2), 107–126. doi:10.1002/j.2161-007X.1996.tb00844.x.

Enright, R. D., & North, J. (Eds.). (1998). *Exploring forgiveness*. Madison, WI: The University of Wisconsin Press.

Enright, R. D., & Zell, R. L. (1989). Problems encountered when we forgive one another. *Journal of Psychology and Christianity*, 8(1), 52–60.

Exline, J. J. (2013). Religious and spiritual struggles. In K. I. Pargament, J. J. Exline, & J. W. Jones (Eds.), *APA handbook of psychology, religion, and spirituality* (Vol. 1, pp. 459–475). Washington, DC: American Psychological Association.

Exline, J. J., & Rose, E. (2005). Religious and spiritual struggles. In R. F. Paloutzian & C. L. Park (Eds.), *Handbook of the psychology of religion and spirituality* (pp. 315–330). New York, NY: Guilford Press.

Exline, J. J., & Rose, E. D. (2013). Religious and spiritual struggles. In R. F. Paloutzian & C. L. Park (Eds.), *Handbook of the psychology of religion and spirituality* (2nd ed., pp. 380–398). New York, NY: Guilford Press.

Exline, J. J., Pargament, K. I., Grubbs, J. B., & Yali, A. M. (2014). The Religious and Spiritual Struggles Scale: Development and initial validation. *Psychology of Religion and Spirituality*, 6 (3), 208–222. doi:10.1037/a0036465

Fincham, F. D. (2000). The kiss of the porcupines: From attributing responsibility to forgiving. *Personal Relationships*, 7(1), 1–23. doi:10.1111/j.1475-6811.2000.tb00001.x.

Frazier, R. E., & Hansen, N. D. (2009). Religious/spiritual psychotherapy behaviors: Do we do what we believe to be important? *Professional Psychology: Research and Practice*, 40(1), 81–87. doi:10.1037/a0011671.

Freud, S. (1989). The future of an illusion. In P. Gay (Ed.), *The Freud reader* (pp. 685–722). New York, NY: W. W. Norton & Co.

Gable, S. L., & Maisel, N. C. (2019). Positive processes in close relationships. In C. R. Snyder, S. J. Lopez, L. M. Edwards, & S. C. Marques (Eds.), *Oxford handbook of positive psychology* (3rd ed.). New York, NY: Oxford University Press.

GESIS (Ed.) (2018). ISSP 2008 - Religion III. Variable Report: Documentation release 2018/10/26, related to the international dataset Archive-Study-No. ZA4950 Version 2.3.0 Variable Reports 2018|17. Cologne: Author.

Handelsman, M. M., Knapp, S., & Gottlieb, M. C. (2009). Positive ethics: Themes and variations. In S. J. Lopez & C. R. Snyder (Eds.), *Oxford handbook of positive psychology* (2nd ed.). New York, NY: Oxford University Press.

Hargrave, T. D., & Sells, J. N. (1997). The development of a forgiveness scale. *Journal of Marital and Family Therapy*, 23(1), 41–63. doi:10.1111/j.1752-0606.1997.tb00230.x.

Harter, S. (2002). Authenticity. In C. R. Snyder & S. J. Lopez (Eds.), *Handbook of positive psychology* (pp. 382–394). New York, NY: Oxford University Press.

Hitchens, C. (2007). *god is not Great: How religion poisons everything*. New York, NY: Twelve.

Hood, R. W., Jr. (2003). The relationship between religion and spirituality. In A. L. Greil & D. Bromley (Eds.), *Defining religion: Investigating the boundaries between the sacred and secular religion and the social order* (Vol. 10, pp. 241–264). Amsterdam: Elsevier Science.

Hooker, E. D., Zoccola, P. M., & Dickerson, S. S. (2018). Toward a biology of social support. In C. R. Snyder, S. J. Lopez, L. M. Edwards, & S. C. Marques (Eds.), *Oxford handbook of positive psychology* (3rd ed.). New York, NY: Oxford University Press.

Hope, D. (1987). The healing paradox of forgiveness. *Psychotherapy: Theory, Research, Practice, Training*, 24(2), 240–244. doi:10.1037/h0085710.

ISSP Research Group (2018). International Social Survey Programme: Religion III - ISSP 2008. GESIS Data Archive, Cologne. ZA4950 Data file Version 2.3.0, doi:10.4232/1.13161..

Journal for the Scientific Study of Religion (1961). An introductory word. *Journal for the Scientific Study of Religion*, 1(1), 3–4.

Kim, J. J., & Enright, R. D. (2016). 'State and trait forgiveness': A philosophical analysis and implications for psychotherapy. *Spirituality in Clinical Practice*, 3(1), 32–44. doi:10.1037/scp0000090.

Kimball, T. G., Shumway, S. T., Austin-Robillard, H., & Harris-Wilkes, K. S. (2017). Hoping and coping in recovery: A phenomenology of emerging adults in a collegiate recovery program. *Alcoholism Treatment Quarterly*, 35(1), 46–62. doi:10.1080/07347324.2016.1256714.

King James Version (1983). *Holy Bible.* Salt Lake City, UT: Church of Jesus Christ of Latter-day Saints.

Koenig, H. G. (2009). Research on religion, spirituality, and mental health: A review. *The Canadian Journal of Psychiatry*, 54(5), 283–291. doi:10.1177/070674370905400502.

Koenig, H. G. (2018). *Religion and mental health: Research and clinical applications.* San Diego, CA: Academic Press.

Koenig, H. G., King, D. E., & Carson, V. B. (2012). *Handbook of religion and health* (2nd ed.). New York, NY: Oxford University Press.

Koenig, H. G., McCullough, M. E., & Larson, D. B. (2001). A history of religion, science, and medicine: Historical timeline. In H. G. Koenig, D. E. King, & V. B. Carson (Eds.), *Handbook of religion and health* (pp. 24–49). New York, NY: Oxford University Press.

Krentzman, A. R. (2013). Review of the application of positive psychology to substance use, addiction, and recovery research. *Psychology of Addictive Behaviors*, 27(1), 151–165. doi:10.1037/a0029897.

Krentzman, A. R. (2019). A full and thankful heart: Writings about gratitude by Alcoholics Anonymous co-founder, Bill Wilson. *Addiction Research & Theory*, 27(6), 451–461. doi:10.1080/16066359.2018.1547816.

Kugelmann, R., & Belzen, J. A. (2009). Historical intersections of psychology, religion, and politics in national contexts. *History of Psychology*, 12(3), 125–131. doi:10.1037/a0016855.

Langer, E. J., & Ngnoumen, C. (2019). Well-being: Mindfulness versus Positive evaluation. In C. R. Snyder, S. J. Lopez, L. M. Edwards, & S. C. Marques (Eds.), *Oxford handbook of positive psychology* (3rd ed.). New York, NY: Oxford University Press.

Levin, J. S., & Vanderpool, H. Y. (1991). Religious factors in physical health and the prevention of illness. *Prevention in Human Services*, 9(2), 41–64. doi:10.1300/J293v09n02_03.

Locke, E. A. (2002). Setting goals for life and happiness. In C. R. Snyder & S. J. Lopez (Eds.), *Handbook of positive psychology* (pp. 299–312). New York, NY: Oxford University Press.

Lopez, S. J., & Snyder, C. R. (Eds.) (2009). *Oxford handbook of positive psychology* (2nd ed.). New York, NY: Oxford University Press.

Los Angeles Times (2001). Obituary: Seymour Zelen (published August 16, 2001).

Lynn, R., Harvey, J., & Nyborg, H. (2009). Average intelligence predicts atheism rates across 137 nations. *Intelligence*, 37(1), 11–15. doi:10.1016/j.intell.2008.03.004.

Maddux, J. E., & Kleiman, E. M. (2016). Self-efficacy: The power of believing you can. In C. R. Snyder, S. J. Lopez, L. M. Edwards, & S. C. Marques (Eds.), *Oxford handbook of positive psychology* (3rd ed.). New York, NY: Oxford University Press.

McCullough, M. E., & Worthington, E. L., Jr. (1994). Encouraging clients to forgive people who have hurt them: Review, critique, and research prospectus. *Journal of Psychology and Theology*, 22(1), 3–20. doi:10.1177/009164719402200101.

McCullough, M. E., & Worthington, E. L., Jr. (1999). Religion and the forgiving personality. *Journal of Personality*, 67(6), 1141–1164. doi:10.1111/1467-6494.00085.

McCullough, M. E., Pargament, K. I., & Thoresen, C. E. (2000a). *Forgiveness: Theory, research, and practice.* New York, NY: Guilford Press.

McCullough, M. E., Pargament, K. I., & Thoresen, C. E. (2000b). The psychology of forgiveness: History, conceptual issues, and overview. In M. E. McCullough, K. I. Pargament, & C. E. Thoresen (Eds.), *Forgiveness: Theory, research, and practice* (pp. 1–14). New York, NY: Guilford Press.

McCullough, M. E., Worthington, E. L., Jr., & Rachal, K. C. (1997). Interpersonal forgiving in close relationships. *Journal of Personality and Social Psychology*, 73(2), 321–336. doi:10.1037/0022-3514.73.2.321.

McMinn, M. R., Hathaway, W. L., Woods, S. W., & Snow, K. N. (2009). What American Psychological Association leaders have to say about Psychology of Religion and Spirituality. *Psychology of Religion and Spirituality*, 1(1), 3–13. doi:10.1037/a0014991.

Mens, M. G., Scheier, M. F., & Carver, C. S. (2016). Optimism. In C. R. Snyder, S. J. Lopez, L. M. Edwards, & S. C. Marques (Eds.), *Oxford handbook of positive psychology* (3rd ed.). New York, NY: Oxford University Press.

Miller, L. J. (Ed.) (2012). *The Oxford handbook of psychology and spirituality.* New York, NY: Oxford University Press.

Nielsen, S. L., Johnson, W. B., & Ellis, A. (2001). *Counseling and psychotherapy with religious persons: A rational emotive behavior therapy approach.* Mahwah, NJ: Lawrence Erlbaum Associates.

North, J. (1998). The "ideal" of forgiveness: A philosopher's explanation. In R. D. Enright & J. North (Eds.), *Exploring forgiveness* (pp. 15–34). Madison, WI: University of Wisconsin Press.

North, R. J., & Swann, W. B., Jr. (2016). What's positive about self-verification. In C. R. Snyder, S. J. Lopez, L. M. Edwards, & S. C. Marques (Eds.), *Oxford handbook of positive psychology* (3rd ed.). New York, NY: Oxford University Press.

O'Connor, S., & Vandenberg, B. (2005). Psychosis or faith? Clinicians' assessment of religious beliefs. *Journal of Consulting and Clinical Psychology*, 73(4), 610–616. doi:10.1037/0022-006X.73.4.610.

Oishi, S., Diener, E., & Lucas, R. E. (2018). Subjective well-being: The science of happiness and life satisfaction. In C. R. Snyder, S. J. Lopez, L. M. Edwards, & S. C. Marques (Eds.), *Oxford handbook of positive psychology* (3rd ed.). New York, NY: Oxford University Press.

Oman, D. (2013). Defining religion and spirituality. In R. F. Paloutzian & C. L. Park (Eds.), *Handbook of the psychology of religion and spirituality* (2nd ed., pp. 23–47). New York, NY: Guilford Press.

Paloutzian, R. F., & Park, C. L. (Eds.) (2013). *Handbook of the psychology of religion and spirituality* (2nd ed.). New York, NY: Guilford Press.

Pargament, K. I. (1997). *The psychology of religious coping: Theory, research, practice.* New York, NY: Guilford Press.

Pargament, K. I. (2007). *Spiritually integrated psychotherapy: Understanding and addressing the sacred.* New York, NY: Guilford Press.

Pargament, K. I. (2013a). Searching for the sacred: Toward a nonreductionistic theory of spirituality. In K. I. Pargament, J. J. Exline, & J. W. Jones (Eds.), *APA handbook of psychology, religion, and spirituality (Vol 1): Context, theory, and research* (pp. 257–273). Washington, DC: American Psychological Association.

Pargament, K. I. (Ed.) (2013b). *APA handbook of psychology, religion, and spirituality* (Vol. 1 & 2). Washington, DC: American Psychological Association.

Pargament, K. I., & Mahoney, A. (2017). Spirituality: The search for the sacred. In C. R. Snyder, S. J. Lopez, L. M. Edwards, & S. C. Marques (Eds.), *Oxford handbook of positive psychology* (3rd ed.). New York, NY: Oxford University Press.

Pargament, K. I., Mahoney, A., Exline, J. J., Jones, J. W., & Shafranske, E. P. (2013). Envisioning an integrative paradigm for the psychology of religion and spirituality. In K. I. Pargament, J. J. Exline, & J. W. Jones (Eds.), *APA handbook of psychology, religion, and spirituality (Vol 1): Context, theory, and research* (pp. 3–19). Washington, DC: American Psychological Association.

Park, C. L., Currier, J. M., Harris, J. I., & Slattery, J. M. (2017). *Trauma, meaning, and spirituality: Translating research into clinical practice.* Washington, DC: American Psychological Association.

Piedmont, R. L. (1999). Does spirituality represent the sixth factor of personality? Spiritual transcendence and the Five-Factor Model. *Journal of Personality*, 67(6), 985–1013. doi:10.1111/1467-6494.00080.

Piedmont, R. L. (2009). Editorial. *Psychology of Religion and Spirituality*, 1(1), 1–2. doi:10.1037/a0015253.

Piedmont, R. L., & Wilkins, T. A. (2013). Spirituality, religiousness, and personality: Theoretical foundations and empirical applications. In K. I. Pargament, J. J. Exline, & J. W. Jones (Eds.), *APA handbook of psychology, religion, and spirituality (Vol 1): Context, theory, and research* (pp. 173–186). Washington, DC: American Psychological Association.

Pincus, H. A. (1998). Preface. In H. G. Koenig (Ed.), *Handbook of religion and mental health* (pp. xxv–xxvi). San Diego, CA: Academic Press.

Pingleton, J. P. (1989). The role and function of forgiveness in the psychotherapeutic process. *Journal of Psychology and Theology*, 17(1), 27–35. doi:10.1177/009164718901700106.

Pury, C. L. S., Brawley, A. M., Lopez, S. J., & Burnett, E. A. (2016). Courage. In C. R. Snyder, S. J. Lopez, L. M. Edwards, & S. C. Marques (Eds.), *Oxford handbook of positive psychology* (3rd ed.). New York, NY: Oxford University Press.

Rand, K. L., & Touza, K. K. (2018). Hope theory. In C. R. Snyder, S. J. Lopez, L. M. Edwards, & S. C. Marques (Eds.), *Oxford handbook of positive psychology* (3rd ed.). New York, NY: Oxford University Press.

Reisner, A. D., & Lawson, P. (1992). Psychotherapy, sin, and mental health. *Pastoral Psychology*, 40(5), 303–311. doi:10.1007/BF01042291.

Richards, P. S., & Bergin, A. E. (Eds.). (2014). *Handbook of psychotherapy and religious diversity* (2nd ed.). Washington, DC: American Psychological Association.

Rye, M. S., Pargament, K. I., Ali, M. A., Beck, G. L., Dorff, E. N., Hallisey, C., … Williams, J. G. (2000). Religious perspectives on forgiveness. In M. E. McCullough, K. I. Pargament, & C. E. Thoresen (Eds.), *Forgiveness: Theory, research, and practice* (pp. 17–40). New York, NY: Guilford Press.

Sandage, S. J., & Shults, F. L. (2007). Relational spirituality and transformation: A relational integration model. *Journal of Psychology and Christianity*, 26(3), 261–269.

Satne, P. (2016). Forgiveness and moral development. *Philosophia*, 44, 1029–1055. doi:10.1007/s11406-016-9727-6.

Scheibe, S., & Kunzmann, U. (2018). Territories of positive life span development: Wisdom and *Sehnsucht* (life longings). In C. R. Snyder, S. J. Lopez, L. M. Edwards, & S. C. Marques (Eds.), *Oxford handbook of positive psychology* (3rd ed.). New York, NY: Oxford University Press.

Schulman, M. (2002a). How we become moral: The sources of moral motivation. In C. R. Snyder & S. J. Lopez (Eds.), *Handbook of positive psychology* (pp. 499–512). New York, NY: Oxford University Press.

Schulman, M. (2002b). The passion to know: A developmental perspective. In C. R. Snyder & S. J. Lopez (Eds.), *Handbook of positive psychology* (pp. 313–326). New York, NY: Oxford University Press.

Seligman, M. E. P. (1998). Building human strength: Psychology's forgotten mission. *APA Monitor*, 29(1). Retrieved December 14, 2001, from http://www.apa.org/monitor/jan98/pres.html (see also, https://nonopp.com/ar/Psicologia/00/pres.htm).

Shapiro, S. L., Jazaieri, H., & de Sousa, S. (2016). Meditation and positive psychology. In C. R. Snyder, S. J. Lopez, L. M. Edwards, & S. C. Marques (Eds.), *Oxford handbook of positive psychology* (3rd ed.). New York, NY: Oxford University Press.

Shontz, F. C., & Rosenak, C. (1988). Psychological theories and the need for forgiveness: Assessment and critique. *Journal of Psychology and Christianity*, 7(1), 23–31.

Shults, F. L., & Sandage, S. J. (2006). *Transforming spirituality: Integrating theology and psychology.* Grand Rapids, MI: Baker Academic.

Shumway, S. T., & Kimball, T. G. (2012). *Six essentials to achieve lasting recovery.* Center City, MN: Hazelden.

Shumway, S. T., Schonian, S., Bradshaw, S., & Hayes, N. D. (2017). A revised multifamily group curriculum: The need for family member recovery from addiction. *Journal of Groups in Addiction & Recovery*, 12(4), 260–283. doi:10.1080/1556035X.2017.1348281.

Snyder, C. R., & Lopez, S. J. (Eds.) (2002). *Handbook of positive psychology.* New York, NY: Oxford University Press.

Snyder, C. R., Lopez, S. J., Edwards, L. M., & Marques, S. C. (Eds.) (2016). *Oxford handbook of positive psychology* (3rd ed.). New York, NY: Oxford University Press.

Sperry, L., & Miller, L. (2014). Spirituality in clinical practice and you: Welcome from the editors. *Spirituality in Clinical Practice*, 1(1), 1–2. doi:10.1037/scp0000011.

Sperry, L., & Shafranske, E. P. (Eds.). (2005). *Spiritually oriented psychotherapy.* Washington, DC: American Psychological Association.

Steger, M. F. (2018). Meaning in life: A unified model. In C. R. Snyder, S. J. Lopez, L. M. Edwards, & S. C. Marques (Eds.), *Oxford handbook of positive psychology* (3rd ed.). New York, NY: Oxford University Press.

Tangney, J. P. (2009). Humility. In S. J. Lopez & C. R. Snyder (Eds.), *Oxford handbook of positive psychology* (2nd ed.). New York, NY: Oxford University Press.

Tangney, J. P., Boone, A. L., & Dearing, R. (2005). Forgiving the self: Conceptual issues and empirical findings. In E. L.Worthington, Jr. (Ed.), *Handbook of forgiveness* (pp. 143–158). New York, NY: Routledge.

Thielman, S. B. (1998). Reflections on the role of religion in the history of psychiatry. In H. G. Koenig (Ed.), *Handbook of religion and mental health* (pp. 3–20). San Diego, CA: Academic Press.

Thompson, S. C. (2017). The role of personal control in adaptive functioning. In C. R. Snyder, S. J. Lopez, L. M. Edwards, & S. C. Marques (Eds.), *Oxford handbook of positive psychology* (3rd ed.). New York, NY: Oxford University Press.

Toussaint, L. L., Webb, J. R., & Keltner, W. (2012). Religion, spirituality, and mental health. In J. D. Aten, K. A. O'Grady, & E. L.Worthington, Jr. (Eds.), *The psychology of religion and spirituality for clinicians: Using research in your practice* (pp. 331–356). New York, NY: Routledge.

Toussaint, L. L., Worthington, E. L., Jr., & Williams, D. R. (Eds.). (2015). *Forgiveness and health: Scientific evidence and theories relating forgiveness to better health.* New York, NY: Springer.

Tsang, J.-A., & Martin, S. R. (2018). Forgiveness. In C. R. Snyder, S. J. Lopez, L. M. Edwards, & S. C. Marques (Eds.), *Oxford handbook of positive psychology* (3rd ed.). New York, NY: Oxford University Press.

Veenhoven, R., Diener, E., & Michalos, A. (2000). Editorial. *Journal of Happiness Studies*, 1(1), 5–8. doi:10.1023/A:101007730.

Wahking, H. (1992). Spiritual growth through grace and forgiveness. *Journal of Psychology and Christianity*, 11(2), 198–206.

Walker, D., & Gorsuch, R. (2002). Forgiveness within the Big Five personality model. *Personality and Individual Differences*, 32(7), 1127–1138. doi:10.1016/S0191-8869(00)00185-9.

Walker, D. F., & Hathaway, W. L. (Eds.) (2013). *Spiritual interventions in child and adolescent psychotherapy.* Washington, DC: American Psychological Association.

Watkins, P. C., & McCurrach, D. (2017). Progress in the science of gratitude. In C. R. Snyder, S. J. Lopez, L. M. Edwards, & S. C. Marques (Eds.), *Oxford handbook of positive psychology* (3rd ed.). New York, NY: Oxford University Press.

Webb, J. R. (2003). Spiritual factors and adjustment in medical rehabilitation: Understanding forgiveness as a means of coping. *Journal of Applied Rehabilitation Counseling*, 34(3), 16–24.

Webb, J. R. (2007). Spiritual factors and adjustment in medical rehabilitation: Understanding forgiveness as a means of coping. In A. E. DellOrto & P. W. Power (Eds.), *The psychological and social impact of illness and disability* (5th ed., pp. 455–471). New York, NY: Springer. (Reprinted from: *Journal of Applied Rehabilitation Counseling*, 34(3), 16–24: 2003).

Webb, J. R., & Toussaint, L. L. (2020). Forgiveness, well-being, and mental health. In E. L. Worthington, Jr. & N. G. Wade (Eds.), *Handbook for forgiveness* (2nd ed., pp. 188–197). New York, NY: Routledge.

Webb, J. R., Hirsch, J. K., & Toussaint, L. L. (2015). Forgiveness as a positive psychotherapy for addiction and suicide: Theory, research, and practice. *Spirituality in Clinical Practice*, 2(1), 48–60. doi:10.1037/scp0000054.

Webb, J. R., Hirsch, J. K., & Toussaint, L. L. (2017). Self-forgiveness and pursuit of the sacred: The role of pastoral-related care. In L. Woodyatt, E. L.Worthington, Jr., M. Wenzel, & B. J. Griffin (Eds.), *Handbook of the psychology of self-forgiveness* (pp. 309–325). New York, NY: Springer.

Webb, J. R., Toussaint, L. L., & Conway-Williams, E. (2012). Forgiveness and health: Psycho-spiritual integration and the promotion of better healthcare. *Journal of Health Care Chaplaincy*, 18(1–2),57–73. doi:10.1080/08854726.2012.667317.

Webb, J. R., Toussaint, L. L., & Dula, C. S. (2014). Ritualistic, theistic, and existential spirituality: Initial psychometric qualities of the RiTE measure of spirituality. *Journal of Religion & Health*, 53(4), 972–985. doi:10.1007/s10943-013-9697-y.

Webb, J. R., Bumgarner, D. J., Conway-Williams, E., Dangel, T., & Hall, B. B. (2017). A consensus definition of self-forgiveness: Implications for assessment and treatment. *Spirituality in Clinical Practice*, 4(3), 216–227. doi:10.1037/scp0000138.

Wehmeyer, M. L., Shogren, K. A., Little, T. D., & Adams, N. (2017). Self-determination. In C. R. Snyder, S. J. Lopez, L. M. Edwards, & S. C. Marques (Eds.), *Oxford handbook of positive psychology* (3rd ed.). New York, NY: Oxford University Press.

Widiger, T. A., & Costa, P. T., Jr. (Eds.) (2013). *Personality disorders and the five-factor model of personality.* Washington, DC: American Psychological Association.

Woodyatt, L., Worthington, E. L., Jr., Wenzel, M., & Griffin, B. J. (Eds.) (2017). *Handbook of the psychology of self-forgiveness.* New York, NY: Springer.

Worthington, E. L., Jr. (2006). *Forgiveness and reconciliation: Theory and application.* New York, NY: Routledge.

Worthington, E. L., Jr. (Ed.) (1998). *Dimensions of forgiveness: Psychological research and theological perspectives.* Philadelphia: Templeton Foundation Press.

Worthington, E. L., Jr. (Ed.) (2005). *Handbook of forgiveness.* New York, NY: Routledge.

Worthington, E. L., Jr., & DiBlasio, F. A. (1990). Promoting mutual forgiveness within the fractured relationship. *Psychotherapy: Theory, Research, Practice, Training*, 27(2), 219–223. doi:10.1037/0033-3204.27.2.219.

Worthington, E. L., Jr., & Sandage, S. J. (2016). *Forgiveness and spirituality in psychotherapy: A relational approach.* Washington, DC: American Psychological Association.

Worthington, E. L., Jr., & Wade, N. G. (Eds.) (2020). *Handbook of forgiveness* (2nd ed.). New York, NY: Routledge.

Yandell, K. E. (1998). The metaphysics and morality of forgiveness. In R. D. Enright & J. North (Eds.), *Exploring forgiveness* (pp. 35–45). Madison, WI: University of Wisconsin Press.

Zinnbauer, B. J., & Pargament, K. I. (2005). Religiousness and spirituality. In R. F. Paloutzian & C. L. Park (Eds.), *Handbook of the psychology of religion and spirituality* (pp. 21–42). New York, NY: Guilford Press.

5 Theory: Forgiveness, Health, and Addiction

> The problems of the world cannot possibly be solved by skeptics or cynics, whose horizons are limited by the obvious realities.
>
> John F. Kennedy (1963, p. 1)

The association of forgiveness with health is receiving considerable attention in the scientific literature. The first edition of the edited volume *Handbook of Forgiveness* (Worthington, 2005) contained summaries of the initial base of scientific theory and empirical evidence regarding forgiveness (and its correlates) in the context of physiology (Witvliet, 2005), physical health (Harris & Thoresen, 2005), and mental health and well-being (Toussaint & Webb, 2005b). The edited volume *Forgiveness and Health: Scientific Evidence and Theories relating Forgiveness to Better Health* (Toussaint et al., 2015) was focused solely on health related topics; that is, 19 chapters, including a chapter dedicated to forgiveness and substance-related addiction (Webb & Jeter, 2015). The second edition of the aforementioned *Handbook of Forgiveness* (Worthington & Wade, 2020) includes the most up-to-date reviews of the state-of-the-science regarding forgiveness and psychophysiology (Witvliet, 2020), physical health (Toussaint et al., 2020), and general psychological adjustment (i.e., mental health and well-being; Webb & Toussaint, 2020).

Regarding physical health (Toussaint et al., 2020), a non-date-restricted search of the scientific psychological and medical literature revealed that, starting in and since the year 2000, 55 empirical studies have been published. Associations of forgiveness with physical health were examined in the context of fibromyalgia, spinal cord injury, chronic heart failure, traumatic brain injury, stroke, chronic pain, HIV, arthritis, chronic obstructive pulmonary disease, diabetes, and posttraumatic stress disorder. Of these 55 studies, 40 observed salubrious associations between forgiveness and physical health (i.e., about 73 percent). Regarding general psychological adjustment (Webb & Toussaint, 2020), a non-date-restricted search of the scientific psychological literature revealed that, starting in and since the year 1947, 714 peer-reviewed journal articles (i.e., theoretical articles, limited literature reviews, empirical studies, and meta-analyses) have been published. Of note, empirical examinations of the association of forgiveness with general psychological adjustment have been conducted in the context of many mental health and well-being related variables (e.g., depression, anxiety, stress, substance use, bulimia, life satisfaction, existential well-being, quality of life, psychiatric diagnosis, posttraumatic symptoms, suicidal behavior, anger, hostility, aggression, empathy, gratitude, hope, self-esteem, fear, prosocial emotions). And, salubrious associations "appear to be frequent, consistent, and robust," such that "associations are present nearly regardless of the particular aspect of well-being and mental health under consideration" (Webb & Toussaint, 2020, pp. 195 & 194, respectively).

There is plenty of empirical evidence to support the notion that multiple dimensions of forgiveness are salubriously associated with many and varied aspects of health. As a result, the question arises: How or why is forgiveness related to health, including addiction (i.e., forgiveness → health/addiction)? Related to this, how is spirituality related to health (i.e., spirituality → health)? That is, to the extent that forgiveness is a component of spirituality (see Chapter 4), and/or, to the extent that spirituality facilitates or is a precursor to forgiveness (see Choe et al., 2020), how are spirituality, forgiveness, and health related to each other (i.e., spirituality → forgiveness → health)? Through the remainder of this chapter, several theoretical models progressively applicable to the forgiveness-addiction association will be discussed in terms of explaining *how or why* such variables are thought to be related to each other. Given that spirituality is – or can be – a precursor to forgiveness, the association of spirituality with health will be addressed first, followed by the association of forgiveness with health and lastly, the association of forgiveness with addiction.

Spirituality and Health

Toussaint et al. (2012) provide an overview of the empirical association of religiousness/spirituality with mental health (i.e., depression, suicide, anxiety, psychosis, and substance use), including theory (as developed by Baetz & Toews, 2009; James & Wells, 2003; Koenig & Larson, 2001; Levin & Chatters, 1998) regarding potential mechanisms to explain how or why religiousness/spirituality and health are related to each other. Considered in more detail by Toussaint et al. (2012), a very brief presentation of said theories is given here.

Baetz and Toews (2009) discuss facilitative relationships between religiousness/spirituality and psychological, social, and biological factors, including motivation, coping, social control of healthy behaviors, genetic predispositions for health, and a biological interface with physiological stress-reaction systems. James and Wells (2003) contend that religiousness/spirituality contributes to the development of adaptive interpretation, appraisal, and self-regulation in the context of stressful life events. Koenig and Larson (2001) propose that religiousness/spirituality can foster positive psychological characteristics, promote prosocial virtues, and facilitate and strengthen social support and familial relationships. Levin and Chatters (1998) maintain that religiousness/spirituality can impact poor health and life stress through various processes, including: (1) a suppressing effect as a function of psychological, social, and behavioral factors, (2) a counterbalancing effect, (3) a preventative effect, based on suppression (see above) as well as a positive impact, and (4) a moderating/mitigating effect. Also, and conversely, so to speak, that poor health and life stress *interfere* with the otherwise positive effect of religiousness/spirituality on health and well-being. Of note, a common characteristic of each of these explanatory models regarding the relationship between religiousness/spirituality and health is the beneficial underlying effect of religiousness/spirituality in reducing stress and thus the negative implications and consequences of long-term stress (ors) on health (i.e., allostatic load; see McEwen, 2005).

Forgiveness and Health

The robust association of forgiveness with better health-related outcomes is thought to be (1) a manifestation of the effect of stress-and-coping on health and (2) a component of the larger association of religiousness/spirituality with health. Indeed, Worthington and colleagues have developed a comprehensive general model of the forgiveness–

health association (see Lavelock et al., 2013; Lavelock et al., 2015; Worthington et al., 2001; Worthington & Scherer, 2004; Worthington et al., 2007), built upon a foundation of stress-and-coping theory (see Lazarus & Folkman, 1984; Strelan, 2020; Strelan & Covic, 2006; Toussaint et al., 2017; Worthington, 2006).

Stress-and-Coping

Strelan (2020; see also Strelan & Covic, 2006) describes the stress-and-coping model of forgiveness in the context of the broad model of stress-and-coping developed by Lazarus and Folkman (1984). That is, after experiencing any given event, humans make an initial appraisal of the stressful nature of the experience/event (i.e., stressful, non-stressful, or irrelevant) and if stressful, whether or not the stress is threatening or an otherwise beneficial opportunity. A secondary appraisal regarding the adequacy of our personal resources (i.e., physical and psychosocial capabilities, and tangible resources) then occurs, followed by our attempts to implement our resources in order to address or cope with the stressor; that is, in a positive, constructive, healthy manner, *or* in a negative, self-defeating, unhealthy manner (see Strelan, 2020). In the specific context of forgiveness and health (Worthington, 2006), when offended, forgiveness is a potential resource available to us to address the stressful impact of unforgiveness – a confluence of negative emotional responses to being offended (e.g., hatred, anger, hostility, resentment, bitterness, and fear (Worthington et al., 2001)). Other options for coping with an offense include justice, avoidance, revenge, retaliation, and denial (Wade & Worthington, 2003). Importantly, forgiveness is not necessarily the default response to unforgiveness. Genuine forgiveness is a thoughtful, reasoned, deliberate choice (Enright, 2001; see also Chapter 3) – one of many alternative solutions available to us when we are offended and experiencing the negative and stressful effects of unforgiveness. Also, forgiveness and unforgiveness are not opposite ends of a spectrum. High or low levels of forgiveness do not necessarily equate with respectively low or high levels of unforgiveness (Worthington et al., 2001). Although related to one another, statistical variance between forgiveness and unforgiveness is not fully shared (Wade & Worthington, 2003). That is, based on analysis of the data (e.g., similar to the relationships between elevation and temperature or height and weight[1]), there is only a partial empirical (and conceptual) overlap between forgiveness and unforgiveness.

Spirituality, Forgiveness, and Health

Worthington and colleagues describe forgiveness as a component of the larger relationship between religiousness/spirituality and health, or one of a variety of intervening variables in this association (see Lavelock et al., 2015; Worthington et al., 2001). Religiousness/spirituality itself as well as the influence of such on culture can lead to conscientiousness-based (e.g., self-control, integrity, sense of justice, and desire for peace) and warmth-based (e.g., other-oriented love, empathy, humility, and gratitude) virtuous dispositions, which can lead to forgiveness, which, in turn, can have an impact on health and well-being (Worthington et al., 2001). Regarding the forgiveness link in this chain, it is thought to have both a relatively direct impact on health through stress-and-coping (see above) and an indirect effect on health through a variety of additional distinctive intervening variables, or mediators (see Toussaint & Webb, 2005b). Such as, *decreasing* negative experiences (e.g., rumination, tension), risky health behaviors, and unhealthy coping, and *increasing* positive experiences (e.g., empathy, compassion), relational well-being (e.g., social support, social skills), and spiritual well-being (e.g., self-transcendence, inner peace) (Lavelock et al., 2015). Underlying the indirect association(s) of forgiveness with health, or the notion that the impact of forgiveness on health can operate through other variables, is the (un)forgiveness-energy hypothesis (Svalina & Webb, 2012; see also, Temoshok & Chandra, 2000; Temoshok & Wald, 2005; Worthington et al., 2001). That is, "the process of forgiveness allows an individual to be more productive, effective and adaptive and, thus, to invest or redirect energy toward facilitating health, rather than toward impeding health through the rumination, stress and negative emotions associated with unforgiveness" (see Svalina & Webb, 2012, p. 384). For example, through engaging in the process of forgiveness, one is able to free up and use one's energy to engage in health promoting behaviors (e.g., stress management and exercise), rather than consuming said energy in a self-defeating manner by ruminating on the offense and all of the negative implications and experiences associated therewith, including the nature of one's relationship with the offender.

Forgiveness and Addiction

Webb and colleagues have expanded upon Worthington and colleagues' modeling of the general Forgiveness–Health Association (see above) to describe the role of forgiveness in addiction and recovery, or the Forgiveness–Addiction–Recovery Association (e.g., Webb et al., 2015; Webb et al., 2017). Webb and colleagues' primary modifications to Worthington and colleagues' work in this regard involve (1) tying the direct effect of forgiveness on addiction recovery to the elemental interface between resentments and addiction inherent to the Twelve-Step Model (Alcoholics Anonymous, 1981, 1998, 2001); that is, forgiveness is likely a critical factor in addressing and coping with the common occurrence of resentments in addiction (see Chapter 9), and (2) the addition of particular mediators and the separation of these distinctive mediators into categories (see below). Such categorical modifications have included *health-related functioning* (i.e., Worthington and colleagues' theorized mediators of the association of forgiveness with health, in general) and *existangst* (i.e., Webb and colleagues' theorized mediators of the association of forgiveness with addiction recovery, more specifically). In the following paragraphs, further description and development of the theoretical modeling regarding the Forgiveness–Addiction–Recovery Association is presented (see Figure 5.1).

Biopsychosocial Functioning

Initial modeling of the general association between forgiveness and health included indirect associations operating through health behavior, social support, and interpersonal functioning (Worthington et al., 2001) – categorized as *health-related functioning* in Webb and colleagues' expanded modeling (Webb et al., 2015). That is, being more forgiving, it was argued, would lead individuals to engage in more healthy behaviors (e.g., stress management, exercise, nutrition), benefit from more social support, and experience better interpersonal functioning, each of which would then lead to better outcomes related to physical health, mental health, and well-being. Over the years, research has supported these predictions (e.g., Webb & Brewer, 2010b; Webb et al., 2013). More recent related modeling has expanded this to include additional likely mediators of the general Forgiveness–Health Association; that is, the general association of forgiveness with health operating through the decrease and increase of various respective negative and positive health and psychosocial related attitudes, activities, and experiences (as briefly described above; see also, Lavelock et al., 2013; Lavelock et al., 2015).

In terms of addiction recovery as the particular health-related outcome and also in the context of self-forgiveness as the particular dimension of forgiveness under consideration,

Webb and colleagues, along with the variables of health behavior, social support, and interpersonal functioning (Worthington et al., 2001), incorporated additional psychosocial variables (e.g., self-blame, hope, and pessimism) and re-labeled their previous category of health-related functioning to be *biopsychosocial variables* (Toussaint et al., 2017; Webb et al., 2017). However, for descriptive purposes, re-labeling this category once again – this time to *biopsychosocial functioning* – will provide more accuracy and parsimonious clarity. Also, in the particular circumstance of self-forgiveness, Webb and colleagues discussed the role of self-condemnation as a contextual factor leading to the explicit need for self-forgiveness (Toussaint et al., 2017; Webb et al., 2017). Related to this, when considering forgiveness more broadly, that is, in its multiple dimensions (e.g., of self, of other, seeking, feeling, etc.), recognizing the contextual effect of condemnation more broadly, is warranted as well. That is, not only is *unforgiveness* a stress-and-coping related underlying contextual factor providing the environment for forgiveness as a possible solution (see above), but so is condemnation. When offense occurs, not only is it common for humans to experience anger, hostility, resentment and so on toward the offender (whether self, others, institutions, etc.), but these negative emotions – otherwise known as unforgiveness – can and often do lead to feelings of condemnation toward the offender (whether self, others, institutions, etc.) (see Figure 5.1).

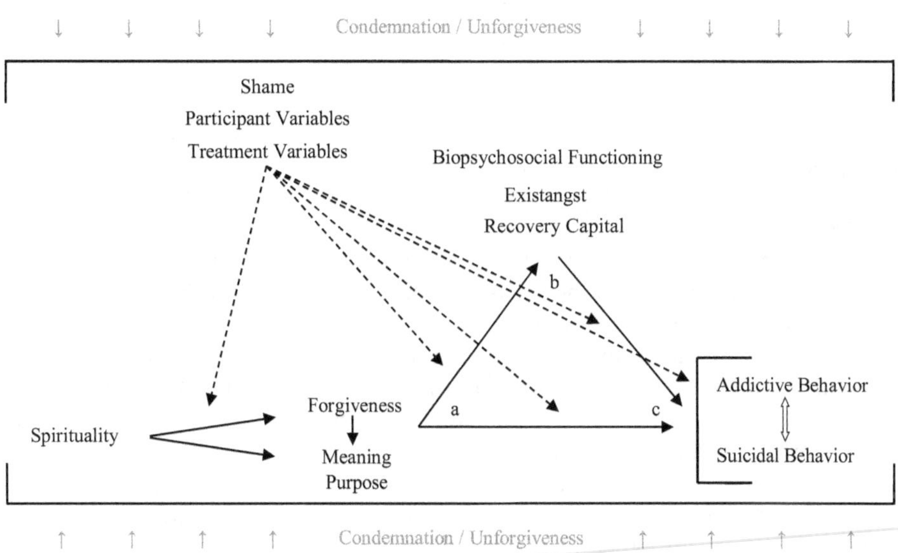

Figure 5.1 The Forgiveness–Addiction–Recovery Association: A Conceptual Model.
Notes
a→c = Direct Effect of Forgiveness on Dependent Variable(s)
a→b = Direct Effect of Forgiveness on Mediator Variable(s)
b→c = Direct Effect of Mediator Variable(s) on Dependent Variable(s)
a→b→c = Indirect Effect of Forgiveness on Dependent Variable(s) through Mediator Variable(s)
dotted→ = Moderation Effect
↕ = potential for a Concomitant, Bidirectional Effect
faded↓↑ = Condemnation and/or Unforgiveness [i.e., a constellation of negative emotions in response to offense experience(s) including, hatred, anger, hostility, resentment, bitterness, and fear (Worthington et al., 2001)] providing the context for forgiveness to become an option in the struggle of addiction recovery
Source: Adapted from Webb et al. (2015)

Existangst

In addition to adopting Worthington and colleagues' inclusion of health behavior, social support, interpersonal functioning and other variables related to biopsychosocial functioning, Webb and colleagues (e.g., Webb, 2018; Webb et al., 2015; Webb et al., 2017) have included another category of mediating variables, particularly related to addictive and suicidal behavior, termed *existangst.* Derived from existential[2] and teleological[3] angst,[4] existangst is defined as "emotionally and philosophically driven psychological distress" (Webb et al., 2015, p. 52). Examples of existangst include, symptoms of depression, anxiety, hopelessness, and/or psychache *when* such symptoms are driven by emotionally and philosophically charged psychological distress. Additional examples of existangst herein incorporated into the model for the first time are anger, loneliness, and temptation (see below).

What is the difference between such symptoms when driven *or not driven* by emotionally and philosophically charged psychological distress? Consider the cases of George and Sally. George, a single, mixed-ethnicity male in his mid 30s, presents with symptoms of depression and anxiety, such that he is struggling with maintaining employment and daily functioning related to eating and sleeping. While his appetite is minimal such that he is losing weight, his sleeping fluctuates between insomnia and hypersomnia. After discussing such issues in depth with his mental health therapist, George discloses that much of his waking hours are spent questioning whether his current employment is worthwhile and honorable and, related to this, whether he has been wasting his life so far – having spent several years in his current career, including obtaining the specialized education for such a career. Alternatively, Sally, a married, caucasian female in her late 20s, presents with symptoms of obsessive/compulsive anxiety, such that she spends considerable amounts of time checking doors and electrical appliances to ensure that they are locked and turned off. She also retraces her pathways when walking and driving to ensure that nobody was hurt (inadvertently by her as she passed by) or otherwise needing help along the way. After discussing such issues with her mental health therapist, Sally reports inevitable symptoms of depression due to intense frustration over her self-identified and self-acknowledged inability to otherwise control her obsessive/compulsive activities. Moreover, she experiences her anxiety and depression as feeding off of each other in a downward spiral and is unable to pinpoint a satisfactory explanation for the origin of her symptoms. While both George and Sally are experiencing personally profound symptoms of depression and anxiety, there is a primary qualitative difference. As with George, for such symptoms and experiences to qualify as existangst, they are also imbued with a particularly different depth and intensity described as "emotionally struggling with affirming one's meaningful existence" (Webb et al., 2015, p. 52).

Psychache

Although previously mentioned (see above) and discussed elsewhere (see Webb et al., 2015) as a manifestation of existangst, psychache, arguably, in all cases exhibits the depth and intensity of emotional struggle as described immediately above. As such, it is an exemplifying hallmark of existangst, and thus is worthy of explicit additional attention here. Shneidman (1993) originally coined the term in the context of suicidal behavior. However, it also seems relevant in the context of addictive behavior (Webb et al., 2015), particularly given the high co-occurrence of suicidal behavior and addictive behavior (Yuodelis-Flores & Ries, 2015). Indeed, empirical evidence has been observed regarding the association of psychache and suicidal behavior in the context of substance use problems among college students (Dangel & Webb, 2018; Webb, 2018).

Psychache is defined as "the hurt, anguish, soreness, aching, psychological pain in the psyche, the mind. … the pain of excessively felt shame, guilt, humiliation, loneliness, fear, angst, dread … or whatever" (Shneidman, 1993, p. 51). Sometimes described as an aching soul (Holden et al., 2001), Shneidman (1993) concluded, as the so-called father of modern suicidology (Jobes & Nelson, 2006) and over 50 years as a suicidologist, that the intense, unrelenting, and unremitting psychological pain of psychache is *the cause* of suicide. Given the aforementioned high co-occurrence of suicidal behavior and addictive behavior (up to 40 percent; Yuodelis-Flores & Ries, 2015), and, particularly from a Twelve-Step Model perspective, the anguish and torment when confronted with one's self-centeredness when seeking recovery (Webb & Toussaint, 2018), psychache has a well-earned place as a likely key contributing factor to addiction and likewise a mediator in the relationship between forgiveness and addiction recovery (i.e., higher levels of multiple dimensions of forgiveness are likely to be associated with lower levels of psychache, and in turn better outcomes related to addictive (and suicidal) behavior; see Figure 5.1).

Anger and Loneliness

From a Twelve-Step Model of addiction and recovery point of view, anger and loneliness are critical factors in the risk of relapse (see Alcoholics Anonymous, 1981, 1998, 2001; see also Nowinski et al., 1994). Indeed, anger is considered a "pivotal emotion" and "a constant threat to sobriety" (Nowinski et al., 1994, p. 83). Also, Nowinski et al. (1994) encourage therapists to ask if their "patients [struggling with addiction] relate to experiencing 'existential anxiety': the feeling of being isolated, of facing difficult decisions and choices but feeling totally alone in making them?" (p. 82). Of note, anger and loneliness may, but do not necessarily, occur in the context of one another. However, in the Twelve-Step Model, they are considered together (and thus discussed here, together), along with hunger and tiredness as a cluster of related risk factors for relapse, and given the acronym HALT (i.e., hungry, angry, lonely, tired). In the Twelve-Step Model, individuals struggling with addiction recovery are encouraged to pay close attention to and monitor whether or not they are feeling: (1) excessively hungry, (2) angry, (3) lonely, and/or (4) excessively tired. These distinct negative experiences are argued to make one particularly vulnerable for relapse as each of these physiological and emotional states lead one to be less able to think clearly and problem solve effectively. When faced with the inherently stressful challenges of addiction recovery *combined* with and thereby compounded by the vulnerabilities associated with feeling excessively hungry, angry, lonely, and/or excessively tired, poor choices are much more likely to occur, as is the risk for relapse. Indeed, when experiencing *anger* and *loneliness*, etc., the Twelve-Step Model recommendation is to "HALT"; that is, to stop what you are doing and take care of and/or resolve these basic needs, so as to reduce your vulnerability and likelihood for relapse.

Regarding anger and addiction related outcomes, research supports the notion of anger and aggression playing a role (see Chapter 12 for a discussion addressing forgiveness, aggression, and addiction), including the more frequent occurrence of such among those struggling with addiction and as a precipitant of substance use disorders and relapse (see Awalt et al., 1997; Coccaro et al., 2016; Shopshire & Reilly, 2013). Likewise, loneliness has been observed to play an important role in addiction related outcomes (see Blevins et al., 2018; Bonin et al., 2000; Xia & Yang, 2019). Enright and Fitzgibbons (2015) discuss the relevance of forgiveness in addiction, particularly in the context of addressing anger as manifested through depression, anxiety, low self-esteem, rebelliousness, and various personality disorders. Lin et al. (2004) observed forgiveness therapy to have a beneficial effect on anger among inpatients struggling with substance dependence. Webb and colleagues have observed salubrious associations between (1) forgiveness (i.e., of self and/or of others) and physical aggression, verbal aggression, anger, and/or hostility among college students, in general (Webb et al, 2012) and (2) forgiveness of self and the variables associated with HALT (i.e., hungry, angry, lonely, and tired; see above) among college student problematic drinkers (Webb & Brewer, 2010a).

Temptation

The psychology of temptation has been examined in the context of social psychology, addiction psychology, and the psychology of religion and spirituality. However, with the exception of the latter, which surprisingly has addressed temptation the least of the three, much of this work has addressed it from a secular point of view. Indeed, despite the close association of temptation with religion and spirituality from a societal and cultural point of view, in the scientific psychological literature, there has been "very little acknowledgment of [temptation's] place, function, and implication in the context of human spirituality" (Webb, 2014, p. 231). From this secular point of view, temptation is considered to be a deep-seated threat to goal-driven activity – a fundamental conflict regarding the pursuit of destructive short-term desires versus constructive long-term ideals – the resolution of which is a function of self-control versus ego-depletion (see Fishbach & Converse, 2011; Muraven, 2012; Myrseth & Fishbach, 2009). In this regard, and in the particular context of addiction, temptation often involves self-indulgence (e.g., sensation seeking, impulsivity, and risk-taking (see Zuckerman, 2012)) versus self-restraint (e.g., impulse control, delayed gratification, and judicious constraint).

Although there has been considerable research conducted and powerfully insightful understanding developed regarding the psychology of temptation, much of this work is in the context of undesirable, yet relatively innocuous behaviors (e.g., eating sweets), rather than activities with illicit and/or transcendent implications (e.g., sexual infidelity). In response to the lack of attention paid to the spirituality of temptation in the scientific psychological literature, Webb (2014) proposed a more comprehensive, inclusive definition of *temptation* such that, it is "the dispositional or situational incidence of being drawn cognitively, affectively, and/or behaviorally to engage in undesirable, illicit, and/or transcendent short-term activities that are inconsistent with personal, societal, and/or transcendent long-term standards" (p. 236).

Many addiction-related studies incorporate the notion of temptation (albeit largely from a secular point of view), particularly when describing and examining the process of restraining associated problematic behaviors (e.g., Bischof et al., 2005; Breitling et al., 2009; Palfai, 2001), including self-control depletion (e.g., Muraven et al., 2002; Muraven & Shmueli, 2006). Given the common (though not necessarily only) struggle of addiction being the conflict between self-indulgence and self-restraint and the ultimately transcendent nature of such (i.e., temptation), the inclusion of temptation as a manifestation of existangst is warranted.

Recovery Capital

A new category of intervening or mediating variables in the Forgiveness–Addiction–Recovery Association (see Figure 5.1) is herein proposed. That is, a broad construct known as *recovery capital*; originally defined as:

> the sum total of one's resources that can be brought to bear in an effort to overcome [addiction]. It is embodied in a number of tangible and intangible resources and relationships, including those that existed prior to a person's [addiction], during the period of [addiction], and conditions likely to prevail in the future. It encompasses attitudes and beliefs that one has toward the past, [the] present, and the future. It also includes one's mental status and other personal characteristics that can be drawn upon to resolve [an addiction] problem.
>
> (Granfield & Cloud, 1999, p. 179)

Of note, recovery capital, at its core, is conceptualized in the context of Natural Recovery from addiction (see Chapter 2) and "represents [the] critical elements that an individual possesses or that exist within his or her immediate surroundings and that function to *promote and sustain a recovery experience*" (emphasis added; Granfield & Cloud, 1999, p. 179).

The original categories of recovery capital have been expanded from social, physical, and human (Granfield & Cloud, 1999) to include capital domains subsumed within ecological levels (Hennessy, 2017). As described, albeit in much more detail, by Hennessy (2017), the individual ecological level includes physical/financial capital (i.e., material resources), human capital (i.e., personal characteristics such as, knowledge and skills), health capital (i.e., physical health and mental health), and growth capital (i.e., innate desire for growth). The micro ecological level includes social capital (i.e., social networks) and family/social recovery capital (i.e., social support). And, the meso ecological level includes cultural capital (i.e., personal qualities such as values and beliefs) and community recovery capital (i.e., community-based attitudes, policies, and resources). Related to this, Groshkova et al. (2013) have developed the *Assessment of Recovery Capital* (ARC), a 50-item, self-report questionnaire measuring 10 subsets of recovery captial: (1) substance use and sobriety, (2) psychological health, (3) physical health, (4) citizenship/community involvement, (5) social support, (6) meaningful activities, (7) housing and safety, (8) risk taking, (9) coping and life functioning, and (10) recovery experience. Importantly, spirituality, religiousness, life meaning, and Twelve-Step affiliation have also been discussed and examined as aspects of recovery capital (Laudet et al., 2006).

Some may argue that recovery capital could be included in the biopsychosocial functioning category of intervening variables in my model of the Forgiveness–Addiction–Recovery Association. Or, perhaps the role of forgiveness in addiction recovery could even be included as an aspect of a larger notion of recovery capital, as it appears that not all domains of recovery capital explicitly accommodate the notion of forgiveness. Nevertheless, given the complex nature of the association of forgiveness with addiction recovery and the reality that certain aspects and/or particular domains of recovery capital are likely *facilitated by* forgiveness, it seems prudent to include recovery capital, broadly speaking, as an intervening variable in a model focused on forgiveness as a priority and relatively unique alternative in addressing the problem of addiction. As such, some may ask, "What is the difference, then, between biopsychosocial functioning and recovery capital in this model of the Forgiveness–Addiction–Recovery Association?" Simply put, biopsychosocial functioning is in the general context of everyday living and recovery capital is in the specific context of the clear, deliberate, and concerted effort to change one's lifestyle from addiction to recovery. But, "Isn't 'the general context of everyday living' and the 'effort to change one's lifestyle' the same set of affairs for the person struggling with addiction recovery?" My answer: in some ways yes, in some ways no. To the extent that a person struggling with addiction recovery is explicitly engaged in-the-moment with the process of recovery, yes, they are likely the same thing. However, if said person is otherwise focused on their daily activities, long-term goals, and over-arching values and responsibilities there will likely be meaningful differences between effective biopsychosocial functioning and the possession of or access to recovery capital.

In this regard, it may be useful to draw a parallel between early recovery and the former (i.e., recovery capital), and likewise to draw a parallel between long-term recovery and the latter (i.e., biopsychosocial functioning). That is, recovery capital is more "obvious" in early recovery or attaining and maintaining recovery, whereas biopsychosocial functioning is more "obvious" during long-term recovery or established and mature recovery. However, recovery capital is also relevant in the context of long-term recovery, and biopsychosocial functioning is also relevant in early recovery. Each likely has a primary versus secondary role in each stage of recovery. In early recovery, recovery capital will likely be primary and biopsychosocial functioning will likely be largely secondary. And, in long-term recovery biopsychosocial functioning will likely be primary and recovery capital will likely be largely secondary.

Demographic and Individual Differences in Forgiveness

Differences in person-level variables or characteristics can be very important when seeking to understand how forgiveness is related to health-related variables, including how best to apply forgiveness in the context of treatment. For example, Toussaint and colleagues have observed: (1) gender differences such that empathy was associated with forgiveness of others for men, but not for women (Toussaint & Webb, 2005a), (2) age related differences such that forgiveness of others was associated with better mental and physical health among middle age and old age adults as opposed to young adults (Toussaint et al., 2001), and (3) race/ethnicity differences such that forgiveness of others was protective of health for elderly Black people, but not elderly White people (McFarland et al., 2012). Griffin, Cowden, and Shawkey (2020) provided a bibliographic overview of narrative reviews and meta-analyses regarding forgiveness, including in the context of various person-level characteristics; for example, sex differences, culture (see also Sandage et al., 2020), personality (see also Hodge et al., 2020), and interpersonal relational qualities.

Notes

1 As an example, height and weight are related to each other, but not entirely so. That is, generally speaking, the taller a person is, the more they are likely to weigh. However, it is not a perfect relationship, as there are exceptions to the rule, so to speak.

2 Merriam-Webster defines *existential* as: "(1): of, relating to, or affirming existence. (2a): grounded in existence or the experience of existence" (https://www.merriam-webster.com/dictionary/existential).

3 Merriam-Webster defines *teleological* as: "exhibiting or relating to design or purpose especially in nature" (https://www.merriam-webster.com/dictionary/teleological).

4 Merriam-Webster defines *angst* as: "a feeling of anxiety, apprehension, or insecurity" (https://www.merriam-webster.com/dictionary/angst).

References

Alcoholics Anonymous (AA) (1981). *Twelve steps and twelve traditions.* New York, NY: Author. See https://www.aa.org/pages/en_US/twelve-steps-and-twelve-traditions.

Alcoholics Anonymous (AA) (1998). *Living sober.* New York, NY: Author.

Alcoholics Anonymous (AA) (2001). *Alcoholics Anonymous* (4th ed.). New York, NY: Author. See https://www.aa.org/pages/en_US/alcoholics-anonymous.

Awalt, R. M., Reilly, P. M., & Shopshire, M. S. (1997). The angry patient: An intervention for managing anger in substance abuse treatment. *Journal of Psychoactive Drugs*, 29(4), 353–358. doi:10.1080/02791072.1997.10400562.

Baetz, M., & Toews, J. (2009). Clinical implications of research on religion, spirituality, and mental health. *The Canadian Journal of Psychiatry/La Revue canadienne de psychiatrie*, 54(5), 292–301.

Bischof, G., Rumpf, H. J., Meyer, C., Hapke, U., & John, U. (2005). Gender differences in temptation to drink, self-efficacy to abstain and coping behavior in treated alcohol-dependent individuals: Controlling for severity of dependence. *Addiction Research & Theory*, 13(2), 129–136. doi:10.1080/16066350412331335305.

Blevins, C. E., Lash, S. J., & Abrantes, A. M. (2018). Adapting substance use motives measures for a clinical population of opiate, alcohol, and stimulant users. *Addiction Research & Theory*, 26(2), 151–158. doi:10.1080/16066359.2017.1338689.

Bonin, M. F., McCreary, D. R., & Sadava, S. W. (2000). Problem drinking behavior in two community-based samples of adults: Influence of gender, coping, loneliness, and depression. *Psychology of Addictive Behaviors*, 14(2), 151–161. doi:10.1037/0893-164X.14.2.151.

Breitling, L. P., Twardella, D., Raum, E., & Brenner, H. (2009). Situational temptation scores and smoking cessation in general care. *Psychology of Addictive Behaviors*, 23(2), 362–367. doi:10.1037/a0015715.

Choe, E., McLaughlin, A., McElroy-Heltzel, S. E., & Davis, D. E. (2020). Forgiveness and religion/spirituality. In E. L.Worthington, Jr. & N. G. Wade (Eds.), *Handbook of forgiveness* (2nd ed., pp. 107–116). New York, NY: Routledge.

Coccaro, E. F., Fridberg, D. J., Fanning, J. R., Grant, J. E., King, A. C., & Lee, R. (2016). Substance use disorders: Relationship with intermittent explosive disorder and with aggression, anger, and impulsivity. *Journal of Psychiatric Research*, 81, 127–132. doi:10.1016/j.jpsychires.2016.06.011.

Dangel, T., & Webb, J. R. (2018). Forgiveness and substance use problems among college students: Psychache, depressive symptoms, and hopelessness as mediators. *Journal of Substance Use*, 23(6), 618–625. doi:10.1080/14659891.2018.1489003.

Enright, R. D. (2001). *Forgiveness is a choice: A step-by-step process for resolving anger and restoring hope.* Washington, DC: American Psychological Association.

Enright, R. D., & Fitzgibbons, R. P. (2015). *Forgiveness therapy: An empirical guide for resolving anger and restoring hope* (2nd ed.). Washington, DC: American Psychological Association.

Fishbach, A., & Converse, B. A. (2011). Identifying and battling temptation. In K. D. Vohs & R. F. Baumeister (Eds.), *Handbook of self-regulation: Research, theory, and applications* (2nd ed.). (pp. 244–260). New York, NY: Guilford Press.

Granfield, R., & Cloud, W. (1999). *Coming clean: Overcoming addiction without treatment*. New York, NY: New York University Press.

Griffin, B. J., Cowden, R. G., & Shawkey, L. (2020). Bibliography of narrative reviews and meta-analyses on forgiveness (2004–2018). In E. L.Worthington, Jr. & N. G. Wade (Eds.), *Handbook of forgiveness* (2nd ed., pp. 335–344). New York, NY: Routledge.

Groshkova, T., Best, D., & White, W. (2013). The Assessment of Recovery Capital: Properties and psychometrics of a measure of addiction recovery strengths. *Drug and Alcohol Review*, 32 (2), 187–194. doi:10.1111/j.1465-3362.2012.00489.x.

Harris, A. H. S., & Thoresen, C. E. (2005). Forgiveness, unforgiveness, health, and disease. In E. L.Worthington, Jr. (Ed.), *Handbook of forgiveness* (pp. 321–333). New York, NY: Brunner-Routledge.

Hennessy, E. A. (2017). Recovery capital: A systematic review of the literature. *Addiction Research & Theory*, 25(5), 349–360. doi:10.1080/16066359.2017.1297990.

Hodge, A. S., Captari, L. E., Mosher, D. K., Kodali, N., Hook, J. N., Davis, D. E., & Van Tongeren, D. R. (2020). Personality and forgiveness: A meta-analytic review. In E. L.Worthington, Jr. & N. G. Wade (Eds.), *Handbook of forgiveness* (2nd ed., pp. 97–106). New York, NY: Routledge.

Holden, R. R., Mehta, K., Cunningham, E. J., & McLeod, L. D. (2001). Development and preliminary validation of a scale of psychache. *Canadian Journal of Behavioural Science/Revue canadienne des sciences du comportement*, 33(4), 224–232. doi:10.1037/h0087144.

James, A., & Wells, A. (2003). Religion and mental health: Towards a cognitive-behavioural framework. *British Journal of Health Psychology*, 8(3), 359–376. doi:10.1348/135910703322370905.

Jobes, D. A., & Nelson, K. N. (2006). Shneidman's contributions to the understanding of suicidal thinking. In T. E. Ellis (Ed.), *Cognition and suicide: Theory, research, and therapy* (pp. 29–49). Washington, DC: American Psychological Association.

Kennedy, J. F. (1963). A journey home: John F. Kennedy in Ireland. Retrieved September 8, 2019, from https://www.jfklibrary.org/visit-museum/exhibits/past-exhibits/a-journey-home-john-f-kennedy-in-ireland.

Koenig, H. G., & Larson, D. B. (2001). Religion and mental health: Evidence for an association. *International Review of Psychiatry*, 13(2), 67–78. doi:10.1080/09540260124661.

Laudet, A. B., Morgen, K., & White, W. L. (2006). The role of social supports, spirituality, religiousness, life meaning and affiliation with 12-step fellowships in quality of life satisfaction among individuals in recovery from alcohol and drug problems. *Alcoholism Treatment Quarterly*, 24(1–2), 33–73. doi:10.1300/J020v24n01_04.

Lavelock, C. R., Griffin, B. J., & Worthington, E. L., Jr. (2013). Forgiveness, religiousness, spirituality, and health in people with physical challenges: A review and a model. *Research in the Social Scientific Study of Religion*, 24, 53–92. doi:10.1163/9789004252073_005.

Lavelock, C. R., Snipes, D. J., Griffin, B. J., Worthington, E. L., Jr., Davis, D. E., Hook, J. N., … Ritter, J. (2015). A conceptual model of forgiveness and health. In L. L. Toussaint, E. L. Worthington, Jr., & D. R. Williams (Eds.), *Forgiveness and health: Scientific evidence and theories relating forgiveness to better health* (pp. 29–42). New York, NY: Springer.

Lazarus, R. S., & Folkman, S. (1984). *Stress, appraisal, and coping*. New York, NY: Springer.

Levin, J. S., & Chatters, L. M. (1998). Research on religion and mental health: An overview of empirical findings and theoretical issues. In H. G. Koenig (Ed.), *Handbook of religion and mental health* (pp. 33–50). San Diego, CA: Academic Press.

Lin, W. F., Mack, D., Enright, R. D., Krahn, D., & Baskin, T. W. (2004). Effects of forgiveness therapy on anger, mood, and vulnerability to substance use among inpatient substance-dependent clients. *Journal of Consulting and Clinical Psychology*, 72(6), 1114–1121. doi:10.1037/0022-006X.72.6.1114.

McEwen, B. S. (2005). Stressed or stressed out: What is the difference? *Journal of Psychiatry and Neuroscience*, 30(5), 315–318.

McFarland, M. J., Smith, C. A., Toussaint, L., & Thomas, P. A. (2012). Forgiveness of others and health: Do race and neighborhood matter? *The Journals of Gerontology: Series B: Psychological Sciences and Social Sciences*, 67(1), 66–75. doi:10.1093/geronb/gbr121.

Muraven, M. (2012). Ego depletion: Theory and evidence. In R. M. Ryan (Ed.), *The Oxford handbook of human motivation* (pp. 111–126). New York, NY: Oxford University Press.

Muraven, M., & Shmueli, D. (2006). The self-control costs of fighting the temptation to drink. *Psychology of Addictive Behaviors*, 20(2), 154–160. doi:10.1037/0893-164x.20.2.154.

Muraven, M., Collins, R. L., & Neinhaus, K. (2002). Self-control and alcohol restraint: An initial application of the Self-Control Strength Model. *Psychology of Addictive Behaviors*, 16(2), 113–120. doi:10.1037/0893-164x.16.2.113.

Myrseth, K. O. R., & Fishbach, A. (2009). Self-control: A function of knowing when and how to exercise restraint. *Current Directions in Psychological Science*, 18(4), 247–252. doi:10.1111/j.1467-8721.2009.01645.x.

Nowinski, J., Baker, S., & Carroll, K. M. (1994). *Twelve step facilitation therapy manual: A clinical research guide for therapists treating individuals with alcohol abuse and dependence.* NIH Publication No. 94–3722. Rockville, MD: National Institute on Alcohol Abuse and Alcoholism.

Palfai, T. P. (2001). Individual differences in temptation and responses to alcohol cues. *Journal of Studies on Alcohol*, 62(5), 657–666.

Sandage, S. J., Crabtree, S. A., & Bell, C. A. (2020). Forgiveness and culture: Conceptual issues. In E. L.Worthington, Jr. & N. G. Wade (Eds.), *Handbook of forgiveness* (2nd ed., pp. 201–211). New York, NY: Routledge.

Shneidman, E. (1993). *Suicide as psychache: A clinical approach to self-destructive behavior.* Northvale, NJ: Jason Aronson.

Shopshire, M. S., & Reilly, P. M. (2013). Anger management treatment and substance use disorders. In E. Fernandez (Ed.), *Treatments for anger in specific populations: Theory, application, and outcome* (pp. 74–91). New York, NY: Oxford University Press.

Strelan, P. (2020). The stress-and-coping model of forgiveness: Theory, research, and the potential of dyadic coping. In E. L.Worthington, Jr. & N. G. Wade (Eds.), *Handbook of forgiveness* (pp. 63–73). New York, NY: Routledge.

Strelan, P., & Covic, T. (2006). A Review of Forgiveness Process Models and a Coping Framework to Guide Future Research. *Journal of Social & Clinical Psychology*, 25(10), 1059–1085. doi:10.1521/jscp.2006.25.10.1059.

Svalina, S. S., & Webb, J. R. (2012). Forgiveness and health among people in outpatient physical therapy. *Disability and Rehabilitation*, 34(5), 383–392. doi:10.3109/09638288.2011.607216.

Temoshok, L. R., & Chandra, P. S. (2000). The meaning of forgiveness in a specific situational and cultural context: Persons living with HIV/AIDS in India. In M. E. McCullough, K. I. Pargament, & C. E. Thoresen (Eds.), *Forgiveness: Theory, research, and practice* (pp. 41–64). New York, NY: Guilford Press.

Temoshok, L. R., & Wald, R. L. (2005). Forgiveness and health in persons living with HIV/AIDS. In E. L.Worthington, Jr. (Ed.), *Handbook of forgiveness* (pp. 335–348). New York, NY: Brunner-Routledge.

Toussaint, L. L., & Webb, J. R. (2005a). Gender differences in the relationship between empathy and forgiveness. *The Journal of Social Psychology*, 145(6), 673–685. doi:10.3200/socp.145.6.673-686.

Toussaint, L. L., & Webb, J. R. (2005b). Theoretical and empirical connections between forgiveness, mental health, and well-being. In E. L.Worthington, Jr. (Ed.), *Handbook of forgiveness* (pp. 349–362). New York, NY: Routledge.

Toussaint, L. L., Webb, J. R., & Hirsch, J. K. (2017). Self-forgiveness and health: A stress-and-coping model. In L. Woodyatt, E. L.Worthington, Jr., M. Wenzel, & B. J. Griffin (Eds.), *Handbook of the psychology of self-forgiveness* (pp. 87–99). New York, NY: Springer.

Toussaint, L. L., Webb, J. R., & Keltner, W. (2012). Religion, spirituality, and mental health. In J. D. Aten, K. A. O'Grady, & E. L.Worthington, Jr. (Eds.), *The psychology of religion and spirituality for clinicians: Using research in your practice* (pp. 331–356). New York, NY: Routledge.

Toussaint, L. L., Worthington, E. L., Jr., & Williams, D. R. (Eds.). (2015). *Forgiveness and health: Scientific evidence and theories relating forgiveness to better health.* New York, NY: Springer.

Toussaint, L. L., Williams, D. R., Musick, M. A., & Everson, S. A. (2001). Forgiveness and health: Age differences in a U.S. probability sample. *Journal of Adult Development*, 8(4), 249–257. doi:10.1023/a:1011394629736.

Toussaint, L. L., Worthington, E. L., Jr., Williams, D. R., & Webb, J. R. (2020). Forgiveness and physical health. In E. L.Worthington, Jr. & N. G. Wade (Eds.), *Handbook of forgiveness* (2nd ed., pp. 178–187). New York, NY: Routledge.

Wade, N. G., & Worthington, E. L., Jr. (2003). Overcoming interpersonal offenses: Is forgiveness the only way to deal with unforgiveness? *Journal of Counseling & Development*, 81(3), 343–353. doi:10.1002/j.1556-6678.2003.tb00261.x.

Webb, J. R. (2014). Incorporating spirituality into the psychology of temptation: Conceptualization, measurement, and clinical implications. *Spirituality in Clinical Practice*, 1(3), 231–241. doi:10.1037/scp0000028.

Webb, J. R. (2018). Forgiveness, addiction, and suicide. In J. K. Hirsch, E. C. Chang, & J. K. Rabon (Eds.), *A positive psychological approach to suicide: Theory, research, and prevention* (pp. 37–58). New York, NY: Springer.

Webb, J. R., & Brewer, K. (2010a). Forgiveness and college student drinking in Southern Appalachia. *Journal of Substance Use*, 15(6), 417–433. doi:10.3109/14659891003706373.

Webb, J. R., & Brewer, K. (2010b). Forgiveness, health, and problematic drinking among college students in Southern Appalachia. *Journal of Health Psychology*, 15(8), 1257–1266. doi:10.1177/1359105310365177.

Webb, J. R., & Jeter, B. R. (2015). Forgiveness and problematic substance use. In L. L. Toussaint, E. L.Worthington, Jr., & D. R. Williams (Eds.), *Forgiveness and health: Scientific evidence and theories relating forgiveness to better health* (pp. 139–154). New York, NY: Springer.

Webb, J. R., & Toussaint, L. L. (2018). Self-forgiveness as a critical factor in addiction and recovery: A 12-step model perspective. *Alcoholism Treatment Quarterly*, 36(1), 15–31. doi:10.1080/07347324.2017.1391057.

Webb, J. R., & Toussaint, L. L. (2020). Forgiveness, well-being, and mental health. In E. L. Worthington, Jr. & N. G. Wade (Eds.), *Handbook for forgiveness* (2nd ed., pp. 188–197). New York, NY: Routledge.

Webb, J. R., Dula, C. S., & Brewer, K. (2012). Forgiveness and aggression among college students. *Journal of Spirituality in Mental Health*, 14(1), 38–58. doi:10.1080/19349637.2012.642669.

Webb, J. R., Hirsch, J. K., & Toussaint, L. L. (2015). Forgiveness as a positive psychotherapy for addiction and suicide: Theory, research, and practice. *Spirituality in Clinical Practice*, 2(1), 48–60. doi:10.1037/scp0000054.

Webb, J. R., Toussaint, L. L., & Hirsch, J. K. (2017). Self-forgiveness, addiction, and recovery. In L. Woodyatt, E. L.Worthington, Jr., M. Wenzel, & B. J. Griffin (Eds.), *Handbook of the psychology of self-forgiveness* (pp. 265–277). New York, NY: Springer.

Webb, J. R., Hirsch, J. K., Visser, P. L., & Brewer, K. G. (2013). Forgiveness and health: Assessing the mediating effect of health behavior, social support, and interpersonal functioning. *Journal of Psychology: Interdisciplinary and Applied*, 147(5), 391–414. doi:10.1080/00223980.2012.700964.

Witvliet, C. v. (2005). Unforgiveness, forgiveness, and justice: Scientific findings on feelings and physiology. In E. L.Worthington, Jr. (Ed.), *Handbook of forgiveness* (pp. 305–319). New York, NY: Routledge.

Witvliet, C. v. (2020). Forgiveness, embodiment, and relational accountability: Victim and transgressor psychophysiology research. In E. L.Worthington, Jr. & N. G. Wade (Eds.), *Handbook of forgiveness* (2nd ed., pp. 167–177). New York, NY: Routledge.

Worthington, E. L., Jr. (Ed.) (2005). *Handbook of forgiveness.* New York, NY: Routledge.

Worthington, E. L., Jr. (2006). *Forgiveness and reconciliation: Theory and application*. New York, NY: Routledge.

Worthington, E. L., Jr., & Scherer, M. (2004). Forgiveness is an emotion-focused coping strategy that can reduce health risks and promote health resilience: Theory, review, and hypotheses. *Psychology & Health*, 19(3), 385–405. doi:10.1080/0887044042000196674.

Worthington, E. L., Jr., & Wade, N. G. (Eds.). (2020). *Handbook of forgiveness* (2nd ed.). New York, NY: Routledge.

Worthington, E. L., Jr., Berry, J. W., & Parrott, L., III. (2001). Unforgiveness, forgiveness, religion, and health. In T. G. Plante & A. C. Sherman (Eds.), *Faith and health: Psychological perspectives* (pp. 107–138). New York, NY: Guilford Press.

Worthington, E. L., Jr., Witvliet, C. v., Pietrini, P., & Miller, A. J. (2007). Forgiveness, health, and well-being: A review of evidence for emotional versus decisional forgiveness, dispositional forgivingness, and reduced unforgiveness. *Journal of Behavioral Medicine*, 30(4), 291–302. doi:10.1007/s10865-007-9105-8.

Xia, M., & Yang, C. (2019). The relationship among social support, self-esteem, affect balance and loneliness in individuals with substance use disorders in China. *Journal of Community Psychology*, 47(5), 1269–1281. doi:10.1002/jcop.22190.

Yuodelis-Flores, C., & Ries, R. K. (2015). Addiction and suicide: A review. *The American Journal on Addictions*, 24(2), 98–104. doi:10.1111/ajad.12185.

Zuckerman, M. (2012). Psychological factors and addiction: Personality. In H. J. Shaffer, D. A. LaPlante, S. E. Nelson, H. J. Shaffer, D. A. LaPlante, & S. E. Nelson (Eds.), *APA addiction syndrome handbook, Vol. 1: Foundations, influences, and expressions of addiction* (pp. 175–194). Washington, DC: American Psychological Association.

6 Research: Forgiveness and Addictive Behavior

Although both the role of resentments in the struggle with addiction and the role of forgiveness in the struggle for addiction recovery have been acknowledged and discussed – albeit in an anecdotal fashion – in the context of the Twelve-Step Model of addiction and recovery since the 1930s (see Alcoholics Anonymous, 2001), the first *scientific* study deliberately and explicitly focused on forgiveness in the context of addiction was not published in the psychological literature until 2001 (see Brenneis, 2001). Webb and colleagues have periodically published systematic reviews of the published scientific psychological literature seeking to understand and track the nature of the empirical evidence regarding the relationship between forgiveness and addictive behavior (see Webb, Hirsch et al., 2011; Webb & Jeter, 2015; Webb & Toussaint, 2018, 2020). Through January 12, 2019, the date of the last comprehensive literature search/review, 44 scientific studies focused on the association of forgiveness with addictive behavior had been published (Webb & Toussaint, 2020). Each of the 44 studies is briefly described below, along with six additional studies from an updated review, and a seventh additional study overlooked in previous reviews. In this regard, there are now 51 scientific psychological studies deliberately and explicitly focused on the empirical association of forgiveness with addictive behavior. The updated review, as with the previous reviews, was conducted by searching the PsycINFO and PUBMED databases using the following search phrase: "(alcohol OR substance OR drug OR addict*) AND forgiv*)" and restricted to peer-reviewed journal articles (one of the 51 studies was published in an edited book). The six new studies were retrieved on August 22, 2020 and are otherwise indicated as such in the descriptions below. Also, in an effort to show the progression of the research over the years, the studies are presented largely in chronological order – within each category.

Forgiveness and Alcohol Use

Twenty-two studies have been conducted that focus on the association of forgiveness with alcohol use, with alcohol being the only substance under consideration (i.e., included in the analyses). Fifteen of these 22 studies were conducted in the context of individuals being in treatment (at least having started treatment) for alcohol related problems and seven were conducted among individuals in other non-treatment based settings (e.g., undergraduate college students).

*Alcohol Among Individuals in Treatment (*n *= 15)*

Webb et al. (2006), in a 6-month longitudinal study among people entering treatment for alcohol related problems, found that self-forgiveness and other-forgiveness, but not feeling forgiven by God, were associated with less frequency and quantity of alcohol use and fewer negative consequences of alcohol use. However, these associations were only observed at treatment entry, and not at 6-month follow-up, nor from treatment entry to 6-month follow-up. Of note, this study also suggested that self-forgiveness – when considering forgiveness in the context of addiction – may be the most difficult dimension of forgiveness to achieve (i.e., lower than the other dimensions measured) and the most important to recovery (i.e., more frequently associated with better outcomes than the other dimensions measured). Knight et al. (2007) in a study of adolescents (12–18 years of age) seeking routine outpatient primary care, observed self-forgiveness, other-forgiveness, and feeling forgiven by God each to be associated with a lower likelihood to drink during the past 90 days. Also, that self-forgiveness seemed to be the most important for the overall sample, with feeling forgiven by God particularly so amongst past-year congregants. Robinson et al. (2007), the aforementioned overlooked study (i.e., in terms of contributing to the overall tally), found that although total forgiveness (i.e., self-forgiveness, other-forgiveness, and feeling forgiven by God, summed together as one total score, and not making a distinction between particular dimensions of forgiveness) increased from treatment entry to 6-month follow-up, this change was not associated with less heavy drinking at the 6-month follow-up. However, in a larger, broader sample Robinson et al. (2011) found these 6-month changes in total forgiveness, as well as changes in self-forgiveness separately measured by an additional self-report instrument, to be associated with less drinking at the 9-month follow-up (i.e., an additional 3 months later).

Webb et al. (2009) examined associations of self-forgiveness, other-forgiveness, and feeling forgiven by God with a variety of indicators of mental health, as measured by the *Brief Symptom Inventory* (Derogatis & Melisaratos, 1983) (e.g., depression, anxiety, somatization, hostility, paranoid ideation, and psychoticism), among people entering outpatient treatment for alcohol problems. Many associations involving self-forgiveness and other-forgiveness with the aspects of mental health were observed. At treatment entry, self-forgiveness and other-forgiveness seemed equally important in relation to mental health. At 6-month follow-up, self-forgiveness seemed most important, and from treatment entry to 6-month follow-up, other-forgiveness seemed most important. Feeling forgiven by God was not observed to be predictive of mental health in this study. Scherer et al. (2011) compared a self-forgiveness intervention against treatment as usual in the context of individuals struggling with alcohol problems. Those receiving the self-forgiveness intervention showed greater improvements on measures of state-based self-forgiveness, drinking refusal self-efficacy, guilt, and shame. Webb et al. (2011) examined social support and mental health as mediators of the association of forgiveness with alcohol use and problems. And, at treatment entry, found that self-forgiveness and other-forgiveness, but not feeling forgiven by God, was predictive of each alcohol-related outcome. At the 6-month follow-up, only self-forgiveness was predictive of fewer negative consequences of alcohol use, and from treatment entry to the 6-month follow-up, only other-forgiveness was predictive of fewer negative consequences of use.

Krentzman et al. (2013) examined the effect of Alcoholics Anonymous (AA), among individuals diagnosed with alcohol dependence, on the frequency and intensity of drinking over the course of 18 months, as mediated by spirituality (including self-forgiveness and other-forgiveness). Involvement with AA at 6 months was predictive of other-forgiveness at 12 months, but not of self-forgiveness at 12 months. However, other-forgiveness at 12 months was not observed to be a mediator of the association of 6-month AA involvement with 18-month drinking related outcomes. Charzyńska (2015) studied sex-based differences in spiritual coping, self-forgiveness, other-forgiveness, forgiveness by God, and gratitude among patients in an alcohol addiction treatment program. In the context of forgiveness, overall, levels of self-forgiveness were the lowest, and at treatment entry, males had higher levels of other-forgiveness, whereas at treatment end (about 5–7 weeks later), females had higher levels of forgiveness by God. Braun et al. (2018), conducted a study among alcohol-dependent individuals who had received in-patient withdrawal treatment 24 months prior and found that patients had lower levels of other-forgiveness than did healthy controls, and that among females only, willingness to forgive a regretful offender was associated with more days before a first readmission.

Krentzman and colleagues have examined associations among various aspects of spirituality and religiousness, including self-forgiveness and other-forgiveness, among individuals diagnosed with alcohol dependence upon entering outpatient treatment and every 6 months for 30 months thereafter. In the context of forgiveness and sex, Krentzman (2017), overall, found that self-forgiveness increased from treatment entry to 6 months, and both self-forgiveness and other-forgiveness increased from 6 months to 30 months. Also, from treatment entry to 6 months, other-forgiveness scores were higher for females than for males. And, from 6 months to 30 months self-forgiveness scores for females rose more quickly than for males. Krentzman et al. (2017) examined drinking and involvement with Alcoholics Anonymous (AA) in association with levels and trajectories of self-forgiveness and other-forgiveness over the 30-month span. Although drinking and self-forgiveness and involvement with AA and other-forgiveness were each associated with each other in a salutary fashion, neither involvement with AA nor drinking were observed to predict any of the trajectories of the forgiveness variables (i.e., forgiveness changing over time). Krentzman et al. (2018) examined the association of the forgiveness variables with each other over the 30-month span. Levels of self-forgiveness were consistently lower than were the levels of other-forgiveness, but self-forgiveness increased more quickly over time. Also, the predictive effect of other-forgiveness on self-forgiveness was twice as strong as was the predictive effect of self-forgiveness on other-forgiveness.

The two new studies, in this category, identified in the updated review conducted for this chapter were both conducted by Charzyńska and colleagues. Charzyńska et al. (2018), in a study of alcohol dependent individuals who were receiving outpatient therapy, examined forgiveness (self-, other-, and feeling forgiven by God) and gratitude trajectories over the course of three time-points. That is, the beginning of treatment, after treatment completion (about 5–7 weeks later), and about 6 months later. In relation to other-forgiveness and feeling forgiven by God, self-forgiveness was observed to be the lowest at treatment entry, and for most of the patients low self-forgiveness did not change whether during or after therapy. This finding led the authors to suggest, while citing the work of Webb and colleagues (see Webb, Hirsch, et al., 2011; Webb et al., 2006), support for the notion that self-forgiveness may be the most difficult dimension of forgiveness to achieve, when considering forgiveness in the context of alcohol addiction recovery. Otherwise, mixed results were observed, such that no obvious patterns in the trajectories could be observed. Although those with high initial levels of forgiveness and gratitude tended to maintain them over time, individuals sufficiently differed in their levels of such at treatment entry, as well as during and after therapy.

Lastly, Charzyńska et al. (2020), in a matched-case study, examined the association of self-forgiveness, other-forgiveness, feeling forgiven by God, and gratitude with health-related quality of life in the context of alcohol-dependent individuals at outpatient treatment entry versus such individuals who have never been in therapy (but were receiving detoxification treatment). Regarding forgiveness, those individuals who had never been in outpatient therapy, had higher levels of self-forgiveness and feeling forgiven by God, but not other-forgiveness, as compared to those who were starting such treatment. In the context of mental health related quality of life (MHQoL), for those never in outpatient treatment, higher levels of self-forgiveness and feeling forgiven by God were associated with better MHQoL. The authors suggested that for those who have never been in therapy (and perhaps are not interested in therapy), self-forgiveness and feeling forgiven by God may be protective of mental health.

*Alcohol Among Individuals Not in Treatment (*n *= 7).*

Ianni et al. (2010), observed shame to be a moderator of the association of forgiveness with alcohol misuse among college students. Self-forgiveness was associated with less alcohol misuse, but only among those students who also had high levels of shame. Webb and Brewer (2010a) observed self-forgiveness and feeling forgiven by God (but not other-forgiveness) to be associated with negative consequences of alcohol use (but not quantity or frequency of use) among college students, as well as better levels of variables associated with the Alcoholics Anonymous recovery slogan, HALT. That is, lower levels of excessive hunger, anger, loneliness, and excessive tiredness – issues thought to be risk factors for relapse in the Twelve-Step Model of addiction recovery. Webb and Brewer (2010b) examined, among college students likely to be hazardous/harmful drinkers, associations of self-forgiveness, other-forgiveness, and feeling forgiven by God with physical health status, mental health status, somatic symptoms, health behavior, social support, and interpersonal functioning. Self-forgiveness was associated with better scores on each of the measures of health (though only marginally with physical health status). Feeling forgiven by God was associated with better social support and better interpersonal functioning, only. And, other-forgiveness was not associated with any of the measures of health. Webb et al. (2012) examined the role of constructive social support versus social undermining as mediators of the association of forgiveness with alcohol related outcomes among college students. Social undermining (but not constructive social support) was observed to play a role in the forgiveness-alcohol association. Such that, for each of self-forgiveness and feeling forgiven by God (but not other-forgiveness) a beneficial association with consumption, dependence symptoms, negative consequences of use, and risk for relapse operated through fewer perceptions of socially undermining behavior from others.

Webb et al. (2013) examined associations of self-forgiveness, other-forgiveness, and feeling forgiven by God with alcohol related outcomes among college students, as mediated by social support and mental health. The alcohol related outcomes again consisted of overall problems with alcohol, consumption, dependence symptoms, negative consequences, and risk of relapse. Self-forgiveness was associated with four of the five outcomes (not consumption) mainly through better mental health status, and feeling forgiven by God maintained a direct only association (i.e., after accounting for the potential mediators) with overall problems, dependence symptoms, and negative consequences. Other-forgiveness was not associated with any of the five alcohol related dependent variables. Lastly, for self-forgiveness, social support and mental health both played a mediating role in association with negative consequences. Ellingwood et al. (2018) examining differences in forgiveness (and self-compassion) among college student binge drinkers, social drinkers, and nondrinkers found no differences in self-forgiveness, other-forgiveness, or forgiveness of uncontrollable situations. However, drinkers (i.e., binge drinkers and social drinkers combined together as one group for analysis) had *higher* levels of self-forgiveness as compared to nondrinkers. Lastly, a new study identified in the updated review conducted for this chapter was in the context of intimate partner violence. Katerndahl et al. (2019), using two multiple time series studies of partner violence, developed a mathematical model seeking to address and predict day-to-day violence between partners in male-female relationships. Increased forgiveness and reduced alcohol use were predictive of less violence for females, but had little effect on violence for males. Yet, in some situations, if the female partner reduced her violent behavior, it was associated with the male partner reducing his behavior related to violence and stalking.

Forgiveness, Alcohol Use, and Other Substance Use

Nine studies have been conducted in the context of the association of forgiveness with alcohol and other substance use. Eight of these nine studies were conducted in the context of individuals being in treatment (at least having started treatment) for substance use problems and the ninth was conducted among individuals in a non-treatment based setting among undergraduate college students.

*Alcohol and Other Substances Among Individuals in Treatment (*n *= 8)*

Brenneis (2001), in a study of clergy seeking treatment for substance use problems or compulsive behavioral problems, found other-forgiveness to be associated with both systolic and diastolic blood pressure in a problematic manner. Lin et al. (2004) compared forgiveness therapy (i.e., other-forgiveness) against treatment as usual among people in residential treatment for substance use problems (whether alcohol or other drugs). Forgiveness therapy was associated with a variety of beneficial health related outcomes including less vulnerability to drug use. Benda and Belcher (2006) examined other-forgiveness in the context of many other psychosocial variables when assessing a broad structural equation based model of said variables in association with alcohol and other drug use, among homeless veterans receiving inpatient treatment in a Domiciliary program at a Veterans Affairs Medical Center. When other-forgiveness was added to the analytical model, the nature of the associations among variables changed; such that, other-forgiveness may be "a salubrious experience in later life that ameliorates adverse feelings such as distress and depression, which may result from insecure caregiver attachments and childhood maltreatment that lead to alcohol and drug abuse" (p. 162). Lyons et al. (2011) examined self-forgiveness, other-forgiveness, receiving forgiveness from others, and receiving forgiveness from God as predictors of resentment and as mediators of the association of spirituality with purpose in life among individuals in substance use treatment. Each dimension of forgiveness measured was associated with less resentment. And, each dimension, except other-forgiveness, was observed to play a role, as a mediator, in the association of daily spiritual experiences with purpose in life. Also, the association of Twelve-Step-Model-based spiritual beliefs with purpose in life was mediated by receiving forgiveness from God.

Deane et al. (2012) examined various predictors of treatment dropout at 3 months, including self-forgiveness and other-forgiveness. Self-forgiveness was associated with higher odds for dropping out of treatment, whereas other-forgiveness was not. Langman and Chung (2013) examined various predictors of PTSD symptoms and psychological comorbidity, including self-forgiveness, other-forgiveness, and forgiveness of uncontrollable situations among recovering individuals in residential treatment and in outpatient treatment. No forgiveness-based associations were observed. McGaffin et al. (2013) examined the association of guilt and shame with self-forgiveness among individuals in residential treatment for substance use problems, as mediated by self-acceptance, empathy, and conciliatory behavior. Self-acceptance was found to mediate the association with self-forgiveness for both guilt and shame. However, in the context of guilt, the association was salutary, whereas for shame the association was deleterious (i.e., ↑ shame → ↓ self-acceptance → ↓ self-forgiveness). Lastly, in a new study identified in the updated review conducted for this chapter, Kerlin (2019) examined relationships among other-forgiveness, attachment styles, and mental health among women in residential treatment for substance use problems. Regarding forgiveness, scores on the revenge and avoidance subscales of the TRIM-12 measure of other-forgiveness (see McCullough et al., 1998) improved from treatment entry to 90 days, and continued for avoidance at a 180-day assessment. Also, at treatment entry, higher levels of avoidance of intimacy with God were associated with higher levels of revenge. And, at 90 days, higher levels of anxiety and anxiety about abandonment by God were associated with higher levels of avoidance.

*Alcohol and Other Substances Among Individuals Not in Treatment (*n = *1)*

Dangel and Webb (2018) examined the association of forgiveness with alcohol related problems and drug related problems, as mediated by psychache, depressive symptoms, and hopelessness, among college students who self-identified with both a history of drinking alcohol and using illicit drugs. Psychache and depressive symptoms (but not hopelessness) were observed as mediators of the association with both alcohol problems and drug problems in the context of each of the dimensions of forgiveness measured. However, for self-forgiveness and forgiveness of uncontrollable situations, the associations were salubrious and for other-forgiveness the associations were deleterious. That is, the former were associated with less psychological distress and in turn fewer substance related problems, whereas the latter was associated with more psychological distress and in turn more substance related problems.

Forgiveness, Alcohol Use, and/or Other Substance Use: Moral Injury and Sexual Abuse

*Moral Injury (*n = *3)*

Three studies have been conducted examining moral injury and outcomes related to alcohol and/or other substance use problems among military personnel, drawn from a community-based sample. In these studies, moral injury is treated as a composite variable comprised of feelings of guilt, feelings of shame, difficulties with self-forgiveness, difficulties with other-forgiveness, and becoming withdrawn. Battles et al. (2018) observed moral injury to be a mediator of the association of morally-injurious experiences with hazardous alcohol use. Braitman et al. (2018) observed moral injury to be associated with alcohol and/or drug problems. And, Kelley et al. (2019) likewise found that moral injury was associated with hazardous alcohol use.

*Sexual Abuse (*n = *1)*

A single study has been published in the context of sexual abuse. Kerlin and Sosin (2017) conducted a qualitative study of ten females, who had completed a residential treatment program, in recovery from childhood sexual abuse, including resultant substance problems, and found other-forgiveness and self-forgiveness to be important factors.

Forgiveness and Other Substance Use

Six studies have been conducted examining the association of forgiveness with substances other than alcohol as the focal point of the study. Two of these six studies were in the context of nicotine as a problematic substance, and four were regarding the use hallucinogens as a potential complement to health – one in the context of psychotherapy with cancer patients, two in the context of addiction, and one in the context of otherwise healthy participants.

*Nicotine (*n *= 2)*

Wohl and Thompson (2011) examined state-based self-forgiveness in the context of Prochaska and DiClemente's model of the Stages of Change (see Prochaska & DiClemente, 1986, 2019) and found a negative association with smoking behavior change among undergraduate students. That is, "self-forgiveness was associated with a reduction in the positive impact of acknowledging smoking's negative effects on motivation to quit" and "predicted the likelihood of being in the preparation compared to the contemplation stage of change" (Wohl & Thompson, 2011, p. 361). In a new study identified in the updated review conducted for this chapter, Hittner et al. (2020) examined substance use, personality variables (including forgiveness), and gender as predictors of e-cigarette use among undergraduate students. Regarding the forgiveness variables, other-forgiveness (but not self-forgiveness or forgiveness of uncontrollable situations) was observed to be negatively associated with e-cigarette use; such that, e-cigarette users were less likely to be forgiving of others.

*Hallucinogens (*n *= 4)*

Three studies regarding psilocybin (a drug with addictive potential) and its *beneficial* effect on levels of forgiveness and thus health have been conducted and reported in the scientific literature. Belser et al. (2017) examined psilocybin-assisted psychotherapy among cancer patients and found it to be associated with other-forgiveness in four of 13 cases, with one case also associated with self-forgiveness. Bogenschutz et al. (2018) examined psilocybin-assisted psychotherapy for alcohol use disorder and found it to be associated with other-forgiveness and self-forgiveness in one of three cases. Griffiths et al. (2018) found psilocybin together with a spiritual practices program to be associated with other-forgiveness among otherwise healthy participants. Lastly, in a new study identified in the updated review conducted for this chapter, Apud (2019) conducted a qualitative study of four individuals being treated for addiction with Ayahuasca, "an Amazon psychoactive compound traditionally used for spiritual, religious, and medical purposes" (p. 133). During the treatment process, two of the four cases were found to have engaged in self-forgiveness with a beneficial effect.

Forgiveness in the Context of Others' Use of Substances

Three studies have been conducted examining forgiveness among those impacted by the problematic use of substances by others. Osterndorf et al. (2011) examined the effect of forgiveness therapy (i.e., other-forgiveness) among adult children of alcoholics. The outcome variables measured included state forgiveness of others, anxiety, depression, anger, self-esteem, and positive relationships with others. Improvements, following forgiveness therapy, on each of these outcome measures were observed, except for anxiety. Scherer et al. (2012) reported two studies, conducted among undergraduate college students, examining associations among state and trait-based other-forgiveness, trust, family cohesion, and perception of another's drinking refusal self-efficacy among people who had a family member who misused alcohol. In one of the studies, trust and state-based other-forgiveness toward a misusing family member were lower when compared to levels of such toward a non-misusing family member. In the second study, beneficial associations were observed; such that, trait-based other-forgiveness and family cohesion were associated with state-based other-forgiveness, which was associated with trust, which was associated – all in sequence – with family members' perception of the drinking refusal self-efficacy of the misusing member of the family. Lastly, Kim and Lee (2014) examined the effect of forgiveness therapy (i.e., other-forgiveness) on the well-being of women whose husbands struggled with alcohol use. Following the intervention, other-forgiveness was associated with better resilience and self-esteem, and more spirituality among participants in the treatment group, as opposed to a control group.

Forgiveness and Compulsive Behaviors

Six studies have been conducted examining the association of forgiveness with behavioral addiction, or compulsive behavioral sets. One study in the context of gambling, the only non-substance related addiction currently recognized by the DSM system (see Chapter 2), three in the context of sexual behavior, and two in the context of problematic internet use.

*Gambling (*n *= 1)*

Squires et al. (2012) examined the role of state-based self-forgiveness in the association of gambling pathology with readiness to change among undergraduate students. Higher levels of gambling pathology were found to be associated with lower levels of self-forgiveness, which, in turn, were associated with higher levels of readiness to change.

*Sexual Behavior (*n *= 3)*

Turner (2008) discussed forgiveness in the context of case studies regarding women struggling with compulsive sexual behavior. Self-forgiveness and other-forgiveness were concluded to be meaningful contributors to successful treatment, along with developing the capacity to bond, tolerating painful disclosure, and being accountable and resilient. Wagner (2009) also described a case study wherein other-forgiveness and self-acceptance were concluded to be meaningful contributors to healing for a man struggling with substance and sexual addiction. Hook et al. (2015) examined associations among state-based-self-forgiveness, shame/guilt, and hypersexual behavior among undergraduate college students. Self-forgiveness was observed to be associated with less shame/guilt, which, in turn was associated with less hypersexual behavior.

*Internet Use (*n *= 2)*

Arslan (2017) examined the association of perceived psychologically abusive parental behaviors with internet addiction among undergraduate students, as mediated by forgiveness and mindfulness. Self-forgiveness, other-forgiveness, and forgiveness of uncontrollable situations were summed together as a total forgiveness score and found to mediate the association between psychological maltreatment and internet addiction. Wang and Qi (2017) examined associations among harsh parenting, problematic internet use, child emotional dysregulation, and child other-forgiveness among parents and their middle school children. For those children with low levels of other-forgiveness for their harsh parents, harsh parenting was associated with emotional dysregulation (i.e., a moderation-based analysis), whereas for those children with high levels of other-forgiveness toward their harsh parents, harsh parenting was not associated with emotional dysregulation.

Forgiveness, Substance Use, and Suicidal Behavior

One study has been published examining forgiveness in the context of addictive behavior and suicidal behavior. Given the concomitant role of addictive behavior and suicidal behavior in the modeling of the Forgiveness–Addiction–Recovery Association presented in Chapter 5, including the view of suicidal behavior as addictive behavior presented in Chapter 2, this single study is briefly presented here, as well as in Chapter 7.Webb (2018) examined the associations of self-forgiveness, other-forgiveness, forgiveness of uncontrollable situations, and feeling forgiven by God with suicidal behavior among college student problematic drinkers, as mediated by alcohol problems, depressive symptoms, and psychache – in sequence. Self-forgiveness, forgiveness of uncontrollable situations, and feeling forgiven by God were each associated with less suicidal behavior, largely through fewer depressive symptoms and/or less psychache. However, other-forgiveness was associated with higher levels of suicidal behavior, operating through higher levels of psychache.

Forgiveness as a Factor in Addictive Behavior

Of the now 51 empirical, data-driven studies published in the peer-reviewed, scientific, psychological literature, 44 or 86.27 percent report a salubrious association (i.e., 44 / 51 = .8627), 9 or 17.65 percent report a deleterious association (i.e., 9 / 51 = .1765), and 1 or 1.96 percent report no forgiveness-based associations observed (i.e., 1 / 51 = .0196). Of note, 44 + 9 + 1 = 54 studies. This is because three studies are counted twice, as they reported both salubrious and deleterious associations. Also, of these 51 studies, 31 or 60.78 percent were conducted in clinical settings (i.e., 31 / 51 = .6078), 14 or 27.45 percent were conducted among college students (i.e., 14 / 51 = .2745), and 6 or 11.76 percent were conducted among community-based participants (i.e., 6 / 51 = .1176).

A few themes can be noticed when seeking to understand the nature of forgiveness as a factor in addictive behavior. Although multiple dimensions of forgiveness are associated with various aspects of addiction, including other health related variables in the context of addiction, it appears that self-forgiveness may be the most consistent. Likewise, when levels of differing dimensions of forgiveness are reported and compared to one another, it appears that self-forgiveness is consistently lowest (though not always). In this regard, when considering forgiveness in the context of addiction, self-forgiveness may be the most difficult to attain, and without self-forgiveness, full recovery may be difficult to achieve (see Charzyńska et al., 2018; Webb, Hirsch, et al., 2011; Webb et al., 2009; Webb et al., 2006).

Unless indicated otherwise (see above), the studies largely have been cross-sectional in design (i.e., data collected at one point in time) and mostly have been conducted in the context of adults (ranging from college students through middle age). Also, these studies are typically conducted in the context of trait-based or dispositional forgiveness. Although trait-based forgiveness (as opposed to state-based forgiveness) is thought most likely to be the level of forgiveness associated with health-related variables in general (Worthington et al., 2001), state-based forgiveness has been examined in the context of addictive behavior in relatively few cases.

Of note, as indicated above, most of the studies have been conducted in clinical settings (about 61 percent), followed by college students (about 27 percent), and community-based participants (about 12 percent). Generally speaking, this is very good news given the common criticism of psychological research too-often being conducted in the context of white, male, undergraduate students and the resultant difficulties associated with applying such results to the wider population. Now, some might say that 27 percent of studies having been conducted among college students is not very good news (even though it is *far less* than what has been done in clinical settings); given another common criticism that college students are a sample of convenience. However, the reality is that alcohol and drug use among college students is common (probably ubiquitous); indeed, so much so that a culture of substance use problems is considered to exist (The National Center on Addiction and Substance Abuse at Columbia University, 2007). Problematic drinking among college students has been described as part of a "widespread and persistent public health and safety problem" (U. S. Department of Health and Human Services, 2007, p. 1). As such, college student problematic drinking and drug use is in need of focused and persistent scientific attention (see Webb et al., 2013; see also, Jackson et al, 2006). Indeed, in this regard, college students are not a sample of convenience.

Lastly, the overwhelming majority of the studies (86.27 percent) support the long-held anecdotal assumption (since the 1930s; Alcoholics Anonymous, 2001; see also, Chapter 9) that forgiveness, in its multiple dimensions, plays a constructive, beneficial role in addiction recovery. However, it is important to recognize that not all studies are supportive of such. Of the nine studies (17.65 percent) finding evidence for a deleterious association, self-forgiveness (five studies) and other-forgiveness (four studies) were found to contribute nearly equally to the problematic outcomes. Although it appears that forgiveness is most likely a useful tool in addressing addiction recovery, it will be important to fully understand those conditions and instances when it may not be.

References

Alcoholics Anonymous (AA) (2001). *Alcoholics Anonymous* (4th ed.). New York, NY: Author. See https://www.aa.org/pages/en_US/alcoholics-anonymous.

Apud, I. (2019). Ayahuasca en el tratamiento de adicciones Estudio de cuatro casos tratados en IDEAA, desde una perspectiva interdisciplinaria = Ayahuasca in the treatment of addictions Study of four cases treated in IDEAA, using an interdisciplinary perspective. *Interdisciplinaria Revista de Psicología y Ciencias Afines*, 36(1), 133–154. doi:10.16888/interd.2019.36.1.10.

Arslan, G. (2017). Psychological maltreatment, forgiveness, mindfulness, and internet addiction among young adults: A study of mediation effect. *Computers in Human Behavior*, 72, 57–66. doi:10.1016/j.chb.2017.02.037.

Battles, A. R., Bravo, A. J., Kelley, M. L., White, T. D., Braitman, A. L., & Hamrick, H. C. (2018). Moral injury and PTSD as mediators of the associations between morally injurious experiences and mental health and substance use. *Traumatology*, 24(4), 246–254. doi:10.1037/trm0000153.

Belser, A. B., Agin-Liebes, G., Swift, T. C., Terrana, S., Devenot, N., Friedman, H. L., ... Ross, S. (2017). Patient experiences of psilocybin-assisted psychotherapy: An interpretative phenomenological analysis. *Journal of Humanistic Psychology*, 57(4), 354–388. doi:10.1177/0022167817706884.

Benda, B. B., & Belcher, J. R. (2006). Alcohol and other drug problems among homeless veterans: A life-course theory of forgiveness. *Alcoholism Treatment Quarterly*, 24(1–2), 147–170. doi:10.1300/J020v24n01_09.

Bogenschutz, M. P., Podrebarac, S. K., Duane, J. H., Amegadzie, S. S., Malone, T. C., Owens, L. T., ... Mennenga, S. E. (2018). Clinical interpretations of patient experience in a trial of psilocybin-assisted psychotherapy for alcohol use disorder. *Frontiers in Psychopharmacology*, 9, 100. doi:10.3389/fphar.2018.00100.

Braitman, A. L., Battles, A. R., Kelley, M. L., Hamrick, H. C., Cramer, R. J., Ehlke, S., & Bravo, A. J. (2018). Psychometric properties of a Modified Moral Injury Questionnaire in a military population. *Traumatology*, 24(4), 301–312. doi:10.1037/trm0000158.

Braun, B., Weinland, C., Kornhuber, J., & Lenz, B. (2018). Religiosity, guilt, altruism and forgiveness in alcohol dependence: Results of a cross-sectional and prospective cohort study. *Alcohol and Alcoholism*, 53(4), 426–434. doi:10.1093/alcalc/agy026.

Brenneis, M. J. (2001). The relationship between forgiveness and physical health indicators in recovering members of the clergy. *Journal of Ministry in Addiction & Recovery*, 7(2), 43–59. doi:10.1300/J048v07n02_04.

Charzyńska, E. (2015). Sex differences in spiritual coping, forgiveness, and gratitude before and after a basic alcohol addiction treatment program. *Journal of Religion and Health*, 54(5), 1931–1949. doi:10.1007/s10943-015-0002-0.

Charzyńska, E., Gruszczyńska, E., & Heszen, I. (2018). Forgiveness and gratitude trajectories among persons undergoing alcohol addiction therapy. *Addiction Research & Theory*, 26(4), 282–293. doi:10.1080/16066359.2018.1429595.

Charzyńska, E., Gruszczyńska, E., & Heszen-Celińska, I. (2020). The role of forgiveness and gratitude in the quality of life of alcohol-dependent persons. *Addiction Research & Theory*, 28 (2), 173–182. doi:10.1080/16066359.2019.1642332.

Dangel, T., & Webb, J. R. (2018). Forgiveness and substance use problems among college students: Psychache, depressive symptoms, and hopelessness as mediators. *Journal of Substance Use*, 23(6), 618–625. doi:10.1080/14659891.2018.1489003.

Deane, F. P., Wootton, D. J., Hsu, C.-I., & Kelly, P. J. (2012). Predicting dropout in the first 3 months of 12-step residential drug and alcohol treatment in an Australian sample. *Journal of Studies on Alcohol and Drugs*, 73(2), 216–225.

Derogatis, L. R., & Melisaratos, N. (1983). The Brief Symptom Inventory: An introductory report. *Psychological Medicine*, 13, 595–605.

Ellingwood, L., Espinoza, M.-A., Acevedo, M., & Olson, L. E. (2018). College student drinkers have higher self-compassion scores than nondrinkers. *International Journal of Mental Health and Addiction*. doi:10.1007/s11469-018-9919-3.

Griffiths, R. R., Johnson, M. W., Richards, W. A., Richards, B. D., Jesse, R., MacLean, K. A., … Klinedinst, M. A. (2018). Psilocybin-occasioned mystical-type experience in combination with meditation and other spiritual practices produces enduring positive changes in psychological functioning and in trait measures of prosocial attitudes and behaviors. *Journal of Psychopharmacology*, 32(1), 49–69. doi:10.1177/0269881117731279.

Hittner, J. B., Penmetsa, N., Bianculli, V., & Swickert, R. (2020). Personality and substance use correlates of e-cigarette use in college students. *Personality and Individual Differences*, 152. doi:10.1016/j.paid.2019.109605.

Hook, J. N., Farrell, J. E., Davis, D. E., Van Tongeren, D. R., Griffin, B. J., Grubbs, J., … Bedics, J. D. (2015). Self-forgiveness and hypersexual behavior. *Sexual Addiction & Compulsivity*, 22 (1), 59–70. doi:10.1080/10720162.2014.1001542.

Ianni, P. A., Hart, K. E., Hibbard, S., & Carroll, M. (2010). The association between self-forgiveness and alcohol misuse depends on the severity of drinker's shame: Toward a buffering model. *Addictive Disorders & Their Treatment*, 9(3), 106–111. doi:10.1097/ADT.0b013e3181f158cd.

Jackson, K. M., Sher, K. J., & Park, A. (2006). Drinking among college students: Consumption and consequences. In M. Galanter (Ed.), *Alcohol problems in adolescents and young adults: Epidemiology, neurobiology, prevention, and treatment* (pp. 85–117). New York, NY: Springer.

Katerndahl, D., Burge, S., Ferrer, R., Becho, J., Wood, R., & Villacampa, M. D. M. (2019). Agent-based modeling of day-to-day intimate partner violence. *Nonlinear Dynamics, Psychology, and Life Sciences*, 23(2), 275–296.

Kelley, M. L., Braitman, A. L., White, T. D., & Ehlke, S. J. (2019). Sex differences in mental health symptoms and substance use and their association with moral injury in veterans. *Psychological Trauma: Theory, Research, Practice, and Policy*, 11(3), 337–344. doi:10.1037/tra0000407.

Kerlin, A. M. (2019). Women in Christian substance abuse treatment; forgiveness, attachment styles, and improvements in co-occurring mental health symptoms. *Journal of Religion and Health*. doi:10.1007/s10943-019-00948-x.

Kerlin, A. M., & Sosin, L. S. (2017). Recovery from childhood sexual abuse: A spiritually integrated qualitative exploration of 10 women's journeys. *Journal of Spirituality in Mental Health*, 19(3), 189–209. doi:10.1080/19349637.2016.1247411.

Kim, H. K., & Lee, M. (2014). Effectiveness of forgiveness therapy on resilience, self-esteem, and spirituality of wives of alcoholics. *Journal of Korean Academy of Nursing*, 44(3), 237–247. doi:10.4040/jkan.2014.44.3.237.

Knight, J. R., Sherritt, L., Harris, S. K., Holder, D. W., Kulig, J., Shrier, L. A., ... Chang, G. (2007). Alcohol use and religiousness/spirituality among adolescents. *Southern Medical Journal*, 100(4), 349–355. doi:10.1097/SMJ.0b013e3180316a32.

Krentzman, A. R. (2017). Longitudinal differences in spirituality and religiousness between men and women in treatment for alcohol use disorders. *Psychology of Religion and Spirituality*, 9 (Suppl 1), S11–S21. doi:10.1037/rel0000096.

Krentzman, A. R., Cranford, J. A., & Robinson, E. A. R. (2013). Multiple dimensions of spirituality in recovery: A lagged mediational analysis of Alcoholics Anonymous' principal theoretical mechanism of behavior change. *Substance Abuse*, 34(1), 20–32. doi:10.1080/08897077.2012.691449.

Krentzman, A. R., Webb, J. R., Jester, J. M., & Harris, J. I. (2018). Longitudinal relationship between forgiveness of self and forgiveness of others among individuals with alcohol use disorders. *Psychology of Religion and Spirituality*, 10(2), 128–137. doi:10.1037/rel0000152.

Krentzman, A. R., Strobbe, S., Harris, J. I., Jester, J. M., & Robinson, E. A. R. (2017). Decreased drinking and Alcoholics Anonymous are associated with different dimensions of spirituality. *Psychology of Religion and Spirituality*, 9(Suppl 1), S40–S48. doi:10.1037/rel0000121.supp.

Langman, L., & Chung, M. C. (2013). The relationship between forgiveness, spirituality, traumatic guilt and posttraumatic stress disorder (PTSD) among people with addiction. *Psychiatric Quarterly*, 84(1), 11–26. doi:10.1007/s11126-012-9223-5.

Lin, W. F., Mack, D., Enright, R. D., Krahn, D., & Baskin, T. W. (2004). Effects of forgiveness therapy on anger, mood, and vulnerability to substance use among inpatient substance-dependent clients. *Journal of Consulting and Clinical Psychology*, 72(6), 1114–1121. doi:10.1037/0022-006X.72.6.1114.

Lyons, G. C. B., Deane, F. P., Caputi, P., & Kelly, P. J. (2011). Spirituality and the treatment of substance use disorders: An exploration of forgiveness, resentment and purpose in life. *Addiction Research & Theory*, 19(5), 459–469. doi:10.3109/16066359.2011.555022.

McCullough, M. E., Rachal, K. C., Sandage, S. J., Worthington, E. L., Jr., Brown, S. W., & Hight, T. L. (1998). Interpersonal forgiving in close relationships: II. Theoretical elaboration and measurement. *Journal of Personality and Social Psychology*, 75(6), 1586–1603. doi:10.1037/0022-3514.75.6.1586.

McGaffin, B. J., Lyons, G. C. B., & Deane, F. P. (2013). Self-forgiveness, shame, and guilt in recovery from drug and alcohol problems. *Substance Abuse*, 34(4), 396–404. doi:10.1080/08897077.2013.781564.

The National Center on Addiction and Substance Abuse at Columbia University (2007). *Wasting the best and the brightest: Substance abuse at America's colleges and universities*. New York, NY: Author. Retrieved December 18, 2020, from https://drugfree.org/reports/wasting-the-best-and-the-brightest-substance-abuse-at-americas-colleges-and-universities/.

Osterndorf, C., Enright, R. D., Holter, A., & Klatt, J. (2011). Treating adult children of alcoholics through forgiveness therapy. *Alcoholism Treatment Quarterly*, 29(3), 274–292. doi:10.1080/07347324.2011.586285.

Prochaska, J. O., & DiClemente, C. C. (1986). Toward a comprehensive model of change. In W. R. Miller & N. Heather (Eds.), *Treating addictive behaviors: Processes of change* (pp. 3–27). New York, NY: Plenum Press.

Prochaska, J. O., & DiClemente, C. C. (2019). The transtheoretical approach. In J. C. Norcross & M. R. Goldfried (Eds.), *Handbook of psychotherapy integration* (3rd ed., pp. 161–183). New York, NY: Oxford University Press.

Robinson, E. A. R., Cranford, J. A., Webb, J. R., & Brower, K. J. (2007). Six-month changes in spirituality, religiousness, and heavy drinking in a treatment-seeking sample. *Journal of Studies on Alcohol and Drugs*, 68(2), 282–290.

Robinson, E. A. R., Krentzman, A. R., Webb, J. R., & Brower, K. J. (2011). Six-month changes in spirituality and religiousness in alcoholics predict drinking outcomes at nine months. *Journal of Studies on Alcohol and Drugs*, 72(4), 660–668.

Scherer, M., Worthington, E. L., Jr., Hook, J. N., & Campana, K. L. (2011). Forgiveness and the bottle: Promoting self-forgiveness in individuals who abuse alcohol. *Journal of Addictive Diseases*, 30(4), 382–395. doi:10.1080/10550887.2011.609804.

Scherer, M., Worthington, E. L., Jr., Hook, J. N., Campana, K. L., West, S. L., & Gartner, A. L. (2012). Forgiveness and cohesion in familial perceptions of alcohol misuse. *Journal of Counseling & Development*, 90(2), 160–168. doi:10.1111/j.1556-6676.2012.00021.x.

Squires, E. C., Sztainert, T., Gillen, N. R., Caouette, J., & Wohl, M. J. A. (2012). The problem with self-forgiveness: Forgiving the self deters readiness to change among gamblers. *Journal of Gambling Studies*, 28(3), 337–350. doi:10.1007/s10899-011-9272-y.

Turner, M. (2008). Female sexual compulsivity: A new syndrome. *Psychiatric Clinics of North America*, 31(4), 713–727. doi:10.1016/j.psc.2008.06.004.

U. S. Department of Health and Human Services (2007). *The Surgeon General's call to action to prevent and reduce underage drinking*. Rockville, MD: U. S. Department of Health and Human Services, Office of the Surgeon General. Retrieved December 18, 2020, from https://www.ncbi.nlm.nih.gov/books/NBK44360/.

Wagner, J. (2009). Sexual Steve: A schema-focused, spiritually based approach. *Journal of Psychology and Christianity*, 28(3), 275–279.

Wang, M., & Qi, W. (2017). Harsh parenting and problematic Internet use in Chinese adolescents: Child emotional dysregulation as mediator and child forgiveness as moderator. *Computers in Human Behavior*, 77, 211–219. doi:10.1016/j.chb.2017.09.005.

Webb, J. R. (2018). Forgiveness, addiction, and suicide. In J. K. Hirsch, E. C. Chang, & J. K. Rabon (Eds.), *A positive psychological approach to suicide: Theory, research, and prevention* (pp. 37–58). New York, NY: Springer.

Webb, J. R., & Brewer, K. (2010a). Forgiveness and college student drinking in Southern Appalachia. *Journal of Substance Use*, 15(6), 417–433. doi:10.3109/14659891003706373.

Webb, J. R., & Brewer, K. (2010b). Forgiveness, health, and problematic drinking among college students in Southern Appalachia. *Journal of Health Psychology*, 15(8), 1257–1266. doi:10.1177/1359105310365177.

Webb, J. R., & Jeter, B. R. (2015). Forgiveness and problematic substance use. In L. L. Toussaint, E. L.Worthington, Jr., & D. R. Williams (Eds.), *Forgiveness and health: Scientific evidence and theories relating forgiveness to better health* (pp. 139–154). New York, NY: Springer.

Webb, J. R., & Toussaint, L. L. (2018). Self-forgiveness as a critical factor in addiction and recovery: A 12-step model perspective. *Alcoholism Treatment Quarterly*, 36(1), 15–31. doi:10.1080/07347324.2017.1391057.

Webb, J. R., & Toussaint, L. L. (2020). Forgiveness, well-being, and mental health. In E. L. Worthington, Jr. & N. G. Wade (Eds.), *Handbook for forgiveness* (2nd ed., pp. 188–197). New York, NY: Routledge.

Webb, J. R., Hill, S. K., & Brewer, K. G. (2012). Dimensions of social support as mediators of the forgiveness-alcohol outcome relationship. *Addictive Disorders & Their Treatment*, 11(2), 64–75. doi:10.1097/ADT.0b013e31822dcd56.

Webb, J. R., Hirsch, J. K., & Toussaint, L. L. (2011). Forgiveness and alcohol problems: A review of the literature and a call for intervention-based research. *Alcoholism Treatment Quarterly*, 29 (3), 245–273. doi:10.1080/07347324.2011.585922.

Webb, J. R., Robinson, E. A. R., & Brower, K. J. (2009). Forgiveness and mental health among people entering outpatient treatment with alcohol problems. *Alcoholism Treatment Quarterly*, 27(4), 368–388. doi:10.1080/07347320903209822.

Webb, J. R., Robinson, E. A. R., & Brower, K. J. (2011). Mental health, not social support, mediates the forgiveness-alcohol outcome relationship. *Psychology of Addictive Behaviors*, 25 (3), 462–473. doi:10.1037/a0022502.

Webb, J. R., Hirsch, J. K., Conway-Williams, E., & Brewer, K. G. (2013). Forgiveness and alcohol problems: Indirect associations involving mental health and social support. *Addiction Research & Theory*, 21(2), 141–153. doi:10.3109/16066359.2012.703267.

Webb, J. R., Robinson, E. A. R., Brower, K. J., & Zucker, R. A. (2006). Forgiveness and alcohol problems among people entering substance abuse treatment. *Journal of Addictive Diseases*, 25(3), 55–67. doi:10.1300/J069v25n03_08.

Wohl, M. J. A., & Thompson, A. (2011). A dark side to self-forgiveness: Forgiving the self and its association with chronic unhealthy behaviour. *British Journal of Social Psychology*, 50(2), 354–364. doi:10.1111/j.2044-8309.2010.02010.x.

Worthington, E. L., Jr., Berry, J. W., & Parrott, L., III. (2001). Unforgiveness, forgiveness, religion, and health. In T. G. Plante & A. C. Sherman (Eds.), *Faith and health: Psychological perspectives* (pp. 107–138). New York, NY: Guilford Press.

7 Research: Forgiveness and Suicidal Behavior

The first scientific study to be published in the psychological literature regarding the association of forgiveness with suicidal behavior was a case study and occurred in 1970 (see Close, 1970). As with forgiveness in the context of addiction (see Chapter 6), Webb and colleagues have periodically published systematic reviews of the published scientific psychological literature seeking to understand and track the nature of the empirical evidence regarding the relationship between forgiveness and suicidal behavior (see Webb, 2018; Webb et al., 2015; Webb & Toussaint, 2020). Through January 12, 2019, the date of the last comprehensive literature search/review, 25 scientific studies focused on the association of forgiveness with suicidal behavior had been published (Webb & Toussaint, 2020). Twenty-four of the 25 studies are briefly described below (upon further reflection, one of the originally identified studies is not sufficiently focused on suicidal behavior), along with ten additional studies from an updated review, and two additional studies overlooked in the previous reviews. In this regard, there are now 36 scientific psychological studies deliberately and explicitly focused on the empirical association of forgiveness with suicidal behavior. The updated review, as with the previous reviews, was conducted by searching the PsycINFO and PUBMED databases using the following search phrase: "forgiv* AND suicid*" and restricted to peer-reviewed journal articles (three of the 36 studies were published in edited books, and one of the studies was an authored book). The ten new studies were retrieved on August 22, 2020 and are otherwise indicated as such in the descriptions below. Also, in an effort to show the progression of the research over the years, the studies are presented largely in chronological order – within each category.

Primary Care (n = 4)

Sansone et al. (2013) examined the association of forgiveness with history of suicide attempts among primary care outpatients. Those participants with a history of attempting suicide (as opposed to those who did not have a history of such) had lower levels of self-forgiveness, other-forgiveness, and forgiveness *by* others, but not forgiveness by God (i.e., there was no difference between the groups for forgiveness by God). Or, in other words, those without a history of attempting suicide had higher levels of said dimensions of forgiveness.

Three studies were conducted, by Hirsch and colleagues, examining forgiveness in the context of suicidal behavior among a sample of rural primary care outpatients. Nsamenang et al. (2013) examined the association of self-forgiveness, other-forgiveness, and feeling forgiven by God with suicidal behavior in this sample, as serially mediated (i.e., in sequence) by depression, thwarted belongingness, and perceived burdensomeness. Each of the three dimensions of forgiveness measured were associated with less suicidal behavior, operating through less depression. Also, self-forgiveness and other-forgiveness (but not feeling forgiven by God) were associated with less suicidal behavior through less depression, less thwarted belongingness, and less perceived burdensomeness, in sequence. And, self-forgiveness and other-forgiveness (but not feeling forgiven by God) were also associated with less suicidal behavior through less thwarted belongingness and less perceived burdensomeness, in sequence. Chang et al. (2014) examined the relationship between domestic abuse and suicidal behavior as mediated by self-forgiveness and other-forgiveness. Self-forgiveness (but not other-forgiveness) was found to play a role in the relationship between domestic abuse and suicidal behavior; such that, self-forgiveness may be important in addressing suicidal behavior among victims of domestic abuse. Rabon et al. (2019) examined the association of self-forgiveness, other-forgiveness, and feeling forgiven by God with suicidal behavior as mediated by future orientation and found future orientation to play a role in the association of each forgiveness dimension with less suicidal behavior.

Community-Based Settings (*n* = 3)

In one of the aforementioned overlooked studies (i.e., in terms of contributing to the overall tally), Hirsch et al. (2017) explored bivariate associations between forgiveness and suicidal behavior among a United States national-level community-based sample (through Amazon's MTURK system; https://www.mturk.com/). Current self-forgiveness and future oriented other-forgiveness were each individually associated with lower levels of lifetime history of suicidal behavior, less suicidal ideation in the past year, and lower likelihood of a future suicide attempt. In a new study identified in the updated review conducted for this chapter, Hall et al. (2020) examined the association of multiple dimensions of spirituality (i.e., ritualistic, theistic, and existential spirituality) with suicidal behavior among the same community-based sample recruited through MTURK as described immediately above, as mediated by self-forgiveness and psychache, in sequence. The association of existential spirituality (but not ritualistic or theistic spirituality) with suicidal behavior was mediated by self-forgiveness and psychache; such that, existential spirituality was associated with higher levels of self-forgiveness, which, in turn, were associated with lower levels of psychache, which, in turn, were associated with lower levels of suicidal behavior (i.e., ↑existential spirituality → ↑self-forgiveness → ↓psychache → ↓suicidal behavior). In another new study identified in the updated review conducted for this chapter, Jung et al. (2019) examined the association of depression with suicidality among a community-based sample, as moderated by self-forgiveness, other-forgiveness, and forgiveness of uncontrollable situations. Self-forgiveness (but not other-forgiveness or forgiveness of uncontrollable situations) was found to be a protective factor in the relationship between depression and suicidality.

College Students (*n* = 4)

Hirsch et al. (2011) examined the association of self-forgiveness, other-forgiveness, and feeling forgiven by God with suicidal behavior among a sample of ethnically diverse college students, as mediated by depression. Self-forgiveness was associated with less depression, which, in turn, was associated with less suicidal behavior. Whereas, other-forgiveness was directly associated with less suicidal behavior *after* accounting for depression (i.e., depression did not mediate the effect). Feeling forgiven by God was not observed to be associated with suicidal behavior directly or indirectly. Hirsch et al. (2012) examined the association of anger expression with suicidal behavior among a sample of ethnically diverse college students, as moderated by self-forgiveness, other-forgiveness, and feeling forgiven by God. Self-forgiveness (but not other-forgiveness or feeling forgiven by God) moderated the association of inward and outward anger with suicidal behavior. That is, "individuals who tend to *internalise* their anger may be at less risk for suicidal behaviour if they are able to forgive themselves. … For those high in self-forgiveness, there is little effect of *outward* anger on suicidal behaviour" (emphasis added; Hirsch et al., 2012, p. 286).

Dangel et al. (2018) examined the association of self-forgiveness, other-forgiveness, and forgiveness of uncontrollable situations with suicidal behavior among undergraduate college students, as mediated by cynicism and psychache, in sequence. Self-forgiveness and forgiveness of uncontrollable situations each were individually associated with less suicidal behavior, operating through lower levels of psychache. Other-forgiveness was associated with less suicidal behavior, operating through lower levels of cynicism and lower levels of psychache, in sequence. In a new study identified in the updated review conducted for this chapter, Noor and Halabi (2018) reported two experimentally designed studies, conducted among two separate samples of university students, examining the effects of perspective taking on prosocial motivation to forgive a radicalized enemy, in the context of a potential suicide bombing. In the first study, perspective taking was associated with motivation to forgive, versus those who remained objective and detached. In the second study, comparing a low-threat condition to a high-threat condition showed that those participants in the low-threat group were more forgiving of the radicalized enemy than were those in the high-threat group. And, comparing a perspective-taking condition to an objective condition showed that those participants in the perspective-taking condition were more forgiving of the radicalized enemy than were those in the objective condition. Also, "perspective-taking had a significant effect on the tendency to like the target individual. In turn, liking him predicted increased forgiveness [mediation analysis]" (Noor & Halabi, 2018, p. 251).

Military and Moral Injury (n = 6)

Bryan et al. (2015) examined the association of posttraumatic stress with suicide ideation and suicide attempts among military personnel and veterans, as moderated by self-forgiveness. Although self-forgiveness was associated with less posttraumatic stress, and levels of self-forgiveness were lower for those with a history of suicide ideation and attempts, self-forgiveness was not observed to moderate the association of posttraumatic stress with suicide ideation and attempts. Kopacz et al. (2016) examined the association of forgiveness with risk for suicide among veterans with posttraumatic stress disorder and found that lower levels of self-forgiveness, other-forgiveness, and feeling forgiven by God – measured together as total forgiveness – were, indeed, associated with higher levels of suicidal thoughts and attempts. In a new study identified in the updated review conducted for this chapter, Smigelsky et al. (2020) examined the association of religious/spiritual factors with suicidal ideation and suicide attempt history among military veterans. Increased odds for suicidal ideation were associated with a diagnosis of major depressive disorder, a diagnosis of posttraumatic stress disorder, and lower levels of both self-forgiveness (but not forgiveness from others or forgiveness from God) and perceived control over one's life. Increased odds for having attempted suicide were associated with age, a diagnosis of posttraumatic stress disorder, problematic substance use, and with perceptions of punishment from God and a lack of meaning/purpose.

In the following studies regarding moral injury among military veterans, moral injury is treated as a composite variable comprised of feelings of guilt, feelings of shame, difficulties with self-forgiveness, difficulties with other-forgiveness, and becoming withdrawn. Kelley et al. (2019) in a study regarding moral injury and hazardous alcohol use among military personnel (see Chapter 6) also found moral injury to be associated with suicidality. Kelley, Bravo, et al. (2019) examined the association of moral injury with suicidality among combat wounded veterans, as moderated by self-compassion and social connectedness. Regarding the association of self-directed moral injury (including difficulty with self-forgiveness) with suicidality, higher levels of over-identification (considered an aspect of a lack of self-compassion) were observed to strengthen the association. Regarding the association of other-directed moral injury (including difficulty with other-forgiveness) with suicidality, higher levels of mindfulness (considered an aspect of self-compassion) were observed to weaken the association. Higher levels of social connectedness were also observed to weaken the association of other-directed moral injury with suicidality. Levi-Belz et al. (2020) examined the association of potentially morally injurious events with suicidal ideation and behaviors among combat veterans, as moderated by self-forgiveness and perceived social support. Among those veterans with a history of suicidal ideation and suicidal behavior, levels of self-forgiveness and perceived social support were lower than such associations among those veterans without a history of suicidal ideation and suicidal behavior. Also, self-forgiveness and perceived social support were negatively associated with suicidal ideation and behaviors. However, although perceived social support was observed as a moderator, self-forgiveness was not. Of note, each of these last two studies were identified in the updated review conducted for this chapter.

Other Groups (*n* = 4)

Cheavens et al. (2016) examined the association of interpersonal needs with suicidal ideation among older adults and found self-forgiveness to weaken the association of perceived burdensomeness with suicidal ideation. Nagra et al. (2016) examined psychological risk and protective factors of suicidality among people with a history of self-harm. Higher levels of self-forgiveness were associated with lower levels of suicidality, and this association was the strongest of the significant predictors observed (i.e., compared to – in descending order – no mental illness diagnosis, emotion coping, social support, and dismissing attachment). Carpenter et al. (2020) examined associations among self-forgiveness, stigma, posttraumatic stress disorder symptoms, depressive symptoms, and suicidality among firefighters participating in a stigma-reduction workshop. Among other dependent, or outcome variables included in the study, self-forgiveness was associated with (predictive of) less suicidality. Khan et al. (2020) conducted qualitative semi-structured interviews with 17 male survivors of suicide (i.e., they attempted suicide themselves). Themes were observed regarding attempts to cope with attempts by others to demean their masculinity post the suicide attempt. In a subset of cases where suicide was attempted in the context of romantic relationship difficulties, some participants coped by seeking revenge, while others coped by forgiving their partner. Again, each of these last two studies were identified in the updated review conducted for this chapter.

Case Studies (*n* = 5)

Five case studies involving various dimensions of forgiveness have been published. As mentioned at the beginning of this chapter, the very first scientific psychological study published regarding forgiveness in the context of suicidal behavior was conducted by Close (1970). This case described a suicidal client struggling to and finally feeling forgiven by God. Carter (1971) described a personal case where he, as the therapist, struggled with self-forgiveness following the death by suicide of one of his clients.

Carter concluded that "self-forgiveness is very important particularly, if it is coupled with an attempt to learn from the event in a constructive and growth producing way" (1971, p. 289). Bottoms (2000) recounted the death by suicide of his brother and his (i.e., the author's) personal need to and the beneficial process of forgiving him. Freeman and Hayes (2002) discuss the beneficial process and outcome, through family therapy, of the case of an individual who had sought and received forgiveness from his family after attempting to kill them and then die by suicide. Sandage (2010) described the case of family member survivors of a father and daughter who died by suicide (years apart) and their processes of coping and meaning-making. Forgiveness was an important theme for a particular family member survivor, as both the father and the daughter (the family member survivor's sister) had asked to be forgiven in their suicide notes.

Adolescents (n = 4)

Liu et al. (2013) examined the association of victimization with suicidal ideation among seventh and eighth grade students, as moderated by other-forgiveness. For those students with low levels of other-forgiveness the association of victimization with suicidal ideation was stronger than for those students with high levels of other-forgiveness. Or, in other words, those victimized students with higher levels of other-forgiveness had lower levels of suicidal ideation.

Quintana-Orts and colleagues have published three studies examining other-forgiveness in the context of suicide among adolescents. Quintana-Orts and Rey (2018a) found that other-forgiveness weakened the association of depression with suicidal ideation for adolescent boys, but not for adolescent girls. Quintana-Orts and Rey (2018b) found other-forgiveness to moderate the association of bullying with suicidal risk; such that, among those adolescents with higher levels of bullying victimization, those with higher levels of other-forgiveness had lower levels of suicide risk. In a new study identified in the updated review conducted for this chapter, Quintana-Orts et al. (2020) examined the association of cybervictimization with suicidal ideation as mediated by perceived stress and further, other-forgiveness (i.e., benevolence, revenge, and avoidance motivations) as a moderator of said mediating relationship. Perceived stress was observed to mediate the association of cyberbullying with suicidal ideation; such that, cyberbullying was associated with perceived stress, which in turn was associated with suicidal ideation. Regarding other-forgiveness, both revenge and avoidance moderated the association of perceived stress with suicidal ideation; such that, lower levels of each weakened the association between perceived stress and suicidal ideation. Benevolence was not observed to play a moderating role in the relationship between perceived stress and suicidal ideation in the context of cyberbullying.

Bereavement (n = 5)

Groos (2012) conducted 20 qualitative face-to-face semi-structured interviews in the context of suicide bereavement and discussed the notion that during bereavement some individuals may "begin to be desperate for change, realise that they are stuck and at risk, need to do something and can subsequently more deeply engage in healing and a forgiving process to return to self and life" (p. 95). Lee et al. (2017) conducted a qualitative study of family member survivors of suicide and found struggling with other-forgiveness and self-forgiveness to be prominent themes, yet forgiveness remained important for healing. Testoni et al. (2019) conducted a 4-year longitudinal qualitative study of family members of suicide. Prominent themes included a continual struggle with self-blame, and although self-forgiveness was very difficult, other-forgiveness seemed to be facilitated when survivors were able to stop self-blaming.

In a new study identified in the updated review conducted for this chapter, Sever and Ozdemir (2019) conducted a qualitative study of seven academic survivors (two administrators and five faculty members) of a colleague who died by suicide. One participant spoke of asking forgiveness from God on the person's behalf as a personal means of coping in response to the stigmatization of suicide. In another new study identified in the updated review conducted for this chapter, Levi-Belz and Gilo (2020) conducted a study among bereaved individuals following the death of others. The association of self-forgiveness with depression and suicidality was examined among these individuals based on whether the death was in the context of suicide, sudden death not related to suicide, or following expected death. Those participants bereaved in the context of suicide and reporting lower levels of self-forgiveness had higher levels of depression and suicidal ideation as compared to those survivors bereaved in the context of sudden death not related to suicide, and those bereaved by expected death. However, across the different types of loss, those bereaved individuals with higher levels of self-forgiveness had lower levels of depression, and suicidal ideation.

Addiction and Suicide (n = 1)

As discussed in Chapter 6 (and repeated here), one study has been published examining forgiveness in the context of addictive behavior and suicidal behavior. Given the concomitant role of addictive behavior and suicidal behavior in the modeling of the Forgiveness–Addiction–Recovery Association presented in Chapter 5, including the view of suicidal behavior as addictive behavior presented in Chapter 2, this single study is briefly presented here, again. Also, this is the second of the aforementioned overlooked studies (i.e., in terms of contributing to the overall tally in the context of suicidal behavior). Webb (2018) examined the associations of self-forgiveness, other-forgiveness, forgiveness of uncontrollable situations, and feeling forgiven by God with suicidal behavior among college student problematic drinkers, as mediated by alcohol problems, depressive symptoms, and psychache – in sequence. Self-forgiveness, forgiveness of uncontrollable situations, and feeling forgiven by God were each associated with less suicidal behavior, largely through fewer depressive symptoms and/or less psychache. However, other-forgiveness was associated with higher levels of suicidal behavior, operating through higher levels of psychache.

Forgiveness as a Factor in Suicidal Behavior

Of the now 36 published scientific psychological studies focused on addressing forgiveness in the context of suicidal behavior, all 36 or 100 percent report a constructive or beneficial association. Of note, one of these studies reported both a beneficial and a deleterious association (i.e., Webb, 2018). Multiple dimensions of forgiveness have been measured across studies and within many studies; however, when only one dimension is included in any particular study, it appears self-forgiveness, followed by other-forgiveness, become the default dimensions of forgiveness examined. As in the context of other aspects of health, trait-level or dispositional forgiveness is the most common measured; yet, state-level or incident-specific forgiveness does seem to be a particular focus in the context of suicide, particularly when considering bereavement related topics. Likewise, as with other areas of forgiveness being studied in the context of health and unless indicated otherwise above, the studies are largely cross-sectional in design (i.e., data collected at one point in time) and mostly have been conducted in the context of adult samples. Lastly, there is a good mix of studies across sample type, including primary care settings (*n* = 4), community-based settings (*n* = 3), college students (*n* = 4; not a sample of convenience, but a segment of the population particularly relevant for the scientific study of suicide), military and moral injury (*n* = 6), other particular groups (e. g., older adults, firefighters; *n* = 4), case studies (*n* = 5), adolescents (*n* = 4), bereaved survivors (*n* = 5), and suicidal behavior in the context of addiction (*n* = 1).

Theories of Suicide

In addition to the Twelve-Step Model of addiction and recovery as applied to suicidal behavior (see Suicide Anonymous, 2010; see also, Chapter 9), how might other, more standard theories of suicide be related to or otherwise incorporate the theory and process of forgiveness? Two particular theories of suicide provide important context for the relevance of forgiveness in addressing suicidal behavior: Shneidman's theory of suicide focused on psychache (Shneidman, 1993) and Joiner and colleagues' Interpersonal Theory of Suicide (IPT) focused on unmet interpersonal needs (Joiner et al., 2009).

Psychache

Considered the founder of contemporary Suicidology (Jobes & Nelson, 2006), Edwin Shneidman, after more than 50 years as a Suicidologist, concluded that psychache, a term he coined, is *the cause* of suicide. Shneidman (1993) defined psychache as:

> the hurt, anguish, soreness, aching, psychological pain in the psyche, the mind. It is intrinsically psychological – the pain of excessively felt shame, or guilt, or humiliation, or loneliness, or fear, or angst, or dread of growing old, or of dying badly, or whatever. When it occurs, its reality is introspectively undeniable. Suicide occurs when the psychache is deemed by that person to be unbearable.
>
> (p. 51)

Of note, the psychological pain that is psychache is intense, unrelenting, and unremitting – so much so that it is sometimes described as an aching soul (Holden et al., 2001).

Shneidman argued that psychache supersedes any and all other possible contributors to suicide, whether demographic, "biological, sociological, psychological (interpersonal and intrapsychic), epidemiological, [or] philosophic [in their underlying nature]" (Shneidman, 1993, p. 56). Expounding on the relative importance of other psychological contributors, Shneidman argued that all other related affective or emotional variables, including depression, hopelessness, shame, guilt, hostility, and/or a variety of basic human needs "are relevant to suicide only as they relate to unbearable psychological pain. … In every case, the psychological pain is created and fueled by frustrated psychological needs" (Shneidman, 1993, p. 56). Regarding the frustration of basic human needs, Shneidman incorporated and referenced Henry Murray's classification of psychological needs (see Shneidman, 1993, pp. 36–39; see also, Murray, 1938), including affiliation and succorance, arguably reciprocal equivalents to IPT's thwarted belongingness and perceived burdensomeness, respectively (see below). Willingness to tolerate and endure pain varies among individuals and continuing to suffer therewith is thought to be an individualized choice. As such, the desire to escape the psychological pain of psychache is a critical risk factor. In sum, Shneidman (1993) described four necessary conditions for death by suicide to occur: (a) extreme, (b) unbearable psychache, (c) the only perceived antidote for which is cessation of consciousness or existence, and (d) sufficiently depleted motivation to endure or sustain the incapacitating pain. When there is heightened risk for suicide, *the* task of a therapist is to "mollify the psychache … no psychache, no suicide" (Shneidman, 1993, pp. 53 & 56).

Interpersonal Needs

Joiner and colleagues, the originators of the Interpersonal Theory of Suicide (IPT; Joiner & Silva, 2012; Joiner et al., 2009) have argued that there are three necessary conditions for death by suicide: thwarted belongingness, perceived burdensomeness, and acquired capability. Suicidal *ideation* is thought to arise from the overwhelming personal experience of two somewhat contradicting yet concurrent unmet psychological needs. That is, intense social alienation (thwarted belongingness) and the sense of being a drain on others' resources (perceived burdensomeness). Such "perceptions – 'I am hopelessly alienated' and 'my death will be worth more than my life to others' … characterize the suicidal mind" (Joiner & Silva, 2012, p. 326).

Thwarted belongingness and perceived burdensomeness are considered to be particular manifestations of emotional pain and hopelessness that can lead to suicidal ideation (or thoughts related to suicide) slowly over time, or quite quickly. However, without thwarted belongingness and perceived burdensomeness, IPT holds that emotional pain and hopelessness will not lead to suicidal ideation. Moreover, without the ability to overcome the instinctual, evolutionarily adaptive, fear of death, thoughts related to suicide will not transition to suicidal *behavior.* In this regard, acquired capability must develop and be present in order for a suicide attempt or death by suicide to occur.

> The only ones who are capable of death by suicide are those who have been through enough past pain and provocation … to have habituated to the fear and pain of self-injury, so much so that the self-preservation urge can be beaten back. … The self-preservation instinct is too strong to be eliminated altogether; it will always rear its head. It usually prevails, but there are a select few who are able to stare it down, and these few have acquired this dangerous capability … through getting used to pain and fear.
>
> (Joiner et al., 2009, p. 5)

Importantly, the capability for self-harm must be paired with desire for self-harm in order for suicide risk to be present.

The Relevance of Forgiveness to Suicidal Behavior

Although empirical research is mounting regarding the helpful role that forgiveness can play in addressing suicidal behavior (see above), less apparent, perhaps, is *why* does forgiveness play a helpful role? There are at least two main reasons. First, forgiveness is negatively associated with many variables that are positively associated with suicidal behavior (e.g., depression, hopelessness, psychache; see Webb & Toussaint, 2020; Webb et al., 2012). For example, higher levels of forgiveness are associated with lower levels of depression (i.e., *higher* levels of one variable being associated with *lower* levels of another variable is, by definition, a negative [statistical] relationship). Whereas, higher levels of depression are associated with higher levels of suicidal behavior (i.e., higher levels of one variable being associated with higher levels of another variable is, by definition, a positive relationship – as is lower levels of one variable being associated with lower levels of another variable). As such, it is likely the case that higher levels of forgiveness will be associated with and/or lead to lower levels of depression, which in turn, will be associated with and/or lead to lower levels of suicidal behavior.

This type of relationship (i.e., mediation; or, forgiveness leads to better levels of a variable, which then leads to less suicidal behavior) is but one way that forgiveness might play a role in addressing suicidal behavior. Another type of relationship is known as moderation; that is, when forgiveness is present, the association between some other variable and suicidal behavior may be weakened. For example, feelings of hopelessness and helplessness are generally associated with suicidal behavior in a positive fashion (i.e., more hopelessness and/or helplessness are associated with more suicidal behavior). However, among such people that also are more forgiving (as opposed to less forgiving), the association of hopelessness/helplessness with suicidal behavior may not be as strong and thus would be less likely to be problematic. Importantly, there are potentially many pathways between forgiveness and improved outcomes in the context of suicidal behavior. Indeed, empirical evidence is beginning to verify these types of explanations for why forgiveness may play a beneficial role in addressing suicidal behavior (see above review of the 36 extant published studies focused on forgiveness in the context of suicide).

The second main reason (and really just another pathway) is that forgiveness is likely to be an antidote – not the only antidote, but likely one of many possible antidotes – to the necessary conditions for suicide proposed by particular theories of suicide, especially those stressing psychological needs as the crux of suicide. Whether it be unmet psychological needs being conceptualized as creating and fueling psychological pain (i.e., psychache; Shneidman, 1993) or the particular unmet needs of thwarted belongingness and perceived burdensomeness instigating suicidal ideation (Joiner et al., 2009). To the extent that these unmet psychological and/or interpersonal needs stem from relational problems with others and/or the self, genuine forgiveness is likely to play a meaningful and powerful role in preventing suicidal ideation and behavior.

References

Bottoms, G. (2000). *Angelhead: My brother's descent into madness.* Norwalk, CT: Crown House Publishing.

Bryan, A. O., Theriault, J. L., & Bryan, C. J. (2015). Self-forgiveness, posttraumatic stress, and suicide attempts among military personnel and veterans. *Traumatology*, 21(1), 40–46. doi:10.1037/trm0000017.

Carpenter, T. P., Pennington, M. L., Seebeck, J., Gomez, D. R., Denman, T. C., Kimbrel, N. A., … Gulliver, S. B. (2020). Dispositional self-forgiveness in firefighters predicts less help-seeking stigma and fewer mental health challenges. *Stigma and Health*, 5(1), 29–37. doi:10.1037/sah0000172.

Carter, R. E. (1971). Some effects of client suicide on the therapist. *Psychotherapy: Theory, Research & Practice*, 8(4), 287–289.

Chang, E. C., Kahle, E. R., Yu, E. A., & Hirsch, J. K. (2014). Understanding the relationship between domestic abuse and suicide behavior in adults receiving primary care: Does forgiveness matter? *Social Work*, 59(4), 315–320. doi:10.1093/sw/swu028.

Cheavens, J. S., Cukrowicz, K. C., Hansen, R., & Mitchell, S. M. (2016). Incorporating resilience factors into the interpersonal theory of suicide: The role of hope and self-forgiveness in an older adult sample. *Journal of Clinical Psychology*, 72(1), 58–69. doi:10.1002/jclp.22230.

Close, H. T. (1970). Forgiveness and responsibility: A case study. *Pastoral Psychology*, 21(6), 19–25.

Dangel, T., Webb, J. R., & Hirsch, J. K. (2018). Forgiveness and suicidal behavior: Cynicism and psychache as serial mediators. *Journal of Psychology: Interdisciplinary and Applied*, 152(2), 77–95. doi:10.1080/00223980.2017.1408555.

Freeman, M. S., & Hayes, B. G. (2002). Clients changing counselors: An inspirational journey. *Counseling and Values*, 47(1), 13–21.

Groos, A. D. (2012). Trauma, grief and guilt in suicide bereavement. In K. Gow & M. J. Celinski (Eds.), *Individual trauma: Recovering from deep wounds and exploring the potential for renewal* (pp. 83–100). Hauppauge, NY: Nova Science Publishers.

Hall, B. B., Webb, J. R., & Hirsch, J. K. (2020). Spirituality and suicidal behavior: The mediating role of self-forgiveness and psychache. *Psychology of Religion and Spirituality*, 12(1), 36–44. doi:10.1037/rel0000182.

Hirsch, J. K., Webb, J. R., & Jeglic, E. L. (2011). Forgiveness, depression, and suicidal behavior among a diverse sample of college students. *Journal of Clinical Psychology*, 67(9), 896–906. doi:10.1002/jclp.20812.

Hirsch, J. K., Webb, J. R., & Jeglic, E. L. (2012). Forgiveness as a moderator of the association between anger expression and suicidal behavior. *Mental Health, Religion & Culture*, 15(3), 279–300. doi:10.1080/13674676.2011.571666.

Hirsch, J. K., Webb, J. R., & Toussaint, L. L. (2017). Self-forgiveness, self-harm, and suicidal behavior: Understanding the role of forgiving the self in the act of hurting one's self. In L. Woodyatt, E. L.Worthington, Jr., M. Wenzel, & B. J. Griffin (Eds.), *Handbook of the psychology of self-forgiveness* (pp. 249–264). New York, NY: Springer.

Holden, R. R., Mehta, K., Cunningham, E. J., & McLeod, L. D. (2001). Development and preliminary validation of a scale of psychache. *Canadian Journal of Behavioural Science/Revue canadienne des sciences du comportement*, 33(4), 224–232. doi:10.1037/h0087144.

Jobes, D. A., & Nelson, K. N. (2006). Shneidman's contributions to the understanding of suicidal thinking. In T. E. Ellis (Ed.), *Cognition and suicide: Theory, research, and therapy* (pp. 29–49). Washington, DC: American Psychological Association.

Joiner, T. E., Jr., & Silva, C. (2012). Why people die by suicide: Further development and tests of the interpersonal-psychological theory of suicidal behavior. In P. R. Shaver & M. Mikulincer (Eds.), *Meaning, morality, and choice: The social psychology of existential concerns* (pp. 325–336). Washington, DC: American Psychological Association.

Joiner, T. E., Jr., Van Orden, K. A., Witte, T. K., & Rudd, M. D. (2009). *The interpersonal theory of suicide: Guidance for working with suicidal clients.* Washington, DC: American Psychological Association.

Jung, M., Park, Y., Baik, S. Y., Kim, C. L., Kim, H. S., & Lee, S. H. (2019). Self-forgiveness moderates the effects of depression on suicidality. *Psychiatry Investigation*, 16(2), 121–129. doi:10.30773/pi.2018.11.12.1.

Kelley, M. L., Braitman, A. L., White, T. D., & Ehlke, S. J. (2019). Sex differences in mental health symptoms and substance use and their association with moral injury in veterans. *Psychological Trauma: Theory, Research, Practice, and Policy*, 11(3), 337–344. doi:10.1037/tra0000407.

Kelley, M. L., Bravo, A. J., Davies, R. L., Hamrick, H. C., Vinci, C., & Redman, J. C. (2019). Moral injury and suicidality among combat-wounded veterans: The moderating effects of social connectedness and self-compassion. *Psychological Trauma: Theory, Research, Practice, and Policy*, 11(6), 621–629. doi:10.1037/tra0000447.

Khan, A. R., Ratele, K., & Arendse, N. (2020). Men's reflections on postsuicide attempt episode in Bangladesh. *Omega: Journal of Death and Dying*. doi:10.1177/0030222820904878.

Kopacz, M. S., Currier, J. M., Drescher, K. D., & Pigeon, W. R. (2016). Suicidal behavior and spiritual functioning in a sample of Veterans diagnosed with PTSD. *Journal of Injury and Violence Research*, 8(1), 6–14. doi:10.5249/jivr.v8i1.728.

Lee, E., Kim, S. W., Kim, J. J., & Enright, R. D. (2017). Family conflict and forgiveness among survivors of suicide. *Journal of Loss and Trauma*, 22(8), 689–697. doi:10.1080/15325024.2017.1388344.

Levi-Belz, Y., & Gilo, T. (2020). Emotional distress among suicide survivors: The moderating role of self-forgiveness. *Frontiers in Psychiatry*, 11, 341. doi:10.3389/fpsyt.2020.00341.

Levi-Belz, Y., Dichter, N., & Zerach, G. (2020). Moral injury and suicide ideation among Israeli combat veterans: The contribution of self-forgiveness and perceived social support. *Journal of Interpersonal Violence*. doi:10.1177/0886260520920865.

Liu, X., Lu, D., Zhou, L., & Su, L. (2013). Forgiveness as a moderator of the association between victimization and suicidal ideation. *Indian Pediatrics*, 50(7), 685–688.

Murray, H. A. (1938). *Explorations in personality.* New York, NY: Oxford University Press.

Nagra, G. S., Lin, A., & Upthegrove, R. (2016). What bridges the gap between self-harm and suicidality? The role of forgiveness, resilience and attachment. *Psychiatry Research*, 241, 78–82. doi:10.1016/j.psychres.2016.04.103.

Noor, M., & Halabi, S. (2018). Can we forgive a militant outgroup member? The role of perspective-taking. *Asian Journal of Social Psychology*, 21(4), 246–255. doi:10.1111/ajsp.12328.

Nsamenang, S. A., Webb, J. R., Cukrowicz, K. C., & Hirsch, J. K. (2013). Depressive symptoms and interpersonal needs as mediators of forgiveness and suicidal behavior among rural primary care patients. *Journal of Affective Disorders*, 149, 282–290. doi:10.1016/j.jad.2013.01.042.

Quintana-Orts, C., & Rey, L. (2018a). Forgiveness, depression, and suicidal behavior in adolescents: Gender differences in this relationship. *Journal of Genetic Psychology.* doi:10.1080/00221325.2018.1434478

Quintana-Orts, C., & Rey, L. (2018b). Traditional bullying, cyberbullying and mental health in early adolescents: Forgiveness as a protective factor of peer victimization. *International Journal of Environmental Research and Public Health*, 15(11). doi:10.3390/ijerph15112389.

Quintana-Orts, C., Rey, L., & Neto, F. (2020). Beyond cyberbullying: Investigating when and how cybervictimization predicts suicidal ideation. *Journal of Interpersonal Violence.* doi:10.1177/0886260520913640.

Rabon, J. K., Webb, J. R., Chang, E. C., & Hirsch, J. K. (2019). Forgiveness and suicidal behavior in primary care: Mediating role of future orientation. *Journal of Spirituality in Mental Health*, 21(1), 1–13. doi:10.1080/19349637.2018.1469454.

Sandage, S. J. (2010). Intergenerational suicide and family dynamics: A hermeneutic phenomenological case study. *Contemporary Family Therapy: An International Journal*, 32(2), 209–227.

Sansone, R. A., Kelley, A. R., & Forbis, J. S. (2013). The relationship between forgiveness and history of suicide attempt. *Mental Health, Religion & Culture*, 16(1), 31–37.

Sever, M., & Ozdemir, S. (2019). How an academic's death by suicide impacts coworkers and an organization. *Death Studies.* doi:10.1080/07481187.2019.1700572.

Shneidman, E. (1993). *Suicide as psychache: A clinical approach to self-destructive behavior.* Northvale, NJ: Jason Aronson.

Smigelsky, M. A., Jardin, C., Nieuwsma, J. A., Brancu, M., Meador, K. G., Molloy, K. G., & Elbogen, E. B. (2020). Religion, spirituality, and suicide risk in Iraq and Afghanistan era veterans. *Depression and Anxiety*, 37(8), 728–737. doi:10.1002/da.23013.

Suicide Anonymous (2010). *Suicide Anonymous, the little book.* Memphis, TN: Author. Retrieved August 7, 2018, from http://www.suicideanonymous.net/uploads/SA_BOOKLET_ok_copy.pdf.

Testoni, I., Francescon, E., De Leo, D., Santini, A., & Zamperini, A. (2019). Forgiveness and blame among suicide survivors: A qualitative analysis on reports of 4-year self-help-group meetings. *Community Mental Health Journal*, 55(2), 360–368. doi:10.1007/s10597-018-0291-3.

Webb, J. R. (2018). Forgiveness, addiction, and suicide. In J. K. Hirsch, E. C. Chang, & J. K. Rabon (Eds.), *A positive psychological approach to suicide: Theory, research, and prevention* (pp. 37–58). New York, NY: Springer.

Webb, J. R., & Toussaint, L. L. (2020). Forgiveness, well-being, and mental health. In E. L. Worthington, Jr. & N. G. Wade (Eds.), *Handbook for forgiveness* (2nd ed., pp. 188–197). New York, NY: Routledge.

Webb, J. R., Hirsch, J. K., & Toussaint, L. L. (2015). Forgiveness as a positive psychotherapy for addiction and suicide: Theory, research, and practice. *Spirituality in Clinical Practice*, 2(1), 48–60. doi:10.1037/scp0000054.

Webb, J. R., Toussaint, L. L., & Conway-Williams, E. (2012). Forgiveness and health: Psychospiritual integration and the promotion of better healthcare. *Journal of Health Care Chaplaincy*, 18(1–2), 57–73. doi:10.1080/08854726.2012.667317.

8 Clinical Application: Models of Forgiveness Intervention

> What is true of individuals is true of nations. One cannot forgive too much. The weak can never forgive. Forgiveness is the attribute of the strong.
>
> Gandhi (1931, p. 59)

As reviewed in the previous two chapters, multiple dimensions of forgiveness have been observed to be associated with better outcomes related to substance addiction, behavioral addiction, and suicidal behavior; thus, warranting the identification of a robust Forgiveness–Addiction–Recovery Association. Much of this work is in the context of cross-sectional research; that is, data-driven studies largely suggest that, *at any given moment in time*, higher levels of differing dimensions of forgiveness are associated with lower levels of and/or better outcomes related to addictive and suicidal behavior. Cross-sectional data is important and provides a base for moving forward with more sophisticated research design and analysis. For example, longitudinal analysis examines *relationships over time*, or levels of forgiveness today predicting fewer problems in the future – say, 6 months from now. Similarly, intervention-based analysis allows for the examination of *the effect of a formalized activity* on an outcome over time. For example, the maintenance of (1) newly acquired knowledge or abilities from an educational module or (2) newly acquired insight or skills from psychotherapeutic intervention, and the effect of such on problems in the future.

Although the aforementioned cross-sectional data is sufficient to justify longitudinal and intervention-based research regarding the effect of forgiveness on addiction recovery, and such has been called for (Webb, Hirsch, & Toussaint, 2011), unfortunately very little work in this regard has been published (e.g., Lin et al., 2004; Scherer et al., 2011; Scherer et al., 2012; Webb, Robinson, et al., 2009, 2011; Webb et al., 2006). Fortunately, a considerable amount of research has been conducted regarding the effect of forgiveness interventions more generally, with consistent beneficial and constructive effects being observed in the context of a variety of health related outcomes (other than addiction related outcomes – see above), and, importantly, promoting forgiveness itself, for both forgiveness *of others* (see Akhtar & Barlow, 2018; Freedman & Enright, 2020; Wade et al., 2014; Wade & Tittler, 2020; Worthington, 2020b) and forgiveness *of self* (see Cornish et al., 2020; Cornish et al., 2017; Griffin et al., 2017; Ruffing et al., 2017; Worthington, Griffin et al., 2017). That is, forgiveness interventions designed to (1) facilitate health and (2) increase other-forgiveness and self-forgiveness have been observed to be successful in doing so. Also, forgiveness of others intervention research has been conducted in the context of cultural adaptations of particular forgiveness models, couples counseling, integration with treatment for specific disorders and clinical concerns, community-based interventions, and self-administered interventions (see Wade & Tittler, 2020). Likewise, forgiveness of self intervention research has been conducted in the context of psychotherapy and both leader-facilitated and self-directed psychoeducation (see Cornish et al., 2020; see also Woodyatt et al., 2017).

Forgiveness of others models developed by Enright (e.g., Enright & Fitzgibbons, 2015) and Worthington (e.g., Worthington, 2006) have been the two most commonly researched forgiveness interventions (Wade et al., 2014; Worthington & Wade, 2020) – regardless of forgiveness target (e.g., self, others, God) or forgiveness method (e.g., offering, seeking, feeling). Additional models of forgiveness of others and forgiveness of self have been developed, examples of which will be discussed below.

The Process Model of Forgiveness

Enright and colleagues (see Enright, 2001; Enright & Fitzgibbons, 2015; Enright et al., 1998; Freedman & Enright, 2020; see also, Enright & The Human Development Study Group, 1991) have developed the Process Model of Forgiveness which consists of 20 steps or units of forgiveness, comprising four phases of forgiveness. The goal of the first phase, *Uncovering*, is to develop "insight into whether and how the injustice and subsequent injury have compromised [one's] life" (Enright & Fitzgibbons, 2015, p. 59). This process happens through scrutinizing and understanding one's counterproductive psychologically based defense mechanisms (Unit 1), and acknowledging, embracing, and working through the justifiable anger (Unit 2) and the relevant shame and/or reasonable guilt (Unit 3) associated with an offense. Related to this, it is important to recognize the dysfunctional investment of emotional energy (Unit 4) and cognitive resources (Unit 5) in one's responses to an offensive experience, including, sometimes, becoming focused on the positive outcomes experienced by the offender compared to the negative consequences of having been offended (Unit 6). For example, the consistent manifestation of emotions in a stressed and strained fashion (Unit 4) and the largely constant mental expression of negative thoughts and experiences in a rehearsed and replayed fashion (Unit 5) can become problematic and self-defeating, including "if the offender has prospered while you have suffered, this disparity in circumstance may become another cause of anger" (Unit 6; Enright, 2001, p. 117). Lastly, in this first of four phases of forgiveness, the offended comes to understand the personal, permanent, and adverse nature of the offensive experience (Unit 7), and the resultant, likely alteration of one's worldview, particularly in the context of what constitutes an otherwise just world (Unit 8).

The goal of the second phase of forgiveness, *Decision*, is to develop "an accurate understanding of the nature of forgiveness and [to make] a decision to commit to forgiving on the basis of this understanding" (Enright & Fitzgibbons, 2015, p. 59). This process is a function of the offended recognizing and accepting that one's default strategies for addressing or coping with offensive experiences are not effective and that an alternative approach is needed (Unit 9). Building upon this recognized need for an alternative approach, consideration is given to forgiveness itself (Unit 10), after informed and consented willingness for such is developed through reasoned understanding of what *is* and *is not* (a) included in the psychological definition of forgiveness and (b) implied by the outcome of forgiveness. For example, forgiveness is a freely chosen reduction of negative responses to an offense and does not require one to view the offensive experience as now good or inconsequential (see Chapter 3). The last task in this second phase of forgiveness is to commit to forgiveness (Unit 11), despite lingering reluctance and hesitation; that is, to commit to begin the process of forgiveness and to trust that it may very well turn out to be the answer to the problem at hand.

The goal of the third phase, *Work*, is to develop "a cognitive understanding of the offender and [to begin] to view the offender in a new light, resulting in [a] positive change in affect [i.e., emotions] about the offender, about the self, and about the relationship" (Enright & Fitzgibbons, 2015, p. 59). This process is facilitated by engaging in a reframing or re-envisioning of the offense and/or offender, through role-taking, such that any relevant context of the experience is recognized and valued (Unit 12). The task here is not to justify in any way what happened; rather, it is to help the offended to gain perspective and to develop empathy and compassion for the offender (Unit 13). Related to this, it is critical for the offended to accept, bear, and absorb the pain (Unit 14). That is, to personally heal, rather than to continue the downward, never-ending spiral of blaming the offender and seeking to externalize the pain through exacting revenge and retribution. All of the above comprises an undeserved, yet moral gift to the offender (Unit 15), who "deserves respect because of [their] humanity, despite [their] actions" (Freedman & Enright, 2020, p. 268).

The goal of the fourth and final phase of forgiveness, *Deepening*, is to develop "increasing meaning in the suffering; [the feeling of being] more connected with others; and [the experiencing of] decreased negative affect [i.e., emotions] and, at times, renewed purpose in life" (Enright & Fitzgibbons, 2015, p. 59). This process occurs when the offended is able to derive meaning from their suffering and from their struggle for forgiveness (Unit 16), which includes recognition of the interdependent nature of forgiveness (Unit 17). That is, as commonly attributed to George Herbert, an Anglican priest who died in 1633, "he that cannot forgive others breaks the bridge over which he himself must pass if he would ever reach heaven, for everyone has need to be forgiven." Related to this is recognizing and embracing the reality that one is not alone in the pain and suffering associated with the need for and struggle of forgiveness (Unit 18); indeed, that others have had similar experiences and are available to provide support. Similarly, endeavoring to discover new-found purpose resulting from the offensive experience can help solidify the progress being made (Unit 19). Lastly, as the outcome of forgiveness begins to coalesce and increasingly transpire, the negative responses to the offense and/or offender will decrease (and positive responses may increase), "likely because of the [deep, inner-core] emotional relief realized on finishing the forgiveness process" (Unit 20; Enright & Fitzgibbons, 2015, p. 82).

In sum, Enright's Process Model of Forgiveness includes four phases (see Enright, 2001; Enright & Fitzgibbons, 2015; Enright et al., 1998; Freedman & Enright, 2020; see also, Enright & The Human Development Study Group, 1991). First, *Uncovering*, or developing an awareness of the problem and the emotional pain following an offense, including recognizing and accepting one's own defense mechanisms, anger, shame, and guilt, as well as the permanent, life-altering nature of the offensive experience. Second, *Decision*, or developing an accurate, reasoned understanding of the definition and outcome of forgiveness, and realizing the need for and committing to the alternate resolution of forgiveness. Third, *Work*, or engaging in processes such as, reframing to gain perspective and developing empathy and compassion for the offender; thereby, facilitating acceptance (rather than externalization) of one's pain, and giving the moral gift of forgiveness to the offender. And, fourth, *Deepening*, or solidifying progress being made through finding meaning and purpose in suffering and the need and struggle for forgiveness, recognizing interdependence, and realizing universality with and support from others.

The REACH Model of Forgiveness

Worthington and colleagues (see Worthington, 2003, 2006, 2020b; Worthington & Sandage, 2016; see also, Worthington, 1998) have developed the REACH Model of Forgiveness which includes five broad components or steps – organized in an acrostic, yet purposefully ordered fashion – designed to attain forgiveness. The first component, *Recalling the Hurt*, involves identifying and separating one's emotional responses from the offensive, wounding experience. That is, to carefully recall the hurt and one's responses to it as objectively and as accurately as possible, including in as much vivid detail as possible, perhaps even visualizing the experience(s). Importantly, one is to judiciously engage in this activity without blaming the offender (keeping in mind that accurately attributing responsibility is different from blaming), without depersonalizing the offender, without embellishing one's own injury, pain, and suffering, and without the otherwise typical emotional responses related to the rage and indignation of having been wounded. In sum, this process of recollection should occur without re-traumatizing one's self through re-living the offensive experience and the pain associated therewith. Rather, when starting on the path toward forgiveness, one is to recall the offensive experience in a different, helpful, sympathetic manner.

The aim of this first step toward forgiveness is not to overlook the pain of the offensive experience, or to deny oneself the experience of unforgiveness (i.e., the confluence of negative emotional responses to an offensive experience such as anger, hatred, hostility, resentment, etc.; see Chapter 3), but to recognize, acknowledge, and embrace the hurt and one's unforgiveness thereof in a healthy, rather than dysfunctional fashion. Worthington (2006) states that "before trying to promote forgiveness, two tasks are necessary. First, … [conducting] a strong assessment of unforgiveness. Second, … [recalling] the hurt more objectively or more compassionately" (p. 174). Related to this, expressing negative emotions in response to an offensive, wounding experience in a healthy manner does not mean suppressing or minimizing such emotions. The offended individual is encouraged to fully experience such emotions, but in a controlled or balanced manner. That is, one must be careful when beginning "to recall the hurt and details surrounding it, [to] monitor yourself to make sure that you are not slipping into rage, fear, or depression" (Worthington, 2003, p. 87). Expressing emotion without an effort to seek and increase understanding is counterproductive and likely destructive and self-defeating.

The second component of the REACH Model of Forgiveness, *Empathy* or emotional reprocessing, entails thinking differently about the offense and feeling differently about the offender (Worthington, 1998, 2003, 2006). That is, "creating cognitive and emotional conditions that activate other emotional systems," thereby leading the victim to experience "a *state of empathy* for the person who harmed [them]" (emphasis in original; Worthington, 1998, p. 118). Once a person has recalled a hurtful experience in an honest, genuine, and balanced fashion (i.e., the first component of the REACH Model), the linchpin to forgiving is to experience *different, positive* emotions in an effort to replace the counterproductive negative emotions associated with unforgiveness (Worthington, 2006, 2020b; Worthington & Sandage, 2016). Empathy, or deliberately and accurately taking the perspective of another, is critical to this process. In the explicit context of seeking to forgive, "to empathize, we must discern why *this* person has hurt *me* in this way" (emphasis in original; Worthington, 2003, p. 106). Moreover, whether or not forgiveness occurs depends heavily on *compassionate empathy*; that is, accurately detecting, understanding, and otherwise sharing the thoughts and feelings of the offender, combined with experiencing compassion and concern for the offender (Worthington, 1998, 2003). Indeed, it is thought "that a strong sense of compassionate empathy … will necessarily change the emotion and experience of unforgiveness" (Worthington, 1998, p. 120).

How does one foster the development of empathy? Worthington (1998, 2003, 2006, 2020a) provides many suggestions; for example, (1) discussing the offense, including speculating about the offender's thoughts and feelings, (2) writing letters of explanation and apology (from the perspective of the offender), assuming genuine accountability and sensible motivation from the offender, and (3) recalling past and imagining future good and positive experiences and interactions with the offender. Although an actual apology from the offender can facilitate forgiveness, it is not required, as vivid imagination of an apology can likewise be a powerful experience. Also, "empathy can be contagious" (Worthington, 2003, p. 99). That is, observing empathy exhibited by another and receiving empathy from another can help one to experience empathy toward an offender. When helping *others* to be empathic, it is important to monitor and reinforce their efforts to transition away from unforgiveness for their offender, as it can be challenging to engage, on one's own, the process of developing empathy. Related to this, given the general difficulty of developing empathy in the context of having suffered an offensive experience, facilitating sympathy, compassion, and love can be productive alternatives (Worthington, 2006, 2020b; Worthington & Sandage, 2016).

The third component, giving an *Altruistic Gift* of forgiveness, is focused on facilitating forgiveness, not because it is good for the forgiver in terms of their physical, mental, relational, or spiritual health (even though it is, see Chapters 5, 6, & 7), but as a selfless, unwarranted gift from the victim to the offender, designed to help the offender in their own struggles of life (Worthington, 2006, 2020b; Worthington & Sandage, 2016). Once a foundation of empathy has been established (i.e., the previous step in the REACH Model), it is important to strengthen and broaden its effect through developing insight regarding the victim's own historical need for forgiveness and focusing on what the experience of being forgiven feels like, including the resultant feelings of being freed from the emotional burdens associated with having harmed a victim (Worthington, 2003, 2006, 2020b). Nevertheless, increased understanding of, identifying with, and developing empathy, as well as sympathy, compassion, and love for an offender may not lead to forgiveness. In such cases, it is important also to encourage humility (see also, Worthington, Davis et al., 2017), thereby fortifying empathy, and leading to healthy guilt (i.e., rather than (1) self-obsessed, excessive guilt or (2) shame), contrition, gratitude, hope, and an increased motivation and willingness to offer the altruistic gift of forgiveness (Worthington, 1998, 2003, 2006). That is, a *humble* recognition of one's own need for and experience of forgiveness – resulting in healthy guilt and contrition for wrongdoing, gratitude for having been forgiven, and hopeful optimism for good relationships moving forward – can facilitate the development of altruism and the motivation for altruistic behavior. Needless to say, altruism is not an easy endeavor, but it can play a crucial role in generating the definitive, compelling conditions for the outcome of forgiveness (Worthington, 2006). If we have need of forgiveness, how can we deny awarding forgiveness to others (Worthington, 2003)? In this regard, the question of whether or not to forgive arguably becomes an ethical consideration.

Worthington (2003) stresses that humility and gratitude are inseparably connected and central to this step; that is, facilitating the altruistic gift of forgiveness. "Humility arises from and reinforces a person's sense of empathy. Empathy is also important to feeling gratitude. Gratitude is a feeling of thanksgiving at having received a gift perceived to be altruistic" (Worthington, 2003, p. 125). Moreover, "empathy plus the [healthy] guilt and gratitude of humility create an aroused motivational state. The person identifies with the experience of the offender (through empathy) and sees the other as needy (through humility)" (Worthington, 1998, p. 125). In sum, "our empathy, humility and gratitude somehow ennoble us. In so doing, they inspire us to step beyond our own self-interest and give altruistic gifts of love to those in need" (Worthington, 2003, p. 127). Indeed, "forgiving is an altruistic gift you can give to someone who *needs* forgiveness" (emphasis in original; Worthington, 2003, p. 128). Once this altruistic gift is under active consideration and seemingly being offered, the process of committing to forgiveness has begun (i.e., the next step in the REACH Model; Worthington, 2006).

The fourth component, *Commitment*, addresses the necessity of making a deliberate and explicit public commitment to forgiveness, including any initial progress that has already been made (Worthington, 1998, 2003, 2006). Without making a *public* commitment to forgive, forgiveness may occur only in one's mind (and perhaps heart, or possibly between a patient and their mental health care provider) and, being private, such forgiveness (even though genuine) may break down when confronted with the inevitable occurrence of doubts (Worthington, 1998, 2003). Doubts about whether or not one has actually forgiven an offender are normal and can arise when one sees their offender again, when a different person hurts you in a similar fashion, when a victim is under stress (even when the stress is unrelated to the original offense), and when hurt again by the same offender (Worthington, 1998, 2003). These types of experiences are common – including in the sense that it is human nature to offend others (and ourselves), whether intentional or not – and potentially painful (Worthington, 2003, 2006; see also, Toussaint & Webb, 2005a). Moreover, recalling a specific offensive experience, and all of its particulars, even when having genuinely forgiven the offender, can be painful; nevertheless, "[re-experiencing the] hurt [associated with an offensive experience] is not unforgiveness," particularly when genuine forgiveness has occurred, and thus does not justify the doubts that can creep in during these times (Worthington, 2003, p. 133; see also, Worthington, 1998).

Worthington (2006) underscores the reality that when assisting a person to make a commitment to forgive, trust between parties is necessary or taking the risk to forgive may not be very likely. Taking this risk and making a commitment to try to forgive suggests that a crossroad for change has been reached. Being at this crossroad is difficult, stressful, and frightening as there is uncertainty about what will happen next and how things will turn out – will things get better or worse? Taking the added step of saying or doing something – getting our intent and commitment to forgive *outside* of ourselves – makes our words and actions regarding forgiveness a matter of public record. Such that, the probability for doubt and denial regarding forgiveness becomes much *less* likely, and the probability for following through with forgiveness becomes much *more* likely (Worthington, 1998, 2003). The prospect of working on forgiveness "is a big commitment," the commitment to forgive (and, making said commitment public) is a risk, taking the risk requires "courage," and such "courage needs to be recognized and honored," perhaps "with a ceremony" (Worthington, 2006, pp. 182–183). Recommendations to help solidify commitment include writing about it (e.g., a *Certificate of Forgiveness*, or a *Letter of Forgiveness* – but not necessarily sending such to the offender), reading what you have written about it to people other than the offender, talking to others about your need for and commitment to forgiveness (e.g., friends, family, and significant others), acting *as if* forgiveness has occurred, and various other rituals and symbols (e.g., burning written descriptions of an offense, or carrying and then, when ready, putting down a rock, etc.) signifying the burden versus relief associated with unforgiveness versus forgiveness (Worthington, 1998, 2003, 2006, 2020b).

The fifth and final step, or broad component of the REACH Model of Forgiveness, *Holding On*, is an extension of the previous step in the model and involves continuing to maintain and strengthen one's commitment to forgiveness – regardless of the inevitable recurrence of doubts (Worthington, 2003, 2006, 2020b; Worthington & Sandage, 2016). Even after successfully engaging in genuine forgiveness and building confidence and resolve through making your commitment to forgiveness public, doubts about whether one has actually forgiven (or not) are natural and likely will persist. Over time, intrusive thoughts, memories, and images are inevitable and act as the fertilizing manure for the seeds of doubt to flourish as weeds in the garden of forgiveness. "[T]he experiences of doubt occur because other negative emotions arise to confuse the person" (Worthington, 2006, p. 184). When encountering a past offender (e.g., seeing them, or being reoffended), when a different person hurts you in a similar fashion, or when under stress (whether related to the original offense or not), the often visceral experiences of anxiety, fear, and anger are "the body's way of warning of a potentially harmful situation, [and] *not* unforgiveness" (emphasis added; Worthington, 2020b, p. 279). Stopping these unwanted experiences and holding on to forgiveness can be very difficult. "Even after we have forgiven, it's not easy to resist unforgiveness. For many people, unforgiveness is the low point to which they automatically roll if left alone. Holding on to forgiveness requires an uphill fight" (Worthington, 2003, p. 149). One must expend focused energy and consistently pay careful attention to engaging in forgiveness *and* the maintenance of one's progress (Worthington, 1998). Worthington (1998, 2003, 2006) suggests several options for addressing doubts and making holding on to forgiveness more likely. Most importantly, the forgiver must understand and fully grasp the notion that unresolved pain related to having been offended (e.g., anxiety, fear, and anger) is not necessarily the same as unforgiveness. Likewise, the forgiver must recognize, interrupt, and reduce any negative feelings, emotions, and rumination associated with the offender and the offensive experience. Related to this, in can be helpful to develop more positive reactions to the offender. Deliberately reminding oneself that forgiveness has taken place, actively seeking support and encouragement from friends and loved ones, and purposefully reading through one's written exercises and documents generated as tools to foster forgiveness can be very effective. Also, one can always return to and study the REACH Model and work through the steps, as needed.

In sum, Worthington's REACH Model of Forgiveness includes five steps (see Worthington, 1998, 2003, 2006, 2020b; Worthington & Sandage, 2016). First, accurately and fully *Recalling* an offense, including the objective nature of the experience and the pain associated therewith, in reasonable, yet vivid detail. Second, developing *Empathy* for the offender so as to be able to reprocess and change for the better the negative emotions and experiences associated with the process of unforgiveness. Third, choosing to give the *Altruistic* gift of forgiveness to the offender through the development of one's own sense of humility and gratitude (i.e., *as* the offended, not for having been offended), thereby viewing the offender as in need of forgiveness. Fourth, making a public, formal *Commitment* to forgive, in order to begin to address the doubts about forgiveness that inevitably come as a result of the otherwise intrusive thoughts, memories, and images associated with the offensive experience. And, fifth, *Holding on* to progress made toward forgiveness. That is, continually addressing recurring doubts about whether or not forgiveness has taken place, including reminding one's self that any unresolved pain associated with having been offended is not necessarily unforgiveness. And, remaining vigilant against negative feelings, emotions, and rumination regarding the offense and the offender.

Fundamental Assumptions Regarding the Nature of Forgiveness

The Process Model of Forgiveness and the REACH Model of Forgiveness, in addition to broad, over-arching conceptual consistency, have much in common. Both, while initially developed as models of inter-personal forgiveness (i.e., forgiveness of others), have been adapted and applied to *intra*-personal forgiveness (i.e., forgiveness of self) – with their foundational essence and core objectives remaining the same (e.g., Enright & The Human Development Study Group, 1996; Worthington, 2006). Also, in both models, as well as with those additional models to be briefly outlined below, it is important to realize that individuals are not encouraged to overlook or minimize any personal thoughts, emotions, or behaviors associated with the offense or being offended, nor to overlook or minimize the gravity of the offense or the accountability of the offender. Likewise, at no point is the offended party to deny the permanently and inherently unjustifiable and unnecessary nature of the offense. As previously stated (see Chapter 3), actual forgiveness does not require a return to vulnerability or a lack of accountability, nor does it necessarily include reconciliation – to forgive, the offended need not view the offense (or the offender) as a good or inconsequential experience. Also, Enright et al. (1998) carefully point out that the overall process of forgiveness is not likely to be linear. That is, individuals may or may not progress through the steps of these models in a start-to-finish, orderly fashion. Similarly, Webb and Trautman (2010) emphasize that levels of forgiveness are likely to fluctuate over the course of the forgiveness process (see also, Krentzman et al., 2018; McCullough et al., 2010; Toussaint & Webb, 2005b). As such, genuine forgiveness is not likely to occur in a smooth, direct, or undeviating fashion, nor is it likely to be an event or an all-or-nothing experience.

Additional Models of Forgiveness

Although the Process Model and the REACH Model described above have received the most attention in the published scientific literature, other scholars also have developed and published models and methods of forgiveness. Following is a brief overview of two alternative models of other-forgiveness and two alternative models of self-forgiveness.

Forgiveness of Others

Luskin (2002, 2007; see also, Toussaint et al., 2019) has developed a four-stage model of forgiveness of others. The model builds on particular prescribed counseling-related techniques designed to facilitate forgiveness of specific offenses and is focused on developing dispositional forgiveness, or the tendency to consistently forgive over time, and, ideally, regardless of the situation at hand. Importantly, Luskin (2002) encourages the potential forgiver to prepare to forgive by satisfying three pre-conditions: "know what your feelings are about what happened, be clear about the action that wronged you, [and] share your [painful] experience with at least one or two trusted people" (p. 65). Once you have met these conditions you are ready to proceed. Without the understanding developed in meeting these pre-conditions forgiveness will be much harder and less enduring. The first stage of becoming a more forgiving person is after having been offended, the victim usually feels justified in the various negative emotional responses they are experiencing. "There is usually both active and submerged anger as well as a great deal of pain" (Luskin, 2002, p. 181). The second stage involves recognizing that said negative emotional responses are not resolving, are counterproductive, and that something needs to change. The third stage involves remembering past positive experiences with forgiveness and making the choice to forgive again. The fourth stage in Luskin's model of becoming a more forgiving person entails making "the decision to forgive first and let many troubling things go. … [Recognizing] that you are responsible for how you feel, … [and that you can choose] to rarely if ever take offense" (Luskin, 2002, pp. 182–183). Of note, Luskin also has applied these principles to self-forgiveness.

Rusbult et al. (2005) describe a three-stage model of forgiveness of others. *Restraint* or resisting impulsive vengeance, which occurs within seconds of an offense. *Forbearance* or choosing to interpret an offense in a prosocial, empathic manner, which occurs within minutes to hours of an offense. And, *extended forgiveness* or engaging in the long-term process of the growth, development, and deepening of forgiveness, which occurs from several hours to several months (perhaps years) following an offense.

Forgiveness of Self

Jacinto and Edwards (2011) outline a four-stage therapeutic model of forgiveness of self. The first stage involves *recognition* of self-forgiveness as a viable choice for conflict resolution. That is, after reflecting upon and understanding one's own role in the difficult experiences one is having, and thereby realizing the need to transition blame attribution away from others and toward the self, one can seek responsible relief through self-forgiveness. Related to this, the second stage includes accepting *responsibility* for one's role in said difficult experiences. This is facilitated by insight, self-empathy, awareness of and compassion for the inherent limitations of self and others. The third stage involves identification and *expression* of any feelings associated with the ruminative self-blame related to taking responsibility for one's actions. Critically, this stage includes the explicit and deliberate goal of finding resolution for such feelings, and reconnection with relevant others. Lastly, the fourth stage is necessitated by a need for *re-creating* the self; that is, developing "a renewed self-image that incorporates the past and gives direction to the future" (Jacinto & Edwards, 2011, p. 429).

Cornish and Wade (2015) developed a four-component model and termed it the *four Rs of genuine self-forgiveness.* The first component entails the recognition, acknowledgment, and acceptance of *responsibility* for an offense without excusing, justifying, rationalizing, or shifting the blame. Next, as a result of realizing one's role in having offended another, one is likely to experience intense negative emotions toward the self, most notably guilt and shame. This *remorse*-laden response is based not only on one's poor behavior (guilt), but also on one's sense of self as being inherently bad for having committed the offense (shame). After experiencing such remorse, for self-forgiveness to occur said remorse also must be addressed and resolved. Taking responsibility for one's offensive actions and experiencing and resolving the deeply remorseful reaction thereto allows for the third and fourth components of genuine forgiveness to occur. The third component, *restoration*, requires "engagement in reparative behaviors and a recommitment to the values damaged by the offense" (Cornish & Wade, 2015, p. 98). Finally, *renewal*, the fourth component, can occur. One is now able, in a responsible manner, to let go of their guilt and shame and experience the empowering regeneration of genuine self-forgiveness.

References

Akhtar, S., & Barlow, J. (2018). Forgiveness therapy for the promotion of mental well-being: A systematic review and meta-analysis. *Trauma, Violence, & Abuse*, 19(1), 107–122. doi:10.1177/1524838016637079.

Cornish, M. A., & Wade, N. G. (2015). A therapeutic model of self-forgiveness with intervention strategies for counselors. *Journal of Counseling & Development*, 93(1), 96–104. doi:10.1002/j.1556-6676.2015.00185.x.

Cornish, M. A., Griffin, B. J., & Morris, G. W. (2020). Promotion of self-forgiveness. In E. L. Worthington, Jr. & N. G. Wade (Eds.), *Handbook of forgiveness* (2nd ed., pp. 288–298). New York, NY: Routledge.

Cornish, M. A., Wade, N. G., & Cikara, A. (2017). Self-forgiveness in individual psychotherapy: Therapeutic models and counseling outcomes. In L. Woodyat, E. L.Worthington, Jr., M. Wenzel, & B. J. Griffin (Eds.), *Handbook of the psychology of self-forgiveness* (pp. 163–177). New York, NY: Springer.

Enright, R. D. (2001). *Forgiveness is a choice: A step-by-step process for resolving anger and restoring hope.* Washington, DC: American Psychological Association.

Enright, R. D., & Fitzgibbons, R. P. (2015). *Forgiveness therapy: An empirical guide for resolving anger and restoring hope* (2nd ed.). Washington, DC: American Psychological Association.

Enright, R. D., & The Human Development Study Group (1991). The moral development of forgiveness. In W. Kurtines & J. Gewirtz (Eds.), *Handbook of moral behavior and development* (Vol. 1, pp. 123–152). Hillsdale, NJ: Lawrence Erlbaum.

Enright, R. D., & The Human Development Study Group (1996). Counseling within the forgiveness triad: On forgiving, receiving forgiveness, and self-forgiveness. *Counseling and Values*, 40(2), 107–126. doi:10.1002/j.2161-007X.1996.tb00844.x.

Enright, R. D., Freedman, S., & Rique, J. (1998). The psychology of interpersonal forgiveness. In R. D. Enright & J. North (Eds.), *Exploring forgiveness* (pp. 46–62). Madison, WI: University of Wisconsin Press.

Freedman, S., & Enright, R. D. (2020). A review of the empirical research using Enright's Process Model of interpersonal forgiveness. In E. L.Worthington, Jr. & N. G. Wade (Eds.), *Handbook of forgiveness* (2nd ed., pp. 266–276). New York, NY: Routledge.

Gandhi, M. K. (1931). The test of faith. *Young India*, 13(14), 58–59.

Griffin, B. J., Worthington, E. L., Jr., Bell, C. M., & Davis, D. E. (2017). Self-directed intervention to promote self-forgiveness. In L. Woodyat, E. L.Worthington, Jr., M. Wenzel, & B. J. Griffin (Eds.), *Handbook of the psychology of self-forgiveness* (pp. 207–218). New York, NY: Springer.

Jacinto, G. A., & Edwards, B. L. (2011). Therapeutic stages of forgiveness and self-forgiveness. *Journal of Human Behavior in the Social Environment*, 21(4), 423–437. doi:10.1080/15433714.2011.531215.

Krentzman, A. R., Webb, J. R., Jester, J. M., & Harris, J. I. (2018). Longitudinal relationship between forgiveness of self and forgiveness of others among individuals with alcohol use disorders. *Psychology of Religion and Spirituality*, 10(2), 128–137. doi:10.1037/rel0000152.

Lin, W. F., Mack, D., Enright, R. D., Krahn, D., & Baskin, T. W. (2004). Effects of forgiveness therapy on anger, mood, and vulnerability to substance use among inpatient substance-dependent clients. *Journal of Consulting and Clinical Psychology*, 72(6), 1114–1121. doi:10.1037/0022-006X.72.6.1114.

Luskin, F. (2002). *Forgive for good: A proven prescription for health and happiness*. New York, NY: HarperOne.

Luskin, F. (2007). *Forgive for love: The missing ingredient for a healthy and lasting relationship.* New York, NY: HarperOne.

McCullough, M. E., Luna, L. R., Berry, J. W., Tabak, B. A., & Bono, G. (2010). On the form and function of forgiving: Modeling the time-forgiveness relationship and testing the valuable relationships hypothesis. *Emotion*, 10(3), 358–376. doi:10.1037/a0019349.

Ruffing, E. G., Moon, S. H., Krier, J., Paine, D. R., Wolff, E., & Sandage, S. J. (2017). Self-forgiveness in couple and family therapy. In L. Woodyat, E. L.Worthington, Jr., M. Wenzel, & B. J. Griffin (Eds.), *Handbook of the psychology of self-forgiveness* (pp. 193–206). New York, NY: Springer.

Rusbult, C. E., Hannon, P. A., Stocker, S. L., & Finkel, E. J. (2005). Forgiveness and relational repair. In E. L.Worthington, Jr. (Ed.), *Handbook of forgiveness* (pp. 185–205). New York, NY: Routledge.

Scherer, M., Worthington, E. L., Jr., Hook, J. N., & Campana, K. L. (2011). Forgiveness and the bottle: Promoting self-forgiveness in individuals who abuse alcohol. *Journal of Addictive Diseases*, 30(4), 382–395. doi:10.1080/10550887.2011.609804.

Scherer, M., Worthington, E. L., Jr., Hook, J. N., Campana, K. L., West, S. L., & Gartner, A. L. (2012). Forgiveness and cohesion in familial perceptions of alcohol misuse. *Journal of Counseling & Development*, 90(2), 160–168. doi:10.1111/j.1556-6676.2012.00021.x.

Toussaint, L. L., & Webb, J. R. (2005a). Gender differences in the relationship between empathy and forgiveness. *The Journal of Social Psychology*, 145(6), 673–685. doi:10.3200/socp.145.6.673-686.

Toussaint, L. L., & Webb, J. R. (2005b). Theoretical and empirical connections between forgiveness, mental health, and well-being. In E. L.Worthington, Jr. (Ed.), *Handbook of forgiveness* (pp. 349–362). New York, NY: Routledge.

Toussaint, L. L., Luskin, F., Aberman, R., & DeLorenzo, A. (2019). Is forgiveness one of the secrets to success? Considering the costs of workplace disharmony and the benefits of teaching employees to forgive. *American Journal of Health Promotion*, 33(7), 1090–1093. doi:10.1177/0890117119866957e.

Wade, N. G., & Tittler, M. V. (2020). Psychological interventions to promote forgiveness of others: Review of empirical evidence. In E. L.Worthington, Jr. & N. G. Wade (Eds.), *Handbook of forgiveness* (2nd ed., pp. 255–265). New York, NY: Routledge.

Wade, N. G., Hoyt, W. T., Kidwell, J. E. M., & Worthington, E. L., Jr. (2014). Efficacy of psychotherapeutic interventions to promote forgiveness: A meta-analysis. *Journal of Consulting and Clinical Psychology*, 82(1), 154–170. doi:10.1037/a0035268.

Webb, J. R., & Trautman, R. P. (2010). Forgiveness and alcohol use: Applying a specific spiritual principle to substance abuse problems. *Addictive Disorders & Their Treatment*, 9(1), 8–17. doi:10.1097/ADT.0b013e318195000d.

Webb, J. R., Hirsch, J. K., & Toussaint, L. L. (2011). Forgiveness and alcohol problems: A review of the literature and a call for intervention-based research. *Alcoholism Treatment Quarterly*, 29 (3), 245–273. doi:10.1080/07347324.2011.585922.

Webb, J. R., Robinson, E. A. R., & Brower, K. J. (2009). Forgiveness and mental health among people entering outpatient treatment with alcohol problems. *Alcoholism Treatment Quarterly*, 27(4), 368–388. doi:10.1080/07347320903209822.

Webb, J. R., Robinson, E. A. R., & Brower, K. J. (2011). Mental health, not social support, mediates the forgiveness-alcohol outcome relationship. *Psychology of Addictive Behaviors*, 25 (3), 462–473. doi:10.1037/a0022502.

Webb, J. R., Robinson, E. A. R., Brower, K. J., & Zucker, R. A. (2006). Forgiveness and alcohol problems among people entering substance abuse treatment. *Journal of Addictive Diseases*, 25 (3), 55–67. doi:10.1300/J069v25n03_08.

Woodyatt, L., Worthington, E. L., Jr., Wenzel, M., & Griffin, B. J. (Eds.). (2017). *Handbook of the psychology of self-forgiveness*. New York, NY: Springer.

Worthington, E. L., Jr. (1998). The pyramid model of forgiveness: Some interdisciplinary speculations about unforgiveness and the promotion of forgiveness. In E. L.Worthington, Jr. (Ed.), *Dimensions of forgiveness: Psychological research and theological perspectives* (pp. 107–137). Philadelphia: Templeton Foundation Press.

Worthington, E. L., Jr. (2003). *Forgiving and reconciling: Bridges to wholeness and hope* (Revised ed.). Downers Grove, IL: InterVarsity Press.

Worthington, E. L., Jr. (2006). *Forgiveness and reconciliation: Theory and application*. New York, NY: Routledge.

Worthington, E. L., Jr. (2020a). *Forgiveness intervention manuals*. Accessed June 19, 2020 from: http://www.people.vcu.edu/~eworth/ & https://evworthington.squarespace.com/diy-workbooks.

Worthington, E. L., Jr. (2020b). An update of the REACH Forgiveness Model: Psychoeducation in groups, do-it-yourself formats, couple enrichment, religious congregations, and as an adjunct to psychotherapy. In E. L.Worthington, Jr. & N. G. Wade (Eds.), *Handbook of forgiveness* (2nd ed., pp. 277–287). New York, NY: Routledge.

Worthington, E. L., Jr., & Sandage, S. J. (2016). *Forgiveness and spirituality in psychotherapy: A relational approach*. Washington, DC: American Psychological Association.

Worthington, E. L., Jr., & Wade, N. G. (2020). How you can benefit from this handbook. In E. L.Worthington, Jr. & N. G. Wade (Eds.), *Handbook of forgiveness* (2nd ed., pp. 1–8). New York, NY: Routledge.

Worthington, E. L., Jr., Davis, D. E., & Hook, J. N. (Eds.). (2017). *Handbook of humility: Theory, research, and applications*. New York, NY: Routledge.

Worthington, E. L., Jr., Griffin, B. J., & Wade, N. G. (2017). Group intervention to promote self-forgiveness. In L. Woodyat, E. L.Worthington, Jr., M. Wenzel, & B. J. Griffin (Eds.), *Handbook of the psychology of self-forgiveness* (pp. 179–192). New York, NY: Springer.

9 Clinical Application: Twelve-Step Model and Twelve-Step Facilitation

Resentments are viewed by the Twelve-Step Model of addiction and recovery as a core factor in the emotional and psychological struggle of addiction. For example, in the context of: (1) Alcoholics Anonymous (AA, 2001, p. 64), "Resentment is the 'number one' offender. It destroys more alcoholics than anything else," (2) Narcotics Anonymous (NA, 2008, p. 4), "Hostile, resentful, self-centered and self-seeking, we cut ourselves off from the outside world," (3) Gamblers Anonymous (GA, 1989, p. 44), "Anger could lead you back to a bet via the hatred and resentment created," and (4) Suicide Anonymous (SA, 2010, p. 33), "Often victims of emotional deprivation in childhood, we had learned to survive on anger and resentment." As such, a logical extension of this is that the resolution of resentments is a core factor in relapse prevention (broadly construed) and recovery. Given the interplay between anger, hostility, hatred, and resentment, otherwise known as *unforgiveness* (see Chapter 5; Worthington et al., 2001), in the context of the Twelve-Step Model of addiction and recovery, forgiveness may be a ready-made antidote for addiction and thus a key facilitator of recovery. Indeed, not only is forgiveness as a goal/outcome directly applicable to the specific steps of the Twelve-Step Model focused on identifying and acknowledging resentments (i.e., Step 4 and Step 5) and resolving resentments through making amends (i.e., Step 8 and Step 9), the underlying principles and procedures of forgiveness (see Chapter 8) are indirectly related to *all* of the steps in the Twelve-Step Model (e.g., Webb et al., 2015). Likewise, the technique, skill, and practice of forgiveness is consistent with the formalized Twelve-Step based treatment of addiction; that is, Twelve-Step Facilitation Therapy (TSF; e.g., Nowinski, 2012; Webb et al., 2015).

Basic Principles of the Twelve-Step Model of Addiction and Recovery

Background

The Twelve-Step Model of addiction and recovery, first manifest in the context of problematic alcohol use as Alcoholics Anonymous (AA; https://www.aa.org/) in the late 1930s, has since been adapted and applied to other substances (e.g., Narcotics Anonymous (NA; https://www.na.org/), Cocaine Anonymous (CA; https://ca.org/), Marijuana Anonymous (MA; https://marijuana-anonymous.org/), and Nicotine Anonymous (NicA; https://nicotine-anonymous.org/)). Likewise, the Twelve-Step Model has been adapted and applied to various behavioral addictions and otherwise compulsive behavioral problems, including Gamblers Anonymous (GA; https://www.gamblersanonymous.org/ga/), Sex Addicts Anonymous (SAA; https://saa-recovery.org/), Overeaters Anonymous (OA; https://oa.org/), and Suicide Anonymous (SA; https://suicideanonymous.net/), among many others (i.e., substances and behaviors; see Schenker,

2009). For over 80 years, the Twelve-Step Model of addiction and recovery has focused on the development, maintenance, and resolution of resentments as the crux of addiction, relapse, and recovery (e.g., AA, 2001; GA, 1989; NA, 2008; SA, 2010; see also, AA, 1981, 1998). Importantly, the Twelve-Step Model, particularly in the context of AA, has been found to be a valuable evidence-based tool in effectively addressing addiction recovery, both in the context of its original intent as mutual-help (i.e., traditional self-help, informal, grass-roots, community-based approaches) and as applied to and integrated with professional treatment (i.e., formal, structured, and (in some cases) manualized counseling and psychotherapy driven approaches) (see Kelly et al., 2020; Lembke & Humphreys, 2012).

Fundamental Assumptions

The five most basic underlying assumptions of the Twelve-Step Model of addiction and recovery are that: (1) addiction is a disease (and not a moral weakness), (2) once a person crosses the threshold of struggling with an addiction, said person will always struggle with addiction, (3) abstinence is critical for recovery, (4) the process of recovery is contingent upon deliberately working through twelve explicit steps, and (5) a person struggling with addiction requires a mentor (i.e., a person in successful Twelve-Step based recovery, commonly known as a *sponsor*) to guide them through the process of recovery (e.g., AA, 2001; GA, 1989; NA, 2008; SA, 2010; see also, AA, 1981, 1998). Of note, although abstinence (i.e., reduced-to-zero addictive behavior; for example, not using a substance(s), only engaging in otherwise acceptable sexual behavior, etc.) is critical for recovery, the twelve steps of The Model are ultimately designed to assist a person struggling with addiction also to become *sober*. That is, in addition to abstinent behavior, sobriety moves beyond reduced-to-zero addictive behavior and necessarily involves changing one's overall lifestyle.[1] In this regard, abstinent behavior refers to reducing use (or other analogous addictive/compulsive behaviors) to zero and sobriety refers to increasing otherwise adaptive and wellness-oriented attitudes and behaviors, not only as directly related to successful addiction recovery, but also in the context of how one lives life more generally. In the Twelve-Step Model, recovery is more than eliminating problematic use/behavior, it necessarily involves addressing the larger issues of problematic living. That is, according to The Model, the problems of life combined with maladaptive coping critically contribute to the development and maintenance of addiction for many individuals (but not necessarily all[2]) and cannot be overlooked when seeking, attaining, and sustaining recovery.

The Twelve Steps

Throughout this chapter (and the book), the primary and representative source material for the Twelve-Step Model to be used will be drawn from AA, NA, GA, and SA publications. However, all adaptations and applications of the Twelve-Step Model (e.g., CA, MA, NicA, SAA, OA) share consistent variations of these common principles. The Twelve-Step Model based principles discussed herein apply to individuals struggling with addiction whether the addiction manifests as related to substance use, an otherwise compulsive behavioral set, or suicide. Listings of the steps in the Twelve-Step Model as applied and adapted to AA, NA, GA, and SA, and formalized, official descriptions and discussions thereof can be found in *Alcoholics Anonymous: The Story of How Many Thousands of Men and Women have Recovered from Alcoholism* (more commonly known as the "Big Book"; AA, 2001, pp. 59–103), *Narcotics Anonymous* (more commonly known as the "Basic Text"; NA, 2008, pp. 17–53), *Gamblers Anonymous: A New Beginning* (GA, 1989, pp. 36–52), and *Suicide Anonymous: The Little Book* (SA, 2010, pp. 25–42). In this regard, the following discussion of the steps in the Twelve-Step Model is based on these aforementioned references as a whole, as interpreted by me,[3] the author of this book (i.e., *Understanding Forgiveness and Addiction: Theory, Research, and Clinical Application*) – unless explicitly cited as coming from a particular reference, whether from said list of four references or otherwise. Also, when discussing the Twelve-Step Model, paraphrasing the material sometimes does not do justice to the ideas and perspectives expressed by the original authors regarding the nature of addiction and recovery. As such, a more-than-usual amount of direct quoting is used in the following overview of the Twelve-Step Model.

Steps 1, 2, and 3

The first three steps of the Model are focused on overcoming barriers to seeking and starting on the path of recovery. The task of these opening steps is often referred to as *acceptance and surrender.* Accepting that there is a problem, recognizing the need for help, identifying a personally suitable power outside of the self to provide said help (i.e., a Higher Power), and surrendering to this Power *and* the process and challenge of addiction recovery.

The first and most important step[4] of the Twelve-Step Model is focused on issues of power and control. Step 1 requires the honest and genuine recognition of one's own (a) addictive behavior, (b) powerlessness over one's addictive behavior, and (c) consequent inability to manage life in the context of one's addiction – and wholeheartedly admitting such to self and others. Importantly, for a person struggling with addiction, there is not necessarily a loss of power and control over all behavior and thus unmanageability in all aspects of life. That is, not all people struggling with an addiction become destitute. Although many hit a low point in their lives, and the Twelve-Step Model posits the need to "hit bottom" before being able to utilize help (NA, 2008, p. 15), the reality is that many people struggling with addiction function well in many areas of life. Recognizing and admitting such powerlessness, unmanageability, and the *need* for help does not imply that a person struggling with addiction is (a) no longer accountable for their addictive behavior, (b) free of the burden to change, or (c) thereby allowed to sit back and let their Higher Power (see Steps 2 and 3) intervene and do everything. The first step simply means that one must become intimately aware of where and when they do and do not have power and control in their life, and admit the need for help to address the areas in which they are struggling.

The second and third steps involve an individual believing in, or choosing to believe in, "a Power greater than [the self]" (Step 2) and making the deliberate *decision* to submit one's will and life to this entity; more precisely, to surrender to a power greater than and external to the self (Step 3) (AA, 2001, p. 59; GA, 1989, pp. 37, 38; NA, 2008, p. 17; SA, 2010, p. 25). In reference to the Power identified in Step 2, some versions of Step 3 include the notion of God (e.g., AA, NA, and SA) and others do not (e.g., GA). Importantly, all variations of the Twelve-Step Model emphasize that the Power identified in Step 2 must be based on personal conceptualization and understanding. Although it is common for Twelve-Step Model adherents to identify this Power as deity (i.e., God(s) and/or Goddess(es), etc.), the Twelve-Step Model is not based in theism, or religious notions of deity, rather it is presented as a spiritual program requiring a connection to a personally identified, *and* chosen, beneficent power greater than and external to the self. Indeed,

> the Higher Power can be anything a member wants it to be, such as God or the psychological and emotional support from the Fellowship or the group. This step does not ask for belief in any organized religion but, more simply, a commitment to personal spirituality.
>
> (GA, 2007, p. 68)

It is not uncommon for people seeking recovery through the Twelve-Step Model to struggle with the notion of having to believe in or accept a power external to and superseding the self, particularly when this notion is perceived as requiring a belief in deity. If the Twelve-Step Model is the only resource available to those struggling with addiction (whether community-based self/mutual-help, or professional, formalized treatment), it becomes critically important to help such individuals realize that believing in God (whether in a traditional or alternative sense) is by no means a requirement for successful recovery. Also, it is not uncommon for self/mutual-help programs and professional, formalized treatment programs based on the Twelve-Step Model to include notions of deity by default (perhaps, inadvertently), due to the widespread belief in deity or a higher power (of some sort) found across the globe (see Chapter 1; GESIS, 2018; ISSP Research Group, 2018). As such, for this and many other reasons, a popular saying heard in the context of the Twelve-Step approach to recovery is the need to *shop around* for resources that are a good ideological fit for the person struggling with addiction recovery. That is, making sure that the Twelve-Step Model is being applied (in any given community-based meeting, or professional treatment program) in a way that is consistent with the beliefs and values of the individual seeking recovery. To those reading this who are struggling with addiction, including those in circumstances where alternatives to the Twelve-Step Model are not readily available, it is OK to look until you find a manifestation of the Twelve-Step Model that works for you. In fact, when other resources are not available, it is imperative to do so, given the need for social support in facilitating recovery (e.g., Hennessy, 2017; Hsu & Marlatt, 2012).

Steps 4, 5, 6, 7, 8, and 9

Steps 4 through 9 are focused on sufficiently addressing the problems associated with one's previous addictive behavior. Once a person struggling with addiction examines, understands, and works through what brought them to where they are – seeking recovery – not only have they started on the journey toward recovery, they are now prepared to use said tools in the perpetual struggle to maintain recovery and move forward.

The first nine steps of the Twelve-Step Model, taken together, are designed to initiate the process of addiction recovery (Steps 1, 2, and 3) and to "clear away the wreckage of [the] past" (Steps 4 through 9; AA, 2001, p. 164). This process allows the person struggling with addiction to attain initial recovery and creates the possibility for long-term recovery.

For its fourth step, the Twelve-Step Model includes conducting a comprehensive and complete personal accounting of one's self; that is, of all interactions with the self, other people, and any other entities, organizations, institutions, or societal principles that give rise to resentments derived from anger, hurt, and perception of threat.

> The purpose of a searching and fearless moral inventory is to sort through the confusion and the contradiction of our lives, so that we can find out who we really

are. We are starting a new way of life and need to be rid of the burdens and traps that controlled us and prevented our growth.

(NA, 2008, p. 27)

This process can be described as the development (and resolution; see Steps 8 and 9) of a "grudge list" (AA, 2001, p. 65). This grudge list is meant to be an actively and constantly evolving, living document; indeed, it must be committed-to-paper and not just thought about. "Looking at what we had done in black and white was an invaluable aid to honesty and objectivity. As we read our version of what happened, we could see through our excuses and our need to blame others" (SA, 2010, p. 31). Without careful, honest, and thorough identification of *all* past, present, and future resentments, one is unlikely to be able to attain and sustain recovery.

In order to be successful, the fourth step is to be a "vigorous and painstaking effort to discover what these liabilities in each of us have been, and are" (AA, 1981, p. 42) and requires "rigorous honesty" (AA, 2001, p. 58). Although other people, as well as other entities, organizations, institutions, and societal principles also contribute to the development of one's resentments, successful identification (and resolution; see Steps 8 and 9) of such involves meaningfully "putting out of our minds the wrongs others [have] done [and] resolutely [looking] for our own mistakes [and not just others']" (AA, 2001, p. 67). Indeed, "first, we searched out the flaws in our make-up which caused our failure. Being convinced that self, manifested in various ways, was what had defeated us, we considered its common manifestations" (AA, 2001, p. 64).

Importantly, the fourth step is not meant to break-down or humiliate the individual struggling with addiction. The aforementioned comprehensive and complete personal accounting of one's self includes one's strengths and good qualities. The task of the fourth step is "to look our past in the face, see it for what it really was and release it so we can live today" (NA, 2008, p. 29); that is, to "face squarely the financial and emotional wrongs that have been done in order to then forgive [ourselves]" (GA, 1989, p. 40). Through this process, "we found the acid test for each relationship: was it selfish or not?" (SA, 2010, p. 32). This all-inclusive, wide-ranging, personal inventory is meant to allow for a thorough examination of "our past performance and our present behavior to see what we want to keep and what we want to discard" (NA, 2008, p. 29). Indeed, through the fourth step, "we begin enjoying our recovery, because we have a way to resolve shame, guilt, or resentment" (NA, 2008, p. 30).

The fifth step involves appropriate, honest, and genuine self-disclosure of the personal inventory/grudge list developed in Step 4. The individual struggling with addiction is to admit "to [our Higher Power], to ourselves, and to another human being the exact nature of our wrongs" (AA, 2001, p. 59; GA, 1989, p. 41; NA, 2008, p. 17; SA, 2010, p. 25). The person that the inventory/grudge list is shared with must be a careful and deliberate choice. A person who knows what is being done and why it is being done. Somebody that can be trusted, respectful, and hold the contents of the self-disclosure confidential. During Step 4, "nothing counted but thoroughness and honesty" (AA, 2001, p. 65). The same holds true during Step 5 as those struggling with addiction "tend to live secret lives" (NA, 2008, p. 33). Honest self-reflection and self-disclosure requires the personal integrity to recognize when one is hiding, or even simply beginning to hide (through dishonesty, and sometimes even less-than-full honesty), and calling oneself out for such – again, admitting such to one's Higher Power, to ourselves, and to others. Such "rigorous honesty" (AA, 2001, p. 58) does not entail obsessive over-disclosure. Rather, it entails *sufficient* disclosure. Arguably, when clear-headed, one cannot escape one's own disingenuousness. In other words, when engaging with the self in a sincere, honest, and authentic manner, we "know" when we are being truthful or not with ourselves and others. Often times this other person is one's sponsor.

The sixth and seventh steps involve active (Step 6) and humble (Step 7) submission to one's Higher Power. Step 6 is focused on taking a "first step toward re-building" (SA, 2010, p. 33); that is, forthrightly becoming willing, ready, and able, and actively following through with submitting to one's Higher Power.

> Do we really want to be rid of our resentments, our anger, our fear? ... [If not,] indulgence in these character defects clouds our ability to think logically. ... [If so,] when we see how our defects exist in our lives and accept them, we can let go of them and get on with our new life.
>
> (NA, 2008, pp. 34–35)

Indeed, many individuals struggling with addiction "slither through life hiding from themselves and now strive to remove the mask so that [they can see, and be seen for, who they are]. ... In Step 6, these defects of character must be worked on and eliminated" in order for recovery from addiction to be successful (GA, 1989, pp. 42–43).

Step 7 is focused on humility. "The main objective of Step Seven is to get out of ourselves and strive to achieve the will of our Higher Power" (NA, 2008, p. 37); indeed, "the basic ingredient of humility is a desire to seek and do [our Higher Power's] will" (SA, 2010, p. 34). In seeking out and striving to live according to the will of one's Higher Power, the Twelve-Step Model encourages its adherents to ask daily for help while continually working to effect change on one's own. That is, consistent with the popular saying (something to the effect of), *pray* [or ask] *as if everything depends on God* [or your Higher Power], *and act as if everything depends on you.* In sum, in Step 7, individuals struggling with addiction are to "ask for help in reducing or removing the defect on which [they] will be working on that day. You must do the leg work so your Higher Power can finish the job as [it] sees fit" (GA, 1989, p. 44). Indeed, the active ingredient, or the mechanism of action, of the Twelve-Step Model is developing a *collaborative* relationship with one's Higher Power. The person struggling with addiction continually is to give their best effort to recovery *and* not only to rely on, but to *allow* their Higher Power to enlighten, strengthen, and empower them in the areas where they fall short.

The eighth and ninth steps have been referred to as the *forgiveness steps* of the Twelve-Step Model (see Hart, 1999). Step 8 involves becoming willing to make amends and Step 9 involves making amends when possible and appropriate. The amends to be made are based on resolving the resentments identified and the resultant grudge list developed in Step 4. Often times, making amends involves discussing with others (i.e., those who the resentments are held against) the nature of the issue, engaging in forgiveness, possibly making restitution, and possibly seeking reconciliation. When seeking to make amends, the default assumption may be that the person struggling with addiction is seeking forgiveness from those they offended during their addiction. However, it can also be important to offer forgiveness to those the person struggling with addiction has been offended by. Seeking forgiveness from one's Higher Power and self-forgiveness also can be important components of making amends. In sum, *multiple* dimensions of forgiveness are important to consider as part of the process of making amends.

"The Eighth Step starts the process of forgiveness. We forgive others; possibly we are forgiven; and finally we forgive ourselves and learn how to live in the world" (NA, 2008, p. 38). "To be forgiven, one must first forgive others and then one's self" (GA, 1989, p. 46). "As we realize our need to be forgiven, we tend to be more forgiving" (NA, 2008, p. 39).

Actually making amends (Step 9) can be difficult, but "we should never fail to contact anyone because of embarrassment, fear or procrastination" (NA, 2008, p. 40). The details and circumstances underlying the development of resentments are often convoluted and confusing to all involved. After a person struggling with addiction develops sufficient self-awareness and comes to a conscientious and reasonably objective understanding of the nature of their addiction – through their work with the Twelve-Step Model – they are ready to proceed with Step 9. In this regard, in understanding one's problematic relations with others (and the respective roles of all involved), it becomes important "to set the record straight" by "laying out the past frankly and fully and asking for forgiveness", thereby acknowledging and taking personal responsibility where applicable and likewise relieving others of relevant burdens (SA, 2010, p. 37). So that, "we [can] step away from further antagonisms and ongoing resentments" (NA, 2008, p. 41).

A critical caveat to Step 9 is making amends *when possible and appropriate.* It is important to realize that it may not be possible to make amends in certain circumstances. For example, a particular person – whether the offended or the offender – may no longer be willing to interact with the person struggling with an addiction. Likewise, a particular person may have passed away, or their whereabouts may be unknown. In such circumstances, it is important to genuinely be willing and ready to make amends if the opportunity were to arise. Also, it is important to realize that it may not be appropriate to make amends with a particular person or under particular circumstances. In some cases, the nature of the offense is such that it may do more harm than good to explicitly address the issue. It is important for the person struggling with addiction not to force their recovery process on others. That is, one's need for peace does not override another's need for peace and right for privacy. The person struggling with addiction and seeking recovery through actively and deliberately making amends must be willing and committed "to go to any lengths ... to do the right thing, no matter what the *personal* consequences may be" (emphasis added; AA, 2001, p. 79). However, although "we want to be free of our guilt, ... we don't wish to do so at the expense of anyone else. ... Sometimes, the only amend we can make is to [remain abstinent and] stay [in recovery]" (NA, 2008, pp. 40–41).

Steps 10, 11, and 12

The concluding steps of the Twelve-Step Model are designed to sustain long-term addiction recovery. "Now that we have progressed through the first nine steps, we should be ready to maintain them with the last three steps. ... Another view is that Steps One through Nine are never done and should be regularly repeated" (GA, 1989, pp. 48–49).

The tenth step involves the steadfast, vigilant, consistent, and *recurrent* examination of past, present, and future concerns in the context of the insights and skills developed in the previous steps, particularly Steps 4 through 9. In this regard, the reality is two-fold: (a) Steps 4 through 9 address the past, and give those struggling with addiction a chance for a different future and (b) aspects of the past are missed, and being imperfect, new issues arise. Related to this, "we learned that our character defects, outrageous in the past, continued in milder form, and that we had to recognize them, realize that they were part of us, and keep them in check" (SA, 2010, p. 38). "In [doing this, we are to], look for personal growth, not perfection" (GA, 1989, p. 48). "Continue to watch for selfishness, dishonesty, resentment, and fear. ... Love and tolerance of others is our code. [Such that], we have ceased fighting anything or anyone" (AA, 2001, p. 84). "The ability to cope is perhaps the most valuable reward which you will receive from the program. … Abstinence combined with physical, mental and emotional healing will give us a logical ability to cope" (GA, 1989, pp. 48–49). "We work this step continuously. This is a preventative action. … By continuing a personal inventory, we are set free, in the here and now, from ourselves and the past" (NA, 2008, pp. 43–44).

As discussed previously in Steps 4 and 5, when investing in Step 10, and thereby revisiting Steps 4 through 9, "nothing [counts] but thoroughness and [rigorous] honesty" (AA, 2001, pp. 65, 58). Once again, however, one needs to be careful and resist the urge to review one's life in an obsessive fashion. Obsessive-compulsive behavior (broadly construed; that is, aside from formal clinical diagnosis) is counterproductive and, unfortunately, is inherent to addiction. It is no wonder that those struggling with obsessive tendencies in addiction also seem to struggle with obsessive tendencies in recovery. "We need to remember that everyone makes mistakes. We will never be perfect. However, we can accept ourselves by using Step 10" (NA, 2008, p. 44). A helpful tool to combat such obsessive tendencies is to realize and become comfortable with the reality that we can only do *our* best and it is OK to be good enough.

The eleventh step requires the continual, deliberate, and purposeful pursuit of and contact with one's Higher Power, including seeking guidance and the strength to follow-through with such. Similar to Step 10 and its focus on revisiting Steps 4 through 9, Step 11 is focused on revisiting Steps 2 and 3, which steps "made us aware that human resources were not enough … . Eventually we came to realize that our addiction meant we must use all possible help. Now we must learn better how to communicate with our Higher Power" (GA, 1989, p. 49).

In the eleventh step of the Twelve-Step Model, communication with one's higher power is defined as occurring "through prayer and meditation" (e.g., AA, 2001, p. 59; GA, 1989, p. 49; NA, 2008, p. 17; SA, 2010, p. 25). Prayer is viewed as a mode of self-instigated, intentional, otherwise cognitively-oriented contact with one's Higher Power (whether out-loud or thoughts-based), that also is consistent with the individual's conceptualization of their Higher Power. To be clear, although prayer can take a traditional faith-based and/or organized-religion form (whether memorized recitation or personalized conversation, etc.), it is by no means a requirement of the Twelve-Step Model to follow any set or pre-existing format for prayer. One's manner of prayer can take *any* form, "the only requirements for our prayers [are] unselfishness and sincerity" (SA, 2010, p. 39). "Prayer is communicating our concerns to a Power greater than ourselves" (NA, 2008, p. 46). "[Each night], we constructively review our day. Were we resentful, selfish, dishonest or afraid? Do we owe an apology? … After making our review we ask [our Higher Power's] forgiveness and inquire what corrective measures should be taken" (AA, 2001, p. 86).

Is prayer sufficient to effect change? That is, do we ask for help and simply go about our day/lives and wait for divine or external intervention to occur? Is our responsibility for action over once we utter our prayer? "Once we talk to [our Higher Power], we must listen carefully for answers" (SA, 2010, p. 40). In the Twelve-Step Model, meditation is viewed as the means by which answers come from one's Higher Power. The Twelve-Step Model acknowledges that answers to prayer are not automatic and that meditation – a learned skill – can be difficult and requires practice. In this regard, how does one identify answers to prayer? Put differently, what do answers to prayer look, feel, and/or sound like? How do we know that we have received an answer to prayer? Can we *reliably* know that we have received an answer? These are age-old, difficult questions – regardless of whether or not one is struggling with addiction. For a state-of-the-science review of the psychology of prayer, see Spilka and Ladd (2013). In the meantime, from the perspective of the Twelve-Step Model of addiction and recovery:

> We find ourselves praying, because it brings us peace and restores our confidence and courage. It helps us to live a life that is free of fear and distrust. When we remove our selfish motives and pray for guidance, we find feelings of peace and serenity. We begin to experience an awareness and an empathy with other people that was not possible before working this step.
>
> (NA, 2008, p. 47)

"Intuitions came to us during these times of meditation and throughout each day. A word from another person, a thought popping into our minds, an idea for action emerging as we worked on our problems" (SA, 2010, p. 40). "Sometimes when we pray, a remarkable thing happens; we find the means, ways and energies to perform tasks far beyond our capacities. We grasp the limitless strength provided for us through our daily prayer and surrender" (NA, 2008, p. 46). "We find that our thinking will, as time passes, be more and more on the plane of [receiving] inspiration [from our Higher Power]" (AA, 2001, p. 87). "*The conscious contact described in this step is the direct result of living the steps*" (emphasis added; NA, 2008, p. 44).[5]

The twelfth step is focused on (a) sharing the message of recovery with those continuing to struggle with active addiction *and* (b) personally striving to broadly apply all of the principles of the Twelve-Step Model of addiction and recovery to all aspects of one's life and everyday living, *not just* in the context of substance use, compulsive behavioral sets, and/or suicide. In order to sustain recovery, one must be of service to others and embrace a new lifestyle.

> Here we turn outward toward [those struggling with addiction] who are still in distress. Here we experience the kind of giving that asks no rewards. Here we begin to practice all Twelve Steps of the program in our daily lives so that we and those about us may find *emotional* sobriety.
>
> (emphasis added; AA, 1981, p. 106)

"Saying it another way, you cannot carry the recovery program to another unless you are practicing the Twelve Steps in your life, one day at a time" (GA, 1989, p. 51). "The message … is meaningless unless WE LIVE IT. As we live it, our lives and actions give it more meaning than our words and literature ever could" (emphasis in original; NA, 2008, p. 49).

Regarding serving others, "by this time, most of us realize that the only way we can keep what was given to us is by sharing this new gift of life [with those still suffering from addiction]" (NA, 2008, p. 50). "[We have discovered] that by the divine paradox of this kind of giving [we, nonetheless, find our] own reward, [whether those still suffering have] yet received anything or not" (AA, 1981, p. 109). "If you give of yourself and try to help another human being, you will gain from the act of giving, even if your effort fails" (GA, 1989, p. 52). Indeed, "we cannot deny [those still struggling with addiction] their pain, but we can carry the message of hope that was given to us" (NA, 2008, p. 52). "Paradoxically, we found no greater satisfaction and no greater joy than that which we received in our selfless giving to others" (SA, 2010, p. 41). "We share the principles of recovery, as they have worked in our lives. [Our Higher Power] helps us as we help each other" (NA, 2008, p. 52).

Regarding seeking to apply the Twelve-Step Model to everyday living and all aspects of life, the reality is that even after a person struggling with addiction (1) attains initial recovery, (2) learns the tools necessary for maintaining recovery, and (3) increases the efficiency of said tools, through consistent and determined personal application and service to others, thereby achieving sustained, long-term recovery, the problems of life and living never go away. The Twelve-Step Model is clearly designed to help individuals struggling with addiction change their negative addictive behaviors and find resolution for the negative consequences associated therewith. Yet, the tools of recovery and the lifestyle modifications effected thereby are readily adaptable and applicable to the inevitable pitfalls and stresses of life. The steps of the Twelve-Step Model are, at their core, meant to provide an effective and efficient system of not only coping with problems, but also a system of preventing unnecessary problems from arising. Moreover, when those things which are outside of our control happen, the habits developed from living the Twelve Steps can prevent such from themselves spiraling out of control, as well as preventing such from exacerbating other problematic situations that may be going on.

> Once we find the [Twelve-Step] way, boredom and complacency have no place in our new life. By [investing in and engaging with long-term recovery], we begin to practice spiritual principles such as hope, surrender, acceptance, honesty, open-mindedness, willingness, faith, tolerance, patience, humility, unconditional love, sharing, and caring. As our recovery progresses, spiritual principles touch every area of our lives, because we simply try to live this program in the here and now. … We feel that our lives have become worthwhile. Spiritually refreshed, we are glad to be alive. When we were [actively engaging in addictive behavior], our lives became an exercise in survival. Now we are doing much more living than surviving. … Practicing spiritual principles in our daily lives leads us to a new image of ourselves. Honesty, humility, and open-mindedness help us to treat our associates fairly. Our decisions become tempered with tolerance. We learn to respect ourselves.
>
> (NA, 2008, pp. 51–52)

The Twelve-Step Model and Twelve-Step Facilitation Therapy

The Twelve-Step Model of addiction and recovery was developed to be a grass-roots, community-based, self/mutual-help program designed to be implemented by laypersons. That is, professional training in relevant treatment modalities (whether related to physical, mental, or spiritual health and/or well-being, etc.) is not required, nor intended to be a part of the method or application of the Twelve-Step Model. The only requirement, in this regard, is that the mutual/self-help, community-based meetings are to be led *by* people struggling with addiction, but in recovery, *for* people struggling with addiction *and* recovery (and, potentially, others interested in learning about addiction and recovery). Twelve-Step Facilitation Therapy (TSF; see Nowinski, 2012; Nowinski et al., 1994) is a formalized treatment modality derived from the Twelve-Step Model and is designed to be delivered by professionally trained mental health care providers. On its own (e.g., through Project MATCH; Longabaugh & Wirtz, 2001) and together with modalities incorporating Motivational Interviewing (see Chapter 10), Cognitive-Behaviorism (see Chapter 11), and medication or pharmacotherapy (e.g., through COMBINE; Miller, 2004; Pettinati et al., 2004), TSF has received a considerable amount of empirical attention (mostly, but not only, in the context of alcohol use), and is viewed as an effective, evidence-based psychotherapeutic treatment for substance-related addiction (see Blonigen et al., 2015; Kelly et al., 2020; Kingree, 2013; Lembke & Humphreys, 2012; Pilkey et al., 2015; for effective medication-based treatments for substance-related addiction, see also, McKay et al., 2015). Likewise, for broad discussions of effective treatments in the context of gambling and compulsive buying, eating related issues, and suicidal behavior, see Grant et al. (2015), Pike et al. (2015), and Bongar and Sullivan (2013), respectively.

Focusing on the first three steps of the Twelve-Step Model, TSF primarily addresses the potentially confounding barriers to recovery related to powerlessness and lack of control (Step 1), and belief in (Step 2) and submission to (Step 3) a Higher Power (see Nowinski, 2012; Nowinski et al., 1994). Taken together, these issues, including the process and task of overcoming them, are commonly known as *acceptance and surrender* and are viewed as core principles underlying the successful completion of the remaining Twelve Steps. Importantly, however, TSF can also include various elective components, thereby incorporating multiple, if not all of the steps in the Twelve-Step Model.

Forgiveness, the Twelve-Step Model, and Twelve-Step Facilitation Therapy

Forgiveness is included in the Twelve-Step Model as an explicit goal and outcome of particular steps (i.e., Steps 8 and 9) and has been shown, conceptually, to be consistent with and thus, underlying many, if not all of the steps in the Twelve-Step Model (e.g., Webb et al., 2015; Webb & Trautman, 2010; see also, Hart, 1999; Lyons et al., 2010). As such, infusing the process of forgiveness into the treatment of addiction, through the principles of TSF and/or the entire Twelve-Step Model, is warranted and herein called for (see Webb et al., 2015; Webb & Jeter, 2015; Webb & Toussaint, 2018, 2020). Following is a more detailed discussion of the consistencies between the Process and REACH models of forgiveness (as developed by Enright and Worthington, respectively; see Chapter 8) and the Twelve-Step Model of addiction and recovery (see Table 9.1), thereby justifying the implicit (and explicit) incorporation of forgiveness into TSF as an evidence-based psychotherapeutic treatment for addiction.

Forgiveness and Steps 1, 2, and 3

The first step in the Twelve-Step Model is consistent with the first phase in each of the models of forgiveness developed by Enright and Worthington; that is, *Uncovering* and *Recalling the Hurt*, respectively (see Chapter 8). The overall goals of Step 1 regarding recognizing, understanding, and admitting (a) one's addictive behavior, (b) one's powerlessness over addiction, and (c) where one does and does not have control over one's life (i.e., the unmanageability of life in the context of addiction) – again, whether concerning substance use, compulsive behavioral sets, or suicide – entails developing accurate and appropriate self-regulation and personal responsibility. This process often involves developing a deep personal understanding of the counterproductive interplay of psychological defenses, anger, and shame in one's life. Indeed, during Enright's *Uncovering* phase, it is important to scrutinize and understand our attempts to deny or defend against what has been going on, and acknowledge and address not only the resultant negative emotions, but one's investment in and reluctance to let go of such. Also, during the process of Uncovering, one must come to terms with how one's life and worldview have permanently changed as a result of one's experiences.

Similarly, during Worthington's *Recalling the Hurt* phase, one is to accurately and objectively recall and understand one's painful experiences and responses in an effort to address them in a more constructive and productive manner. That is, to recognize, acknowledge, and embrace one's problematic experiences in a beneficial, rather than

Table 9.1 Forgiveness and the Twelve-Step Model

Forgiveness Phase		*Corresponding Aspects of the Twelve-Step Model adapted to Addictive Behavior*[a]	
Process Model[b]	*REACH Model*[b]	*Step*	*Descriptor*
Uncovering	Recalling the Hurt	Step 1[c]	Acceptance
Decision	Empathy	Step 2 & Step 3	Surrender
Work	Altruistic Gift		
	Commitment		
Work	Commitment	Step 4	Personal Moral Inventory
		Step 5	Appropriate Self-Disclosure
		Step 6 & Step 7	Active Submission
		Step 8	Willing to Make Amends
		Step 9	Making Amends
Deepening	Holding On	Step 10	Proactive Self-Awareness
		Step 11	Consistent Pursuit of Higher Power
		Step 12	Service and Twelve-Step based Lifestyle

Source: Adapted from Webb et al. (2015).

[a] That is, as related to substance use, compulsive behavior sets, and suicide.
[b] See Chapter 9
[c] Although Uncovering and Recall are overwhelmingly associated with Step 1, they also are likely associated with Steps 2 through 12, albeit to a lesser degree. Likewise, Step 1 is overwhelmingly associated with Uncovering and Recall, but likely comes into play with each of the phases of the models of forgiveness developed by Enright and Worthington.

dysfunctional fashion. Inherent to the task of Recalling the Hurt in a healthy manner is that separating one's negative emotional responses from one's difficult experiences helps break through the denial of and resistance to addressing the life altering nature of said difficult experiences. Such separation can occur through accepting the negative responses as normal reactions – when expressed accurately, objectively, and judiciously – to difficult experiences; thereby, leading to self-empathy, rather than self-condemnation. That is, otherwise normalizing any anger, fear, guilt, shame, etc. associated with poor behavior and/or failure (whether directed at or perpetuated by self or others) can prevent defensive, counterproductive, self-defeating attempts at resolution.

A critical common feature between Step 1, Enright's Uncovering phase, and Worthington's Recalling the Hurt phase is the notion of a counterintuitive effect regarding the issue of control. Coleman (1998), in the context of forgiveness, yet, it holds true also for addiction, describes this paradoxical effect. That is, often when faced with a profoundly disillusioning, life-altering offensive experience (whether in the context of addiction or not, but *particularly so with addiction*), our default assumption is that an active, unyielding determination to re-establish unquestionable control over said situation is the only hope for resolution, repair, and a return to normalcy. In this regard, forgiveness, as well as admitting powerlessness and unmanageability, are typically viewed as signs of weakness. That engaging in such processes allows the offender off the hook (i.e., the self, other people, or any other entities, organizations, institutions, or societal principles – again, whether in the context of addiction or not), or not to be held responsible or accountable. Yet, when holding on to all of the negative responses to said negative experiences, one becomes consumed with rumination, or obsessively thinking about the situation, at the expense of being able to actually address and solve the problem in an efficient and effective manner. By choosing to forgive, as well as choosing to admit powerlessness and unmanageability, one becomes free of the overwhelming weight of rumination and thus more able to redirect one's energy and efforts toward more productive solutions.

The second and third step of the Twelve-Step Model, believing in a personally identified Higher Power (Step 2) and making a decision to surrender one's life and will thereto (Step 3), together involve recognizing, considering, and accepting the personal need for transformation *and* the inability to do so without the help of one's Higher Power. This process is consistent with the second phase and initial aspects of the third phase of Enright's model (i.e., *Decision* and *Work*, respectively) and the second and third phase, and initial aspects of the fourth phase of Worthington's model (i.e., *Empathy, Altruistic Gift*, and *Commitment*, respectively). Regarding Enright's Decision phase, it is important to realize that one's current and default methods are not working and that something different needs to happen (i.e., similar to the transformation involved in Steps 2 and 3). After gaining sufficient understanding of the proposed alternative (i.e., forgiveness or the help of a Higher Power), the individual makes an informed and intentional choice to proceed therewith, and formally commits to such. During Enright's Work phase, one starts to reframe the difficult experience, gain perspective, and develop empathy and compassion for the offender (i.e., more transformation) in order to work towards giving the moral gift of forgiveness, or in the context of addiction, the opportunity for a different future.

Regarding Worthington's Empathy phase, the task is to recognize the need to reprocess one's emotions (i.e., the need for a different, more effective means of problem solving) and to do so by replacing negative, counterproductive emotions and reactions with positive, productive alternatives (i.e., similar to the transformation involved in Steps 2 and 3). Moreover, specifically to develop empathy through perspective taking, and to combine such with compassion and concern for the offender (i.e., more transformation). Completion of the Empathy phase enables progression toward giving an Altruistic Gift of forgiveness (or the opportunity for a different future); nevertheless, empathy alone may not be sufficient. Facilitating humility and gratitude (along with empathy) may also be necessary (i.e., even more transformation). Part of the process here is to develop insight into one's own needs in these areas, including the experience of being relieved of the burdens associated with the guilt and shame of having harmed self or others, and/or the struggle of addiction. Again, success to this point includes the initial commitment to the process of forgiveness and to moving forward (i.e., Worthington's Commitment phase).

In sum, working through the first three steps in the Twelve-Step Model constitutes (a) one's initial commitment to pursue recovery and (b) the necessary preparation to be successful in the hard work of *following through* with recovery. Similarly, Enright's Uncovering and Decision phases, along with initial aspects of the Work phase, and Worthington's Recalling the Hurt, Empathy, and Altruistic Gift phases, along with initial aspects of the Commitment phase, constitute (a) one's initial commitment to pursue forgiveness and (b) the necessary preparation to be successful in the hard work of following through with forgiveness. In a sense, the Higher Power in the process of forgiveness is: *forgiveness*, itself. Often, one must trust with spiritual-level conviction that forgiveness will fulfill its promise of relief from profound difficulties and loss. Just as, in recovery, one must surrender to the will and guidance of one's Higher Power.

Forgiveness and Steps 4, 5, 6, 7, 8, and 9

Focused on addressing the problems created by one's active period(s) of addiction, Steps 4 through 9 are consistent with moving forward and completing the phases of forgiveness begun in Steps 2 and 3; that is, Enright's *Work* phase and Worthington's *Commitment* phase. Step 4, developing a personal moral inventory (remember: written down as a grudge list) involves identifying resentments and beginning the process of finding resolution through forgiveness. The fundamental interplay between resentments and forgiveness in the Twelve-Step Model can employ various methods (i.e., offering, seeking, and feeling) and various targets (e.g., self, others, conceptions of one's Higher Power, uncontrollable circumstances, and/or any other entities, organizations, institutions, or societal principles, etc.; see above, and Chapter 3). Step 5, involves appropriate, honest, and genuine self-disclosure of one's grudge list, including "the exact nature of our wrongs" to another person, to ourselves, and to our Higher Power (AA, 2001, p. 58; GA, 1989, p. 41; NA, 2008, p. 17; SA, 2010, p. 25). If we have developed and written down our grudge list (Step 4), what does it mean to then self-disclose it to ourselves? The process of talking out loud to others – hearing ourselves telling another – provides additional perspective and connection to the reality and gravity of our behavior. Step 6 and Step 7 respectively entail active and humble submission to one's Higher Power. Steps 5, 6, and 7 working together involve continued, focused, and deliberate efforts to logically and objectively reframe, accept, and find resolution to the "wreckage of [the] past" (AA, 2001, p. 164) created by our active period(s) of addiction, as identified in Step 4.

Step 8 involves becoming willing to make amends and Step 9 involves making amends when possible. Merriam-Webster (2020) defines *amends* as "compensation for a loss or injury [or] recompense" and further defines *recompense* as "an equivalent or a return for something done, suffered, or given." Hart (1999) describes Steps 8 and 9 as the *forgiveness steps* and discusses their connection to Steps 3 and 4. Equating forgiveness with amends and recompense suggests that relief *through* forgiveness of the burdens associated with the guilt and shame of having harmed self or others, and/or the struggle of addiction may be payment-in-kind for such difficulties, particularly when one has "ceased fighting anything or anyone" (AA, 2001, p. 84).

Regarding the completion of Enright's *Work* phase, the transformative process described above continues, yet also moves forward through accepting, enduring, and absorbing the painful experiences. Thereby, working towards healing, rather than continuing the self-destructive process of seeking to externalize the pain through seeking revenge and retribution, or in the context of addiction, seeking to avoid the nature and consequences of one's addictive behavior and admitting the struggle therewith. Similarly, completing Worthington's Commitment phase continues the transformative process through making a *public* commitment to forgiveness (or recovery) as a means of addressing the inevitable occurrence of doubts and increasing the likelihood of following through. The Commitment phase includes getting the process of transformative change *outside of the self* through written exercise and disclosure to others. Also, a critical component of this continued transformative process is understanding that continuing to feel the pain of difficult experiences or continuing to struggle with addictive behavior and the recovery process is not necessarily indicative of a lack of progress with forgiveness or recovery. Rather, it is indicative that both forgiveness and recovery are not simple or easy-flowing processes nor is either likely to be an event or an all-or-nothing experience. Considering Steps 4 through 9 together, much time, reasoned thought, and whole-hearted effort is required to be invested in Enright's Work phase and Worthington's Commitment phase.

Forgiveness and Steps 10, 11, and 12

After initial recovery is attained through the first nine steps of the Twelve-Step Model, the concluding steps of the Model are designed to foster vigilance, thereby serving to strengthen, sustain, and solidify recovery for the long term. Step 10 involves the proactive continuation of the intra- and inter-personal processes and procedures learned, particularly in Steps 4 and 5, but also in Steps 6 through 9. That is, sufficiently – and within reason – examining, re-examining, and addressing the past, present, and future (Step 10) for missed and new resentments (see Step 4), honest and genuine self-disclosure of such (see Step 5), active and humble submission to the guidance and intervention of one's Higher Power (see Steps 6 and 7, respectively), and willingly making amends when possible and appropriate (see Steps 8 and 9, respectively). Step 11 is designed to increase efficient contact and collaboration (see also Step 7) with one's Higher Power through proactive, consistent, and persistent pursuit, and Step 12 involves assisting and providing service to peers in and struggling for recovery, *and* broad personal application of the entire Twelve-Step Model in all areas of life and living.

Regarding Enright's *Deepening* phase, one is to derive new-found meaning and purpose from their suffering, including recognizing and embracing the reality that one is not alone in their struggle for change. That strength can come through interdependence and sharing one's experiences with others. Regarding Worthington's *Holding On* phase, one is to continue the process of maintaining and strengthening one's commitment to more effective coping and a different future. That is, vigilance is necessary against the inevitable recurrence of doubts arising from the intrusive thoughts, memories, and images of past difficulties. Likewise, it is important always to revisit and rework the phases of forgiveness, as needed.

In sum, achieving the outcome of forgiveness and the outcome of addiction recovery – through working and reworking each and every phase of forgiveness and each and every step of the Twelve-Step Model – are both deeply transformative processes. Indeed, those that are successful are able to "clear away the wreckage of [the] past" (AA, 2001, p. 164) and "to exceed even their most optimistic expectations for themselves" (Worthington & Wade, 2020, p. 1).

Notes

1 A common term that is still used in popular culture is "clean and sober." However, with concerns over language usage / non-stigmatizing terminology, "clean" is a problematic term. See Chapter 2 for more related discussion.

2 That is, The Twelve-Step Model acknowledges that not all individuals will develop addictive behavior in response to problematic life circumstances and maladaptive coping therewith.

3 For an additional / other perspective on Twelve-Step Model interpretation/theory, see Wallace (2012).

4 Of note, sometimes there is the issue of *Two-Stepping* versus *Twelve-Stepping*. That is, the notion of Two-Stepping implies that Step 1 and Step 12 are most important, that Steps 2 through 11 are not so important when one "has time in recovery" versus working and reworking all 12 Steps (i.e., Twelve-Stepping) is actually what is critical for sustaining recovery (see Alcoholics Anonymous, 1981, p. 113).

5 This notion is consistent with the sentiment expressed in *John* 7:17: "If any [person] will do his will, [said person] shall know of the doctrine, whether it be of God, or whether I speak of myself" (KJV, 1983).

References

Alcoholics Anonymous (AA) (1981). *Twelve steps and twelve traditions.* New York, NY: Author. See https://www.aa.org/pages/en_US/twelve-steps-and-twelve-traditions.

Alcoholics Anonymous (AA) (1998). *Living sober.* New York, NY: Author.

Alcoholics Anonymous (AA) (2001). *Alcoholics Anonymous* (4th ed.). New York, NY: Author. See https://www.aa.org/pages/en_US/alcoholics-anonymous.

Blonigen, D. M., Finney, J. W., Wilbourne, P. L., & Moos, R. H. (2015). Psychosocial treatments for substance use disorders. In P. E. Nathan & J. M. Gorman (Eds.), *A guide to treatments that work* (4th ed., pp. 731–761). New York, NY: Oxford University Press.

Bongar, B., & Sullivan, G. (2013). Outpatient management and treatment of the suicidal patient. In *The suicidal patient: Clinical and legal standards of care* (3rd ed., pp. 157–199). Washington, DC: American Psychological Association.

Coleman, P. W. (1998). The process of forgiveness in marriage and the family. In R. D. Enright & J. North (Eds.) *Exploring forgiveness* (pp. 75–94). Madison, WI: University of Wisconsin Press.

Gamblers Anonymous (GA) (1989). *A new beginning.* Los Angeles, CA: Author.

Gamblers Anonymous (GA) (2007). *Sharing recovery through gamblers anonymous* (Revised ed.). Los Angeles, CA: Author.

GESIS (Ed.) (2018). ISSP 2008 – Religion III. Variable Report: Documentation release 2018/10/26, related to the international dataset Archive-Study-No. ZA4950 Version 2.3.0 Variable Reports 2018|17. Cologne: Author.

Grant, J. E., Odlaug, B. L., & Potenza, M. N. (2015). Treatments for gambling disorder and impulse control disorders. In P. E. Nathan & J. M. Gorman (Eds.), *A guide to treatments that work* (4th ed., pp. 801–826). New York, NY: Oxford University Press.

Hart, K. E. (1999). A spiritual interpretation of the 12-steps of Alcoholics Anonymous: From resentment to forgiveness to love. *Journal of Ministry in Addiction & Recovery*, 6(2), 25–39. doi:10.1300/J048v06n02_03.

Hennessy, E. A. (2017). Recovery capital: A systematic review of the literature. *Addiction Research & Theory*, 25(5), 349–360. doi:10.1080/16066359.2017.1297990.

Hsu, S. H., & Marlatt, G. A. (2012). Addiction syndrome: Relapse and relapse prevention. In H. Shaffer, D. A. LaPlante, & S. E. Nelson (Eds.), *APA addiction syndrome handbook, Vol. 2: Recovery, prevention, and other issues* (pp. 105–132). Washington, DC: American Psychological Association.

ISSP Research Group (2018). *International Social Survey Programme: Religion III - ISSP 2008.* GESIS Data Archive, Cologne. ZA4950 Data file Version 2.3.0, doi:10.4232/1.13161.

Kelly, J. F., Humphreys, K., & Ferri, M. (2020). Alcoholics Anonymous and other 12-step programs for alcohol use disorder. *Cochrane Database of Systematic Reviews*, (3). doi:10.1002/14651858.CD012880.pub2.

King James Version (1983). *Holy Bible.* Salt Lake City, UT: Church of Jesus Christ of Latter-day Saints.

Kingree, J. B. (2013). Twelve-step facilitation therapy. In P. M. Miller, S. A. Ball, M. E. Bates, A. W. Blume, K. M. Kampman, D. J. Kavanagh, M. E. Larimer, N. M. Petry, & P. De Witte (Eds.), *Comprehensive addictive behaviors and disorders, Vol. 3: Interventions for addiction* (pp. 137–146). San Diego, CA: Elsevier Academic Press.

Lembke, A., & Humphreys, K. (2012). What self-help organizations tell us about the syndrome model of addiction. In H. Shaffer, D. A. LaPlante, & S. E. Nelson (Eds.), *APA addiction syndrome handbook, Vol. 2: Recovery, prevention, and other issues* (pp. 157–168). Washington, DC: American Psychological Association.

Longabaugh, R., & Wirtz, P. W. (Eds.). (2001). *Project MATCH: Hypotheses, results, and causal chain analyses.* NIH Publication No. 01–4238. Rockville, MD: National Institute on Alcohol Abuse and Alcoholism.

Lyons, G. C. B., Deane, F. P., & Kelly, P. J. (2010). Forgiveness and purpose in life as spiritual mechanisms of recovery from substance use disorders. *Addiction Research & Theory*, 18(5), 528–543. doi:10.3109/16066351003660619.

McKay, J. R., Kranzler, H. R., Kampman, K. M., Ashare, R. L., & Schnoll, R. A. (2015). Psychopharmacological treatments for substance use disorders. In P. E. Nathan & J. M. Gorman (Eds.), *A guide to treatments that work* (4th ed., pp. 763–800). New York, NY: Oxford University Press.

Merriam-Webster (2020). Amends; Recompense. Retrieved from https://www.merriam-webster.com/dictionary/amends; and https://www.merriam-webster.com/dictionary/recompense.

Miller, W. R. (Ed.) (2004). *COMBINE Monograph Series, Volume 1. Combined behavioral intervention manual: A clinical research guide for therapists treating people with alcohol abuse and dependence.* DHHS Publication No. (NIH) 04–5288. Bethesda, MD: National Institute on Alcohol Abuse and Alcoholism.

Narcotics Anonymous (NA) (2008). *Narcotics Anonymous* (6h ed.). Chatsworth, CA: Author.

Nowinski, J. (2012). Facilitating 12-Step recovery from substance abuse. In S. T. Walters & F. Rotgers (Eds.), *Treating substance abuse: Theory and technique* (3rd ed., pp. 191–223). New York, NY: Guilford Press.

Nowinski, J., Baker, S., & Carroll, K. M. (1994). *Twelve step facilitation therapy manual: A clinical research guide for therapists treating individuals with alcohol abuse and dependence.* NIH Publication No. 94–3722. Rockville, MD: National Institute on Alcohol Abuse and Alcoholism.

Pettinati, H. M., Weiss, R. D., Miller, W. R., Donovan, D., Ernst, D. B., & Rounsaville, B. J. (2004). *COMBINE Monograph Series, Volume 2. Medical management treatment manual: A clinical research guide for medically trained clinicians providing pharmacotherapy as part of the treatment for alcohol dependence.* DHHS Publication No. (NIH) 04–5289. Bethesda, MD: National Institute on Alcohol Abuse and Alcoholism.

Pike, K. M., Gianni, L. M., Loeb, K. L., & Le Grange, D. (2015). Treatments for eating disorders. In P. E. Nathan & J. M. Gorman (Eds.), *A guide to treatments that work* (4th ed., pp. 641–658). New York, NY: Oxford University Press.

Pilkey, D., Steinberg, H., & Martino, S. (2015). Evidence-based treatments for substance use disorders. In A. D. Kaye, N. Vadivelu, & R. D. Urman (Eds.), *Substance abuse: Inpatient and outpatient management for every clinician* (pp. 209–227). New York, NY: Springer.

Schenker, M. D. (2009). *A clinician's guide to 12-Step recovery.* New York, NY: W. W. Norton & Co.

Spilka, B., & Ladd, K. L. (2013). *The psychology of prayer: A scientific approach.* New York, NY: Guilford Press.

Suicide Anonymous (SA) (2010). *Suicide Anonymous, the little book.* Memphis, TN: Author. Retrieved August 7, 2018, from http://www.suicideanonymous.net/uploads/SA_BOOKLET_ok_copy.pdf.

Wallace, J. (2012). Theory of 12-step-oriented treatment. In S. T. Walters, & F. Rotgers (Eds.), *Treating substance abuse: Theory and technique* (3rd ed., pp. 167–190). New York, NY: Guilford Press.

Webb, J. R., & Jeter, B. R. (2015). Forgiveness and problematic substance use. In L. L. Toussaint, E. L.Worthington, Jr., & D. R. Williams (Eds.), *Forgiveness and health: Scientific evidence and theories relating forgiveness to better health* (pp. 139–154). New York, NY: Springer.

Webb, J. R., & Toussaint, L. L. (2018). Self-forgiveness as a critical factor in addiction and recovery: A 12-step model perspective. *Alcoholism Treatment Quarterly*, 36(1), 15–31. doi:10.1080/07347324.2017.1391057.

Webb, J. R., & Toussaint, L. L. (2020). Forgiveness, well-being, and mental health. In E. L. Worthington, Jr. & N. G. Wade (Eds.), *Handbook for forgiveness* (2nd ed., pp. 188–197). New York, NY: Routledge.

Webb, J. R., & Trautman, R. P. (2010). Forgiveness and alcohol use: Applying a specific spiritual principle to substance abuse problems. *Addictive Disorders & Their Treatment*, 9(1), 8–17. doi:10.1097/ADT.0b013e318195000d.

Webb, J. R., Hirsch, J. K., & Toussaint, L. L. (2015). Forgiveness as a positive psychotherapy for addiction and suicide: Theory, research, and practice. *Spirituality in Clinical Practice*, 2(1), 48–60. doi:10.1037/scp0000054.

Worthington, E. L., Jr., & Wade, N. G. (2020). How you can benefit from this handbook. In E. L.Worthington, Jr. & N. G. Wade (Eds.), *Handbook of forgiveness* (2nd ed., pp. 1–8). New York, NY: Routledge.

Worthington, E. L., Jr., Berry, J. W., & Parrott, L., III. (2001). Unforgiveness, forgiveness, religion, and health. In T. G. Plante & A. C. Sherman (Eds.), *Faith and health: Psychological perspectives* (pp. 107–138). New York, NY: Guilford Press.

10 Clinical Application: Motivational Interviewing and Stages of Change

A shared, core theme of the Twelve-Step Model of addiction recovery (see Chapter 9), Enright's Process Model of Forgiveness (see Chapter 8), and Worthington's REACH Model of Forgiveness (see Chapter 8), is the notion that one must recognize and accept the reality that one's current attempts at change are not effective and likely counterproductive. Moreover, that one must then identify an effective alternative course of action and commit to a determined pursuit thereof. Underlying this last component (i.e., committed and determined pursuit) is the need for sufficient *motivation* in order to be able to follow through with the overwhelming difficulty of *changing* one's attitudes and behavior, particularly in the context of addiction, as well as in response to experiencing deeply offense experiences (whether in the context of addiction or not). Such change is difficult in the context of (1) addiction, as evidenced by the common notion that "relapse is part of recovery" and (2) forgiveness, as evidenced by Enright's *Work* phase and Worthington's *Commitment* phase, and the explicit need then to continue on with Enright's *Deepening* phase and Worthington's *Holding On* phase. Of note, each of said successive forgiveness phases, whether from Enright's model or Worthington's model, acknowledges the inherent struggle and required vigilance to maintain one's progress.

In this regard, the conceptual and empirical insights initially developed in the early 1980s regarding motivation (Miller, 1983) and change (Prochaska & DiClemente, 1982) have been game-changers for the field of addiction and recovery, and psychotherapy and behavior change more generally. Miller and colleagues have developed Motivational Interviewing (see Miller et al., 2019; Miller & Rollnick, 2013) and Prochaska and DiClemente have developed the Transtheoretical Model of intentional behavior change, which includes a particular component known as the Stages of Change (see DiClemente, 2018; Prochaska & DiClemente, 2019). Regarding forgiveness and addiction, Webb and colleagues have outlined consistencies between the process of forgiveness and the principles of Motivational Interviewing and the Stages of Change (Webb & Jeter, 2015; Webb & Trautman, 2010). Following will be a more detailed discussion of Motivational Interviewing, the Stages of Change, and their relationship to Enright's Process Model of Forgiveness and Worthington's REACH Model of Forgiveness.

Basic Principles of Motivational Interviewing

For a brief outline of Motivational Interviewing (MI) see Miller et al. (2019). For the originators' comprehensive presentation of MI, which the following overview draws from, see Miller and Rollnick (2013). Given the popularity and universal appeal of MI (not to mention its effectiveness), one way to introduce MI is first to understand what it is not. Some issues that may arise include whether MI is a technique, a way to manipulate people, and/or a panacea (Miller & Rollnick, 2013). Perhaps most importantly is to understand that although MI can be viewed as a set of clinical skills, it is not a technique or set thereof to be used on people. It is an intentional and purposeful manner of interaction between a therapist, or healthcare practitioner, and their clients or patients. This manner of interaction may be perceived as being *warm and fuzzy*, but it is by no means simply being polite or friendly. Although there is a relaxed, easygoing quality to it, it is about a healthcare provider being genuine and respectful with those seeking their care, and being careful not to come across as an authority figure with all of the answers – somebody the client should just be quiet and listen to. Yet, as the healthcare provider is being sought out for their expertise, guidance and definitive answers are expected (and there is a time and place for such). Nevertheless, the approach to be taken is one of collaboration. That the therapist and client are to work together to find the solutions in the best interest of the client. Similarly, MI, being based in a genuine and respectful form of professional collaboration, is not intended as a means of manipulating clients to engage in or pursue a particular behavior or goal. If a healthcare provider does not interact in a genuine, respectful, and collaborative manner it can easily come across as a gimmick or trick designed to manipulate.

Lastly, MI is not intended to be a panacea, or cure-all. Although it is effective in the context of facilitating and promoting many health and wellness related issues (see the Guilford Press website – a major publisher of books and resources for MI; https://www. guilford. com/browse/psychology-psychiatry-social-work/applications-motivational-interviewing-series), it was "never intended [to be] a 'school' of psychotherapy or counseling to which people would be converted and swear allegiance, forsaking all others" (Miller & Rollnick, 2013, p. 35). The genuine, respectful, and collaborative manner of MI can be incorporated into any method of or approach to counseling and psychotherapy. It is a "*style* [or way] of being with people" … "developed specifically for the purpose of helping people resolve ambivalence and strengthen motivation for change" (emphasis in original; Miller & Rollnick, 2013, p. 35).

As Conversation

Miller and Rollnick (2013) begin by describing MI as a conversation about change; that is, "arranging conversations so that people talk themselves into change, based on their own values and interests" (p. 4). In this regard, Miller and Rollnick (2013) discuss conversation styles, what they call the *righting reflex*, ambivalence (including change talk versus sustain talk), and conversation dynamics. Regarding the conversations between a healthcare provider and patient, three styles are discussed: *directing, following*, and *guiding*. A directing style involves the healthcare provider doing most of the talking, providing formalized, structured (even sterile) advice, and playing the role of having all of the answers. A following style involves the healthcare provider mostly listening, being agreeable, and largely playing the role of a friend. A guiding style involves being "a good listener and [offering] expertise where needed" (p. 5). When engaging in professional, helping conversations informed by MI, one is to take the guiding style.

The righting reflex is defined as the default response given when an otherwise conscientious human being observes another human being in obvious distress – to jump in and save the person from the problem being faced (Miller & Rollnick, 2013). That is, when trying to help someone in obvious distress we tend to think that a succinct, facts-laid-out, one-sided conversation about what is going on and what the necessary solution is will quickly solve the problem and get the person in distress on their way, never to look back. A classic example of this is a parent giving a lecture to their teenager learning to drive about the dangers of speeding and not wearing a seat belt. Or, in the context of addiction, a therapist discussing, following the client presenting with having just received a DUI, all of the dangers of excessive alcohol use including, harming others in an accident, blackouts, physiological dependence, alcohol poisoning, and death. Indeed, presenting all of the dangers in an escalating fashion as a stern warning of what is in store if the client does not stop drinking. The problem with a healthcare provider engaging in this type of interaction based in the righting reflex is that the patient is likely to resist, even though they intellectually already know and understand all of the well-intentioned advice *and* the gravity of the situation.

Both the righting reflex (on the part of the healthcare provider) and the patient's resistance to such are argued to be a function of human nature. Healthcare providers want to provide help in an efficient manner, and patients, when lectured to and made to feel even more bad about what they already know is a problem, tend to become defensive and seek to resist the advice given, even though they would otherwise agree with it. Going back to the teenager being lectured about speeding and not wearing a seat belt, remember yourself as a teenager being lectured by your parents, about anything, and the all-but-automatic response is to resist and want to do it anyway, even though you know it is problematic. In sum, even though the righting reflex is based in the good intentions of the healthcare provider, it tends to be perceived as finger-wagging, in-your-face advice to be resisted at all costs. In this regard, MI is designed to avoid this pitfall and other forms of arguing and traditional confrontation and to work with the patient to draw their own conclusions regarding the necessity for more constructive, adaptive behavior to address the problem at hand (see below sections on *essence: evocation* and *procedures: evoking*).

Miller and Rollnick (2013) discuss ambivalence, in the context of behavior change, as the notion that a person, although aware of the negatives associated with a particular behavior and equally aware of the positives associated with a corresponding more constructive, adaptive behavior is nonetheless reluctant, hesitant, and/or conflicted about choosing which way to go. Moreover, that this *and* ambivalence about the need to *actually* change is a function of human nature. Indeed, "other motives conflict with doing the right thing, even when you know what it is" (p. 6). Related to this, as a therapist it becomes important to learn to identify the client's *change talk*, or "the person's own statements that favor change" versus the client's *sustain talk*, or "the person's own arguments for not changing, for sustaining the status quo" (p. 7), and to guide (rather than force) the conversation to be focused on said change talk. Related to this is what Miller and Rollnick used to call *rolling with resistance* (see Miller & Rollnick, 1991, 2002). Realizing that resistance, in this regard, was more about a problem in the relationship between the therapist and client, Miller and Rollnick (2013) now discuss this type of resistance in terms of change talk versus sustain talk. That is, when a client continues to favor the status quo, rather than the therapist assuming it to be an inherent problem (or, resistance), it is more conducive to facilitating motivation for the therapist to take a non-judgmental stance. For the therapist to help the client focus on change talk, rather than the therapist to confront the sustain talk (or, the client's resistance). The former helping to develop *partnership* through *engaging* with the client (see below sections on *essence* and *procedures*, respectively) and the latter inadvertently deterring from such due to the therapist communicating their criticism of the client's viewpoint – whether abruptly or subtly.

A natural way to guide the conversation in this regard is to focus on the dynamics of the conversation. That is, to pay attention to the interactive nature of the conversation. In addition to guiding, indeed as a *function* of guiding, the healthcare provider should seek to have a person-centered conversation. For example, recognizing that the patient has likely already had these conversations many times, either in their head with themselves (i.e., self-talk, or inner voice) or out loud with other well-meaning friends and/or loved ones (i.e., they already know everything being said and the logic behind it, etc.), it becomes important to focus the conversation on the clients' perspective. After agreement is reached between a therapist and client, that a problem needs to be addressed, rather than the therapist telling the client what, when, and how to do it, person-centered questions can be asked, thereby facilitating the client's internal motivation to change and thus increasing the likelihood for change. Importantly, Miller and Rollnick (2013) stress that the following questions are not MI, per se, but the essence, or "spirit and style of MI" (p. 11). That is, you may or may not ask these questions specifically, but these types of client-driven questions. For example, "why would you want to make this change?" … "how might you go about it in order to succeed?" … "So, what do you think you'll do?" (p. 11).

In Essence

Miller and Rollnick (2013) focus on four fundamental factors as underlying the essence of MI. Although there are some basic clinical skills associated with MI (as mentioned above, and to be discussed below), the four aspects mentioned here are not necessarily skills, but principles that underlie the MI style or way of being with one's clients. That is, *partnership, acceptance, compassion*, and *evocation*. Regarding partnership, the bottom line is that the patient is the recognized expert on themselves and the healthcare provider is an expert in their healthcare specialty. The task is for these two experts to collaborate and together apply their knowledge and expertise to the problem at hand. Added responsibilities of the healthcare provider are to facilitate the patient's expression of their expertise and to avoid falling into the *expert trap*, or assuming and/or communicating to the client that professional expertise implies an *overriding* expertise. "Avoiding this trap includes letting go of the assumption that you are *supposed* to have and provide all the right answers. In truth, you don't necessarily have them when the topic is personal change" (emphasis in original; Miller & Rollnick, 2013, p. 16). In sum, the essence of partnership is respect and empathy for the client. "Your purpose is to understand the life before you, to see the world through this person's eyes rather than superimposing your own vision" (Miller & Rollnick, 2013, p. 16).

Related to partnership is the need for acceptance of one's client. Miller and Rollnick (2013) incorporate the humanistic perspective of Carl Rogers (see Rogers, 1989) in this regard. That is, acceptance entails a deep recognition of and respect for another's individuality and humanity. However, acceptance does not necessarily include approval or agreement. For example, one can feel absolute acceptance and love from their parents regardless of poor behavior, but at the same time understand that their parents may be disappointed in said behavior. When this type of acceptance is present, behavior – good or bad – has no impact on the relationship between persons. Moreover, this kind of acceptance is facilitated by honoring the absolute worth and autonomy of others, actively affirming others' positive qualities, and engaging in *accurate*, or active empathy. Again, empathy is critically important. It is to take another's perspective – accurately *and* for their sake. Of note, empathy is not necessarily sympathy, or identification with another. It is seeking to understand another's point of view.

As with partnership and acceptance, compassion and evocation are critical components of the essence of MI. In being compassionate, the healthcare provider is primarily focused on meeting, promoting, and prioritizing the needs of the client. The client's best interests are to be the goal of the healthcare provider and any deviation from this path undermines and threatens the efforts for partnership and acceptance critical to

MI. Regarding evocation, we return to our previous discussion about avoiding the righting reflex, and the importance of the client-centered dynamics of conversation. Miller and Rollnick (2013) discuss the default approach in effecting change as being focused of deficits, or what is missing; whereas, the MI approach is focused on strengths. Again, in MI, a core assumption is that the client, in a very salient and poignant way, already knows what the problem is and what needs to be done. They may not know how to go about it in an efficient manner, etc., and they may be ambivalent, but they nonetheless know, in the big-picture sense, that what is going on is not working for them and an alternative solution is needed. Evocation is the principle that the person struggling for change has the answers within them and it is the therapist's job to help their client (re)discover their own answers and to reconnect with their own values and priorities.

Procedures

In describing the clinical skills employed by MI (keeping in mind that MI is not intended to be technique driven or a formal school of therapy, but a way of being or interacting when seeking to help others; see discussion above), Miller and Rollnick (2013) discuss four related processes inherent to MI: *engaging, focusing, evoking*, and *planning*; and core skills related thereto: open-ended questions, affirmative statements, reflective listening, summarizing, and informing and advising. The first process involves engaging, or connecting with a client and is the foundation for the three additional processes. Engaging with a client is referring to developing a genuine relationship of trust and can happen within seconds, but for various reasons may not happen for several weeks (or ever; if never, then referral to a different therapist is likely needed). Sometimes this process and outcome of engaging with a client is referred to as a therapeutic relationship, or a therapeutic alliance. Importantly, this professional, trusting relationship allows for meaningful interaction and conversation to occur – a safe place where whatever needs to be expressed can be. The process of focusing is referring to the healthcare provider and patient making a concerted and fruitful effort to identify and focus on a specific agenda; usually, objectives regarding the nature of their conversation concerning change, and goals for change. Focusing is important as sometimes counseling and psychotherapy can wander into areas that although important and relevant (e.g., extensive historical details) may not be conducive to an efficient pursuit of change, in the moment.

Evoking, as mentioned above, is critical for personal change. The therapist must prioritize their efforts toward drawing out of their clients their own ideas, values, reasons, and thus motivation for change, rather than the therapist convincing them of the need for change. Two particular examples of evoking are the notions of *development of discrepancy*, and *self-efficacy*. Developing discrepancy, is the process of helping a client to recognize and experience "a discrepancy between present and desired states, the *distance* between a personal goal and the status quo" (Miller & Rollnick, 2013, p. 243), with the intent of the client being nudged toward increased motivation through the weight of the personal conflict brought forth. For example, a person struggling with addiction may simultaneously value – though express such at different points (seconds, minutes, days, weeks, or months apart) in therapy – attending and supporting their child's after-school, evening-based sporting activities, and spending time after work relaxing with friends by having a few drinks at their favorite restaurant. A way to develop discrepancy and therefore facilitate internal motivation for change is to point out these "conflicting values" – especially in the context of seeking addiction recovery – and ask the client how they personally reconcile both interests or concerns. The natural response is likely to be an internal drive to reprioritize one's children rather than maintain the status quo of continuing to miss said activities by continuing to prioritize drinking. Not that developing discrepancy necessarily makes it easy to make the change, but that the internal scales of motivation will be starting to tip – more and more with each recognition that one's behaviors are out of alignment with one's values. That is, things are not working and alternative solutions are necessary.

Self-efficacy, in the context of evoking, involves developing confidence in one's ability to make changes, and hope that through change, a different, better future is possible (Miller & Rollnick, 2013). When struggling with addiction, low self-efficacy (including, in this regard, lack of confidence and hopelessness) is very common. Most individuals struggling with addiction, whether or not having ever been in treatment, are intimately aware of their seeming near-inability to make any headway toward change. Having repeatedly committed to themselves and others to change and eliminate the problem, only to repeatedly return to the same problematic behaviors, many people struggling with addiction tend to resign themselves to failure. That is, under these circumstances – being consumed by the *big picture* – it is very normal to lack confidence in one's abilities and to be hopeless for a better tomorrow. Miller and Rollnick (2013) discuss many ways to help clients develop self-efficacy (i.e, confidence and hope) including giving appropriate, timely information and advice, identifying and affirming strengths, reviewing past successes, brainstorming, reframing, and hypothetical thinking.

Regarding the process of planning, Miller and Rollnick (2013) note that "when people's motivation reaches a threshold of readiness, the balance tips and they begin thinking and talking more about when and how to change and less about whether and why" (p. 29). Sometimes the planning occurs with the help of the healthcare provider. However, sometimes the patient, when as a function of their *own* efforts (i.e., ideas, values, and reasons) attains sufficient motivation for change, not surprisingly decides that additional help is not needed and proceeds to develop sufficient plans of their own.

Miller and Rollnick (2013) are careful to point out that the core clinical skills employed by MI are not unique to MI, but broadly common to many other approaches to counseling and psychotherapy, and are derived from person-centered modalities (e.g., Carl Rogers; see above). Open-ended questions give an opportunity for clients to provide more-detailed, contemplative responses, rather than a simple "yes or no." Affirmative statements from a therapist can help to reinforce a client's efforts and help remind the client (and therapist) that the perspective, efforts, and self-determination of the client are most important. Indeed, Miller and Rollnick (2013) remind us that "making people feel terrible doesn't help them change" (p. 33). Also, reflective listening, or making a brief consolidating statement about what may be going on with the client (see below), and summarizing, or tactfully repeating back to a client particularly meaningful statements they have made, can be very effective at helping clients remain engaged in thoughtful dialogue with the therapist, to the end of the therapist helping the client identify their own ideas, values, reasons, etc., and thus evoking the client's own motivation for change. In both of these examples (i.e., reflective listening and summarizing), clients are provided with an opportunity to acquire more precise understanding for themselves and a deepening of the connection or partnership with the therapist.

Lastly, although evocation is an imperative clinical skill in MI, Miller and Rollnick (2013) stress that there are times when a therapist must engage in giving information and advice, particularly when it is asked for. That is, if a therapist never engages a client by answering and addressing their direct questions and concerns, it can become frustrating and disillusioning to a client and can be perceived by the client as the therapist playing games, or perhaps not actually being an expert in their field. Although the therapist is always to reinforce the notion of genuinely sharing collaborative expertise with their clients, there are times when a therapist must play the role of an authoritative expert, but *only* when appropriate.

A cautionary note is warranted regarding some of the person-centered clinical skills described herein. Affirmative statements, reflective listening, and summarizing can come across as insincere. Indeed, popular culture will often mock such counseling and psychotherapy related methods as disingenuous and/or superficial. And, justifiably so when not used in an appropriate or applicable manner. Sometimes therapists learn these techniques and use them as default responses, without much thought for therapeutic engagement or partnership (see above), context, or relevance. For example, the stereotypical scenario where a client finishes up complaining about their frustrations with their partner – with raised voice and dramatic animation – whereupon a therapist reflects back to the client, "It sounds like you are angry with your partner." If a sufficient therapeutic alliance (partnership, engagement, etc.) has not been established, this can come across as a canned response and can be quite counterproductive. However, if the therapeutic alliance is sufficient and the timing is correct, it can be a powerful experience for the client as it can spur continued reflection and thus, further discussion and insight into relevant underlying concerns.

Although the procedures of MI are related to and build upon each other, they may not happen sequentially. In fact, for most people there is a fluctuating process inherent to MI. That is, MI although very effective, is not a simple linear process. Progress is made and setbacks occur, such that the progression to internally motivated change is not necessarily an easily tracked event, or an all-or-nothing experience. It can happen that the client recognizes and experiences milestones, but sometimes it is a matter of hind-sight being 20/20 (see Miller & Rollnick, 2013). In sum, Motivational Interviewing is defined as:

> a collaborative, goal-oriented style of communication with particular attention to the language of change. It is designed to strengthen personal motivation for and commitment to a specific goal by eliciting and exploring the person's own reasons for change within an atmosphere of acceptance and compassion.
>
> (Miller & Rollnick, 2013, p. 29)

Basic Principles of the Stages of Change

The Transtheoretical Model (TTM; DiClemente, 2018; see also, Prochaska & DiClemente, 2019) of intentional behavior change includes four general dimensions of change: stages of change, processes of change, markers (or, pros and cons) of change, and context (or, levels) of change. The *stages* of change refer to the otherwise sequential attitudes and actions needed to progress through the process of actually changing behavior. "The stages depict a person's movement through the process of change in terms of the motivational, temporal, and coping elements needed to create a successfully sustained pattern of behavior" (DiClemente, 2018, p. 25). The *processes* of change refer to the affective (i.e., emotional), behavioral, and/or cognitive (i.e., thinking) modifications needed in order to address problems (Prochaska & DiClemente, 2019). The *markers* of change represent evidence for or against a person's readiness to make a decision about change and said person's perceived ability to successfully make the change, and the *context* of change refers to the influence of life's circumstances on the individual's functioning, whether it be related to symptoms or situations, beliefs, systemic issues (e.g., family or social systems), and/or inter-/intra-personal issues (DiClemente, 2018). Most relevant to understanding forgiveness in the context of addiction and recovery are the TTM dimensions of change regarding the stages of change and the processes of change.

Stages of Change

The TTM's five stages of change include: (1) precontemplation, (2) contemplation, (3) preparation, (4) action, and (5) maintenance (DiClemente, 2018). Any given stage includes attitude and action-oriented tasks and goals that need to be met prior to an individual advancing to the next otherwise sequential stage in the process of making a change.

Stages One, Two, and Three

A person in the *precontemplation* stage of change has no meaningful or personally relevant recognition of a problem needing to be addressed and thus no intention of making a change. The task for a person in this stage is to develop awareness and relative uneasiness about a particular behavior(s) and an interest in modifying or stopping the behavior(s). The goal is begin to seriously consider the need for change. A person in the *contemplation* stage of change begins to struggle with instability and ambivalence. That is, beginning to recognize the need for change and the subsequent recognition and weighing of the reasons for and against both the old and new behaviors leads to uncertainty about how to move forward. The task is to weigh one's options and to come down on the side of discarding the old and embracing the new. The goal, therefore, is to make the decision to change. The *preparation* stage involves "developing a plan of action and creating the commitment needed to implement the plan" (DiClemente, 2018, p. 29). Making a decision to change is one thing, but following through is another. "Planning is the activity that organizes the environment and develops the strategies for making a change" (DiClemente, 2018, p. 29). The task is to develop a level of commitment to tip the balance toward engaging the process of change and to craft a workable and capable plan, and the goal is to carry out said plan without unreasonable delay.

Stages Four and Five

The *action* stage "represents a clear, visible shift from the first half of the change process that focused on intentions, considerations, and plans to the second half of the process, actual behavior change" (DiClemente, 2018, p. 30). That is, the action stage involves actually putting into play the plan developed in the preparation stage. The goal during this stage is to maintain the new behavior. And, depending on the frequency and intensity of the old behavior the process of establishing the new behavior can take between 3 to 6 months. The task is not only to employ one's plan from the preparation stage, but to do so in a persistent, yet reasonably flexible manner. Persistence is required when unexpected obstacles and difficulties arise (e.g., an unsupportive family, or a spontaneous work-related cocktail party). Flexibility is necessary in order to recognize what is and is not working, and adjusting and adapting the plan, as applicable, appropriate, and necessary. Lastly, the *maintenance* stage involves lifestyle change. The goal is long-term behavior change – for the new behavior to become automatic and habitual. The task "is to sustain and integrate the specific behavior change into the total life context so that it becomes normative, familiar, and recurrent" (DiClemente, 2018, p. 31); such that, returning to the old behavior no longer holds appeal.

Processes of Change

The underlying mechanisms responsible for allowing an individual to progress through the stages of change are known as the *processes* of change (DiClemente, 2018). Importantly, the processes of change are not the techniques that therapists use to effect change with their clients. Nevertheless, such techniques, in order to be effective, do rely on the processes of change. The "processes of change represent the internal and external experiences and activities that enable individuals to move from stage to stage [of behavior change]" (DiClemente, 2018, p. 34). These experiences and activities can be divided into two broad categories: (1) "cognitive and experiential processes" or "ways of thinking and feeling that create change" and (2) "action-oriented processes" that "involve behavioral commitment and actions to create or break a habit" (DiClemente, 2018, p. 35). The first category includes consciousness raising, emotional arousal, self-reevaluation, environmental reevaluation, and social liberation. And, the second category includes self-liberation, stimulus generalization or control, conditioning or counterconditioning, reinforcement management, and helping relationships.

Cognitive and Experiential Processes

The first two underlying mechanisms or processes of change, *consciousness raising* and *emotional arousal*, respectively involve increases in intellectual awareness regarding the problematic behavior and the need for change, *and* responding thereto in an emotionally charged, connected, or invested manner; that is, having an "ah-hah" type of experience regarding the profound nature of what one is facing. The next two mechanisms, *self-reevaluation* and *environmental reevaluation*, respectively involve personal-level evaluations of how the behavior in question fits with one's own belief and value systems (e.g., how will the old or new behavior impact my commitment to honesty?), and within one's practical environment (e.g., how will the new or old behavior impact family members' well-being?). Lastly, *social liberation* is a mechanism or "process [that] promotes realization and acceptance of social norms and societal sanctions, and helps the individual to view change as possible and to experience viable alternatives" (DiClemente, 2018, p. 36).

Action-Oriented Processes

The first behavioral process of change discussed by DiClemente (2018), *self-liberation*, involves recognition of and investment in one's individual autonomy, including self-determination and personal responsibility. There is an almost-paradoxical power to personally effect change when one recognizes that no one can force *real* change upon us – it is entirely up to us if we want to pursue change. Linked with the process of self-liberation are the behavioral processes of *stimulus generalization or control, conditioning or counterconditioning*, and *reinforcement management*, each of which are principles of the scientific field of Behaviorism, or the psychology of learning. Each of these three mechanisms of learning allow for old habits to be broken and new habits to be developed through the manipulation of stimuli, whether through managing the occurrence, frequency, or pleasure of particular interactions with things or people, etc. For a discussion of Behaviorism, particularly in this broad context of counseling and psychotherapy related behavior change, see Antony and Roemer (2011). Lastly, *helping relationships*, as a mechanism or process of change, involves developing and utilizing support systems to start, stop, change, and/or maintain behavior.

As with MI and the process of forgiveness, there is a broad, sequential nature to the stages and processes of change in the TTM. Fluctuation within and among the stages and processes of change can and does occur, such that behavior change is not necessarily a linear process, nor is it likely to be an all-or-nothing process (DiClemente, 2018). Indeed, sometimes a sixth stage of change is mentioned: *relapse*. That is, at any point during the struggle for behavior change (whether related to addictive behavior, suicidal behavior, or any other behavior), a relapse, or return to previous behavior can occur, and is very common. It may not take as long for the person to return to a previous stage of change (e.g., they may briefly cycle through *contemplation* and *preparation* and settle back into the intentional and deliberate work associated with *action*), but a return to previous stages is needed rather than resumption of the previous stage one was in when the relapse occurred. When a return to previous, unwanted behavior occurs, it is always important to sufficiently examine and understand what lead to the relapse and to incorporate it into the application of the stages of change, especially the development, implementation, and maintenance of one's plan for change.

In sum, all of these TTM *processes* of change, whether cognitive/experiential or action-oriented, underlie the ability to progress through the TTM *stages* of change. The TTM processes of change are not the tools used to animate or extract change, but they are the foundation or the structural framework to build upon for change. Much like a skyscraper cannot stand without sufficient footings engineered into the bedrock (nor is it stable in a storm), successful progression through the stages of change cannot occur without the facilitating nature of the processes of change.

Motivational Interviewing and the Stages of Change

Although Motivational Interviewing and the Transtheoretical Model of intentional behavior change were developed during the same time period, conceptually complement each other, were both game-changers in the field of addiction and recovery, and are commonly considered to be components of the same model, they are separate models of motivation itself and change itself and are not dependent upon each other. Indeed, Miller and Rollnick (2013) describe them as " 'kissing cousins who never married' " (pp. 35–36). Similarly, DiClemente and Velasquez (2002) discuss the distinct, yet compatible nature of the two models.

Motivational Interviewing, the Stages of Change, and Motivational Enhancement Therapy

Motivational Enhancement Therapy (MET) is derived from particular principles drawn from both Motivational Interviewing (MI) and the Transtheoretical Model (TTM) of intentional behavior change (Miller et al., 1994). The principles of MI that MET is primarily focused on include, the expression of empathy, the development of discrepancy, avoiding arguing (confrontation), rolling with resistance (change talk versus sustain talk), and supporting self-efficacy. The main aspect of the TTM that MET is focused on includes the Stages of Change; that is, precontemplation, contemplation, determination (preparation), action, and maintenance. However, just as MI and the Stages of Change are highly compatible with each other, but two distinct models, MET, although derived from MI and the TTM's Stages of Change, is a separate adaptation designed as a brief intervention to be tested in Project MATCH (see Longabaugh & Wirtz, 2001) – a large, multi-site, clinical research project funded by the National Institute on Alcohol Abuse and Alcoholism (NIAAA; https://www.niaaa.nih.gov/), a component agency of the United States National Institutes of Health. Similarly, MET was also used in a follow-up NIAAA study called COMBINE (Miller, 2004; Pettinati et al., 2004). Both Project MATCH and COMBINE examined Twelve-Step Facilitation Therapy (TSF; see Chapter 9), MET, and Cognitive-Behavioral Coping Skills Therapy (CBCST; see Chapter 11) – COMBINE also included medication as a treatment option for alcohol related problems. Miller and Rollnick (2013) point out that a main difference between MI and MET, is that MET includes pretreatment-based assessment feedback as part of the clinical intervention and that such "is not a necessary or sufficient component of MI" (p. 36).

Forgiveness, Motivation, and Change

The process of forgiveness has been identified as consistent with the basic principles and processes of Motivational Interviewing (MI) and the Stages of Change (SofC) component of the Transtheoretical Model (TTM) of intentional behavior change (see Webb & Jeter, 2015; Webb & Trautman, 2010). Following is a more detailed discussion of said consistencies between the Process Model of Forgiveness and the REACH Model of Forgiveness (as developed by Enright and Worthington, respectively; see Chapter 8) and MI and the TTM's SofC (see Table 10.1).

Forgiveness and Motivational Interviewing

Enright's *Uncovering* phase and Worthington's *Recalling the Hurt* phase are both focused on the person pursuing forgiveness (i.e., the client) developing, with the assistance of a therapist, facilitator, or workbook, a self-determined, personally relevant, objective awareness of the problem and the pain associated with the difficulties experienced. From an MI point of view, this is consistent with the therapist (1) recognizing the ambivalence of the client (i.e., the client beginning to recognize a problem, that default methods of coping are not working, and an alternative (forgiveness) may be needed), (2) taking a guiding style of conversation, and (3) avoiding the righting reflex, or the urge to tell the client what the problem is and what to do about it. A therapist helping a client uncover (Enright) or recall (Worthington) cannot dominate the conversation, but must allow for the client to discover what is going on. Related to this is making sure that the conversation dynamic is client-centered, such that the therapist is engaging the client and building a partnership so that the information and insights regarding the problem and associated pain is evoked from the client (sometimes through *developing discrepancy*); that is, self-determined, personally relevant, and objective. All of this is driven by the client (i.e., person-centered) in a collaborative manner, rather than by the authoritative expertise of the therapist (or workbook) giving all the answers.

Enright's *Decision* phase and initial aspects of the *Work* phase and Worthington's *Empathy* and *Altruistic Gift* phases and initial aspects of the *Commitment* phase are focused on recognizing that an alternative solution *is* needed, understanding what forgiveness actually is *and* that it is an option, and starting the process of committing to giving forgiveness as a gift, through reframing the difficult experience(s) and developing positive emotions and responses such as empathy, compassion, humility, gratitude, and acceptance. From an MI point of view, this is consistent with ambivalence (see above),

Table 10.1 Forgiveness, Motivational Interviewing, and the Transtheoretical Model of Intentional Behavior Change

Forgiveness Phase		*Corresponding Aspects of MI and the TTM to Addictive Behavior*[a]				
		Motivational Interviewing			*Transtheoretical Model*[b]	
Process Model[c]	*REACH Model*[c]	*As Conversation*	*In Essence*	*Procedures*	*Stages of Change*	*Processes of Change*
Uncovering	Recalling the Hurt	Guiding Style	Partnership	Engaging	*Precontemplation*	Cognitive/ Experiential
		avoid Righting Reflex	*Acceptance*[d]	*Focusing*	Contemplation	Action-Oriented
		Ambivalence	*Compassion*	Evoking		
		Client-Centered	Evocation	*Planning*		
Decision	Empathy	Guiding Style	Partnership	Engaging	Preparation	Cognitive/ Experiential
	Altruistic Gift	*avoid Righting Reflex*	Acceptance	*Focusing*		Action-Oriented
Work	Commitment	Ambivalence	*Compassion*	Evoking		
		Client-Centered	Evocation	*Planning*		
Work	Commitment	Guiding Style	*Partnership*	Engaging	Action	*Cognitive/ Experiential*
		avoid Righting Reflex	Acceptance	Focusing		Action-Oriented
		Ambivalence	Compassion	Evoking		
		Client-Centered	Evocation	Planning		
Deepening	Holding On	*Guiding Style*	*Partnership*	Engaging	Maintenance	*Cognitive/ Experiential*
		avoid Righting Reflex	*Acceptance*	*Focusing*		Action-Oriented
		Ambivalence	*Compassion*	Evoking		
		Client-Centered	*Evocation*	Planning		

Source: Adapted from Webb and Trautman (2010)

[a] That is, as related to substance use, compulsive behavior sets, and suicidal behavior.

[b] Precontemplation and Relapse are consistent with the ebb and flow of forgiveness.

[c] See Chapter 8

[d] Each of the principles of the MI-related Conversation, Essence, and Procedures are listed, but the appearance of those not readily discussed in the body of the text has been italicized. Similarly, the pre-contemplation stage of change has been italicized as it is not deliberately discussed in the body of the text.

including identifying and focusing on change talk (as opposed to sustain talk), partnership (see above), recognizing autonomy, developing respect and empathy, and through evocation/evoking (including through developing discrepancy), continuing to recognize the need for change and alternative solutions.

The completion of Enright's *Work* and Worthington's *Commitment* phases builds upon the process described above, yet also with a particular focus on maintaining the preliminary commitment, particularly through addressing initial reservations and doubts about making said commitment. From an MI point of view, this is consistent with recognition and acceptance of autonomous behavior, compassionate prioritization of the needs of the client, and evoking self-efficacy or confidence in one's ability to change and hope for a different future. Also, concentrating on and reinforcing (i.e., evoking) strengths for moving forward, rather than faltering due to the distracting and counterproductive nature of doubts. Similarly, focusing on developing a specific agenda or goals as a way of minimizing doubts and likewise developing and implementing a practical plan (i.e., a plan with measurable objectives/milestones) for achieving one's agenda.

Enright's *Deepening* phase and Worthington's *Holding On* phase are focused on solidifying and sustaining the progress heretofore made through finding meaning and purpose, recognizing the need for and utilizing social support, continuing to address inevitable doubts, and maintaining vigilance against risk factors for returning to previous behavior(s). From an MI point of view, this is consistent with engaging in meaningful, respectful, and collaborative (evoking) professional interactions and conversations, including continued development of self-efficacy and implementing and adapting one's plans as applicable and appropriate (see above).

There is much overlap among the principles of MI and thus each can be recognized to some degree or another when looking at the process of forgiveness. As such, in Table 10.1, each of the principles of the MI-related Conversation, Essence, and Procedures are listed, but the appearance of those not readily highlighted in the above discussion has been italicized in the listing.

Lastly, some aspects of how MI and the process of forgiveness are related to each other are similar to the notion of two sides of the same coin; for example, empathy. In MI the development of empathy is largely in the context of the therapist, whereas in the process of forgiveness it is largely in the context of the client. However, in both cases a therapist modeling empathy will help the client manifest their own natural inclinations for empathy, thereby leading to motivation for change whether regarding addiction or following through with forgiveness.

Forgiveness and the Stages and Processes of Change

The Stages of Change (SofC) as well as the Processes of Change (PofC) components of the Transtheoretical Model (TTM) of intentional behavior change are both consistent with Enright's Process Model of Forgiveness (see Chapter 8) and Worthington's REACH Model of Forgiveness (see Chapter 8). As stated above in the Forgiveness and MI section, Enright's *Uncovering* and Worthington's *Recalling the Hurt* phases are both focused on the person pursuing forgiveness (i.e., the client) developing, with the assistance of a therapist, facilitator, or workbook, a self-determined, personally relevant, objective awareness of the problem and the pain associated with the difficulties experienced. From the point of view of SofC and PofC, this is consistent with both the precontemplation and contemplation stages of change and both the cognitive/experiential and action-oriented processes of change, respectively. That is, starting with no recognition of a problem and no intention for change, the task and goal of precontemplation is to develop a preliminary level of awareness of and uneasiness regarding a problem and to begin to seriously consider the need for change. Contemplation involves the task and goal of weighing one's options and making a decision to pursue change. Regarding the processes of change, consciousness raising and emotional arousal are facilitative of Enright's Uncovering and Worthington's Recalling the Hurt through enabling intellectual awareness and emotional investment in said awareness. Self-reevaluation and environmental reevaluation are also facilitative of forgiveness through enabling the evaluative processes regarding consistencies between one's behavior and one's (a) beliefs and values and (b) practical environment. Likewise, *self*-liberation facilitates self-determination and personal responsibility to recognize one's dilemma regarding the need for change and what to do about it.

As stated above in the Forgiveness and MI section, Enright's *Decision* and *Work* (initial) and Worthington's *Empathy, Altruistic Gift*, and *Commitment* (initial) phases are focused on recognizing that an alternative solution *is* needed, understanding what forgiveness actually is *and* that it is an option, and starting the process of committing to giving forgiveness as a gift, through reframing the difficult experience(s) and developing positive emotions and responses such as empathy, compassion, humility, gratitude, and acceptance. From the point of view of SofC and PofC, this is consistent with the contemplation and preparation stages of change and both the cognitive/experiential and action-oriented processes of change, respectively. That is, the decision aspect of contemplation (see above) and then continuing on with the task and goal of preparation regarding making a commitment to change and crafting a workable, capable, and timely plan for change. Regarding the processes of change, consciousness raising and emotional arousal again come into play, as do self-reevaluation and environmental reevaluation (see above). Also, *social*-liberation facilitates the commitment to change by enabling confidence in change as a possibility and consideration of feasible options for change.

As stated above in the Forgiveness and MI section, the completion of Enright's *Work* and Worthington's *Commitment* phases builds upon the processes described above, yet also with a particular focus on maintaining the preliminary commitment, particularly through addressing initial reservations and doubts about making said commitment. From the point of view of SofC and PofC, this is consistent with the action stage of change and the action-oriented process of change, respectively. That is, the task and goal of the action stage of change is to employ one's plan from the preparation stage in a persistent, yet flexible manner, thereby maintaining the new behavior. Regarding the processes of change, in conjunction with self-liberation (see above; see also Chapter 11 for a discussion of Viktor Frankl and the notion that regardless of what happens to us, we always have the ability to choose how we respond), the principles of Behaviorism (i.e., stimulus generalization/control, (counter)conditioning, and reinforcement management) are facilitative of forgiveness (pursuing needed change) through enabling one to break old and establish new habits. Similarly, helping relationships as a process of change facilitate the commitment to change through the empowering effect of social support.

As stated above in the Forgiveness and MI section, Enright's *Deepening* phase and Worthington's *Holding On* phase are focused on solidifying and sustaining the progress heretofore made through finding meaning and purpose, recognizing the need for and utilizing social support, continuing to address inevitable doubts, and maintaining vigilance against risk factors for returning to previous behavior(s). From the point of view of SofC and PofC, this is consistent with the maintenance stage of change and the action-oriented process of change, respectively. That is, the task and goal of the maintenance stage of change is to change one's entire lifestyle, such that the new behavior becomes habitual and automatic. Regarding the processes of change, the principles of Behaviorism in the context of habitual processes and the impact of helping relationships on social support (see above) remain critical for long-term, sustainable change.

References

Antony, M. M., & Roemer, L. (2011). *Behavior therapy.* Washington, DC: American Psychological Association.

DiClemente, C. C. (2018). *Addiction and change: How addictions develop and addicted people recover* (2nd ed.). New York, NY: Guilford Press.

DiClemente, C. C., & Velasquez, M. M. (2002). Motivational Interviewing and the stages of change. In W. R. Miller & S. Rollnick (Eds.), *Motivational interviewing: Preparing people for change* (2nd ed., pp. 201–216). New York, NY: Guilford Press.

Longabaugh, R., & Wirtz, P. W. (Eds.). (2001). *Project MATCH: Hypotheses, results, and causal chain analyses.* NIH Publication No. 01–4238. Rockville, MD: National Institute on Alcohol Abuse and Alcoholism.

Miller, W. R. (1983). Motivational interviewing with problem drinkers. *Behavioural Psychotherapy,* 11(2), 147–172. doi:10.1017/S0141347300006583.

Miller, W. R. (Ed.) (2004). *COMBINE Monograph Series, Volume 1. Combined behavioral intervention manual: A clinical research guide for therapists treating people with alcohol abuse and dependence.* DHHS Publication No. (NIH) 04–5288. Bethesda, MD: National Institute on Alcohol Abuse and Alcoholism.

Miller, W. R., & Rollnick, S. (1991). *Motivational interviewing: Preparing people for change.* New York, NY: Guilford Press.

Miller, W. R., & Rollnick, S. (2002). *Motivational interviewing: Preparing people for change* (2nd ed.). New York, NY: Guilford Press.

Miller, W. R., & Rollnick, S. (2013). *Motivational interviewing: Helping people change* (3rd ed.). New York, NY: Guilford Press.

Miller, W. R., Forcehimes, A. A., & Zweben, A. (2019). *Treating addiction: A guide for professionals* (2nd ed.). New York, NY: Guilford Press.

Miller, W. R., Zweben, A., DiClemente, C. C., & Rychtarik, R. G. (1994). *Motivational enhancement therapy manual: A clinical research guide for therapists treating individuals with alcohol abuse and dependence.* NIH Publication No. 94–3723. Rockville, MD: National Institute on Alcohol Abuse and Alcoholism.

Pettinati, H. M., Weiss, R. D., Miller, W. R., Donovan, D., Ernst, D. B., & Rounsaville, B. J. (2004). *COMBINE Monograph Series, Volume 2. Medical management treatment manual: A clinical research guide for medically trained clinicians providing pharmacotherapy as part of the treatment for alcohol dependence.* DHHS Publication No. (NIH) 04–5289. Bethesda, MD: National Institute on Alcohol Abuse and Alcoholism.

Prochaska, J. O., & DiClemente, C. C. (1982). Transtheoretical therapy: Toward a more integrative model of change. *Psychotherapy: Theory, Research & Practice,* 19(3), 276–288. doi:10.1037/h0088437.

Prochaska, J. O., & DiClemente, C. C. (2019). The transtheoretical approach. In J. C. Norcross & M. R. Goldfried (Eds.), *Handbook of psychotherapy integration* (3rd ed., pp. 161–183). New York, NY: Oxford University Press.

Rogers, C. R. (1989). *On becoming a person.* New York, NY: Houghton Mifflin.

Webb, J. R., & Jeter, B. R. (2015). Forgiveness and problematic substance use. In L. L. Toussaint, E. L.Worthington, Jr., & D. R. Williams (Eds.), *Forgiveness and health: Scientific evidence and theories relating forgiveness to better health* (pp. 139–154). New York, NY: Springer.

Webb, J. R., & Trautman, R. P. (2010). Forgiveness and alcohol use: Applying a specific spiritual principle to substance abuse problems. *Addictive Disorders & Their Treatment,* 9(1), 8–17. doi:10.1097/ADT.0b013e318195000d.

11 Clinical Application: Cognitive-Behaviorism

The fundamental underlying assumption of cognitive-behavioral approaches to change is the notion that thoughts, feelings, and behaviors are intimately connected to each other and that intervention in one area in turn impacts each of the other areas. Most notably that changing one's thoughts or cognitions about a particular issue, concern, or problem will change how one feels and how one behaves in response thereto. Importantly, the notion of changing one's thoughts is not in reference to the content or topic of thoughts, beliefs or values, but to thought processes, or, more precisely, *how* one thinks about whatever they think about. Our thought processes, or *metacognitions*, can have a profound effect on how we address or cope with problems. This can go both ways. Metacognitions can contribute to the development of problems or they can contribute to the development of effective and efficient coping and problem solving skills. Similarly, a fundamental component of both the Process Model of Forgiveness and the REACH Model of Forgiveness (developed by Enright and Worthington, respectively; see Chapter 8) is learning to change how one thinks about or approaches both the offender and the offense. For example, if one can develop perspective about what happened and develop empathy for the offender, then one will be more likely to forgive. In this regard, forgiveness can be viewed as an effective coping or problem solving skill. As such, in the context of addiction, the process of forgiveness has been argued to be consistent with the process of cognitive-behavioral approaches to change (see Webb & Jeter, 2015; Webb & Trautman, 2010). Following will be a brief overview of two originating approaches to cognitive-behaviorism, a particular adaptation of cognitive-behaviorism to addiction, and a more detailed review of the consistencies between the process of forgiveness and cognitive-behavioral approaches to change, as applied to addiction.

Basic Principles of Cognitive-Behavioral Approaches to Change

Albert Ellis, a psychologist, and Aaron Beck, a psychiatrist, are considered two of the early pioneers of cognitive-behavioral approaches to psychotherapy and behavior change. Both were originally trained in psychoanalysis (regarding psychoanalysis, see Safran & Hunter, 2020) and after becoming disillusioned with it early in their careers, started to develop, in the 1960s, what has become commonly known as cognitive-behaviorism (Hollon & DiGiuseppe, 2011).

> Both Ellis and Beck based their psychotherapy on the idea that emotional disturbance emerged from thoughts that were illogical, anti-empirical, irrational, or incorrect. More scientific, accurate methods of thinking would free people from their disturbed emotions. Both cognitive therapies focused on what people think in

> the present, incorporated directive techniques into practice, and *initiated a number of the specific methods used today.*
>
> (emphasis added; Hollon & DiGiuseppe, 2011, p. 207)

When Ellis and Beck were in the process of founding cognitive-behaviorism, the popular culture and science of psychotherapy (i.e., the scientists and practitioners) were against them (Hollon & DiGiuseppe, 2011). Nevertheless, cognitive-behaviorism has since become one of the most popular systems of psychotherapy as it has garnered considerable empirical attention and support, making it the sort-of default, evidence-based approach to counseling and psychotherapy (see DeRubeis et al., 2019; DiGiuseppe & Doyle, 2019; Ellis & Ellis, 2019; Hollon & Beck, 2013; Hollon & DiGiuseppe, 2011), unless there is specific empirical evidence to pursue an alternative approach in a particular case or circumstance. Ellis' approach has become known as Rational Emotive Behavior Therapy (see DiGiuseppe & Doyle, 2019; Ellis & Dryden, 1997; Ellis & Ellis, 2019). And, Beck's approach has become known as Cognitive Behavior Therapy (see Beck, 2011; DeRubeis et al., 2019).

Rational Emotive Behavior Therapy

Originally known as *rational therapy* and then as *rational emotive therapy*, Albert Ellis' system of psychotherapy is now known as *Rational Emotive Behavior Therapy* (REBT) (Hollon & DiGiuseppe, 2011). Four of its most essential principles (i.e., those that distinguish it from other non-cognitive systems of psychotherapy) include (1) the ABC Model, (2) positive versus negative emotions, (3) constructive versus destructive emotions, and (4) absolutist thinking (see Ellis & Dryden, 1997; Ellis & Ellis, 2011, 2019). The ABC Model, itself explicitly incorporates many fundamental aspects of what REBT is all about, including the origin of psychological dysfunction deriving from the irrational (i.e., self-defeating versus self-helping) nature of demands and expectations that humans tend to place on themselves, others, and the world. Moreover, that the metacognitions (i.e., how we think about whatever it is that we think about – see above) that we have about our experiences in life – rather than the experiences themselves – are largely what determine our feelings and behaviors.

The first component of the *ABC Model*, is *A*, which stands for *activating event*. The second component, *B*, stands for *belief*, and the third component, *C*, stands for *consequent emotion and / or behavior* (see Ellis & Dryden, 1997; Ellis & Ellis, 2011, 2019). Ellis argues that the ABC Model, or the nature of the relationship between the concepts represented by the letters in the model, underlies every aspect of our lives as human beings and that our *default assumption* is that A leads to C (i.e., A → C). For example, when I am walking across the room and stub my toe on a chair, my response of, say, yelling and screaming in pain and picking up the chair and throwing it across the room was initiated by having stubbed my toe. However, what is really happening, according to Ellis, is that my belief *about* A, leads to C (i.e., A → B → C, or perhaps: A ↔ B → C); such that, my thoughts and beliefs about having stubbed my toe are what leads me to be angry and throw the chair across the room in pain. In this regard, our beliefs and thoughts – more accurately, our thought processes or metacognitions – about our experiences are driving our emotions and behaviors, and thus our coping and problem solving skills. If I believe that I should never stub my toe, that I am stupid for not paying close enough attention to what I am doing, and that the pain is unbearable, especially since I could have avoided it by paying better attention, I am more likely to feel frustrated, embarrassed, and angry, and to lose my temper and throw the chair across the room.

However, if I believe that stubbing my toe was an accident, it happens to everybody from time to time, and it is not that big of a deal (both the fact that it happened and the relatively minor pain experienced), I am much less likely to become angry, etc. and throw the chair across the room. Ellis took the acronym of the ABC Model further, to include *D* (*disputing* said problematic beliefs, which he described as irrational, or self-defeating) and *E* (replacing our irrational beliefs with more *effective* beliefs).

Importantly, our ABC Model based beliefs – whether rational or irrational – are not necessarily in our immediate awareness and thus, have to be uncovered and examined. But, like automatic beliefs or thoughts from a Cognitive Behavior Therapy point of view (see below), they are rooted in our assumptions about life and living, based on our lifetime of interpreted experiences.

Ellis argued that the irrational Bs (i.e., self-defeating beliefs) versus the rational Bs (i.e., self-helping beliefs) in the ABC Model constituted the primary source of cognitive function/dysfunction, and thus human ability/difficulty with emotional functioning and effective coping and problem solving. That is, it is not what happens to us (A, or an activating event) that bothers us, but what we think about what happens to us (B, or belief) that bothers us. Ellis did not claim to be the originator of this fundamental insight into human nature, but attributed it to early philosophers, such as Epictetus (50–135 CE) (see Ellis & Ellis, 2011, 2019).

A caveat here, is warranted. Generally speaking, this fundamental assumption of the ABC Model holds true regardless of the experiences that one may have (i.e., our thoughts about our experiences are what cause emotional problems for us, rather than the experiences themselves). Arguably, however, it is reasonable to acknowledge that there may be some exceptions; that is, some experiences that are so horrific and traumatic that negative emotional responses are the default outcome. For example, child abuse and family neglect can have life-long negative consequences, even if a person is not readily aware of what happened (see Benoit & Coolbear, 2004; Child Welfare Information Gateway, 2019). Nevertheless, it is still fair to acknowledge that, depending on how one thinks about these types of experiences, once they become aware of them, can have an impact on the nature of the emotional response moving forward. And, similar to forgiveness (see Chapters 3, 4, and 8), thinking differently about the experience does not then mean that the experience (and/or offender) must now be viewed as somehow good or inconsequential, or that the offender is no longer to be held accountable, or reconciliation must occur, etc. Rather, the fundamental issue of *how* we think about our experiences is always there, as is how such thoughts impact our emotional response(s) to said experiences. A similar perspective was put forth by Viktor Frankl, an Austrian psychiatrist and Holocaust survivor; that is, "everything can be taken from [us] but one thing: the last of the human freedoms – to choose one's attitude in any given set of circumstances, to choose one's own way" (Frankl, 1992, p. 75).

Related to the dysfunctional nature of irrational beliefs, is the notion that (resultant) emotions can exist on two inter-related spectrums; *positive versus negative emotions* and *constructive versus destructive emotions* (see Ellis & Dryden, 1997; Ellis & Ellis, 2011, 2019). Regarding positive versus negative emotions, intuitively, emotions such as feeling happy, cheerful, or excited can be considered positive, whereas emotions such as feeling frustrated, disappointed, or sad can be considered negative. Regarding constructive versus destructive emotions, any given emotion can be constructive or destructive in terms of whether it leads a person to be adaptive and able to effectively cope and/or problem-solve, or maladaptive and unable to effectively cope and/or problem-solve. In the context of addiction, while it makes sense that a positive emotion such as feeling excited is likely to be a constructive emotion in that it will likely lead to motivation to change (i.e., feeling excited about treatment, will likely constructively promote motivation to change), positive emotions are not always constructive, nor are negative emotions always destructive. In the case of excitement, it may wind up being a distraction in that a person may not be able to focus on treatment (or, excited about the prospect of treatment, but not necessarily about doing the work of treatment). In this case, excitement would be a positive, yet destructive emotion.

Related to this, every expressed emotion can be considered a manifestation of a larger set, or class of related emotions. For example, worry is related to concern on one end of the spectrum and anxiety on the other end of the same spectrum. The spectrum that worry is on could move from concern → worry → nervousness → anxiety (or in the case of excited (see above), the spectrum might be satisfied → happy → cheerful → excited). In this regard, any given emotion could move along its class of emotions and shift between constructive or destructive. For example, in the context of addiction, a person may slip/lapse (i.e., have a half of a beer at a surprise work-related cocktail party) after several months of sobriety and be concerned that the slip will turn into a relapse (i.e., starting to have a few drinks on the weekend, progressing to drinks every evening after work, etc.). As long as this person is feeling concerned about the slip, they are able to cope and problem-solve by seeking advice from their sponsor (i.e., Twelve-Step Model based recovery) or resume seeing their therapist on a weekly basis, etc. Over time, however, if this person continues to think about the slip and becomes worried, then nervous, then anxious that it will turn into a relapse; that is, the progression of emotions may lead to the relapse. Arguably, at some point along this class of emotions, a line is crossed and it shifts from being a constructive emotion (i.e., still able to cope and problem-solve, and still able to function and to help one's self) to a destructive emotion (i.e., no longer able to cope and problem-solve, and quite literally stuck, or unable to function and help one's self). That is, a negative, but constructive emotion (i.e., concern), based on thought processes (i.e., metacognitions) can shift and become a destructive emotion.

The challenge with positive versus negative emotions and constructive versus destructive emotions is to learn to recognize them, understand the process, and work to change them, or to manage our emotions on the spectrums. That is, monitoring our metacognitions and modifying them as needed to prevent emotions – whether positive or negative – from crossing the line from being constructive (i.e., rational or self-helping) to destructive (i.e., irrational or self-defeating).

Regarding *absolutist thinking*, irrational beliefs tend to take on an extreme quality such that said irrational beliefs become absolutistic demands and/or expectations (see Ellis & Dryden, 1997; Ellis & Ellis, 2011, 2019). A typical manifestation of this is the use of words such as should, must, and ought in our everyday language and communication. That is, such words carry fundamental assumptions about anticipated outcomes. If we use the word *should*, the implication is that there is an expectation that something will turn out a certain way and if it does not, then there is something inherently wrong or bad about it. For example, if I believe that I *should not* engage in addictive behavior and I do, then I have violated some otherwise objective, accepted standard and therefore something is wrong with me, and/or I am inherently bad. Believing that we *should* do things is the same as believing that said things are *supposed* to be done. For example, if we have children, we should take care of them, because we are supposed to take care of them. That is what parents do. In our culture/society, if parents do not take care of their kids like they should (i.e., like they are supposed to), they risk having their kids taken away from them, and being considered as not only bad parents, but inherently bad human beings.

The problem with absolutist thinking is that being human and imperfect, we set ourselves up for failure by engaging in irrational, absolutistic thinking. If, as a person struggling with addiction (especially in early recovery), I tell myself that I *must* never have a slip, or my loved ones should never get upset with me – because, after all, I am trying to recover – the reality is that I likely will have a slip and my loved ones likely will become upset with me (they are human and imperfect too). And, if I absolutely expect or demand these things not to happen, when they do, I likely will feel, behave, cope, and problem-solve in a much different way than if I could back away from absolutely demanding/expecting such to happen (see the ABC Model, above). This does not mean that we cannot have preferences (or even strong preferences), but preferences are not absolutistic in that a preference recognizes that things may or may not happen.

Cognitive Behavior Therapy

Originally known as *cognitive therapy*, Aaron Beck's system of psychotherapy is now commonly called *Cognitive Behavior Therapy* (CBT), and four of its most essential principles (again, those that distinguish it from other non-cognitive systems of psychotherapy) consist of (1) the cognitive triad, (2) the source of cognitive dysfunction, (3) the relationship between core beliefs, intermediate beliefs, and automatic thoughts, and (4) the issue of cognitive errors (see Beck, 2011). The cognitive triad is in reference to the human tendency to become focused on beliefs and perceptions about themselves (including sense of self, experiences, and the future), others, and the world (Beck et al., 1979; Beck, 2011). Whether these beliefs and perceptions become problematic or not tends to be related to their qualitative nature. When our beliefs and perceptions in this regard are largely positive, judiciously favorable, and optimistic we tend to be adaptive and able to cope and problem-solve effectively. When said beliefs and perceptions are largely negative, critical, or pessimistic we tend to have difficulty adapting to novel circumstances and thus develop problems with coping and problem solving. Regarding *the source of cognitive dysfunction*, our perceptions of situations influence how we feel, rather than the situation itself. That is, "how [we] interpret and think about a situation. *The situation itself does not directly determine how* [we] *feel or what* [we] *do*; [our] emotional response is mediated by [our] perception of the situation" (emphasis in original; Beck, 2011, p. 31). Again, as Ellis (2011, 2019) and Frankl (1992) both argued, it is not what happens to us that bothers us, but what we think about what happens to us that bothers us (see above). In a very fundamental way (keeping in mind that there are exceptions – see above), it is our thought processes, or our metacognitions that lead us into emotional difficulties, including maladaptive coping and problem solving skills.

Before addressing the relationship between core beliefs, intermediate beliefs, and automatic beliefs, it is critical to understand what is meant by each of these terms (see Beck, 2011). *Core beliefs* are deeply held ideas and assumptions about self, others, and the world (i.e., the cognitive triad) and are based on messages we receive, beginning at a very young age, from our interactions with others and our experiences in life. Things that, for whatever reason, occur repeatedly, such that our potentially idiosyncratic interpretations of them become themes. Objectively, these core beliefs may or may not be accurate or true, but are perceived and accepted by the individual holding them as absolutely and undeniably true. Every individual develops core beliefs, some are positive and/or helpful and some are negative and/or unhelpful. When a core belief of either type is activated by a current experience there can be a cascading wave of emotional, cognitive, and/or behavioral consequences, similarly positive or negative, helpful or unhelpful. Core beliefs are also known as *schemas*, "the underlying cognitive structures that organize the patient's experience and that therefore form the basis for the individual instances of bias or distortion. … [and] represent the core of the cognitive disturbance" (DeRubeis et al., 2019, p. 221).

Intermediate beliefs are attitudes, rules, and assumptions derived from our core beliefs or schemas and influence how we perceive and interpret a situation and thus, how we respond to it, whether through thoughts, feelings, and/or behaviors. *Automatic beliefs* are one of two initial responses we have to any given experience. When having an experience, on one level we are paying attention to the information conveyed by the experience, or the raw data. "At another level, however, [we] may be having some quick evaluative thoughts. These thoughts are called *automatic thoughts* and are not the result of deliberation or reasoning" (emphasis in original; Beck, 2011, p. 31).

Each of these three types of beliefs (i.e., core, intermediate, and automatic) are beliefs that we are not readily or actively aware of. However, core beliefs are the hardest to access and identify, followed by intermediate beliefs, with automatic beliefs/thoughts being the easiest – relatively speaking. Put another way, when seeking to intervene in cognitive dysfunction, starting and having success with automatic beliefs can lead to tracing backwards through intermediate beliefs and ultimately addressing the core beliefs, which can prevent problematic responses in the first place. In sum,

> *Core beliefs* are the most fundamental level of belief; they are global, rigid, and overgeneralized. *Automatic thoughts*, the actual words or images that go through a person's mind, are situation specific and may be considered the most superficial level of cognition. … [Of note,] core beliefs influence the development of an intermediate class of beliefs, which consists of (often unarticulated) attitudes, rules, and assumptions.
>
> (emphasis in original; Beck, 2011, pp. 34–35)

As an example, in the struggle of addiction, we often lie to our loved ones. Consider the context of holding a core belief that making mistakes means you are a bad person. When someone lies they may tell themselves that (1) it is horrible to be dishonest (attitude), (2) any level of dishonesty constitutes a lie (rule), and (3) when asked a question (i.e., in a given situation) it is better to be vague and evasive thereby avoiding a lie, than to start any level of disclosure and risk being asked a follow-up question and needing to be dishonest/lie (assumption). In this scenario, the person avoids telling a lie, strictly speaking, but still perceives themselves as having been dishonest, ostensibly knowing in their heart that there is little difference between avoiding a situation and being dishonest about a situation (automatic belief), which leads the person to feel bad about the whole interaction, frustrated, and pessimistic about the future and their ability to change (reaction). In this example, we see the relationship between these types of beliefs and their ultimate influence on our responses to any given situation. That is, core beliefs → intermediate beliefs ↔ a situation occurs → automatic beliefs/thoughts → reaction (see Beck, 2011).

Lastly, when problematic automatic beliefs become systematic they can manifest as cognitive errors, cognitive distortions, or distorted thinking (synonymous terms). Being at the level of automatic beliefs, although not obvious to begin with, such cognitive errors can become easily recognizable for a person through psychotherapy and/or psychoeducation. If we are able to identify and understand the nature of these cognitive errors it can serve as a reminder that we "may be prone to exaggeration or other biased thinking. At these times, [we] can discount the improbable or illogical reference, reframe it in a less extreme form, or [conduct a cost-benefit type of analysis]" (DeRubeis et al., 2019, p. 228).

Three of the most common cognitive errors are called *all-or-nothing thinking, overgeneralizing*, and *fortune telling* (also known as *catastrophizing*) (see Beck, 2011; DeRubeis et al., 2019). All-or-nothing thinking can also be described as either-or thinking; that is, narrowing an explanation down to two options, typically at opposite ends of a spectrum. Only this or that can be true, ignoring the often multitude of options in the middle. For example, "If I am going to be one minute late for an appointment, I may as well not go." Overgeneralization is in reference to making a broad assumption or coming to a profound conclusion based on one experience. For example, my therapist was late for my appointment, so they must not be very trustworthy. And, fortune telling, or catastrophizing, is in reference to assuming the worst (for the future) based on little evidence. For example, after interviewing for a job and not getting it, believing that no one will hire you. It is important to remember, however, that not all cognitive errors are devoid of truth. The problem is that whatever truth there may be in the basic thought process, said truth is distorted to an unreasonable and often an extreme degree.

REBT, CBT, and Evaluating Metacognitions

Given the central assumptions of both REBT and CBT regarding "the idea that emotional disturbance [emerges] from thoughts that [are] illogical, anti-empirical, irrational, or incorrect. [And,] more scientific, accurate methods of thinking [will] free people from their disturbed emotions" (Hollon & DiGiuseppe, 2011, p. 207), various approaches to evaluating and disputing such problematic metacognitions have been developed. In this regard, two typical approaches of REBT and CBT are addressing the relationship between one's sense of self and their behavior, and Socratic-style questioning, respectively. Both of these approaches can be viewed as consistent with the Motivational Interviewing notion of evocation and evoking, or drawing out insights and commitments from those we are helping rather than imparting information (see Chapter 10; Miller & Rollnick, 2013).

Sense of Self and Behavior

"Since its beginning, REBT has taught people not to rate their self or personhood, but only their acts, deeds, and performances in relation to their goals and purposes" (Ellis & Ellis, 2011, p. 34) and has discussed the importance of unconditional self-acceptance (Ellis & Dryden, 1997; Ellis & Ellis, 2011, 2019). Given the inherent imperfection of the human condition, no human being can expect perfection from themselves, or that they will never make any mistakes. Nevertheless, a common irrational belief stems from self-evaluative behavior and the notion that if I make a mistake, I must be bad or worthless. In this regard, a fundamental assumption of REBT is that someone will be better off if they are able to separate their sense of self, self-worth, self-acceptance, etc. from their behavior. If we connect our sense of self-worth or self-value to our behavior and therefore feel good when we do good and feel bad when we do bad, being imperfect, our sense of self and thus our mood, will fluctuate based on our behavior. Related to this is that our ability to be adaptive and effectively cope and problem-solve will fluctuate based on when we are feeling good or bad about ourselves.

REBT holds that in order to stabilize our mood and our ability to function in a healthy manner, we need to separate our sense of self from our behavior. However, this can be very difficult to do because society is largely based on rewarding and punishing good and bad behavior. Such that, we are good if we are otherwise successful in life and we are bad if not. In the context of addiction, a person is often thought of as good as long as they are on the path of recovery and bad when they are actively struggling with addictive behavior. This is not only a message communicated by society, but as individuals we tend to live by this same creed. As long as we buy into this societal-level irrational (i.e., self-defeating) belief, it is considerably more difficult to change our behavior for the better, because we are spending time feeling bad about ourselves rather than investing our time and efforts in the future.

How do we separate our sense of self from our behavior? REBT encourages us to find a stable, inherent sense of self that is not dependent on behavior. For some people this may entail finding or reconnecting with spirituality. Some spiritual belief systems teach, for example, that humans are the offspring of deity and therefore they always have worth and are loved, even when making mistakes. There can be consequences for poor behavior, but acceptance, love, and the potential for redemption are always present and possible. Others that may not be traditionally spiritual may find a stable sense of value in an existential context. That is, since I exist I have value and nobody can take that away from me.

When self-rating becomes evident in a person's life, which REBT would argue is inevitable given popular culture, it becomes important to learn to identify that it is happening and to evaluate one's personal assumptions and dispute the problematic, illogical thinking. An example of disputing the human tendency for self-rating and the assumed connection between self-worth and behavior comes from my clinical training as a psychologist. One of my pre-doctoral clinical supervisors, Stevan Lars Nielsen, Ph.D., was a so-called REBTer and would often talk about the following conundrum to illustrate the fallacy of such thinking. If self-worth is contingent upon our behavior, then it would make sense for us to go to all of the hospitals and round up all of the newborn babies and jettison them to outer space, never to be heard from again. After all, they have done nothing and thus, are worthless. Obviously this is a thought experiment, as nobody would consider doing such a thing. However, the logic of self-worth as contingent upon behavior is there. But, we can clearly see that it is a logical fallacy. All of this in *not to say* that behavior does not matter, that there is no right or wrong, or that guilt is unwarranted, etc. It is to say that behavior does matter, etc., but it is related to rewards and punishments, not self-worth. For example, if I do not graduate from High School, my opportunities in life are likely to be impacted in a negative way, but it certainly does not mean that I am a bad person or unlovable, etc. Similarly, if I struggle with addiction, I may lose my job (and deservedly so, perhaps), but it does not mean that I am unworthy of respect or unworthy to be treated with basic human decency and dignity. Which person is more likely to be successful in recovery? The person made to feel (by society and/or themselves) that they are a bad, weak person for relapsing or the person supported and encouraged by their loved ones after a relapse? Obviously, healthy boundaries are important and sometimes enforcing boundaries means consequences for a relationship, but there is a difference between relationships based on unconditional positive regard, and conditions of worth (see Rogers, 1989). As a side note, the humanistic, person-centered style of Carl Rogers is consistent with REBT, even though Ellis' public persona was edgy, brash, and borderline abrasive (see Hollon & DiGiuseppe, 2011).

Socratic-Style Questioning

"Perhaps the most distinctive stylistic feature of cognitive [behavior] therapy … is the judicious and persistent use of … leading yet open questions, of helping patients to arrive at new perspectives that challenge their faulty conclusions" (DeRubeis et al., 2019). Beck stresses that "patients need a structured method to evaluate their thinking;

otherwise, their responses to automatic thoughts can be superficial and unconvincing and will fail to improve their mood or functioning" (Beck, 2011, p. 170). This style of questioning is meant to facilitate patients drawing their own conclusions about their problematic metacognitions, or otherwise illogical or incorrect thought processes. The questions can be leading, but not in an overly predetermined way. The questions are meant to be thought-provoking, not thought-providing. The themes addressed during this style of questioning include (1) focusing on the nature of and weighing the evidence for and against the automatic thought, (2) alternative explanations, (3) decatastrophizing the situation, or moving away from the worst-case scenario, (4) the impact or implications of the automatic thought – if true, and (5) distancing or perspective-inducing, or discussing what you would say to someone else in a similar situation (Beck, 2011; see also, DeRubeis et al., 2019). Indeed, this manner of Socratic-style questioning can be described as a sort-of cost-benefit analysis.

For example, return to the example above regarding the illustration of the Cognitive Behavior Therapy notion of the relationship between core beliefs, intermediate beliefs, and automatic beliefs. That is, in the context of a person struggling with addiction lying to their loved ones and the automatic belief of there being little difference between avoiding a situation and being dishonest about a situation. Socratic-style questioning or a cost-benefit style of analysis may include questions such as: (1) What makes you say that reasonably avoiding a topic and being dishonest about a topic are the same thing – different forms of lying? (2) Related to the first question, what are some reasons why avoiding a topic may not be the same as being dishonest? (3) What else could it mean when a person is trying to make a distinction between avoiding a topic and being dishonest about a topic? and (4) If your best friend was expressing the same concern to you, what would you tell them? Regarding the first and second question, when we have to think of similarities and differences, sometimes it is hard to put into words why we view something as similar and thus realize that we are being too hard on ourselves. With the third question, this may actually help the person to open up and think more deeply about their concerns and fears. For example, they may realize that they fear that others will not believe anything they say unless it is a confession of the stark truth or that the "avoiding" answer will be transparent, rather than be perceived by the other as a reasonable response along the lines of "Well, maybe whatever I am asking about is none of my business." Regarding the fourth question, often when we stop and think of how we would discuss the issue if a friend was expressing the same concern to us, we suddenly realize that there are many possible answers and solutions.

Cognitive-Behavioral Coping Skills Therapy

Designed to last up to 12 sessions, including eight core sessions and up to four elective sessions (selected from 14 possible electives), Cognitive-Behavioral Coping Skills Therapy (CBCST; Kadden et al., 1994) was one of three psychosocial treatment modalities for alcohol related problems tested in Project MATCH (Longabaugh & Wirtz, 2001), and a component of treatment tested in COMBINE (Miller, 2004; Pettinati et al., 2004), two large-scale, multi-site clinical research projects funded by the National Institute on Alcohol Abuse and Alcoholism (https://www.niaaa.nih.gov/), a component agency of the United States National Institutes of Health (https://www.nih.gov/). CBCST "is based on a cognitive-behavioral model, with a focus on the training of interpersonal and self-management skills," specifically adapted and applied to alcohol-related problems (Kadden et al., 1994, p. 7). Related to this, CBCST includes the development of relapse prevention and problem solving skills, and self-control skills to help replace maladaptive habits with healthy behaviors. Also, while the CBCST therapist is very directive and focused on developing behaviorally based skills during treatment, the therapist must also be mindful of developing a trusting, therapeutic relationship or alliance with their clients, including interacting with clients in a warm, genuine, and empathic manner. Indeed, "there is a danger that, with such a full agenda and such highly structured sessions, the clients may come to feel that the therapist's agenda is more important than their own needs" (Kadden et al., 1994, p. 12). Obviously, this needs to be avoided at all costs! Following is an overview of the CBCST sessions, drawn from the CBCST Manual developed by Kadden et al. (1994).

The first of the eight core sessions of CBCST is the *Introduction* session, which involves building rapport with the client and helping the client understand the rationale for coping skills, including discussing reasons why people engage in addictive behavior and why people have difficulty changing addictive behavior. Also, during this first session it is important for the therapist to come to an understanding of the client's patterns of addictive behavior and motivation to be in treatment and motivation to consider and seek change. The second CBCST session, *Cravings and Urges*, involves understanding, recognizing, and addressing triggers, or the learned associations that lead to use and relapse. Related to this is developing an understanding that cravings and urges are normal, to be expected, and not to be viewed as something being wrong. That they typically only last for a brief period of time, especially if identified as triggers, or cues that remind you of engaging in addictive behavior (e.g., smells, music, relationship-based situations, etc.). And, that cravings and urges occur less frequently and with less intensity over time as one is more and more successful with their coping and problem solving skills. Critical for this session is helping the client to identify, challenge, reframe, and/or change problematic thought processes regarding their cravings and urges.

The third CBCST session, *Managing Thoughts*, builds on the previous session by adding general attitudes and thought processes that can be dangerous for maintaining behavior change.

> Stinking thinking, as the saying goes, leads to [addictive behavior related] thinking, and then, usually, to [addictive behavior] without thinking. It is not the thinking itself that creates the problem, but how people deal with it. If [people struggling with addiction] can learn to dismiss this thinking from their minds whenever it appears, recognize it for what it is, or counter it with contrary thoughts, it need not lead to a relapse.
>
> (Kadden et al., 1994, p. 35)

Once again, identifying, challenging, reframing, and changing problematic thought processes is necessary. However, now in a more general sense as related to particular situations that may lead to thoughts of engaging in addictive behavior as a means of coping or problem solving. For example, wanting to escape stressful situations, wanting to relax, wanting to be able to overcome socially awkward situations, self-image issues, etc. Part of this process, again, normalizes these types of experiences (i.e., they are not the only ones that have these types of experiences – everyone does), but also as these types of experiences are common and persistent, it becomes important to face and counter these issues, keeping in mind that one must work to maintain commitment to recovery and vigilance against such problematic thinking. The fourth session, *Problem Solving*, involves improving interpersonal conflict resolution skills with people, in general. Also, this session can include learning how to identify and manage problematic responses to experiences and situations that are outside one's influence and control.

The fifth core session of CBCST, *Refusal Skills*, entails addressing social and peer pressure in the explicit context of refusing to engage in one's addictive behavior. Particularly when experiencing old and new relationship-based pressures. For example, managing old friendships that are not supportive of one's recovery, and developing new friendships that are not based on or related to addictive behavior. The sixth session, *Emergencies and Relapse*, involves addressing the immediate and long-term effects of guilt and shame after relapse, including learning to recognize and understand what leads to the relapse.

The seventh session, *Irrelevant Decisions*, involves working with the client to ensure vigilant decision making, including the avoidance of self-defeating circumstances, rationalization, and minimization of risk. That is, as one is making progress in their recovery, it becomes tempting to let one's guard down through over-confidence. For example, at some point in longer-term recovery, it is likely that maintaining vigilance against going to a restaurant with a bar with friends will become unnecessary. However, early in recovery, there is no need to test oneself, or to maintain an image for friends. The focus here is to learn not to set oneself up for failure. The eighth and final core session of CBCST, *Termination*, entails the process of appropriately ending treatment.

Also, throughout the core sessions of CBCST are common general themes and practices of universality, reframing, and role-playing. In an effort to normalize the experience and thereby reduce some of the stress associated with the change process, clients are reminded of and encouraged to recognize and remember that cognitive and behavior based struggles are typically experienced by those seeking recovery; that is, they are not alone (universality). Reframing – developing alternative explanations – is a technique used consistently throughout treatment to challenge and modify problematic thought processes. And, role-playing newly acquired coping and problem solving skills is very effective for developing confidence and hope for a better future.

As mentioned previously, in addition to the eight core sessions of CBCST, up to four elective sessions – tailored to a particular client's needs – can be selected from a formal list of 14 possible electives. These elective topics include, but are not limited to: non-verbal communication, assertiveness, receiving criticism, awareness and management of anger, awareness and management of negative thinking, managing negative moods and depression, and enhancing social support networks.

Forgiveness and Cognitive-Behavioral Approaches to Change

The process of forgiveness has been identified as consistent with the practice of Cognitive-Behavioral Coping Skills Therapy (CBCST) in the explicit context of addiction (Webb & Jeter, 2015; Webb & Trautman, 2010). Following is a more detailed discussion of said consistencies between the Process Model of Forgiveness and the REACH Model of Forgiveness (as developed by Enright and Worthington, respectively; see Chapter 8) and the fundamental principles of cognitive-behaviorism itself, as well as the particulars of such as applied to addiction through CBCST (see Table 11.1). As a side note, the brief statements summarizing each of the phases of forgiveness (based on the work of Enright and Worthington; see Chapter 8), as initially presented in the "Forgiveness and motivational interviewing" section of Chapter 10, will be restated at the beginning of each forgiveness phase-based discussion below.

Enright's *Uncovering* phase and Worthington's *Recalling the Hurt* phase are both focused on the person pursuing forgiveness (i.e., the client) developing, with the assistance of a therapist, facilitator, or workbook, a self-determined, personally relevant, objective awareness of the problem and the pain associated with the difficulties experienced. From

Table 11.1 Forgiveness and Cognitive-Behavioral Principles and Cognitive-Behavioral based Coping Skills

Forgiveness Phase		*Corresponding Aspects of Cognitive-Behavioral based Coping Skills adapted to Addictive Behavior*[a]		
Process Model[b]	*REACH Model*[b]	*REBT*	*CBT*	*CBCST*
Uncovering	Recalling the Hurt	Metacognitions	Metacognitions	Introduction
		Irrational Bs	Cognitive Triad	Cravings and Urges
		Pos/Neg Emotions[c]	Cognitive Dysfunction	Emergencies and Relapse
		Cons/Destr Emotions[d]	Co/In/Au Beliefs[e]	
Decision	Empathy	Metacognitions	Metacognitions	Managing Thoughts
Work	Altruistic Gift	ABC Model	Cognitive Dysfunction	Irrelevant Decisions
	Commitment			Refusal Skills
Work	Commitment	ABC Model	Co/In/Au Beliefs	Cravings and Urges
		Absolutist Thinking	Cognitive Errors	Managing Thoughts
		Evaluating Thoughts	Evaluating Thoughts	Irrelevant Decisions Problem Solving Refusal Skills (Reframing)[f] (Role Playing)
Deepening	Holding On	Absolutist Thinking	Cognitive Errors	Managing Thoughts
		Evaluating Thoughts	Evaluating Thoughts	Irrelevant Decisions (Universality)

Source: Adapted from Webb and Trautman (2010)

[a] That is, as related to substance use, compulsive behavior sets, and suicide.
[b] See Chapter 8
[c] Positive Emotions versus Negative Emotions
[d] Constructive Emotions versus Destructive Emotions
[e] Core, Intermediate, and Automatic Beliefs
[f] Parentheses indicate that the principle is general to CBCST, rather than necessarily a component of a particular core session.

the point of view of rational emotive behavior therapy (REBT), this is consistent with the central role of metacognitions, irrational beliefs (i.e., the B in the ABC Model), positive versus negative emotions, and constructive versus destructive emotions. And, likewise, from the point of view of Cognitive Behavior Therapy (CBT) this is consistent with metacognitions, the cognitive triad, cognitive dysfunction, and the relationship between core, intermediate, and automatic beliefs. The need to recognize that we have metacognitions in the first place (or, that humans have thoughts about what they think about) and that we need to understand their influence on how we feel and behave (irrational Bs;

cognitive dysfunction) is related to the need to understand our negative experiences and uncover/recall any underlying pain, defense mechanisms, etc. (positive/negative emotions; constructive/destructive emotions; core, intermediate, and automatic beliefs). That there are things influencing us that are outside of and need to be brought into our immediate awareness. Also, that Beck's discussion of the cognitive triad, or the human tendency to become focused on beliefs and perceptions about ourselves, others, and the world (Beck et al., 1979; Beck, 2011), and Ellis' similar notion that humans tend to place demands and expectations on ourselves, others, and the world (Ellis & Dryden, 1997), underlie emotional function and dysfunction, and in turn impact our ability to cope and problem-solve effectively.

From the point of view of CBCST, Enright's Uncovering phase and Worthington's Recalling the Hurt phase are consistent with the core sessions of Introduction, Cravings and Urges, and Emergencies and Relapse. Building rapport and understanding issues related to the need for coping skills and the common struggles of addiction and behavior change (Introduction) can help facilitate the processes of Uncovering and Recalling the Hurt through identifying patterns, motivations, and defenses contributing to addiction and recovery. Addressing triggers for relapse or the learned associations that lead to a return to use (Cravings and Urges) facilitates the processes of Uncovering and Recall through continued recognition of problematic thoughts and thought processes (metacognitions). If relapse occurs, the process of preventing sustained relapse (Emergencies and Relapse) necessitates a return to Uncovering and Recall, including in the context of issues related to guilt and shame.

Enright's *Decision* phase and initial aspects of the *Work* phase and Worthington's *Empathy* and *Altruistic Gift* phases and initial aspects of the *Commitment* phase are focused on recognizing that an alternative solution *is* needed, understanding what forgiveness actually is *and* that it is an option, and starting the process of committing to giving forgiveness as a gift, through reframing the difficult experience(s) and developing positive emotions and responses such as empathy, compassion, humility, gratitude, and acceptance. From the point of view of REBT, this is consistent with metacognitions and the ABC Model. And, likewise from the point of view of CBT this is consistent with metacognitions and cognitive dysfunction. Returning to metacognitions, the notion that we think about what we think about and the subsequent influence of feelings and behavior truly does underlie much of life and living. Recognizing and applying this insight is similar to realizing that our default coping and problem solving skills are not working and that we need alternative solutions. More specifically, that our experiences and the situations that we find ourselves in are not what causes our emotional difficulties (and related problems with coping and problem solving), but that our perceptions, demands, and expectations regarding such are (ABC Model; cognitive dysfunction). Similarly, developing these insights and reframing our thoughts (or reorienting our metacognitions, or thinking differently) can help us develop positive emotions in the context of ourselves, others, and the world, as well as learn acceptance for the foibles of humanity. In this regard, understanding the ABC Model and the nature of cognitive dysfunction can bring us to making a decision to change and make an initial commitment thereto.

From the point of view of CBCST, Enright's Decision and Work (initial) and Worthington's Empathy, Altruistic Gift, and Commitment (initial) phases are consistent with the core sessions of Managing Thoughts, Irrelevant Decisions, and Refusal Skills. Managing Thoughts and Irrelevant Decisions is related to these phases of forgiveness as it helps to establish one's initial commitment to and vigilance for recovery through identifying, recognizing, and countering relapse provoking thought processes. Refusal Skills are also related to these phases of forgiveness given the need to avoid high-risk situations and to be quick to refuse immediate demands arising from social and peer pressure.

The completion of Enright's *Work* and Worthington's *Commitment* phases builds upon the process described above, yet also with a particular focus on maintaining the preliminary commitment, particularly through addressing initial reservations and doubts about making said commitment. Likewise, Enright's *Deepening* phase and Worthington's *Holding On* phase are focused on solidifying and sustaining the progress heretofore made through finding meaning and purpose, recognizing the need for and utilizing social support, continuing to address inevitable doubts, and maintaining vigilance against risk factors for returning to previous behavior(s). From the point of view of REBT, this is consistent with the ABC Model (see above), absolutist thinking, and evaluating thoughts. And, from the point of view of CBT this is consistent with the relationship between core, intermediate, and automatic beliefs (see above), cognitive errors, and evaluating thoughts.

Throughout Enright's Work and Deepening phases and Worthington's Commitment and Holding On phases and the associated principles of absolutist thinking (e.g., demands, expectations; should, musts, oughts), cognitive errors (e.g., all-or-nothing thinking, overgeneralization, catastrophizing), and evaluating thoughts, whether through separating self-worth from behavior (REBT) or Socratic-Style questioning/cost-benefit analyses (CBT), the individual is continually monitoring, evaluating, and modifying their problematic metacognitions. Each of these types of processes, whether conceptualized in REBT or CBT terms, are describing similar problems or cognitive-behavioral short-circuits that are almost human nature and although we may get better at addressing them, they tend to occur throughout our lives. In fact, Ellis argued that these faulty thought processes were a function of not only conditioning through social learning (broadly construed; that is, being raised in a common culture – for example, linking good/bad self-worth to good/bad behavior), but also as a function of our biology and genetics (Ellis & Dryden, 1997). Indeed, Ellis also acknowledged that he, even in later life, had to maintain constant vigilance against falling into these types of counterproductive cognitive traps (see Ellis & Ellis, 2011).

From the point of view of CBCST, Enright's Work and Deepening phases and Worthington's Commitment and Holding On phases are consistent with sessions 2, 3, 4, 5, and 7. That is, in order to enable said newly acquired skills to take root and mature, it is important to continually (1) accept and reframe urges and thoughts (Cravings and Urges), (2) maintain a firm and vigilant commitment to recovery through identifying, recognizing, and countering relapse provoking thought processes (Managing Thoughts and Irrelevant Decisions), and (3) manage interpersonal tensions and reframe social situations (Problem Solving and Refusal Skills). Just as genuine and lasting forgiveness is not an event or an all-or-nothing experience, so too is the struggle for recovery. New skills developed and progress made must be maintained and sustained. Also, although long-term recovery and long-term forgiveness at some point may not require indefinite vigilance, it requires enduring vigilance. And, enduring vigilance includes knowing when to engage in what might be described as temporary indefinite vigilance.

References

Beck, A. T., Rush, A. J., Shaw, B. F., & Emery, G. (1979). *Cognitive therapy of depression*. New York, NY: Guilford Press.

Beck, J. S. (2011). *Cognitive behavior therapy: Basics and beyond* (2nd ed.). New York, NY: Guilford Press.

Benoit, D., & Coolbear, J. (2004). Disorders of attachment and failure to thrive. In L. Atkinson & S. Goldberg (Eds.), *Attachment issues in psychopathology and intervention* (pp. 49–64). Mahwah, NJ: Lawrence Erlbaum.

Child Welfare Information Gateway (2019). *Long-term consequences of child abuse and neglect.* Washington, DC: U.S. Department of Health and Human Services, Administration for Children and Families, Children's Bureau.

DeRubeis, R. J., Keefe, J. R., & Beck, A. T. (2019). Cognitive therapy. In K. S. Dobson & D. J. A. Dozois (Eds.), *Handbook of cognitive-behavioral therapies* (4th ed., pp. 218–248). New York, NY: Guilford Press.

DiGiuseppe, R. A., & Doyle, K. A. (2019). Rational emotive behavior therapy. In K. S. Dobson & D. J. A. Dozois (Eds.), *Handbook of cognitive-behavioral therapies* (4th ed., pp. 191–217). New York, NY: Guilford Press.

Ellis, A., & Dryden, W. (1997). *The practice of rational emotive behavior therapy* (2nd ed.). New York, NY: Springer.

Ellis, A., & Ellis, D. J. (2011). *Rational emotive behavior therapy.* Washington, DC: American Psychological Association.

Ellis, A., & Ellis, D. J. (2019). *Rational emotive behavior therapy* (2nd ed.). Washington, DC: American Psychological Association.

Frankl, V. E. (1992). *Man's search for meaning: An introduction to logotherapy* (I. Lasch, Trans. 4th ed.). Boston, MA: Beacon Press.

Hollon, S. D., & Beck, A. T. (2013). Cognitive and cognitive-behavioral therapies. In M. J. Lambert (Ed.), *Bergin and Garfield's handbook of psychotherapy and behavior change* (6th ed., pp. 393–442). Hoboken, NJ: John Wiley & Sons.

Hollon, S. D., & DiGiuseppe, R. (2011). Cognitive theories of psychotherapy. In J. C. Norcross, G. R. VandenBos, & D. K. Freedheim (Eds.), *History of psychotherapy: Continuity and change* (2nd ed., pp. 203–241). Washington, DC: American Psychological Association.

Kadden, R., Carroll, K. M., Donovan, D., Cooney, N., Monti, P., Abrams, D., … Hester, R. (1994). *Cognitive-behavioral coping skills therapy manual: A clinical research guide for therapists treating individuals with alcohol abuse and dependence.* NIH Publication No. 94–3724. Rockville, MD: National Institute on Alcohol Abuse and Alcoholism.

Longabaugh, R., & Wirtz, P. W. (Eds.). (2001). *Project MATCH: Hypotheses, results, and causal chain analyses.* NIH Publication No. 01–4238. Rockville, MD: National Institute on Alcohol Abuse and Alcoholism.

Miller, W. R. (Ed.) (2004). *COMBINE Monograph Series, Volume 1. Combined behavioral intervention manual: A clinical research guide for therapists treating people with alcohol abuse and dependence.* DHHS Publication No. (NIH) 04–5288. Bethesda, MD: National Institute on Alcohol Abuse and Alcoholism.

Miller, W. R., & Rollnick, S. (2013). *Motivational interviewing: Helping people change* (3rd ed.). New York, NY: Guilford Press.

Pettinati, H. M., Weiss, R. D., Miller, W. R., Donovan, D., Ernst, D. B., & Rounsaville, B. J. (2004). *COMBINE Monograph Series, Volume 2. Medical management treatment manual: A clinical research guide for medically trained clinicians providing pharmacotherapy as part of the treatment for alcohol dependence.* DHHS Publication No. (NIH) 04–5289. Bethesda, MD: National Institute on Alcohol Abuse and Alcoholism.

Rogers, C. R. (1989). *On becoming a person.* New York, NY: Houghton Mifflin.

Safran, J. D., & Hunter, J. (2020). *Psychoanalysis and psychoanalytic therapies* (2nd ed.). Washington, DC: American Psychological Association.

Webb, J. R., & Jeter, B. R. (2015). Forgiveness and problematic substance use. In L. L. Toussaint, E. L.Worthington, Jr., & D. R. Williams (Eds.), *Forgiveness and health: Scientific evidence and theories relating forgiveness to better health* (pp. 139–154). New York, NY: Springer.

Webb, J. R., & Trautman, R. P. (2010). Forgiveness and alcohol use: Applying a specific spiritual principle to substance abuse problems. *Addictive Disorders & Their Treatment*, 9(1), 8–17. doi:10.1097/ADT.0b013e318195000d.

12 Clinical Application: Other Modalities and Processes

In addition to the Twelve-Step Model, Motivational Interviewing, aspects of the Transtheoretical Model of intentional behavior change, and classic cognitive-behavioral approaches to change, many additional theories and methods of counseling and psychotherapy are relevant to the treatment of addictive behaviors and likewise share consistencies with the process of forgiveness (see Webb & Trautman, 2010). In this chapter, acceptance/mindfulness-based, systemic-based, and psychodynamic-based systems of counseling and psychotherapy will briefly be addressed, as well as the related issue of aggression in the context of addiction.

Acceptance/Mindfulness-Based Modalities

Originating in the early to mid-1900s with the work of Pavlov, Watson, Skinner, and others regarding the development of learning theory related to classical and operant conditioning, the now-called First Wave of Behavior Therapy took root in the 1950s (Antony & Roemer, 2011; Fishman et al., 2011). As behaviorism continued to evolve and to incorporate explicit cognitive processes, the Second Wave began in the 1960s with the development of Rational Emotive Behavior Therapy and Cognitive Behavior Therapy (see Chapter 11). While still focused on behaviorism and/or cognitive processes, in the late 1980s to early 1990s, the Third Wave of evolving behaviorism began to emerge with the development of various modalities deliberately incorporating aspects of Eastern-oriented philosophy and/or spirituality. Though "no one factor unites these new methods, … all have ventured into areas … of clinical intervention and analysis, emphasizing such issues as acceptance, mindfulness, cognitive defusion, dialectics, values, spirituality, and relationship" (Hayes, 2016, p. 869).

Three particular Third Wave modalities, arguably tied together by a shared prioritization of principles related to acceptance and mindfulness, are: Acceptance and Commitment Therapy, Dialectical Behavior Therapy, and Mindfulness-based Cognitive Therapy (see Fruzzetti et al., 2019). Consistent with the process of forgiveness (see Chapter 8), "the ability to be present with a painful experience without altering or denying the pain is a key component of acceptance-based approaches" (Orcutt, 2006, p. 359). Likewise, integrating the processes of acceptance, mindfulness, and forgiveness likely will allow individuals "to transcend the narrow focus on self and symptoms that prevent connection to others" (Sesan, 2009, p. 236), thereby working to address problems related to self-centeredness in addiction (e.g., Alcoholics Anonymous, 1981, 1998, 2001).

Acceptance and Commitment Therapy

A defining feature of Acceptance and Commitment Therapy (ACT: pronounced as a word) is its grounding in functional contextualism, including the use of language (see Hayes, 2016; Hayes & Lillis, 2012). As such,

> the general clinical goals of ACT are to undermine the grip of the literal verbal content of cognition that occasions avoidance behavior and to construct an alternative context where behavior in alignment with one's values is more likely to occur. … What the client is feeling, thinking, remembering, or otherwise experiencing is never assumed to be the core difficulty, even though human beings will initially focus on difficult content as the core of their problems. … It is the tendency [of the client] to take these experiences literally and then to fight against them that is viewed as harmful.
>
> (Hayes, 2016, p. 876)

As discussed in the context of Second Wave, classic cognitive-behavioral therapy (i.e., Rational Behavioral Therapy (REBT) and Cognitive Behavior Therapy (CBT); see Chapter 11), so it is in ACT as well that, it is not so much what happens to us that causes problems for us as much as it is how we respond to what happens to us that causes problems for us (see also, Frankl, 1992). However, in ACT (as opposed to REBT and CBT), the focus is on helping the client understand the futility of traditional, head-on confrontation of distorted thinking and problematic thought processes (i.e., metacognitions, or thoughts about thoughts; see Chapter 11) and adopt a compassionate, acceptance-oriented approach when addressing problematic metacognitions.

A primary task of ACT is to divest oneself from the quest for control over automatic thoughts, feelings, and memories, and mindfulness and acceptance are viewed as critical resources in this process (Hayes, 2016). ACT defines *mindfulness* as "present moment non-judgmental awareness, as an alternative to our dominant mode of being" (Hayes & Lillis, 2012, p. 96) and *acceptance* as "not merely tolerance – it is the active non-judgmental embracing of experience in the here and now" (Hayes, 2016, p. 879). Explicit clarification of values and deliberate facilitation of commitment can extend the gains achieved through mindfulness and acceptance into everyday living. In this regard,

> Various evocative exercises are used to develop more clarity about fundamental values. … Values dignify the need for acceptance of specific painful thoughts and feelings because it is only that they have arisen as barriers that requires that they be embraced. … ACT involves learning a generalized strategy of moving forward toward valued ends, dissolving psychological barriers through defusion and acceptance and dissolving situational barriers through direct action. … Clients may be asked to establish specific goals, to make public and concrete commitments, and to work toward these goals in small steps.
>
> (Hayes, 2016, pp. 879–880)

Critical to achieving these general clinical objectives in ACT, indeed a common factor across counseling and psychotherapy modalities (Gelso et al., 2018; Norcross & Lambert, 2011; Wampold & Ulvenes, 2019; see also, Rowe & Mac Isaac, 1991), is developing a strong therapeutic relationship/alliance, including empathic responsiveness (Hayes, 2016).

Dialectical Behavior Therapy

Originally developed for the treatment of suicidal patients and in the context of Borderline Personality Disorder, Dialectical Behavior Therapy (DBT) arose when *classic* cognitive-behavioral therapy was found to be ineffective therewith (Linehan & Wilks, 2015; Neacsiu et al., 2012) and has since been adapted to a wide range of psychological and emotional difficulties (see Chapman & Dixon-Gordon, 2020). Although behaviorism remained a component of DBT, aspects of Zen and dialectical philosophy were incorporated in an effort to address the simultaneous priorities of the need for acceptance and change (Neacsiu et al., 2012), given "that the secret to survival was in the ability of the individual in excruciating pain to somehow 'radically' accept the fact or reality of the painful situation" (Linehan, 2011, p. 430).

In addition to acceptance and dialectics, DBT is focused on emotional regulation, validation, and mindfulness (Linehan, 2011; Neacsiu et al., 2012; see also, Chapman & Dixon-Gordon, 2020). Regarding the basic principles of DBT,

> To put these two opposing approaches together (i.e., acceptance and change) a dialectical philosophy emphasizing the synthesis of opposites was adopted. … [the] essential movement toward change generates the need to convey acceptance and validation of the client. … Clients often report how in the midst of a crisis they find themselves seeing what is happening from the prisms of their emotion. … At the same time, clients report perceiving how they are exaggerating the situation, how other people would not get so [emotional], and how it would be better if they just 'got out of it.' … With few skills to integrate the emotion and the reason, clients vacillate from one extreme to the other, struggling with the tension between these opposites [i.e., emotion regulation versus dysregulation]. One way to integrate the opposites … is to accept the emotional arousal and the difficulty of solving the problem in this state while, at the same time, accepting the need to problem solve.
>
> (Neacsiu et al., 2012, pp. 1005–1006)

To help facilitate said synthesis of opposites and dissipate the tension associated therewith, mindfulness practice has become a central component of DBT "so that, in moments of need, attentional control can be easily gained and effective behavior can be more easily attained" (Neacsiu et al., 2012, p. 1005).

Mindfulness-Based Cognitive Therapy

Originally developed in the context of preventing relapse to depression, Mindfulness-based Cognitive Therapy (MBCT) is "designed to foster awareness of the typical ruminative, automatic patterns of thoughts, emotions, and sensations and to teach a way to intentionally switch to a more decentered, non-judgmental present-focused mind" (Felder et al., 2012, p. 180). Not only effective in the context of depression, MBCT also has been adapted to various other health related concerns with promising results being observed (Segal et al., 2013).

Regarding the basic principles of MBCT, clients are taught, through a dyadic, yet collaborative and evoking process,

> mindfulness practices focused on paying attention, noticing mind wandering, and intentionally directing attention to a single, relatively neutral focus. … Therapists are strongly encouraged to have their own mindfulness practice so that they can guide practices and inquiry from within, rather than responding intellectually to participants' experiences. … The MBCT therapist does not attempt to fix or solve participants' difficulties, thereby embodying an important essence of mindfulness of focusing on being with difficulties rather than automatically and ineffectively fixing them. … During the practice of mindfulness, participants are invited to investigate the patterns of thoughts, emotions, and sensations that may appear in the mind and to see whether they can be approached nonjudgmentally and with curiosity.
>
> (Felder et al., 2012, p. 180)

The acceptance-oriented stance imbued in the process of mindfulness, allows us to realize that:

> it can be enormously empowering to discover that we can simply be with unpleasant experiences without being overwhelmed by them, and that, sooner or later, in their own good time, these feelings will pass. With this insight also comes the possibility of choosing behaviors that are more likely to deal skillfully with the situation before us, rather than having our actions automatically driven by fear or old mental habits.
>
> (Segal et al., 2013, p. 232)

By collaboratively modeling the processes of mindfulness and *inquiry from within*, therapists can provide support to their clients and, likewise, help to identify the universal nature of problematic metacognitions (and related behaviors), thereby facilitating change (Felder et al., 2012).

Systemic-Based Modalities

Family based issues can be critical to the recovery process, including (1) the family providing social support for their loved one struggling with addiction *and* (2) the family members themselves as they struggle with the personal and environmental collateral effects of having a loved one struggling with addiction (Lam et al., 2012; McCrady et al., 2012; Miller et al., 2019; Shumway et al., 2019; Shumway et al., 2017). Before adequate support can be provided and received, it is likely that sufficient repair and reconciliation of family relationships must take place. The re-establishment and maintenance of functional and healthy relationship boundaries can be facilitated by the process of forgiveness (given and received) and likely will play a central role in fostering supportive relationships.

Structural Family Therapy

In the early 1990s, as a graduate student in a program designed to meet the requirements for the marriage, family, and child counselor license in the State of California (now known as the marriage and family therapist license), I attended a professional workshop presented by Salvador Minuchin, an early pioneer of family therapy and the originator of structural family therapy (see Minuchin, 1974; Minuchin & Fishman, 1981). A comment that he made during that workshop that has stayed with me all of these years was something to the effect of, "The three most important things about family relationships are: boundaries, boundaries, and boundaries!"

Structural family therapy holds that "the family is normally determined by structure, power, function, boundaries between subsystems [example subsystems include: executive/parents, children, siblings], and degrees of functional attachment among individuals" (Chabot, 2011, p. 179). Minuchin (1974) discussed family structure and boundaries as follows:

> Family structure is the invisible set of functional demands that organizes the ways in which family members interact. A family is a system that operates through transactional patterns. Repeated transactions establish patterns of how, when, and to whom to relate, and these patterns underpin the system. … The boundaries of a

> subsystem are the rules defining who participates, and how. … The function of boundaries is to protect the differentiation of the system. … For proper family functioning, the boundaries of subsystems must be clear [and appropriate].
>
> (Minuchin, 1974, pp. 51, 53, 54)

Moreover, "families experience trouble when their boundaries are too porous (enmeshed) or too rigid (disengaged)" (Doherty & McDaniel, 2010, p. 15), and "a therapist often functions as a boundary maker, clarifying diffuse boundaries and opening inappropriately rigid boundaries" (Minuchin, 1974, p. 56). "The first phase of therapy is joining/accommodating [i.e., developing a therapeutic alliance/relationship] …. The second phase is restructuring problematic family patterns through altering perceptions of the problem" (Doherty & McDaniel, 2010, pp. 15–16).

Internal Family Systems Therapy

Initially excited and then increasingly frustrated by classical approaches to family therapy (such as structural family therapy – see above), Richard Schwartz developed a systemic approach to therapy based on profound, unexpected insights gleaned through exploratory questions and experiences with particular clients when traditional family therapy was not working (see Schwartz & Sweezy, 2020). That is,

> Internal Family Systems (IFS) therapy is a synthesis of two paradigms: the plural mind, or the idea that we all contain many different parts [i.e., intrapsychic aspects of our personality], and systems thinking. … And because we view people as having all the resources they need rather than having deficits or a disease, it is nonpathologizing. Instead of seeing people as lacking resources, we assume people are constrained from using their innate strengths by polarized relationships, both within [i.e., among their intrapsychic parts] and with the people around them.
>
> (Schwartz & Sweezy, 2020, pp. 4–5)

Moreover, "each [part has] a full range of feelings and beliefs … [and together] function as a system, thereby allowing the therapist to use the same [systemic] principles used to treat family members to treat the subparts of an individual" (Chabot, 2011, p. 196).

Schwartz also discovered what he called the *Self*, or the transcendent, spiritual-level essence of who we truly are as human beings. This Self is often pushed into the background (in effect, by the intrapsychic parts seeking to protect said Self), due to traumatic experiences including neglect, abandonment, violence, and abuse (Schwartz & Sweezy, 2020). However,

> inner leadership problems paralleled what [is] seen in dysfunctional families. Various coalitions of extreme parts vied for power over the course of clients' day-to-day lives. And what we usually consider 'thinking' was often a contentious inner dialogue. … [None of the intrapsychic parts] seemed capable of earning the trust of [the others] and taking leadership. As a result, despite good intentions, these parts could not rally together or manage life's challenges.
>
> (Schwartz & Sweezy, 2020, p. 15)

As such,

> the goal of IFS therapy is to help clients [regain access to their true Self and] become Self-led, which means that their [otherwise well-intentioned, but dysfunctional intrapsychic] parts feel loved by the Self and trust the Self's leadership.
>
> (Schwartz & Sweezy, 2020, p. 23)

"When the [Self] is in charge it can balance and heal the parts of the individual and thereby not be at the mercy of extreme behavior from any one part" (Chabot, 2011, p. 196).

Alcohol-Focused Behavioral Couples Therapy

Utilizing cognitive-behavioral approaches to change, together with behavioral couples therapy, alcohol-focused behavioral couples therapy (ABCT) addresses the individual, dyadic, familial, and other social/environmental issues believed to contribute to an individual struggling with alcohol use (McCrady et al., 2016). In the context of this couples-based treatment, cognitive-behavioral approaches to change are used (1) to address the drinking of the identified patient and (2) to strengthen the significant other's ability to support behavior change in their partner, and behavioral couples therapy is used to support and strengthen the relationship between the partners (McCrady et al., 2019). Regarding relationship issues in particular,

> The ABCT model assumes a reciprocal relation between drinking and relationship functioning. … Families in which alcohol problems are present often have evolved poor patterns of communication and problem solving and have developed a variety of relationship, sexual, financial, and child-rearing problems over time. All of these can serve as antecedents to further drinking.
>
> (McCrady et al., 2016, pp. 444–445)

In this regard, "at the couple level, ABCT should result in a greater frequency of positive interactions, greater positive reciprocity in interactions, increased positive and supportive communication in the dyad, decreased negative communication, and better problem-solving skills" (McCrady et al., 2012, p. 243). Also, important components of therapy include the therapeutic alliance, empathy, hope, compassion, acceptance, and anger management (see Magill et al., 2015).

Psychodynamic-Based Modalities

Background

The common thread running through all psychodynamic approaches to psychotherapy and behavior change is the notion that human personality and behavior is driven by unconscious determinants, or processes that are outside of our awareness and thus, not directly accessible to us (i.e., to one degree or another). As such, a counselor or psychotherapist (or psychoanalyst, in Freudian terms – see below) is needed, as a detective of sorts, to uncover and understand the unconscious origins and drivers of our emotional struggles and problematic behavior. The focus on unconscious processes had its heyday with Freud (see Gay, 1989a) and many others, obviously, but became controversial and gave rise to many competing approaches, including behaviorism, humanistic-existential, and cognitive-behaviorism (see Norcross et al., 2011). For many decades now, psychodynamic approaches have been fairly unpopular, with attempts to relegate them as an artifact of a bygone day when empiricism was less developed and less valued (both of which are hindsight-based propositions), *and* given the common assumption *and* otherwise ostensible conclusion that there is little, if any scientific support for fundamental psychodynamic principles, processes, and techniques (see Hansell, 2004; Shedler, 2010).

For those willing to look, there is much evidence to suggest that psychodynamic modalities enjoy as much scientific support (not in sheer quantity of studies, but in critical mass; see Barber et al., 2013; Shedler, 2010), as do other [currently more popular] psychotherapy modalities (e.g., cognitive-behaviorism; Hollon & Beck, 2013; see also, Lambert, 2013). Of note, some of the data-driven principles commonly accepted as efficacious and applied across modalities originated with Freud (e.g., the fundamental importance of (a) the therapeutic relationship/alliance and (b) insight[1]), yet modern practitioners and academicians arguably have lost sight of this fact (Shedler, 2010). Having a cultural awareness of his work, or a background in mental health related fields does not necessarily equate with having an accurate knowledge or understanding of Freud; that is, "before we can speak [about Freud] with *authority*, we must read *his* writings attentively" (emphasis added; Gay, 1989b, p. xi; see also, Gay, 1989a).

Nevertheless, there are scholars working to "reconcile the seemingly conflicting formulations of [psychodynamic], cognitive-behavioral, systemic, and humanistic-experiential orientations" (Wachtel & Gagnon, 2019, p. 184) in an effort to integrate modalities based on shared principles among these otherwise competing schools of psychotherapy and behavior change. Related to this, the originator of Internal Family Systems (IFS) therapy (see above), Richard Schwartz stated:

> For years I did not want to accept that psychodynamic therapists were absolutely right on certain topics. The past does affect the present profoundly; people are driven by unconscious phenomena, which is to say phenomena that remain out of awareness; emotion and the body are key to effective therapy; and, finally, the therapeutic relationship is also key, including both transference and countertransference processes. After swallowing enough pride to privilege data over preconceptions, I also realized that the perspective of IFS provides a different understanding of – and way of working with – these traditionally psychoanalytic observations.
>
> (Schwartz & Sweezy, 2020, p. 19)

Although there may be differences in understanding and application of certain psychodynamic principles, many of Freud's fundamental ideas still resonate today – anecdotally *and* empirically.

Psychodynamic Approaches to Behavior Change

Since the early days of Psychoanalysis – not a catch-all term, but the term used by Freud to denote *his* particular, deliberate, formalized approach to psychotherapy – many variations, derivatives, and also loosely associated relatives have developed (*and* come and gone). Moreover, Psychoanalysis itself has evolved (even Freud's own view of Psychoanalysis evolved during his lifetime), such that there are present-day adherents to classical psychoanalysis, but also arguably more so to *contemporary* psychoanalysis. Many of the modern descendants of Psychoanalysis, though still focused on unconscious/outside-of-awareness drivers of personality and behavior, are sufficiently different from one another in terms of what particular drivers are viewed as most important to focus on. In this regard, it is more appropriate to describe said variants using the umbrella term, *psychodynamic*.

Although psychodynamic approaches to behavior change may differ in their view of what unconscious mechanisms are most important to focus on (e.g., in simple terms, the relative importance of id, ego, or superego related issues), they continue to value and employ many of the same technique-level methods. Regardless of the particular psychodynamic approach under consideration, methods related to the therapeutic relationship/alliance, empathy, psychological defense mechanisms, insight, and interpretation [of alternatives] are commonly used (see Levenson, 2017; Safran & Hunter, 2020; Summers & Barber, 2010; Weiner & Bornstein, 2009).

The Process of Forgiveness is Consistent with Counseling and Psychotherapy

Elements of the process of forgiveness (see Chapter 8), as described in the models of forgiveness developed by Enright (Process Model) and Worthington (REACH Model), are consistent with the fundamental principles of many systems of counseling and psychotherapy including acceptance/mindfulness-based modalities, systemic-based modalities, and psychodynamic-based modalities. The phases of these models of forgiveness were discussed in some detail in Chapter 8. As such, the summarized descriptive statements thereof used in Chapters 10 and 11 are again restated here for reference and introduction to this discussion of the consistencies between said systems of psychotherapy and the principles of forgiveness.

Enright's *Uncovering* phase and Worthington's *Recalling the Hurt* phase are both focused on the person pursuing forgiveness (i.e., the client) developing, with the assistance of a therapist, facilitator, or workbook, a self-determined, personally relevant, objective awareness of the problem and the pain associated with the difficulties experienced. Enright's *Decision* phase and initial aspects of the *Work* phase and Worthington's *Empathy* and *Altruistic Gift* phases and initial aspects of the *Commitment* phase are focused on recognizing that an alternative solution *is* needed, understanding what forgiveness actually is *and* that it is an option, and starting the process of committing to giving forgiveness as a gift, through reframing the difficult experience(s) and developing positive emotions and responses such as empathy, compassion, humility, gratitude, and acceptance. The completion of Enright's *Work* and Worthington's *Commitment* phases builds upon the process described above, yet also with a particular focus on maintaining the preliminary commitment, particularly through addressing initial reservations and doubts about making said commitment. Likewise, Enright's *Deepening* phase and Worthington's *Holding On* phase are focused on solidifying and sustaining the progress heretofore made through finding meaning and purpose, recognizing the need for and utilizing social support, continuing to address inevitable doubts, and maintaining vigilance against risk factors for returning to previous behavior(s).

Acceptance/Mindfulness-Based Modalities and the Process of Forgiveness

Consistent with Enright's Uncovering and Worthington's Recalling the Hurt phases, are the ACT processes of undermining the grip that language has on cognition and the prioritization of the therapeutic alliance in terms of using it to evoke recognition and understanding of the connection between language and cognition. Also, the DBT processes of recognizing the competition between emotions and thoughts, the need to bring balance through acceptance and change, and the evoking nature of the therapeutic alliance through the facilitation of acceptance and validation. And, the MBCT processes of fostering awareness of typical automatic patterns of thoughts, emotions and sensations, and the evoking nature of the therapeutic alliance through collaborative modeling of inquiry from within.

Consistent with Enright's Decision and Work (initial) phases, and Worthington's Empathy, Altruistic Gift, and Commitment (initial) phases, are the ACT processes of constructing an alternative context, recognizing and addressing the metacognitive process of "fighting" against one's experiences and thus recognizing the need for an alternate resolution through acceptance and mindfulness, and beginning the work of aligning one's behavior with one's values. Also, the DBT processes of embracing the need for acceptance and change, embracing validation and the need for an alternate resolution, and beginning the work of synthesizing opposites. And, the MBCT processes of intentionally switching to a non-judgmental and curious state of mind after having recognized the need for a more effective alternative, and beginning the committed work of mindfulness-based investigation and acceptance of counterproductive thoughts, emotions, and sensations.

Consistent with the completion of Enright's Work and Worthington's Commitment phases, as well as the longer-term pursuits involved in Enright's Deepening and Worthington's Holding On phases, are the ACT processes of divesting control over automatic thoughts, feelings, and memories, clarification of values and facilitation of commitment – which extends the gains achieved through the initial and continued practice of mindfulness-based acceptance, and dissolution of psychological and situational barriers. Also, continuing the DBT process and practice of synthesizing opposites through mindfulness, thereby facilitating the dissolution of the tension associated with emotional dysregulation, and adopting mindfulness-based acceptance as a long-term means of easily gaining attentional control and attaining more adaptive behavior and thus effective emotional regulation. And, maintaining and sustaining the MBCT process of inquiry from within through the continual work of mindfulness-based investigation and acceptance of counterproductive thoughts, emotions, and sensations, as well as understanding the universality of struggling with such, and utilizing support from others.

Systemic-Based Modalities and the Process of Forgiveness

Consistent with Enright's Uncovering and Worthington's Recalling the Hurt phases, are the structural family therapy (SFT) processes of prioritizing the therapeutic alliance or joining with the family and facilitating the process of bringing to light invisible problematic interactional demands, transactional patterns, and boundaries-based rules of interaction, thereby functioning as a healthy boundary maker. Also, the IFS processes of developing a trusting therapeutic alliance and facilitating the recognition of constrained and polarized relationships among one's intrapsychic parts as well as one's relationships with others. And, the ABCT processes of likewise developing an empathic therapeutic alliance and facilitating the recognition of poor communication and problem solving skills, and relational problems, and thus the need for an alternate solution.

Consistent with Enright's Decision and Work (initial) phases, and Worthington's Empathy, Altruistic Gift, and Commitment (initial) phases, are the SFT processes of the therapist working to alter the family members' perceptions of the problem(s) thereby facilitating the recognition of the need for an alternate solution, and beginning the work of clarifying diffuse and opening up rigid boundaries, which leads to initiating the restructuring of problematic interactional patterns. Also, the IFS processes of understanding, identifying, and reconnecting with one's true Self – especially in the context of the phenomenon of frequent, contentious inner dialogue among one's intrapsychic parts (i.e., problematic metacognitions), and thus the need for the alternate resolution of re-establishing one's Self as in charge of the system through beginning to re-establish boundaries among one's parts. And, the ABCT processes of working to develop and instill hope, compassion, and acceptance.

Consistent with the completion of Enright's Work and Worthington's Commitment phases, as well as the longer-term pursuits involved in Enright's Deepening and

Worthington's Holding On phases, are the SFT processes of continued vigilance toward understanding, identifying, restructuring, and maintaining adaptive and healthy boundaries. Also, the IFS processes of regaining access to the Self and becoming Self-led. And, the ABCT processes of developing and maintaining longer-term skills to work toward positive interactions and positive reciprocity in relationships, supportive and adaptive communication and problem solving skills, and effective anger management.

Psychodynamic-Based Modalities and the Process of Forgiveness

Consistent with Enright's Uncovering and Worthington's Recalling the Hurt phases, is the psychodynamic process of establishing a strong therapeutic alliance so as to further enable the process of the therapist being able to detect and evoke the client's understanding of the unconscious origins and drivers of their emotional struggles and problematic behaviors, including developing initial insight, and examining defense mechanisms designed to protect them against such (e.g., denial). Consistent with Enright's Decision and Work (initial) phases, and Worthington's Empathy, Altruistic Gift, and Commitment (initial) phases, are the psychodynamic processes of developing empathy and continuing insight regarding underlying connections between and themes of dysfunctional thoughts, feelings, and behaviors, thus recognizing the need for alternative solutions. And, consistent with the completion of Enright's Work and Worthington's Commitment phases, as well as the longer-term pursuits involved in Enright's Deepening and Worthington's Holding On phases, are the psychodynamic processes of continuing to uncover defense mechanisms, strengthening insight-related processes and skills, and facilitating longer-term skills related to interpreting one's experiences more clearly and accurately; that is, increasingly free of distortion stemming from unconscious mechanisms or processes outside of active awareness.

To the extent that psychodynamic modalities share underlying principles and processes with cognitive-behavioral and systemic modalities (Wachtel & Gagnon, 2019; see above), said consistencies of such modalities with the process of forgiveness are also realized. In sum, the process of forgiveness is consistent with many and otherwise varied systems of counseling and psychotherapy in the service of behavior change.

Forgiveness, Aggression, and Addiction

Aggressive behavior has been linked to addiction in terms of an association between the two (e.g. higher levels of one being associated with higher levels of the other), as well as consistencies in underlying processes and mechanisms (i.e., aggression may have addiction-like qualities) (see Elmquist et al., 2016; Golden et al., 2019; National Institute on Alcohol Abuse and Alcoholism, 2000, 2018). Similarly, empirical evidence suggests a negative association between forgiveness and aggression, especially anger (e.g., higher levels of forgiveness associated with lower levels of anger), and the theory and process of aggression has been argued to be consistent with the theory and process of (un)forgiveness (Webb et al., 2012). Following is a brief overview of two theories of aggression and a brief discussion of said underlying consistencies with the theory (see Chapters 3, 4, and 5) and process of forgiveness (see Chapter 8).

Aggression

The general aggression model (GAM; DeWall & Anderson, 2011) and the I^3 theory (pronounced as I-cubed; Slotter & Finkel, 2011) are both designed to address generalities rather than specificities; that is, principles generally applicable to the prediction of aggression as opposed to specific explanations for particular examples of aggressive behavior. The GAM synthesizes aspects of different theoretical perspectives and includes situation and person level variables, as well as biological considerations (DeWall & Anderson, 2011). Regarding difficult or problematic interpersonal interactions, self- and situation-based variables impact internal processes related to affect (i.e., our feelings or emotions) and cognition (i.e., our thought processes or metacognitions), as well as our arousal levels or responsiveness to such stimuli. These internal states impact our appraisal and decision-making processes, which in turn will lead to more or less thoughtful or impulsive outcomes (i.e., adaptive versus aggressive responses or reactions). All of which provides feedback for subsequent related experiences and episodes (see DeWall & Anderson, 2011).

Similar to the GAM, the I^3 theory, seeking a broad, overarching, comprehensive understanding, also integrates aspects of different theoretical perspectives. However, in contrast to the GAM, the I^3 theory is more focused on self-regulation and the interaction of three risk factors for aggression (Slotter & Finkel, 2011). That is, understanding the relative frequency of aggression based on *instigating* triggers, *impelling* forces, and/or *inhibiting* forces, and prioritizing the preventative effect of inhibiting forces on aggressive thoughts and behavior. Of note, impelling forces and inhibiting forces are each comprised of four categories: evolutionary and cultural, personal, dyadic, and situational.

Forgiveness and Aggression

Consistent with Enright's Uncovering, Decision, and Work (initial) phases and Worthington's Recalling the Hurt, Empathy, Altruistic Gift, and Commitment (initial) phases (see above, and Chapter 8), the GAM process of (re)appraisal involves an individual formulating judgments regarding the adequacy of their appraisals, including decisions about corresponding levels of importance and satisfaction (DeWall & Anderson, 2011). Also, consistent with the (un)forgiveness-energy hypothesis (i.e., forgiveness frees up energy – otherwise invested in the ruminative process of unforgiveness – to be utilized for health promoting purposes; see Chapter 5), DeWall and Anderson (2011) referencing the work of others, argue "that the ability to override unwanted impulses depends on a limited energy resource that becomes depleted after prior exertion" (p. 22). Such that, impulsive outcomes are more likely if we "lack the resources and motivation to alter [our] immediate appraisal of the situation. If [we] possess the resources and motivation, however, [we] may reappraise the situation and act in a more thoughtful fashion" (Slotter & Finkel, 2011, p. 36).

Consistent with the four categories of impelling and inhibiting forces described by the I^3 theory (Slotter & Finkel, 2011) are several aspects of the theory and process of forgiveness. For example, McCullough et al. (2011) in discussing the development of forgiveness from an evolutionary perspective, describe revenge (impellor) and forgiveness (inhibitor) as adaptive solutions to adaptive problems. Regarding the I^3 personal category of impellors and inhibitors, the association of (un)forgiveness with interpersonal functioning in the context of health (Worthington et al., 2001; see also, Chapter 5) can be viewed as a personal impellor, whereas self-control, also associated with (un)forgiveness (e.g., Pronk et al., 2010; Wilkowski et al., 2010) can be viewed as a personal inhibitor of aggression. The positive associations of forgiveness with empathy, perspective taking, and relational closeness, commitment, and satisfaction (Fehr et al., 2010; see also, Chapter 8) are consistent with dyadic inhibitors, and associations with lower levels of rumination (Fehr et al., 2010) and higher levels of self-control, as well as the (un)forgiveness-energy hypothesis are consistent with situational inhibitors.

Important aspects of the theory and process of (un)forgiveness appear to map onto comprehensive approaches to understanding the nature of aggressive behavior. At this point, this is largely an analysis of consistencies between theoretical underpinnings. However, just as forgiveness may be a ready-made antidote for addiction (due to its consistency with the Twelve-Step Model of addiction and recovery, and many systems of counseling, psychotherapy, motivation, and behavior change), it may *also* be a ready-made antidote for aggression. Given the empirical links between aggression and addiction (see above), forgiveness and addiction (see Chapters 6 and 7), and the clear conceptual complementary fit between the theories and processes of forgiveness and aggression (including promising initial empirical ties; see Webb et al., 2012), not only may forgiveness be a key for the lock of aggression, it may be a critical key in decoupling the association of aggression with addiction.

Note

1 Insight is the term for what I am talking about when pointing out all these approaches to counseling and psychotherapy prioritizing, valuing, and employing the process of facilitating the recognition of underlying/unaware, etc. connections between issues – whether affective, cognitive, or behavioral – and the need for an alternate resolution because our default coping and problem solving skills, etc. are not working. Indeed, APA (2015) defines insight as:

> 1. the clear and often sudden discernment of a solution to a problem by means that are not obvious and may never become so, even after one has tried hard to work out how one has arrived at the solution. … 2. in psychotherapy, an awareness of underlying sources of emotional, cognitive, or behavioral responses and difficulties in oneself or another person.
> (p. 544)

Also, see the edited volume, *Insight in Psychotherapy* (Castonguay & Hill, 2007), for comprehensive coverage of this particular subject matter.

References

Alcoholics Anonymous (AA) (1981). *Twelve steps and twelve traditions.* New York, NY: Author. See https://www.aa.org/pages/en_US/twelve-steps-and-twelve-traditions.

Alcoholics Anonymous (AA) (1998). *Living sober.* New York, NY: Author.

Alcoholics Anonymous (AA) (2001). *Alcoholics Anonymous* (4th ed.). New York, NY: Author. See https://www.aa.org/pages/en_US/alcoholics-anonymous.

American Psychological Association (2015). *APA dictionary of psychology* (2nd ed.). Washington, DC: Author.

Antony, M. M., & Roemer, L. (2011). *Behavior therapy.* Washington, DC: American Psychological Association.

Barber, J. P., Muran, J. C., McCarthy, K. S., & Keefe, J. R. (2013). Research on dynamic therapies. In M. J. Lambert (Ed.), *Bergin and Garfield's handbook of psychotherapy and behavior change* (6th ed., pp. 443–494). Hoboken, NJ: John Wiley & Sons.

Castonguay, L. G., & Hill, C. (Eds.). (2007). *Insight in psychotherapy.* Washington, DC: American Psychological Association.

Chabot, D. R. (2011). Family systems theories of psychotherapy. In J. C. Norcross, G. R. VandenBos, & D. K. Freedheim (Eds.), *History of psychotherapy: Continuity and change* (2nd ed., pp. 173–202). Washington, DC: American Psychological Association.

Chapman, A. L., & Dixon-Gordon, K. L. (2020). *Dialectical behavior therapy.* Washington, DC: American Psychological Association.

DeWall, C. N., & Anderson, C. A. (2011). The general aggression model. In P. R. Shaver & M. Mikulincer (Eds.), *Human aggression and violence: Causes, manifestations, and consequences* (pp. 15–33). Washington, DC: American Psychological Association.

Doherty, W. J., & McDaniel, S. H. (2010). *Family therapy.* Washington, DC: American Psychological Association.

Elmquist, J., Shorey, R. C., Anderson, S., & Stuart, G. L. (2016). The relation between compulsive sexual behaviors and aggression in a substance-dependent population. *Journal of Aggression, Maltreatment & Trauma*, 25(1), 110–124. doi:10.1080/10926771.2015.1081664.

Fehr, R., Gelfand, M. J., & Nag, M. (2010). The road to forgiveness: A meta-analytic synthesis of its situational and dispositional correlates. *Psychological Bulletin*, 136(5), 894–914. doi:10.1037/a0019993.

Felder, J. N., Dimidjian, S., & Segal, Z. V. (2012). Collaboration in mindfulness-based cognitive therapy. *Journal of Clinical Psychology: In Session*, 68(2), 179–186. doi:10.1002/jclp.21832.

Fishman, D. B., Rego, S. A., & Muller, K. L. (2011). Behavioral theories of psychotherapy. In J. C. Norcross, G. R. VandenBos, & D. K. Freedheim (Eds.), *History of psychotherapy: Continuity and change* (2nd ed., pp. 101–140). Washington, DC: American Psychological Association.

Frankl, V. E. (1992). *Man's search for meaning: An introduction to logotherapy* (I. Lasch, Trans. 4th ed.). Boston, MA: Beacon Press.

Fruzzetti, A. E., McLean, C., & Erikson, K. M. (2019). Mindfulness and acceptance interventions in cognitive-behavioral therapy. In K. S. Dobson & D. J. A. Dozois (Eds.), *Handbook of cognitive-behavioral therapies* (4th ed., pp. 271–296). New York, NY: Guilford Press.

Gay, P. (1989a). Preface and Introduction sections. In P. Gay (Ed.), *The Freud reader*. New York, NY: W. W. Norton & Company.

Gay, P. (1989b). *Sigmund Freud: A brief life. A biographical introduction in The ego and the id*. 1960. Revised and Edited by J. Strachey (J. Riviere, Trans.). New York, NY: W. W. Norton & Company.

Gelso, C. J., Kivlighan, D. M., Jr., & Markin, R. D. (2018). The real relationship and its role in psychotherapy outcome: A meta-analysis. *Psychotherapy*, 55(4), 434–444. doi:10.1037/pst0000183.

Golden, S. A., Jin, M., & Shaham, Y. (2019). Animal models of (or for) aggression reward, addiction, and relapse: Behavior and circuits. *The Journal of Neuroscience*, 39(21), 3996–4008. doi:10.1523/JNEUROSCI.0151-19.2019.

Hansell, J. (2004). Writing an undergraduate textbook: An analyst's enlightening journey. *Psychologist-Psychoanalyst*, 34(4), 37–38.

Hayes, S. C. (2016). Acceptance and commitment therapy, relational frame theory, and the third wave of behavioral and cognitive therapies. *Behavior Therapy*, 47(6), 869–885. doi:10.1016/j.beth.2016.11.006.

Hayes, S. C., & Lillis, J. (2012). *Acceptance and commitment therapy*. Washington, DC: American Psychological Association.

Hollon, S. D., & Beck, A. T. (2013). Cognitive and cognitive-behavioral therapies. In M. J. Lambert (Ed.), *Bergin and Garfield's handbook of psychotherapy and behavior change* (6th ed., pp. 393–442). Hoboken, NJ: John Wiley & Sons.

Lam, W. K. K., O'Farrell, T. J., & Birchler, G. R. (2012). Family therapy techniques for substance abuse treatment. In S. T. Walters & F. Rotgers (Eds.), *Treating substance abuse: Theory and technique* (3rd ed. (pp. 256–280). New York, NY: Guilford Press.

Lambert, M. J. (Ed.) (2013). *Bergin and Garfield's handbook of psychotherapy and behavior change* (6th ed.). Hoboken, NJ: John Wiley & Sons.

Levenson, H. (2017). *Brief dynamic therapy* (2nd ed.). Washington, DC: American Psychological Association.

Linehan, M. M. (2011). University of Washington Behavioral Research and Therapy Clinics. In J. C. Norcross, G. R. VandenBos, & D. K. Freedheim (Eds.), *History of psychotherapy: Continuity and change* (2nd ed., pp. 428–435). Washington, DC: American Psychological Association.

Linehan, M. M., & Wilks, C. R. (2015). The course and evolution of dialectical behavior therapy. *American Journal of Psychotherapy*, 69(2), 97–110.

Magill, M., Kiluk, B. D., McCrady, B. S., Tonigan, J. S., & Longabaugh, R. (2015). Active ingredients of treatment and client mechanisms of change in behavioral treatments for alcohol use disorders: Progress 10 years later. *Alcoholism: Clinical and Experimental Research*, 39(10), 1852–1862. doi:10.1111/acer.12848.

McCrady, B. S., Ladd, B. O., & Hallgren, K. A. (2012). Theoretical bases of family approaches to substance abuse treatment. In S. T. Walters & F. Rotgers (Eds.), *Treating substance abuse: Theory and technique* (3rd ed., pp. 224–255). New York, NY: Guilford Press.

McCrady, B. S., Wilson, A. D., Muñoz, R. E., Fink, B. C., Fokas, K., & Borders, A. (2016). Alcohol-focused behavioral couple therapy. *Family Process*, 55(3), 443–459. doi:10.1111/famp.12231.

McCrady, B. S., Tonigan, J. S., Ladd, B. O., Hallgren, K. A., Pearson, M. R., Owens, M. D., & Epstein, E. E. (2019). Alcohol Behavioral Couple Therapy: In-session behavior, active ingredients and mechanisms of behavior change. *Journal of Substance Abuse Treatment*, 99, 139–148. doi:10.1016/j.jsat.2019.01.018.

McCullough, M. E., Kurzban, R., & Tabak, B. A. (2011). Evolved mechanisms for revenge and forgiveness. In P. R. Shaver & M. Mikulincer (Eds.), *Human aggression and violence: Causes, manifestations, and consequences* (pp. 221–239). Washington, DC: American Psychological Association.

Miller, W. R., Forcehimes, A. A., & Zweben, A. (2019). *Treating addiction: A guide for professionals* (2nd ed.). New York, NY: Guilford Press.

Minuchin, S. (1974). *Families & family therapy*. Cambridge, MA: Harvard University Press.

Minuchin, S., & Fishman, H. C. (1981). *Family therapy techniques*. Cambridge, MA: Harvard University Press.

National Institute on Alcohol Abuse and Alcoholism (2000). Alcohol, violence, and aggression – Alcohol Alert N. 38–1997. Rockville, MD: Author. Retrieved August 20, 2020, from https://pubs.niaaa.nih.gov/publications/aa38.htm.

National Institute on Alcohol Abuse and Alcoholism (2018). Fall semester – A time for parents to discuss the risks of college drinking. Rockville, MD: Author. Retrieved August 20, 2020, from https://pubs.niaaa.nih.gov/publications/CollegeFactSheet/NIAAA_BacktoCollege_Fact_sheet.pdf.

Neacsiu, A. D., Ward-Ciesielski, E. F., & Linehan, M. M. (2012). Emerging approaches to counseling intervention: Dialectical behavior therapy. *The Counseling Psychologist*, 40(7), 1003–1032. doi:10.1177/0011000011421023.

Norcross, J. C., & Lambert, M. J. (2011). Psychotherapy relationships that work II. *Psychotherapy*, 48(1), 4–8. doi:10.1037/a0022180.

Norcross, J. C., VandenBos, G. R., & Freedheim, D. K. (Eds.). (2011). *History of psychotherapy: Continuity and change* (2nd ed.). Washington, DC: American Psychological Association.

Orcutt, H. K. (2006). The prospective relationship of interpersonal forgiveness and psychological distress symptoms among college women. *Journal of Counseling Psychology*, 53(3), 350–361. doi:10.1037/0022-0167.53.3.350.

Pronk, T. M., Karremans, J. C., Overbeek, G., Vermulst, A. A., & Wigboldus, D. H. J. (2010). What it takes to forgive: When and why executive functioning facilitates forgiveness. *Journal of Personality and Social Psychology*, 98(1), 119–131. doi:10.1037/a0017875.

Rowe, C. E., Jr., & Mac Isaac, D. S. (1991). *Empathic attunment: The "technique" of psychoanalytic self psychology*. Northvale, NJ: Jason Aronson.

Safran, J. D., & Hunter, J. (2020). *Psychoanalysis and psychoanalytic therapies* (2nd ed.). Washington, DC: American Psychological Association.

Schwartz, R. C., & Sweezy, M. (2020). *Internal family systems therapy* (2nd ed.). New York, NY: Guilford Press.

Segal, Z. V., Williams, J. M. G., & Teasdale, J. D. (2013). *Mindfulness-based cognitive therapy for depression* (2nd ed.). New York, NY: Guilford Press.

Sesan, R. (2009). Forgiveness: The final frontier in recovery from an eating disorder. In M. Maine, W. N. Davis, & J. Shure (Eds.), *Effective clinical practice in the treatment of eating disorders: The heart of the matter* (pp. 235–248). New York, NY: Routledge.

Shedler, J. (2010). The efficacy of psychodynamic psychotherapy. *American Psychologist*, 65(2), 98–109. doi:10.1037/a0018378.

Shumway, S. T., Schonian, S., Bradshaw, S., & Hayes, N. D. (2017). A revised multifamily group curriculum: The need for family member recovery from addiction. *Journal of Groups in Addiction & Recovery*, 12(4), 260–283. doi:10.1080/1556035X.2017.1348281.

Shumway, S. T., Bradshaw, S. D., Hayes, N., Schonian, S., & Kimball, T. G. (2019). Prefrontal cortex functioning of family members of those with a substance use disorder. *Alcoholism Treatment Quarterly*, 37(1), 75–98. doi:10.1080/07347324.2018.1488549.

Slotter, E. B., & Finkel, E. J. (2011). I^3 theory: Instigating, impelling, and inhibiting factors in aggression. In P. R. Shaver & M. Mikulincer (Eds.), *Human aggression and violence: Causes, manifestations, and consequences* (pp. 35–52). Washington, DC: American Psychological Association.

Summers, R. F., & Barber, J. P. (2010). *Psychodynamic therapy: A guide to evidence-based practice*. New York, NY: Guilford Press.

Wachtel, P. L., & Gagnon, G. J. (2019). Cyclical psychodynamics and integrative relational psychotherapy. In J. C. Norcross & M. R. Goldfried (Eds.), *Handbook of psychotherapy integration* (3rd ed., pp. 184–203). New York, NY: Oxford University Press.

Wampold, B. E., & Ulvenes, P. (2019). Integration of common factors and specific ingredients. In J. C. Norcross & M. R. Goldfried (Eds.), *Handbook of psychotherapy integration* (3rd ed., pp. 69–87). New York, NY: Oxford University Press.

Webb, J. R., & Trautman, R. P. (2010). Forgiveness and alcohol use: Applying a specific spiritual principle to substance abuse problems. *Addictive Disorders & Their Treatment*, 9(1), 8–17. doi:10.1097/ADT.0b013e318195000d.

Webb, J. R., Dula, C. S., & Brewer, K. (2012). Forgiveness and aggression among college students. *Journal of Spirituality in Mental Health*, 14(1), 38–58. doi:10.1080/19349637.2012.642669.

Weiner, I. B., & Bornstein, R. F. (2009). *Principles of psychotherapy: Promoting evidence-based psychodynamic practice* (3rd ed.). Hoboken, NJ: John Wiley & Sons.

Wilkowski, B. M., Robinson, M. D., & Troop-Gordon, W. (2010). How does cognitive control reduce anger and aggression? The role of conflict monitoring and forgiveness processes. *Journal of Personality and Social Psychology*, 98(5), 830–840. doi:10.1037/a0018962.

Worthington, E. L., Jr., Berry, J. W., & Parrott, L., III. (2001). Unforgiveness, forgiveness, religion, and health. In T. G. Plante & A. C. Sherman (Eds.), *Faith and health: Psychological perspectives* (pp. 107–138). New York, NY: Guilford Press.

13 Conclusions and Recommendations

Forgiveness is Important in the Context of Addiction … Now What?

Addictive behavior and suicidal behavior are clear and present problems for the health and well-being of not only the individuals that experience either or both, but also for society and public health. In fact, it may be more appropriate to think of and approach addictive behavior and suicidal behavior in terms of each being a dangerous crisis (rather than merely problems) when we consider the worldwide prevalence and associated human costs, including death, disability, and economic burden (see Chapter 1). Forgiveness may be a valuable tool in addressing this crisis. Anecdotal evidence, initially through the Twelve-Step Model of addiction and recovery, suggests that "where there has been wrong, the program teaches us the spirit of forgiveness" (Narcotics Anonymous, 2008, p. 12; see also, Chapter 9). Indeed, although still in its early stages, scientific evidence also suggests that forgiveness is very likely to play an important role in healing from, and perhaps preventing addiction. In the preceding chapters, much information has been presented and discussed in an effort to bring together in one place the justification for understanding and applying forgiveness as an alternative, and yet, also a complementary approach to addressing addictive and suicidal behavior. Moreover, the information herein presented is intended to shine a light on the path forward toward full-fledged acceptance and implementation of forgiveness as an effective and efficient treatment for addiction whether related to substances, compulsive behavioral sets, or suicidal behavior – or one or more in conjunction with each other. To close this volume, brief discussions of particularly important issues to remember in the context of theory, research, and clinical application will be (re-)presented, as will recommendations for next steps for theory and research, and guidelines for clinical application. And, lastly, some thoughts on self-advocacy.

Theory

When seeking to treat addiction and facilitate recovery therefrom, it is critically important to understand what is meant by addiction and recovery and what constitutes addiction and recovery. Likewise, when seeking to apply forgiveness to addiction and recovery, it is critically important to understand what forgiveness is (and is not) and how it may foster health and well-being.

Defining and Diagnosing Addiction

One of the most fundamental issues for effective and efficient healthcare is accurate diagnosis. However, before we can accurately diagnose, we must be able to know what we are looking at. That is, before we can diagnose in the most effective and efficient way, we must be able to define the issue(s) we are faced with as healthcare providers. Early on, when seeking to understand and treat addictive disorders, the DSM-I (American Psychiatric

Association, 1952) offered the following guidance: Alcoholism "[includes] … cases in which there is well established addiction to alcohol" and "Drug addiction is usually symptomatic of a personality disorder" (p. 39). Regarding evidence for alcohol addiction, the DSM-II (American Psychiatric Association, 1968) added "the inability of the patient to go one day without drinking" (p. 45). Fortunately, over the years our understanding of addiction has improved – through rigorous application of the scientific method – and the DSM-5 (American Psychiatric Association, 2013), the current edition of the diagnostic system used worldwide by healthcare providers to understand, describe, and diagnose mental illness, considers 11 common symptoms for Substance-Related and Addictive Disorders, as well as severity qualifiers of mild, moderate, and severe, and course specifiers (see below for more discussion about diagnosis).

Definitions related to diagnosis have improved quite considerably. But, accurate definition is more than using consistent, informative diagnostic criteria; indeed, accurate and precise definitional *concepts* underlie the creation of useful diagnostic terminology. In this regard, at its most fundamental level, the essence of addiction is usefully understood not as a quality inherent to or arising from a substance [or behavioral set], but an experiential relationship (Albanese & Shaffer, 2012). That is, "experience is the currency of addiction. When a particular pattern of behavior reliably and robustly changes emotional experience, the potential for addiction emerges. … *Addiction* is the description of a relationship between organisms and objects within their environment" (emphasis in original; Albanese & Shaffer, 2012, p. 6). Moreover, "as far as the brain is concerned, a reward's a reward, regardless of whether it comes from a chemical or an experience. And where there's a reward, there's the risk of the vulnerable brain getting trapped in a compulsion" (Holden, 2001, p. 890; also cited in Albanese & Shaffer, 2012, p. 4).

Regarding diagnosis itself, as mentioned above in the DSM-5 (American Psychiatric Association, 2013), there are 11 common criteria considered when diagnosing Substance-Related and Addictive Disorders. Importantly, two of the 11 criteria must be met for a [Substance] Use or Gambling Disorder to be considered to exist and to be mild in severity, four of 11 for moderate, and six of 11 for severe. Also, only two of the 11 symptoms are physiological in nature: #10 – Tolerance, and #11 – Withdrawal. Taken together, one of the most critical realities here for accurate and efficient diagnosis (and definition, for that matter) is that a person struggling with addiction can have a severe addictive disorder *without any physiological symptoms.* Although it is reasonably "understandable" – or, not surprising – that society and popular culture may not comprehend or accept this, it is very unfortunate when healthcare providers seemingly need to be reminded of this fact. When addiction is overlooked because the so-called hallmarks of addiction – tolerance and withdrawal – are not present or obvious, what level of *unnecessary* exacerbation does this have on the human costs of addiction, including death, disability, and economic burden? Related to this is the reality that the physiological aspects of addiction can be managed through the medical detoxification process in a matter of days, and what remains, and thus in many ways the crucible of addiction-related treatment, are the long-term psychological risk factors for addiction-related problems, without resolution of such, the problem of addiction will never be solved (see Leshner, 1997).

Related to accurate definitions and diagnoses, are issues regarding understanding the origins of addiction and issues regarding how we – both as a society, and as healthcare providers – otherwise *talk* about addiction. Humans have been trying to understand the origins of addiction for over 200 years (but more likely since Day One, so to speak), and the many explanations can be categorized as either *Moral, Biological, Psychological, Sociological*, or *Etiological Multidimensional* (Albanese & Shaffer, 2012). Consistent with the Etiological Multidimensional Model regarding the origins of addiction, the American Psychological Association's two-volume *Addiction Syndrome Handbook* (Shaffer et al, 2012a, 2012b) explicitly addresses a variety of specific contributors to addiction and barriers to recovery. For example, neurobiology, psychiatric comorbidity, self-control, personality, and externalizing spectrum related issues. Also, social, sociological, developmental, infectious disease, homelessness, and technology related issues. Indeed, the Etiological Multidimensional Model views addiction as a syndrome or the confluence of various multifaceted pressures on a vulnerable individual.

Lastly, how we speak of addiction, not only as a society, but as healthcare providers, can have a profoundly meaningful impact on the definition, description, diagnosis, and treatment of addiction, if in no other way than as a function of reducing the stigma associated with addiction. Rather than using terms such as *substance abuser, addict, alcoholic, clean, dirty*, etc., using person-centered language is critical (e.g., Broyles et al., 2014; Robinson, 2017; Saitz, 2016); that is, when warranted and applicable, referring to someone as *a person struggling with an addiction*. Thereby, allowing for a person to *have* a problem rather than *to be* a problem (Kelly et al., 2016). In sum, the "consistent use of agreed-upon terminology will aid precise and unambiguous clinical and scientific communication and help reduce stigmatizing and discriminatory public health and social policies" (Kelly et al., 2016, p. 116).

Behavioral Addiction

Gambling Disorder is the only non-substance related addictive disorder recognized in the DSM system. Although Internet Gaming Disorder has been identified as a Condition for Further Study in the DSM-5 (American Psychiatric Association, 2013; see pp. 783 & 795–798), other behavioral addictions, though thought to exist (see below), have not been included in the DSM system "because *at this time* there is insufficient peer-reviewed evidence to establish the diagnostic criteria and course descriptions needed to identify these behaviors as mental disorders" (emphasis added; p. 481).

Nevertheless, consistent with definitional and diagnostic issues for substances (and gambling), scholars have described common features of addiction. For example, (1) salience; that is, an activity governs and dictates one's thinking, feelings, and behavior, (2) mood modification; that is, an activity produces subjective feelings of arousal (e.g., "buzz" or "high" or "rush") and/or tranquility (e.g., "escape" or "numbing"), (3) tolerance, (4) withdrawal symptoms; whether psychological or physiological, (5) conflict related to the activity; whether interpersonal or intrapsychic, and (6) relapse (see Griffiths, 2005, pp. 193–195; see also, Griffiths et al., 2014; Király et al., 2014). Similarly, Sussman and Sussman (2011; see also, Sussman, 2017) describe five features of addictive behaviors: (1) feeling different; that is, "[pursuit of] some course of action for appetitive effects or motives (e.g., pain reduction, affect enhancement, arousal manipulation, or fantasy)," (2) preoccupation with the behavior, (3) temporary satiation, (4) loss of control, and (5) negative consequences (see Sussman & Sussman, 2011, pp. 4026–4030). In sum, said in the context of behavioral addiction, but consistent with addictive behavior more broadly, "the *individual's inability to curtail the activity despite the negative consequences* is what stands as the hallmark of the addiction process" (emphasis in original; Rosenberg & Feder, 2014a, p. 4).

Many scholars, in seminal works on behavioral addiction, have identified many problematic behaviors as candidates for diagnosis (see Petry, 2016; Rosenberg & Feder, 2014b; Sussman, 2017). For example, Sussman (2017) identified 16 categories of addictive behavior (only one of which includes substance use) with over 60 subcategories. However, he only addresses 11 focal addictions given their relatively common presence in scientific research and discussion, and their higher prevalence rates. That is, (1) cigarette smoking, (2) alcohol use, (3) illicit drug use (including marijuana), (4) eating/food, (5) gambling, (6) Internet, (7) love, (8) sex, (9) exercise, (10) work, and (11) shopping (see pp. 91 & 101).

Suicidal Behavior

When discussing addiction, although suicidal behavior is highly comorbid with addictive behavior (up to 40 percent, Yuodelis-Flores & Ries, 2015), it is not typically considered a manifestation of addiction. However, the Twelve-Step Model of addiction and recovery has been explicitly adapted to suicidal behavior (see Suicide Anonymous, 2010). Also, addiction has been described as a microsuicidal behavior (Firestone, 2006; Firestone, 1986; Firestone & Seiden, 1987) and cognitive processes involved in suicidal behavior have been described as analogous to those involved in the cycle of addiction (Firestone, 2006). Most importantly, in this regard, theory has been developed and empirical evidence observed in support of suicidal behavior as addictive behavior (Blasco-Fontecilla, 2016; Blasco-Fontecilla et al., 2014; Blasco-Fontecilla et al., 2016; Hatteschweiler et al., 2015; Tullis, 1998; see also, da Silva et al., 2018; Ellis, 2006; Shneidman, 1993). As such, integrating relevant principles related to the understanding, prevention, and treatment of addictive behaviors into the understanding, prevention, and treatment of suicidal behavior – and vice versa – is warranted.

As with addiction and addictive behavior, definitions and language used when researching and discussing suicide and suicidal behavior are important (see Ackerman et al., 2018; O'Carroll et al., 1996; Silverman et al., 2007a, 2007b). In particular, the American Association of Suicidology (AAS) has developed guidelines for appropriate language to use, in order to describe suicide and suicidal behavior in an ethical, respectful, and constructive manner (Ackerman et al., 2018). For example, rather than using the phrase *commit* suicide (and its variations), it is better to use *die by* suicide, or *death by* suicide, etc. That is, this and other *traditional* types of phrasing reinforce stigma associated with suicide, including implications regarding criminalization and moral failure (see Ackerman et al., 2018).

Of particular relevance to the psychology of forgiveness and suicidal behavior are two theories of suicide: Shneidman's theory of suicide focused on psychache (Shneidman, 1993) and Joiner and colleagues' Interpersonal Theory of Suicide (IPT) focused on unmet interpersonal needs (Joiner et al., 2009). These theories, as put forth by Shneidman and Joiner, describe similar fundamental issues thought to be the focal drivers of suicide and suicidal behavior; that is, emotional pain, social alienation and drain, and the desire for escape. Although these theories are quite similar at their core, each prioritizes the crucible of suicide differently. For Shneidman it is psychache, or the intense, unrelenting, unremitting psychological pain sometimes described as an aching soul (Holden et al., 2001), and for Joiner it is unmet interpersonal, psychological needs manifesting as thwarted belongingness and perceived burdensomeness.

Conceptualizing Recovery

Just as there are many models attempting to understand and describe the origin(s) of addiction (see above), many models have been developed to address addiction recovery. Abstinence models are focused on the lifetime cessation of the use of substances and/or engagement in other addictive behaviors. While the Twelve-Step Model (e.g., Alcoholics Anonymous (https://www.aa.org/), Narcotics Anonymous (https://www.na.org/), Gamblers Anonymous (http://www.gamblersanonymous.org/ga/)) is the most commonly thought of model of abstinence-based recovery and the most accessible in most communities across the globe, other models also exist where the priority is abstinence (e.g., SMART Recovery (https://www.smartrecovery.org/), LifeRing Secular Recovery (https://www.lifering.org/), Secular Organizations for Sobriety (http://www.sossobriety.org/), and Women for Sobriety (https://womenforsobriety.org/)) (see Miller et al., 2019). Relapse Prevention is focused on preventing a return to problematic use and/or other addictive behavior once abstinence has been reasonably established (see Hsu & Marlatt, 2012). Harm Reduction is focused on managing and reducing addictive behaviors, high-risk behaviors, and/or the negative consequences of such behaviors (Marlatt et al., 2011). Consistent with Harm Reduction, Moderation Management (MM) is designed to assist "problematic drinkers who are not alcohol-dependent. … MM's definition of the 'nondependent' problem drinker is based on the individual's ability to adhere to MM guidelines [regarding frequency and quantity of alcohol consumption]" (Lembke & Humphreys, 2012, p. 130). And, if one decides or discovers that moderated drinking is not a self-determined practical outcome, abstinence is encouraged and supported by the MM program and community (MM, 2019). Of note, each of these models of recovery can be effective in helping individuals struggling with addiction to find healing and long-term recovery.

Lastly, the reality is that most people struggling with addictive behavior do not seek treatment (Bischof et al., 2012; see also, Cohen et al., 2007); moreover, "most [expressions of] addictive behavior … resolve in the general population without [the] use of formal treatment" (Bischof et al., 2012, p. 150). This does not mean that treatment is unnecessary or not useful. Rather, in hindsight, it has been discovered that many people do not or cannot access treatment, for various reasons. As such, the predictors of Natural Recovery must be understood, prioritized, and disseminated to the population at large.

A particular model of recovery that is derived from Natural Recovery is known as Recovery Capital, which consists of those

> critical elements that an individual possesses or that exist within his or her immediate surroundings and that function to *promote and sustain a recovery experience*. … [Or,] the sum total of one's resources that can be brought to bear in an effort to overcome [addiction]. It is embodied in a number of tangible and intangible resources and relationships, including those that existed prior to a person's [addiction], during the period of [addiction], and conditions likely to prevail in the future. It encompasses attitudes and beliefs that one has toward the past, [the] present, and the future. It also includes one's mental status and other personal characteristics that can be drawn upon to resolve [an addiction] problem.
>
> (emphasis added; Granfield & Cloud, 1999, p. 179)

Related to this, Groshkova et al. (2013) have developed the *Assessment of Recovery Capital* (ARC), a 50-item, self-report questionnaire measuring ten subsets of recovery captial: (1) substance use and sobriety, (2) psychological health, (3) physical health, (4) citizenship/community involvement, (5) social support, (6) meaningful activities, (7) housing and safety, (8) risk taking, (9) coping and life functioning, and (10) recovery experience.

Defining Forgiveness

Forgiveness is a broad construct consisting of multiple dimensions. It can be considered in trait-based terms (i.e., dispositional) and/or state-based terms (i.e., situational) (Toussaint & Webb, 2005). Also, a person may (or may not) have a general tendency toward engaging in forgiveness, but may (or may not) have difficulty in the context of particular offenses. Forgiveness can involve a variety of targets (e.g., self, others, deity) and methods (e.g., offering, seeking, feeling) (Toussaint & Webb, 2005). In this regard, one can offer, seek, and/or feel forgiveness in the context of the self, others, and/or conceptions of deity – whether in trait-based and/or state-based terms.

Although forgiveness is receiving ever-increasing attention in the scientific, psychological literature (see Woodyatt et al., 2017; Worthington & Wade, 2020), including in the particular context of health and well-being (see Toussaint et al., 2015), commonly accepted definitions have remained elusive. Unfortunately, the definition for forgiveness of others largely has served as the default definition for all dimensions of forgiveness (Webb et al., 2013). This otherwise de facto use of other-forgiveness as the definition for the broad multidimensional construct of forgiveness may be generally innocuous. However, in the particular case of forgiveness of self, using the definition for other-forgiveness is problematic given critical differences based on the self being both the offender and the offended, such as the inability to avoid the self and the need for self-reconciliation (Enright & The Human Development Study Group, 1996; Tangney et al., 2005), as reconciliation is commonly recognized as optional in the context of other-forgiveness (e.g., Enright & The Human Development Study Group, 1996).

Given this use of other-forgiveness as a default, de facto definition for the broad multidimensional construct of forgiveness and the particular difficulties associated with applying it to self-forgiveness, Webb, Bumgarner et al. (2017) reviewed the extant scientific psychological literature focused on self-forgiveness (i.e., 177 peer-reviewed studies) in an effort to reliably distinguish self-forgiveness from other-forgiveness in explicit and succinct definitional terms. Of the 19 consistently identified definitional components of forgiveness drawn from said extant literature, 14 were in the context of forgiveness in general, and five were unique to the context of self-forgiveness in particular. That is, (1) self-reconciliation, (2) self-acceptance, (3) personal accountability, (4) re-connection with humanity, and (5) genuine efforts to change.

Webb, Bumgarner, et al. (2017) concluded that, in definitional terms, all dimensions of forgiveness derive from the 14 general aspects and that particular dimensions incorporate unique components, as necessary. As such, as a broad construct – that is, applicable to all dimensions of forgiveness, including other-forgiveness – Webb, Bumgarner, et al. (2017) defined *forgiveness* such that it:

> occurs over time and is a deliberate, volitional process involving a fundamental shift in affect, cognition, and/or behavior in response to negative feelings regarding an acknowledged offensive experience, without condoning, excusing, or denying the transgression(s) – at a minimum, an absence of ill will toward an offender.
>
> (p. 220)

In the context of the five otherwise unique qualities identified, and building upon their general definition, Webb, Bumgarner, et al. (2017) defined *self-forgiveness* as:

> initiated in response to one's own negative feelings in the context of a personally acknowledged self-instigated wrong, that results in ready accountability for said wrong and a fundamental, constructive shift in one's relationship to, reconciliation with, and acceptance of the self through human-connectedness and commitment to change.
>
> (p. 221)

In this regard, Webb, Bumgarner, et al. (2017) have laid a foundation for the basic definition of the broad multidimensional construct of forgiveness, and provided specific definitions for other-forgiveness and self-forgiveness. Also, said basic definition can be adjusted to accommodate particular nuances associated with additional dimensions of forgiveness, as necessary (e.g., seeking forgiveness, feeling forgiven; see Chapter 3).

Forgiveness and Spirituality

Forgiveness is both a spiritual and a positive psychological construct. What this means is that forgiveness is potentially applicable to all human beings whether (1) religious and spiritual, (2) religious, but not spiritual, (3) spiritual, but not religious, or (4) not religious and not spiritual (see Connors et al., 1996; GESIS, 2018). Also, whether an individual is spiritual in terms of ritualistic spirituality (i.e., a structured connection with deity), theistic spirituality (i.e., a non-structured connection with deity), or existential spirituality (i.e., a transcendent, yet non-theistic search for meaning and purpose) (see Figure 13.1; Webb et al., 2014), forgiveness can be applied in spiritual terms as a belief in deity or theism is not a pre-requisite for healthy (or balanced) spiritual endeavors (see Pargament, 2013a; Piedmont & Wilkins, 2013; Webb et al., 2014). Indeed, spirituality may be usefully described as a *Transcendent Thread*, consisting of those apparent – though sometimes vague – external, guiding, empowering, and unifying aspects of the human condition which are beyond ordinary experience and explanation, yet are commonly and seemingly universally accessible. Related to this, at its most basic (not necessarily theistic) level, spirituality has been defined as a search for the sacred (Pargament, 2013a; Pargament & Mahoney, 2017).

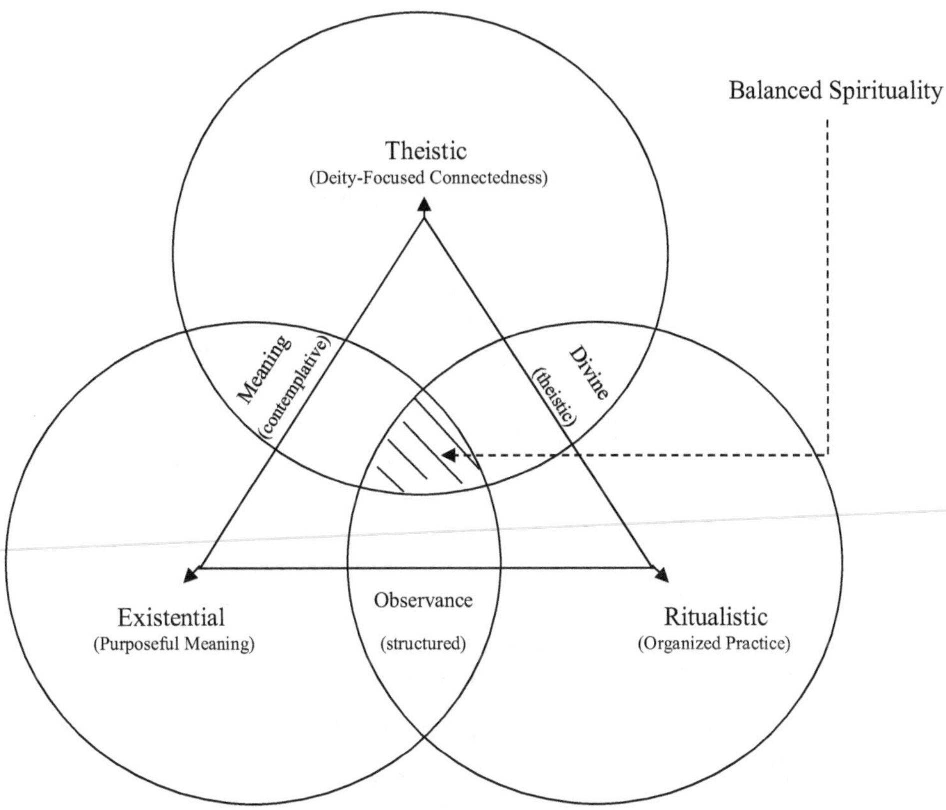

Figure 13.1 The RiTE Model of Spirituality.
Source: Adapted from Webb et al. (2014)
Note. This figure was originally presented and discussed in much more detail in Chapter 4.

Forgiveness, Addiction, and Recovery

The robust association of forgiveness with better health-related outcomes, including addictive behavior and suicidal behavior (see Toussaint et al., 2015; Toussaint et al., 2020; Webb & Toussaint, 2020) is thought to be (1) a manifestation of the effect of stress-and-coping on health (see Strelan, 2020; Strelan & Covic, 2006) and (2) a component of the larger association of religiousness/spirituality with health (see Lavelock et al., 2015; Worthington et al., 2001).

Webb and colleagues have expanded upon Worthington and colleagues' modeling of the general forgiveness–health association to describe the role of forgiveness in addiction and recovery, or the Forgiveness–Addiction–Recovery Association (e.g., Webb et al., 2015; Webb, Toussaint, et al., 2017). The primary modifications to Worthington and colleagues' work in this regard involve (1) tying the direct effect of forgiveness on addiction recovery to the elemental interface between resentments and addiction inherent to the Twelve-Step Model (Alcoholics Anonymous, 1981, 1998, 2001) (see Chapter 9), and (2) the addition and separation into categories of particular, distinctive mediators, including biopsychosocial functioning, existangst, and recovery capital (see Figure 13.2).

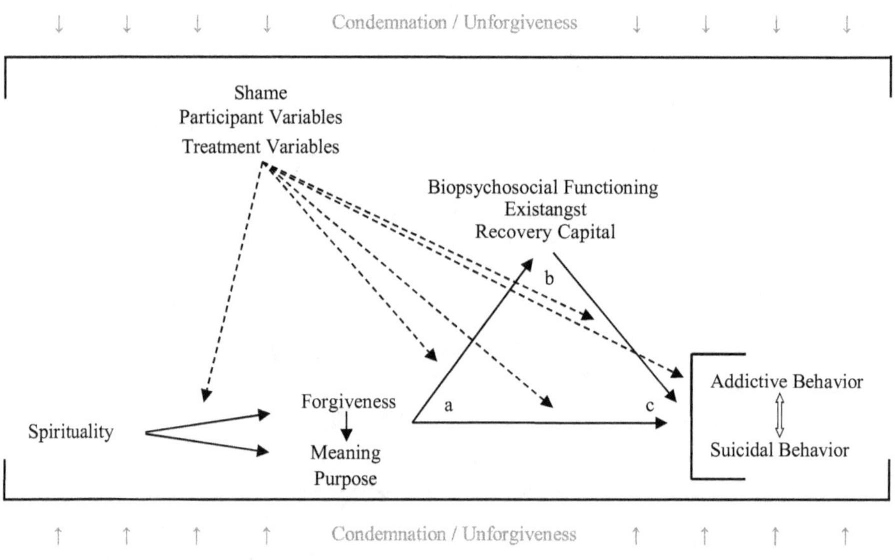

Figure 13.2 The Forgiveness–Addiction–Recovery Association: A Conceptual Model.

Notes

a→c = Direct Effect of Forgiveness on Dependent Variable(s)
a→b = Direct Effect of Forgiveness on Mediator Variable(s)
b→c = Direct Effect of Mediator Variable(s) on Dependent Variable(s)
a→b→c = Indirect Effect of Forgiveness on Dependent Variable(s) through Mediator Variable(s)
dotted→ = Moderation Effect
↕ = potential for a Concomitant, Bidirectional Effect
faded↓↑ = Condemnation and/or Unforgiveness [i.e., a constellation of negative emotions in response to offense experience(s) including, hatred, anger, hostility, resentment, bitterness, and fear (Worthington et al., 2001)] providing the context for forgiveness to become an option in the struggle of addiction recovery.

This figure was originally presented and discussed in much more detail in Chapter 5.
Source: Adapted from Webb et al. (2015)

Biopsychosocial Functioning

When building upon Worthington and colleagues' aforementioned modeling by focusing on addiction recovery as the particular health-related outcome, Webb and colleagues, along with the variables of health behavior, social support, and interpersonal functioning (Worthington et al., 2001), incorporate additional psychosocial variables (e.g., self-blame, hope, and pessimism) and label this category of intervening variables, biopsychosocial functioning (see Chapter 5; see also, Toussaint et al., 2017; Webb, Toussaint, et al., 2017). Also, in the particular circumstance of self-forgiveness, Webb and colleagues have discussed the role of self-condemnation as a contextual factor leading to the explicit need for self-forgiveness (Toussaint et al., 2017; Webb, Toussaint, et al., 2017). Related to this, when considering forgiveness in its multiple dimensions (e.g., of self, of other, seeking, feeling, etc.), recognizing the contextual effect of condemnation more broadly, is warranted as well. When offense occurs, not only is it common for humans to experience anger, hostility, resentment and so on toward the offender (whether self, others, institutions, etc.), but these negative emotions – otherwise known as unforgiveness – can and often do lead to feelings of condemnation toward the offender (whether self, others, institutions, etc.).

Existangst

In addition to including variables related to biopsychosocial functioning, Webb and colleagues (e.g., Webb, 2018; Webb et al., 2015; Webb, Toussaint, et al., 2017) have included another category of mediating variables, particularly related to addictive and suicidal behavior, termed *existangst*. Derived from existential and teleological angst (see Chapter 5), existangst is defined as "emotionally and philosophically driven psychological distress" (Webb et al., 2015, p. 52). Examples of existangst include, symptoms of depression, anxiety, hopelessness, psychache, anger, loneliness, and/or temptation *when* such symptoms are driven by emotionally and philosophically charged psychological distress. That is, "emotionally struggling with affirming one's meaningful existence" (Webb et al., 2015, p. 52).

Anger and Loneliness

From a Twelve-Step Model of addiction and recovery point of view, anger and loneliness are critical factors in the risk for relapse (see Alcoholics Anonymous, 1981, 1998, 2001; see also Nowinski et al., 1994). Indeed, anger is considered a "pivitol emotion" and "a constant threat to sobriety" (Nowinski et al., 1994, p. 83). Also, Nowinski et al. (1994) encourage therapists to ask if their "patients [struggling with addiction] relate to experiencing 'existential anxiety': the feeling of being isolated, of facing difficult decisions and choices but feeling totally alone in making them" (p. 82). Of note, anger and loneliness may, but do not necessarily, occur in the context of one another. However, in the Twelve-Step Model, they are considered together (and thus discussed here, together), along with hunger and tiredness as a cluster of related risk factors for relapse, and given the acronym HALT (i.e., hungry, angry, lonely, tired). When experiencing *anger* and *loneliness*, etc., the Twelve-Step Model recommendation is to "HALT"; that is, to stop what you are doing and take care of and/or resolve these basic needs, so as to reduce your vulnerability and likelihood for relapse.

Temptation

Considered to be a deep-seated threat to goal-driven activity, temptation is a fundamental conflict regarding the pursuit of destructive short-term desires versus constructive long-term ideals; the resolution of which is thought to be a function of self-control versus ego-depletion (see Fishbach & Converse, 2011; Muraven, 2012; Myrseth & Fishbach, 2009). In this regard, and in the particular context of addiction, temptation often involves self-indulgence [e.g., sensation seeking, impulsivity, and risk-taking (see Zuckerman, 2012)] versus self-restraint (e.g., impulse control, delayed gratification, and judicious constraint).

Although there has been considerable research conducted and powerfully insightful understanding developed regarding the psychology of temptation, much of this work is in the context of undesirable, yet relatively innocuous behaviors (e.g., eating sweets), rather than activities with illicit and/or transcendent implications (e.g., sexual infidelity). In response to this, Webb (2014) proposed a more comprehensive, inclusive definition of *temptation* such that, it is "the dispositional or situational incidence of being drawn cognitively, affectively, and/or behaviorally to engage in undesirable, illicit, and/or transcendent short-term activities that are inconsistent with personal, societal, and/or transcendent long-term standards" (p. 236). Given the common (though not necessarily only) struggle of addiction being the conflict between self-indulgence and self-restraint and the ultimately transcendent nature of such (i.e., temptation), the inclusion of temptation as a manifestation of existangst is warranted.

Recovery Capital

As a particular model for conceptualizing addiction recovery, recovery capital is discussed above in more detail. Suffice to say, here, is that although recovery capital is similar to biopsychosocial functioning (see above), in a model focused on forgiveness as a driver of addiction recovery, as well as the likelihood that forgiveness is a predictor of various aspects of recovery capital, there are meaningful distinctions to be made between biopsychosocial functioning and recovery capital. That is, it is useful to draw a parallel between early recovery and recovery capital, and likewise to draw a parallel between long-term recovery and biopsychosocial functioning. Recovery capital may be more "obvious" in early recovery or attaining and maintaining recovery, whereas biopsychosocial functioning may be more "obvious" during long-term recovery or established and mature recovery. Yet, recovery capital is also relevant in the context of long-term recovery, and biopsychosocial functioning is also relevant in early recovery. As such, it may be most useful to consider that each likely has a primary versus secondary role in each stage of recovery. In early recovery, recovery capital will likely be primary and biopsychosocial functioning will likely be largely secondary. And, in long-term recovery biopsychosocial functioning will likely be primary and recovery capital will likely be largely secondary.

Next Steps

Regarding theory, the main next step is to test the many aspects of the theoretical modeling that have been developed. This may sound like one step or a simplistic recommendation, but in truth very little research has examined the myriad details included in the theory of the Forgiveness–Addiction–Recovery Association and all of the related theories drawn from and discussed in support thereof (e.g., theory related to addiction, recovery, spirituality, positive psychology, biopsychosocial functioning, existangst, etc.). Importantly, as all of these theories are examined in the context of the Forgiveness–Addiction–Recovery Association, the explicit basic theory of the Forgiveness–Addiction–Recovery Association as presented and discussed in Chapter 5 will no doubt be modified as particular points already proposed are confirmed or disconfirmed and new points are discovered.

Research

Take Home Messages

Although *anecdotally* associated with addiction recovery for well over three-quarters of a century (see Alcoholics Anonymous, 2001), the *empirical* examination of the role of forgiveness in addiction recovery is really just in its beginning stages. While 87 published scientific reports is a good start and an excellent foundation justifying continued research, much work remains to be done (see below for a brief discussion of limitations and next steps). Nevertheless, in the context of addictive behavior, the take home message derived from the 51 extant, peer-reviewed, scientific psychological studies is that the vast majority (86.27 percent) of the data points to the likely reality that forgiveness, in its multiple dimensions, plays a meaningful and powerful role in addiction recovery. Moreover, that when considering forgiveness as a tool for addiction recovery, self-forgiveness may be the most difficult dimension of forgiveness to achieve, and yet the most important for healing, such that without self-forgiveness (when forgiveness is relevant to addiction recovery), full and lasting recovery may be elusive. Similarly, in the context of suicidal behavior, the take home message derived from the 36 extant, peer-reviewed, scientific psychological studies is that essentially all (100 percent) of the data points to the likely reality that forgiveness, in its multiple dimensions, plays a meaningful and powerful role in promoting healthy and life-preserving outcomes. Importantly, though, one study found both a salutary and deleterious effect of forgiveness in the context of suicidal behavior, thereby warranting careful attention not to overlook the potential for deleterious effects moving forward – both in the context of addictive behavior (i.e., less than 100 percent beneficial associations observed (see above)) and suicidal behavior.

Limitations and Next Steps

In previous reviews of the scientific psychological evidence-base regarding the psychology of forgiveness and both addictive behavior (see Webb et al., 2011; Webb & Jeter, 2015; Webb & Toussaint, 2018, 2020) and suicidal behavior (see Webb, 2018; Webb et al., 2015; Webb & Toussaint, 2020), many basic and nuanced limitations have been identified, as have many basic and nuanced recommendations for future directions been made. Although scholars have begun to examine empirical associations and a good start to the research has been achieved including justifying continued research, the basic weaknesses and recommended remedies discussed in some detail in said previous reviews largely have not been addressed.

Suffice to say, here, is that (1) a large majority of the extant research is cross-sectional in design (i.e., data collected at one point in time) and (2) the nuances of theory have received little attention. Regarding research design, what this means is that all we can really say about forgiveness in the context of both addictive behavior and suicidal behavior – based on an over-reliance on cross-sectional research design – is that forgiveness is *associated* with better levels of many variables directly and indirectly related to addictive behavior and suicidal behavior. In order to be able to say that forgiveness *leads* to better outcomes related to addictive behavior and suicidal behavior over time, we must prioritize research utilizing longitudinal designs (i.e., the same data collected at multiple time-points from the same participants, in order to track any changes over time). Likewise, research utilizing experimental designs will give us critical and necessary data in order to draw *causal* conclusions (i.e., engaging in forgiveness causes …). However, experimental research in the social sciences is a sensitive endeavor. That is, it can only be considered and conducted in appropriate and justified circumstances and settings. For example, it would be inappropriate and unethical to cause serious emotional offense/injury in a laboratory setting in order to observe the effects of (un)forgiveness. Indeed, projects generally analogous to classic and notorious research studies conducted by Milgram (obedience study; see Baumrind & Milgram, 2010) and Zimbardo (prison study; see Zimbardo, 1973), for example, likely can never occur again given advances in the standards for conducting ethical (and humane) research.

Lastly, as mentioned in the next steps regarding the advancement of theory in the context of the Forgiveness–Addiction–Recovery Association (see above), much more work has gone into the development of said comprehensive theoretical modeling than has gone into actually testing the myriad aspects and nuances of the modeling. Although the initial research is promising, much, much more work needs to be done. A hallmark of the scientific method (i.e., empiricism) regarding theoretical modeling is that as models are examined through hypothesis testing (i.e., conclusions drawn from replicable and falsifiable scientific statements regarding identifiable relationships among specific variables), they are either discarded due to a lack of evidence or refined as evidence accumulates. Initial theoretical modeling, especially in the social sciences, is never confirmed without meaningful and salient changes or adjustments. The theory of the Forgiveness–Addiction–Recovery Association will be no different.

Clinical Application

The extensive theoretical modeling and promising scientific evidence base provide ample support for not only continued empirical examination and delineation of the Forgiveness–Addiction–Recovery Association, but also for the deliberate, explicit, and focused clinical application of forgiveness as an active ingredient in the treatment of addiction, whether in the context of substances, compulsive behavioral sets, or suicidal behavior. The question is, how do we go about doing this; that is, how do we include forgiveness in the treatment of addiction?

Assess Forgiveness

One of the very first things clinicians working with those struggling with addiction can do is to assess for forgiveness. During the intake process, patients can be asked about their understanding of forgiveness, attitudes about forgiveness, and experiences with forgiveness. This does not necessarily need to take a lot of time during the intake process. It can be included in an assessment about the patient's background in the context of religiousness and spirituality. As mentioned above and discussed in more detail in Chapter 4, forgiveness is a common factor across mainstream world religions and is consistent with spirituality, more broadly, whether ritualistic, theistic, or existential in nature. Also, religiousness and spirituality, again, whether ritualistic, theistic, or existential is certainly a part of human culture (Cohen, 2009) and arguably is a part of human nature, as well (see Chapter 1 and Chapter 4); that is, the search for the sacred (see Pargament, 2013a; Pargament & Mahoney, 2017). And, it is important to always remember that spirituality, particularly existential spirituality, does not require a belief in deity.

Of equal importance is the reality that religiousness and spirituality can be important and useful tools when addressing addiction (see Koenig et al., 2012). However, sometimes there is a discrepancy when comparing the religiousness and spirituality of healthcare providers, especially mental healthcare providers, to that of their patients (i.e., patients tend to be much more religious/spiritual than healthcare providers). As such, it becomes important for healthcare providers to become sufficiently familiar with spiritual belief systems and sufficiently comfortable with discussing – in an appropriate manner – spiritual topics in a healthcare setting. Toussaint et al. (2012) offer some very explicit guidance in this regard, as do many others (e.g., Aten et al., 2012; Pargament, 2013b; Richards & Bergin, 2014).

Including the topic of forgiveness in the intake assessment in general, and as a component of a larger religiousness/spirituality assessment in particular is a good start. However, it may be that, during the intake process a patient may otherwise appear not to be a candidate for forgiveness. While this is definitely a reality and must be respected, as with any other topic initially addressed during the intake process, once a sufficient therapeutic relationship or alliance is developed, a patient may become more willing to engage with the topic of forgiveness. As such, it is appropriate to return to the topic of forgiveness from time to time, as applicable and appropriate, during the course of healthcare provision.

Is the only way to assess for the relevance of forgiveness by using the word *forgiveness*, or variants thereof? The short answer is No. Assessing for mental health concerns can be an alternative approach. Patients struggling with depression, anxiety, or stress, for example, may be struggling with issues amenable to forgiveness. Likewise, patients with a history of trauma may find forgiveness to be helpful. Indeed, higher levels of forgiveness are beneficially associated with myriad mental health related variables (Webb & Toussaint, 2020). Also, a healthcare provider can listen for issues related to hatred, anger, hostility, resentment, bitterness, and fear. While in and of themselves, these issues are candidates for the process of forgiveness, the confluence of these particular negative emotions, in terms of the psychology of forgiveness, is known as *unforgiveness* (see Chapter 5; see also, Worthington et al., 2001). While each of these negative emotions, that comprise unforgiveness, are associated with addiction-related problems, of particular relevance to addiction, at least in the context of the Twelve-Step Model, is: resentment. One of my favorite quotes from the so-called *Big Book* (the primary, authoritative text of Alcoholics Anonymous – upon which the variants of the Twelve-Step Model are built) is: "Resentment is the 'number one' offender. It *destroys* more [people struggling with addiction] than anything else" (emphasis added; Alcoholics Anonymous, 2001, p. 64). Nevertheless, as with any other aspect of spirituality, a healthcare provider must never force the issue, or impose their values (for or against religiousness/spirituality, including forgiveness) on a patient or client. Periodically returning to the topic of forgiveness can be appropriate; whereas, pushing the topic of forgiveness is never appropriate.

Discuss Forgiveness

During the initial intake process when conducting a forgiveness assessment, or *any other time* during the treatment process, when forgiveness is relevant and the patient is open to the topic, the next step is to *discuss* forgiveness. The assessment process described above can include a brief discussion of a patient or client's understanding, attitudes, and experiences regarding forgiveness, of course. What I am describing here is having an in-depth, comprehensive discussion about forgiveness. When the topic of forgiveness is discussed in a clinical setting, it is not enough to use variants of the *word*: forgiveness. Patients may have pre-conceived notions about forgiveness – whether good or bad, positive or negative, accurate or inaccurate, etc. As such, it is important to discuss the scientific definition of forgiveness, including as pertaining to the many different dimensions of forgiveness, etc. (see above, and Chapter 3), as well as what forgiveness is and is not (see also Chapter 4).

Also, discuss the research evidence supporting the beneficial effect of forgiveness in the context of addictive behavior and suicidal behavior (see above, and Chapter 6 and Chapter 7). *Introduce* the comprehensive models of the process of forgiveness – particularly those exposed to the most research scrutiny and in possession of the most research support (i.e., Enright's Process Model (e.g., Enright & Fitzgibbons, 2015; Freedman & Enright, 2020) and Worthington's REACH Model (e.g., Worthington, 2006, 2020)) – or the steps and "how-to"s of forgiveness (see Chapter 8). Likewise, *introduce* the notion that the process of forgiveness is consistent with many other evidence-based approaches to and principles of counseling and psychotherapy, and behavior change (see Chapters 9, 10, 11, and 12).

In sum, having sufficiently specialized and professional discussions with our patients about the science of forgiveness, rather than surface-level, colloquial exchanges in passing, likely will help tip the scales toward serious consideration of forgiveness as an option to facilitate a different future for those struggling with addiction. The next two sections move beyond *introducing* the models of forgiveness and their similarities with other treatment modalities and address guidelines regarding encouraging and implementing forgiveness.

Encourage Forgiveness

First and foremost, when I recommend encouraging and implementing forgiveness, I am not endorsing pushing or imposing forgiveness. Rather, when appropriate – that is, when a client or patient is open to it – as healthcare providers we can urge or recommend it for their consideration; that is, in a very real way, we can prescribe forgiveness. When a physician prescribes a medication for a patient, the implication is that it is not only an appropriate treatment, but it is the gold-standard for the concern at hand. Likewise, as mental healthcare providers, whether with traditional prescription privileges or not, we can strongly recommend, or prescribe forgiveness as an effective option for the treatment of addictive and suicidal behavior. Granted, more research needs to be done to precisely understand everything about the Forgiveness–Addiction–Recovery Association, but there is a sufficient evidence-base to recommend or prescribe forgiveness, especially for those readily open to it.

What about those who are not readily open to it? Can we still prescribe forgiveness to them? The short answer is Yes. We may need to return to assessing and discussing forgiveness first, but we can definitely work with our patients to encourage their consideration of forgiveness. Moving beyond discussing the basics regarding definitions, reviewing research, and introducing the "how-to"s or steps of forgiveness and the similarities between forgiveness and other scientifically supported treatments for addiction, as healthcare providers we can encourage the use of publicly available forgiveness-based resources, build related/facilitative-of-forgiveness positive psychological characteristics, and explicitly discuss similarities with other treatment modalities (see Chapters 9, 10, 11, and 12) *when implementing* other said modalities.

Regarding encouraging the use of publicly available forgiveness-based resources, Everett L. Worthington, Jr., Ph.D., a world leader in the psychology of forgiveness, the originator of a comprehensive, empirically supported model of the Forgiveness-Health Association (e.g., Lavelock et al., 2015; Worthington et al., 2001), and founder of the REACH Model of Forgiveness (e.g., Worthington, 1998, 2006) – all of which are discussed and cited extensively in this volume – has created self-directed workbooks and made them freely available on his website (http://www.evworthington-forgiveness.com/; see also, http://www.people.vcu.edu/~eworth/). Secular and Christian versions of the workbooks focused on self-forgiveness and other-forgiveness are available, as are 6-hour and 2-hour versions. Also, facilitator-led, group-based manuals are available which include over 20 hours of forgiveness-based exercises. While the self-directed workbooks are exactly that – self-directed – the group-based manuals are also designed to be administered by lay persons; that is, one does not have to be a professionally trained mental healthcare provider to administer the group-based approach to facilitating forgiveness through Worthington's REACH Model.

Not only can healthcare providers point patients to these resources and encourage their use, but healthcare providers can also "walk through" these resources with their patients. Walking though these resources with patients can include encouraging their use and following up with patients on a weekly basis regarding progress being made, seeking to clarify any confusion, answering particular questions, etc. Also, healthcare providers can spend time during portions of or entire treatment sessions addressing and walking through these materials with their patients.

Regarding building related/facilitative-of-forgiveness positive psychological characteristics, healthcare providers can focus on helping their clients develop empathy, compassion, and gratitude - arguably *precursors* to developing the ability to forgive (see Chapter 8). Related to this, many positive psychological characteristics are beneficial in the context of addiction recovery, and, just as with forgiveness, share many similarities with spirituality (see Chapter 4), can be assessed in the initial intake procedures, can be discussed in more detail throughout treatment, and, as applicable and appropriate, can be more actively encouraged and implemented (see Krentzman, 2013; Lopez & Snyder, 2009; Shumway & Kimball, 2012).

Lastly, as healthcare providers become sufficiently familiar with and conversant in the shared principles and processes between forgiveness and other methods of counseling and psychotherapy, and behavior change, deliberate, explicit, and purposeful, in-depth discussion of such can occur when implementing said *other* modalities. What does this look like? In my experience in working with patients as a licensed clinical psychologist, I have found that it can be helpful to facilitate the genuine experience of seeing behind the curtain of counseling and psychotherapy, so to speak. That is, in my view, sometimes a phenomenon occurs in counseling and psychotherapy where there is a certain mystique assumed or created (superficially in popular culture, but also genuinely among patients) about what we do as therapists. In some theories or schools of psychotherapy this can be considered a useful tool; for example, originating in psychodynamic theory/therapy (but, present, in effect (and outright) in other modalities) is the notion of transference, or, in simple terms, the patient treating the therapist in a similar fashion (at least symbolically) as they do other important others in their life. When a patient recognizes this dynamic occurring in their relationship with their therapist it can be a strangely fascinating (and meaningfully therapeutic) experience. Alternatively, an unfortunate example of the mystique of therapy is the common, albeit erroneous assumption (obviously!) in our culture that mental health care workers can read minds!

Regardless, this mystique to counseling and psychotherapy can exist for some and when we, as therapists, let our patients in on the theory and principles underlying what we do as therapists, it can facilitate investment from the patient in the process of counseling and psychotherapy, and behavior change. In this regard, for those open to forgiveness, and when applicable and appropriate, it can be useful to discuss similarities between forgiveness and the principles, methods, and techniques of other modalities of counseling and psychotherapy. As an individual experiences change through one modality, confidence to invest in other similar modalities (in this case, forgiveness) can be facilitated and synergies between modalities can occur.

Implement Forgiveness

So far, some guidelines for assessing forgiveness, discussing forgiveness, and encouraging forgiveness have been presented. Arguably these have all been indirect methods for bringing forgiveness into treatment as a complementary approach, or as an augmentation to treatment. But, how do we go about actually implementing forgiveness into treatment or as a treatment, when applicable and appropriate, in its own right? In previous reviews of the literature regarding the association of forgiveness with addictive behavior and suicidal behavior (e.g., Webb, 2018; Webb et al., 2015), I, along with colleagues, have described the direct implementation of forgiveness through *incorporating* it into the principles, methods, and techniques of conceptually consistent, otherwise traditional counseling and psychotherapy modalities, and approaches to behavior change. For example (and expanded upon in this volume), acceptance related, cognitive-behavioral related, and psychodynamic modalities, and principles related to motivational interviewing and aggression (see Chapters 10, 11, and 12). And, in this volume systemic-based modalities have also been included (see Chapter 12). Also, *infusing* forgiveness into pre-existing aligned modalities (e.g., Twelve-Step Facilitation Therapy; see Chapter 9), and with the empirical evidence-base developing regarding the Forgiveness–Addiction–Recovery Association, *stand-alone* forgiveness treatment modalities (see Chapter 8) are warranted.

How do we incorporate and infuse forgiveness into other modalities? Moving beyond in-depth discussion about forgiveness when implementing conceptually consistent and pre-existing aligned therapies (see above section on *encouraging* forgiveness), as mental health care providers we can actively apply the principles, methods, and techniques of the process of forgiveness when working with our patients. Rather than talking *about* forgiveness or discussing at an intellectual or academic level, we can implement forgiveness as *the* active intervention. Focusing on the steps and processes of forgiveness (see Chapter 8) as we are employing any particular conceptually consistent and/or pre-existing aligned "other" therapeutic modality. Using the other modality as the vehicle to implement the steps, processes, and content specific to forgiveness.

What about forgiveness as a stand-alone therapy for the treatment of addictive behavior and/or suicidal behavior? Clearly the methods and models of forgiveness developed by others (see Chapter 8) not only can be incorporated and infused into other modalities, but can serve as the basis of treatment itself. For example, forgiveness modules can be used in treatment facilities, whether intensive outpatient, residential, or aftercare settings. Likewise, forgiveness of specific individuals (including the self), situations (including traumatic experiences), or multiples thereof in sequence (with consideration for appropriate timing) can be the focus of treatment. Also, as the science becomes clearer regarding the exact role of forgiveness in promoting healing and recovery in the context of addictive behavior and suicidal behavior (e.g., for who and under what circumstances is forgiveness most effective, how is forgiveness best facilitated, what is the best length of forgiveness treatment, etc.) it may be the case that adjusting said existing methods and models of forgiveness-based treatment itself becomes necessary. Such that, the development of a unique, stand-alone forgiveness-addiction-recovery specific treatment is warranted.

Importantly, the application of forgiveness to the treatment of addictive behavior and/or suicidal behavior may not always be applicable or appropriate. That is why, you may have noticed, I have worked to consistently use this type of language when discussing these topics! Firstly, as I have mentioned, patients may not be open to the idea of forgiveness. Related to this, forgiveness is a choice (e.g., Enright, 2001) and but one way to address the confluence of negative emotions, otherwise known as *un*forgiveness (e.g., hatred, anger, hostility, resentment, bitterness, and fear), that typically arise in response to offensive experiences (Worthington et al., 2001). Forgiveness is one option for coping with an offensive experience and addressing the process of unforgiveness; whereas, justice, avoidance, revenge, retaliation, and denial are others (Wade & Worthington, 2003). Secondly, for those individuals open to forgiveness, seeking to implement it during a crisis is likely inappropriate and may be counterproductive. For example, if a patient is highly suicidal (e.g., impending lethality), the most important intervention in-the-moment, is to do essentially whatever is necessary to de-escalate the crisis (Joiner et al., 2009; Shneidman, 1993). That is, to "mollify the psychache … no psychache, no suicide," and "when the person is no longer highly suicidal – the usual methods of psychotherapy can be usefully employed" (Shneidman, 1993, pp. 53, 56, 142).

Self-Advocacy

For the most part, this volume has been focused on understanding the Forgiveness–Addiction–Recovery Association from an academic and scientific point of view. That is, a fairly *intellectual* approach to the theory, research, and clinical relevance of forgiveness to addictive behavior and suicidal behavior. Some case-examples and applied scenarios have been sprinkled in to help provide a face, so to speak, to some of the topics; not only to illustrate the concepts and principles, but also to allow those readers struggling with addiction, whether in the context of substances, compulsive behavioral sets, and/or suicidal behavior, to connect with the material and provide hope for a different future.

I have a three-fold vision for this project – each of which is of equal importance and passion for me. The first is to move the scientific field of the psychology of forgiveness and addiction forward; indeed, to move the scientific field of the psychology of addiction forward through the application of the psychology of forgiveness to addiction recovery. The second is to spur public and private funding agencies to prioritize sufficient grant funding for both research and service grants. Lastly, and, I suppose, in *some* ways more important to me, is that for those struggling with addiction, my hope is that you can use the information contained herein to self-advocate for an effective alternative and/or complementary treatment, when warranted and/or necessary. Quite literally, in this regard, I envision you being able to arm yourself with this information – indeed, carrying this book under your arm – as you walk with confidence through the metaphorical or literal door seeking help or treatment for addiction. That we can use the power of forgiveness as both a shield and a weapon as we face our demons in the uphill, relentless battle for addiction recovery.

References

Ackerman, J., Cannon, E. A., Stage, D. R. L., Singer, J. B., & Young, N. (2018). Suicide reporting recommendations: Media as partners in suicide prevention. Washington, DC: American Association of Suicidology. Retrieved August 16, 2019, from https://suicidology.org/wp-content/uploads/2018/12/Suicide-Media-Reporting-Extended-4-merged-1.pdf.

Albanese, M. J., & Shaffer, H. J. (2012). Addiction: The genesis and evolution of an idea and its consequences. In H. J. Shaffer, D. A. LaPlante, & S. E. Nelson (Eds.), *APA addiction syndrome handbook, Vol. 1: Foundations, influences, and expressions of addiction* (pp. 3–25). Washington, DC: American Psychological Association.

Alcoholics Anonymous (AA) (1981). *Twelve steps and twelve traditions.* New York, NY: Author. See https://www.aa.org/pages/en_US/twelve-steps-and-twelve-traditions.

Alcoholics Anonymous (AA) (1998). *Living sober.* New York, NY: Author.

Alcoholics Anonymous (AA) (2001). *Alcoholics Anonymous* (4th ed.). New York, NY: Author. See https://www.aa.org/pages/en_US/alcoholics-anonymous.

American Psychiatric Association (1952). *Diagnostic and statistical manual of mental disorders.* Washington, DC: Author.

American Psychiatric Association (1968). *Diagnostic and statistical manual of mental disorders* (2nd edition). Washington, DC: Author.

American Psychiatric Association (2013). *Diagnostic and statistical manual of mental disorders* (5th edition). Washington, DC: Author.

Aten, J. D., O'Grady, K. A., & Worthington, E. L., Jr. (Eds.). (2012). *The psychology of religion and spirituality for clinicians: Using research in your practice.* New York, NY: Routledge.

Baumrind, D., & Milgram, S. (2010). Classic dialogue: Was Stanley Milgram's study of obedience unethical? In B. Slife (Ed.), *Clashing views on psychological issues* (16th ed., pp. 26–42). New York, NY: McGraw-Hill.

Bischof, G., Rumpf, H.-J., & John, U. (2012). Natural recovery from addiction. In H. J. Shaffer, D. A. LaPlante, & S. E. Nelson (Eds.), *APA addiction syndrome handbook, Vol. 2: Recovery, prevention, and other issues* (pp. 133–155). Washington, DC: American Psychological Association.

Blasco-Fontecilla, H. (2016). The addiction to suicidal behavior. In P. Courtet (Ed.), *Understanding suicide: From diagnosis to personalized treatment* (pp. 53–61). New York, NY: Springer.

Blasco-Fontecilla, H., Fernández-Fernández, R., Colino, L., Fajardo, L., Perteguer-Barrio, R., & de Leon, J. (2016). The addictive model of self-harming (non-suicidal and suicidal) behavior. *Frontiers in Psychiatry*, 7. doi:10.3389/fpsyt.2016.00008.

Blasco-Fontecilla, H., Artieda-Urrutia, P., Berenguer-Elias, N., Garcia-Vega, J., Fernandez-Rodriguez, M., Rodriguez-Lomas, C., … de Leon, J. (2014). Are major repeater patients addicted to suicidal behavior? *Adicciones*, 26(4), 321–333. doi:10.20882/adicciones.38.

Broyles, L. M., Binswanger, I. A., Jenkins, J. A., Finnell, D. S., Faseru, B., Cavaiola, A., … Gordon, A. J. (2014). Confronting inadvertent stigma and pejorative language in addiction scholarship: A recognition and response. *Substance Abuse*, 35(3), 217–221. doi:10.1080/08897077.2014.930372.

Cohen, A. B. (2009). Many forms of culture. *American Psychologist*, 64(3), 194–204. doi:10.1037/a0015308.

Cohen, E., Feinn, R., Arias, A., & Kranzler, H. R. (2007). Alcohol treatment utilization: Findings from the National Epidemiologic Survey on Alcohol and Related Conditions. *Drug and Alcohol Dependence*, 86(2–3),214–221. doi:10.1016/j.drugalcdep.2006.06.008.

Connors, G. J., Tonigan, J. S., & Miller, W. R. (1996). A measure of religious background and behavior for use in behavior change research. *Psychology of Addictive Behaviors*, 10(2), 90–96. doi:10.1037/0893-164x.10.2.90.

da Silva, A. G., Malloy-Diniz, L. F., Garcia, M. S., Figueiredo, C. G. S., Figueiredo, R. N., Diaz, A. P., & Palha, A. P. (2018). Cognition as a therapeutic target in the suicidal patient approach. *Frontiers in Psychiatry*, 9. doi:10.3389/fpsyt.2018.00031.

Ellis, T. E. (2006). *Cognition and suicide: Theory, research, and therapy.* Washington, DC: American Psychological Association.

Enright, R. D. (2001). *Forgiveness is a choice: A step-by-step process for resolving anger and restoring hope.* Washington, DC: American Psychological Association.

Enright, R. D., & Fitzgibbons, R. P. (2015). *Forgiveness therapy: An empirical guide for resolving anger and restoring hope* (2nd ed.). Washington, DC: American Psychological Association.

Enright, R. D., & The Human Development Study Group (1996). Counseling within the forgiveness triad: On forgiving, receiving forgiveness, and self-forgiveness. *Counseling and Values*, 40(2), 107–126. doi:10.1002/j.2161-007X.1996.tb00844.x.

Firestone, L. (2006). Suicide and the Inner Voice. In T. E. Ellis (Ed.), *Cognition and suicide: Theory, research, and therapy* (pp. 119–147). Washington, DC: American Psychological Association.

Firestone, R. W. (1986). The 'inner voice' and suicide. *Psychotherapy: Theory, Research, Practice, Training*, 23(3), 439–447. doi:10.1037/h0085636.

Firestone, R. W., & Seiden, R. H. (1987). Microsuicide and suicidal threats of everyday life. *Psychotherapy: Theory, Research, Practice, Training*, 24(1), 31–39. doi:10.1037/h0085688.

Fishbach, A., & Converse, B. A. (2011). Identifying and battling temptation. In K. D. Vohs & R. F. Baumeister (Eds.), *Handbook of self-regulation: Research, theory, and applications* (2nd ed., pp. 244–260). New York, NY: Guilford Press.

Freedman, S., & Enright, R. D. (2020). A review of the empirical research using Enright's Process Model of interpersonal forgiveness. In E. L.Worthington, Jr. & N. G. Wade (Eds.), *Handbook of forgiveness* (2nd ed., pp. 266–276). New York, NY: Routledge.

GESIS (Ed.) (2018). ISSP 2008 – Religion III. Variable Report: Documentation release 2018/10/26, related to the international dataset Archive-Study-No. ZA4950 Version 2.3.0 Variable Reports 2018|17. Cologne: Author.

Granfield, R., & Cloud, W. (1999). *Coming clean: Overcoming addiction without treatment*. New York, NY: New York University Press.

Griffiths, M. D. (2005). A 'components' model of addiction within a biopsychosocial framework. *Journal of Substance Use*, 10(4), 191–197. doi:10.1080/14659890500114359.

Griffiths, M. D., Kuss, D. J., & Demetrovics, Z. (2014). Social networking addiction: An overview of preliminary findings. In K. P. Rosenberg & L. C. Feder (Eds.), *Behavioral addictions: Criteria, evidence, and treatment* (pp. 119–141). San Diego, CA: Elsevier Academic Press.

Groshkova, T., Best, D., & White, W. (2013). The Assessment of Recovery Capital: Properties and psychometrics of a measure of addiction recovery strengths. *Drug and Alcohol Review*, 32(2), 187–194. doi:10.1111/j.1465-3362.2012.00489.x.

Hatteschweiler, C., Graziani, P., Bon, M., & Charbonnier, E. (2015). Addiction et passage à l'acte suicidaire: Des processus cognitifs similaires? = Addiction and passage to the suicidal act: Similar cognitive processes? *Revue Francophone de Clinique Comportementale et Cognitive*, 20(3), 35–44.

Holden, C. (2001). 'Behavioral' addictions: Do they exist? *Science*, 294(5544), 980–982. doi:10.1126/science.294.5544.980.

Holden, R. R., Mehta, K., Cunningham, E. J., & McLeod, L. D. (2001). Development and preliminary validation of a scale of psychache. *Canadian Journal of Behavioural Science/Revue canadienne des sciences du comportement*, 33(4), 224–232. doi:10.1037/h0087144.

Hsu, S. H., & Marlatt, G. A. (2012). Addiction syndrome: Relapse and relapse prevention. In H. Shaffer, D. A. LaPlante, & S. E. Nelson (Eds.), *APA addiction syndrome handbook, Vol. 2: Recovery, prevention, and other issues* (pp. 105–132). Washington, DC: American Psychological Association.

Joiner, T. E., Jr., Van Orden, K. A., Witte, T. K., & Rudd, M. D. (2009). *The interpersonal theory of suicide: Guidance for working with suicidal clients*. Washington, DC: American Psychological Association.

Kelly, J. F., Saitz, R., & Wakeman, S. (2016). Language, substance use disorders, and policy: The need to reach consensus on an 'addiction-ary'. *Alcoholism Treatment Quarterly*, 34(1), 116–123. doi:10.1080/07347324.2016.1113103.

Király, O., Nagygyörgy, K., Griffiths, M. D., & Demetrovics, Z. (2014). Problematic online gaming. In K. P. Rosenberg & L. C. Feder (Eds.), *Behavioral addictions: Criteria, evidence, and treatment* (pp. 61–97). San Diego, CA: Elsevier Academic Press.

Koenig, H. G., King, D. E., & Carson, V. B. (2012). *Handbook of religion and health* (2nd ed.). New York, NY: Oxford University Press.

Krentzman, A. R. (2013). Review of the application of positive psychology to substance use, addiction, and recovery research. *Psychology of Addictive Behaviors*, 27(1), 151–165. doi:10.1037/a0029897.

Lavelock, C. R., Snipes, D. J., Griffin, B. J., Worthington, E. L., Jr., Davis, D. E., Hook, J. N., … Ritter, J. (2015). A conceptual model of forgiveness and health. In L. L. Toussaint, E. L. Worthington, Jr., & D. R. Williams (Eds.), *Forgiveness and health: Scientific evidence and theories relating forgiveness to better health* (pp. 29–42). New York, NY: Springer.

Lembke, A., & Humphreys, K. (2012). Moderation management: A mutual-help organization for problem drinkers who are not alcohol-dependent. *Journal of Groups in Addiction & Recovery*, 7(2–4), 130–141. doi:10.1080/1556035X.2012.705657.

Leshner, A. I. (1997). Addiction is a brain disease, and it matters. *Science*, 278(5335), 45–47. doi:10.1126/science.278.5335.45.

Lopez, S. J., & Snyder, C. R. (Eds.) (2009). *Oxford handbook of positive psychology* (2nd ed.). New York, NY: Oxford University Press.

Marlatt, G. A., Larimer, M. E., & Witkiewitz, K. (Eds.) (2011). *Harm reduction: Pragmatic strategies for managing high-risk behaviors* (2nd ed.). New York, NY: Guilford Press.

Miller, W. R., Forcehimes, A. A., & Zweben, A. (2019). *Treating addiction: A guide for professionals* (2nd ed.). New York, NY: Guilford Press.

Moderation Management (MM) (2019). What is moderation management? Retrieved December 15, 2019, from https://www.moderation.org/about_mm/whatismm.html#.

Muraven, M. (2012). Ego depletion: Theory and evidence. In R. M. Ryan (Ed.), *The Oxford handbook of human motivation* (pp. 111–126). New York, NY: Oxford University Press.

Myrseth, K. O. R., & Fishbach, A. (2009). Self-control: A function of knowing when and how to exercise restraint. *Current Directions in Psychological Science*, 18(4), 247–252. doi:10.1111/j.1467-8721.2009.01645.x.

Narcotics Anonymous (NA) (2008). *Narcotics Anonymous* (6th ed.). Chatsworth, CA: Author.

Nowinski, J., Baker, S., & Carroll, K. M. (1994). *Twelve step facilitation therapy manual: A clinical research guide for therapists treating individuals with alcohol abuse and dependence.* NIH Publication No. 94–3722. Rockville, MD: National Institute on Alcohol Abuse and Alcoholism.

O'Carroll, P. W., Berman, A., Maris, R. W., Moscicki, E. K., Tanney, B. L., & Silverman, M. M. (1996). Beyond the tower of Babel: A nomenclature for suicidology. *Suicide and Life-Threatening Behavior*, 26(3), 237–252.

Pargament, K. I. (2013a). Searching for the sacred: Toward a nonreductionistic theory of spirituality. In K. I. Pargament, J. J. Exline, & J. W. Jones (Eds.), *APA handbook of psychology, religion, and spirituality (Vol 1): Context, theory, and research* (pp. 257–273). Washington, DC: American Psychological Association.

Pargament, K. I. (Ed.) (2013b). *APA handbook of psychology, religion, and spirituality* (Vol. 1 & 2). Washington, DC: American Psychological Association.

Pargament, K. I., & Mahoney, A. (2017). Spirituality: The search for the sacred. In C. R. Snyder, S. J. Lopez, L. M. Edwards, & S. C. Marques (Eds.), *Oxford handbook of positive psychology* (3rd ed.). New York, NY: Oxford University Press.

Petry, N. M. (Ed.) (2016). *Behavioral addictions: DSM-5® and beyond.* New York, NY: Oxford University Press.

Piedmont, R. L., & Wilkins, T. A. (2013). Spirituality, religiousness, and personality: Theoretical foundations and empirical applications. In K. I. Pargament, J. J. Exline, & J. W. Jones (Eds.), *APA handbook of psychology, religion, and spirituality (Vol 1): Context, theory, and research* (pp. 173–186). Washington, DC: American Psychological Association.

Richards, P. S., & Bergin, A. E. (Eds.) (2014). *Handbook of psychotherapy and religious diversity* (2nd ed.). Washington, DC: American Psychological Association.

Robinson, S. M. (2017). 'Alcoholic' or 'Person with alcohol use disorder'? Applying person-first diagnostic terminology in the clinical domain. *Substance Abuse*, 38(1), 9–14. doi:10.1080/08897077.2016.1268239.

Rosenberg, K. P., & Feder, L. C. (2014a). An introduction to behavioral addictions. In K. P. Rosenberg & L. C. Feder (Eds.), *Behavioral addictions: Criteria, evidence, and treatment* (pp. 1–17). San Diego, CA: Elsevier Academic Press.

Rosenberg, K. P., & Feder, L. C. (Eds.) (2014b). *Behavioral addictions: Criteria, evidence, and treatment.* San Diego, CA: Elsevier Academic Press.

Saitz, R. (2016). International statement recommending against the use of terminology that can stigmatize people. *Journal of Addiction Medicine*, 10(1), 1–2. doi:10.1097/ADM.0000000000000178.

Shaffer, H. J., LaPlante, D. A., & Nelson, S. E. (Eds.) (2012a). *APA addiction syndrome handbook, Vol. 1: Foundations, influences, and expressions of addiction*. Washington, DC: American Psychological Association.

Shaffer, H. J., LaPlante, D. A., & Nelson, S. E. (Eds.) (2012b). *APA addiction syndrome handbook, Vol. 2: Recovery, prevention, and other issues*. Washington, DC: American Psychological Association.

Shneidman, E. (1993). *Suicide as psychache: A clinical approach to self-destructive behavior*. Northvale, NJ: Jason Aronson.

Shumway, S. T., & Kimball, T. G. (2012). *Six essentials to achieve lasting recovery*. Center City, MN: Hazelden.

Silverman, M. M., Berman, A. L., Sanddal, N. D., O'Carroll, P. W., & Joiner, T. E., Jr. (2007a). Rebuilding the Tower of Babel: A revised nomenclature for the study of suicide and suicidal behaviors: Part 1: Background, rationale, and methodology. *Suicide and Life-Threatening Behavior*, 37(3), 248–263. doi:10.1521/suli.2007.37.3.248.

Silverman, M. M., Berman, A. L., Sanddal, N. D., O'Carroll, P. W., & Joiner, T. E., Jr. (2007b). Rebuilding the Tower of Babel: A revised nomenclature for the study of suicide and suicidal behaviors: Part 2: Suicide-related ideations, communications and behaviors. *Suicide and Life-Threatening Behavior*, 37(3), 264–277. doi:10.1521/suli.2007.37.3.264.

Strelan, P. (2020). The stress-and-coping model of forgiveness: Theory, research, and the potential of dyadic coping. In E. L.Worthington, Jr. & N. G. Wade (Eds.), *Handbook of forgiveness* (pp. 63–73). New York, NY: Routledge.

Strelan, P., & Covic, T. (2006). A review of forgiveness process models and a coping framework to guide future research. *Journal of Social & Clinical Psychology*, 25(10), 1059–1085. doi:10.1521/jscp.2006.25.10.1059.

Suicide Anonymous (SA) (2010). *Suicide Anonymous, the little book*. Memphis, TN: Author. Retrieved August 7, 2018, from http://www.suicideanonymous.net/uploads/SA_BOOKLET_ok_copy.pdf.

Sussman, S. (2017). *Substance and behavioral addictions: Concepts, causes, and cures*. New York, NY: Cambridge University Press.

Sussman, S., & Sussman, A. N. (2011). Considering the definition of addiction. *International Journal of Environmental Research and Public Health*, 8, 4025–4038. doi:10.3390/ijerph8104025.

Tangney, J. P., Boone, A. L., & Dearing, R. (2005). Forgiving the self: Conceptual issues and empirical findings. In E. L.Worthington, Jr. (Ed.), *Handbook of forgiveness* (pp. 143–158). New York, NY: Routledge.

Toussaint, L. L., & Webb, J. R. (2005). Theoretical and empirical connections between forgiveness, mental health, and well-being. In E. L.Worthington, Jr. (Ed.), *Handbook of forgiveness* (pp. 349–362). New York, NY: Routledge.

Toussaint, L. L., Webb, J. R., & Hirsch, J. K. (2017). Self-forgiveness and health: A stress-and-coping model. In L. Woodyatt, E. L.Worthington, Jr., M. Wenzel, & B. J. Griffin (Eds.), *Handbook of the psychology of self-forgiveness* (pp. 87–99). New York, NY: Springer.

Toussaint, L. L., Webb, J. R., & Keltner, W. (2012). Religion, spirituality, and mental health. In J. D. Aten, K. A. O'Grady, & E. L.Worthington, Jr. (Eds.), *The psychology of religion and spirituality for clinicians: Using research in your practice* (pp. 331–356). New York, NY: Routledge.

Toussaint, L. L., Worthington, E. L., Jr., & Williams, D. R. (Eds.) (2015). *Forgiveness and health: Scientific evidence and theories relating forgiveness to better health*. New York, NY: Springer.

Toussaint, L. L., Worthington, E. L., Jr., Williams, D. R., & Webb, J. R. (2020). Forgiveness and physical health. In E. L.Worthington, Jr. & N. G. Wade (Eds.), *Handbook of forgiveness* (2nd ed., pp. 178–187). New York, NY: Routledge.

Tullis, K. (1998). A theory of suicide addiction. *Sexual Addiction & Compulsivity*, 5(4), 311–324. doi:10.1080/10720169808402339.

Wade, N. G., & Worthington, E. L., Jr. (2003). Overcoming interpersonal offenses: Is forgiveness the only way to deal with unforgiveness? *Journal of Counseling & Development*, 81(3), 343–353. doi:10.1002/j.1556-6678.2003.tb00261.x.

Webb, J. R. (2014). Incorporating spirituality into the psychology of temptation: Conceptualization, measurement, and clinical implications. *Spirituality in Clinical Practice*, 1(3), 231–241. doi:10.1037/scp0000028.

Webb, J. R. (2018). Forgiveness, addiction, and suicide. In J. K. Hirsch, E. C. Chang, & J. K. Rabon (Eds.), *A positive psychological approach to suicide: Theory, research, and prevention* (pp. 37–58). New York, NY: Springer.

Webb, J. R., & Jeter, B. R. (2015). Forgiveness and problematic substance use. In L. L. Toussaint, E. L.Worthington, Jr., & D. R. Williams (Eds.), *Forgiveness and health: Scientific evidence and theories relating forgiveness to better health* (pp. 139–154). New York, NY: Springer.

Webb, J. R., & Toussaint, L. L. (2018). Self-forgiveness as a critical factor in addiction and recovery: A 12-step model perspective. *Alcoholism Treatment Quarterly*, 36(1), 15–31. doi:10.1080/07347324.2017.1391057.

Webb, J. R., & Toussaint, L. L. (2020). Forgiveness, well-being, and mental health. In E. L. Worthington, Jr. & N. G. Wade (Eds.), *Handbook for forgiveness* (2nd ed., pp. 188–197). New York, NY: Routledge.

Webb, J. R., Hirsch, J. K., & Toussaint, L. L. (2011). Forgiveness and alcohol problems: A review of the literature and a call for intervention-based research. *Alcoholism Treatment Quarterly*, 29 (3), 245–273. doi:10.1080/07347324.2011.585922.

Webb, J. R., Hirsch, J. K., & Toussaint, L. L. (2015). Forgiveness as a positive psychotherapy for addiction and suicide: Theory, research, and practice. *Spirituality in Clinical Practice*, 2(1), 48–60. doi:10.1037/scp0000054.

Webb, J. R., Toussaint, L. L., & Dula, C. S. (2014). Ritualistic, theistic, and existential spirituality: Initial psychometric qualities of the RiTE measure of spirituality. *Journal of Religion & Health*, 53(4), 972–985. doi:10.1007/s10943-013-9697-y.

Webb, J. R., Toussaint, L. L., & Hirsch, J. K. (2017). Self-forgiveness, addiction, and recovery. In L. Woodyatt, E. L.Worthington, Jr., M. Wenzel, & B. J. Griffin (Eds.), *Handbook of the psychology of self-forgiveness* (pp. 265–277). New York, NY: Springer.

Webb, J. R., Hirsch, J. K., Visser, P. L., & Brewer, K. G. (2013). Forgiveness and health: Assessing the mediating effect of health behavior, social support, and interpersonal functioning. *The Journal of Psychology: Interdisciplinary and Applied*, 147(5), 391–414. doi:10.1080/00223980.2012.700964.

Webb, J. R., Bumgarner, D. J., Conway-Williams, E., Dangel, T., & Hall, B. B. (2017). A consensus definition of self-forgiveness: Implications for assessment and treatment. *Spirituality in Clinical Practice*, 4(3), 216–227. doi:10.1037/scp0000138.

Woodyatt, L., Worthington, E. L., Jr., Wenzel, M., & Griffin, B. J. (Eds.) (2017). *Handbook of the psychology of self-forgiveness.* New York, NY: Springer.

Worthington, E. L., Jr. (1998). The pyramid model of forgiveness: Some interdisciplinary speculations about unforgiveness and the promotion of forgiveness. In E. L.Worthington, Jr. (Ed.), *Dimensions of forgiveness: Psychological research and theological perspectives* (pp. 107–137). Philadelphia: Templeton Foundation Press.

Worthington, E. L., Jr. (2006). *Forgiveness and reconciliation: Theory and application.* New York, NY: Routledge.

Worthington, E. L., Jr. (2020). An update of the REACH Forgiveness Model: Psychoeducation in groups, do-it-yourself formats, couple enrichment, religious congregations, and as an adjunct to psychotherapy. In E. L.Worthington, Jr. & N. G. Wade (Eds.), *Handbook of forgiveness* (2nd ed., pp. 277–287). New York, NY: Routledge.

Worthington, E. L., Jr., & Wade, N. G. (Eds.) (2020). *Handbook of forgiveness* (2nd ed.). New York, NY: Routledge.

Worthington, E. L., Jr., Berry, J. W., & Parrott, L., III. (2001). Unforgiveness, forgiveness, religion, and health. In T. G. Plante & A. C. Sherman (Eds.), *Faith and health: Psychological perspectives* (pp. 107–138). New York, NY: Guilford Press.

Yuodelis-Flores, C., & Ries, R. K. (2015). Addiction and suicide: A review. *The American Journal on Addictions*, 24(2), 98–104. doi:10.1111/ajad.12185.

Zimbardo, P. G. (1973). On the ethics of intervention in human psychological research: With special reference to the Stanford prison experiment. *Cognition*, 2(2), 243–256. doi:10.1016/0010-0277(72)90014-5.

Zuckerman, M. (2012). Psychological factors and addiction: Personality. In H. J. Shaffer, D. A. LaPlante, S. E. Nelson, H. J. Shaffer, D. A. LaPlante, & S. E. Nelson (Eds.), *APA addiction syndrome handbook, Vol. 1: Foundations, influences, and expressions of addiction* (pp. 175–194). Washington, DC: American Psychological Association.

Index

For Product Safety Concerns and Information please contact our EU representative GPSR@taylorandfrancis.com
Taylor & Francis Verlag GmbH, Kaufingerstraße 24, 80331 München, Germany

www.ingramcontent.com/pod-product-compliance
Lightning Source LLC
LaVergne TN
LVHW080809011026
849160LV00015B/1577